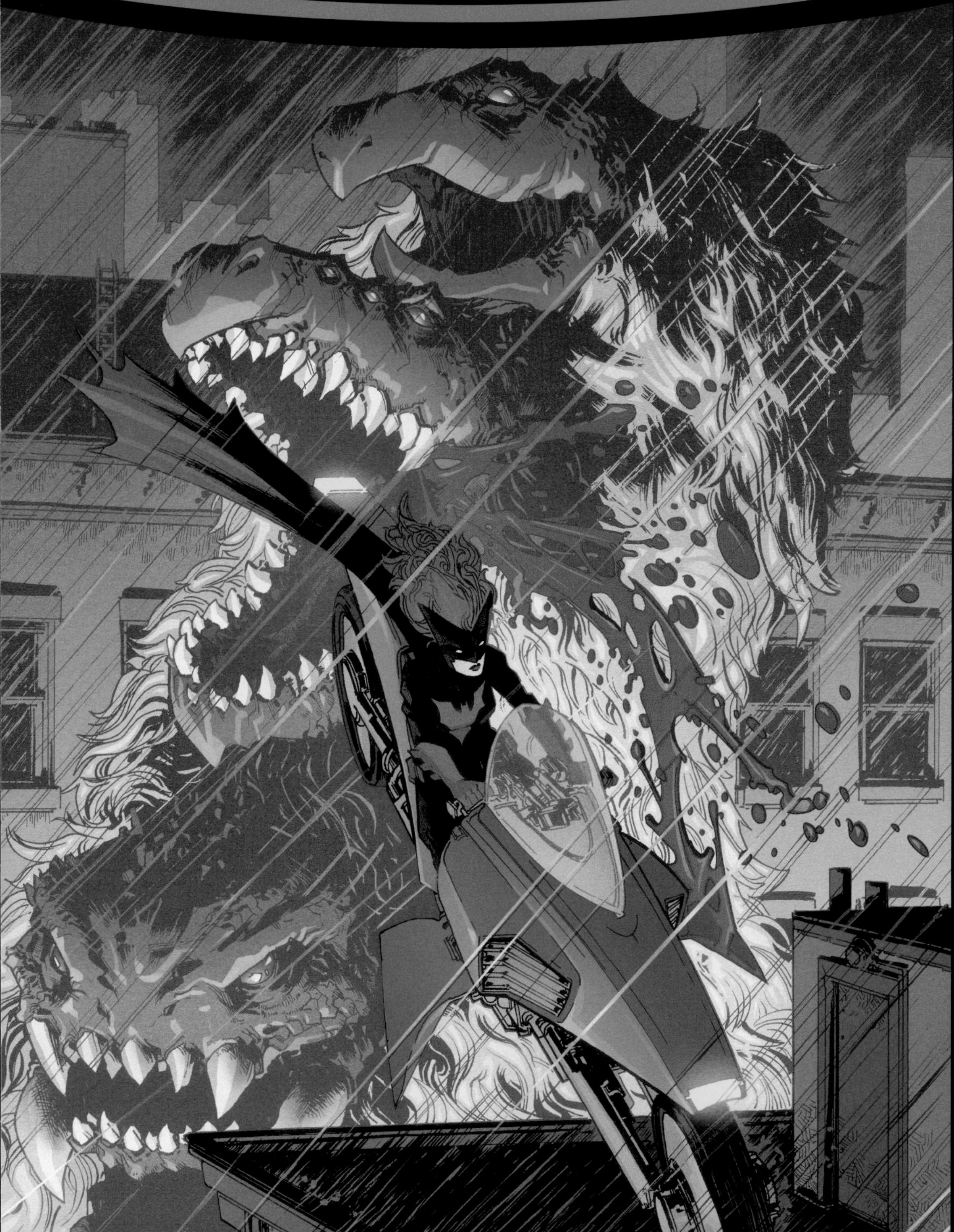

BATMAN
NIGHT OF THE MONSTER MEN

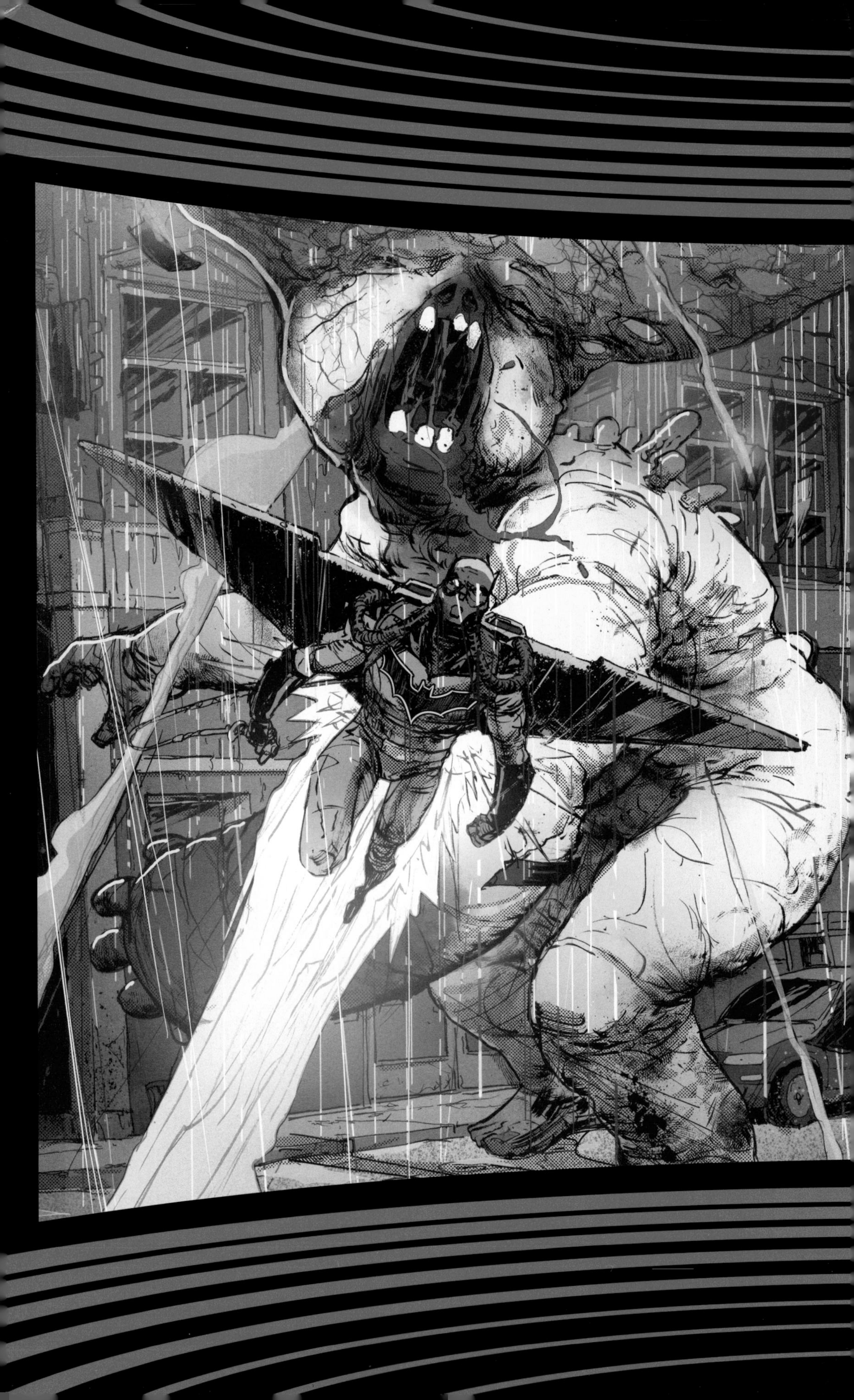

BATMAN
NIGHT OF THE MONSTER MEN

STEVE ORLANDO * **TOM KING**
TIM SEELEY * **JAMES TYNION IV**
story plotters

STEVE ORLANDO
scripter

RILEY ROSSMO * **ROGE ANTONIO** * **ANDY MacDONALD**
artists

IVAN PLASCENCIA * **CHRIS SOTOMAYOR** * **JOHN RAUCH**
colorists

DERON BENNETT * **CARLOS M. MANGUAL** * **MARILYN PATRIZIO**
letterers

YANICK PAQUETTE and **NATHAN FAIRBAIRN**
original series cover artists

RILEY ROSSMO
collection cover artist

Special thanks to **SCOTT SNYDER**

BATMAN created by **BOB KANE** with **BILL FINGER**
NIGHTWING created by **MARV WOLFMAN** and **GEORGE PÉREZ**

MARK DOYLE CHRIS CONROY REBECCA TAYLOR Editors - Original Series
DAVE WIELGOSZ Assistant Editor - Original Series
JEB WOODARD Group Editor - Collected Editions ● **ROBIN WILDMAN** Editor - Collected Edition
STEVE COOK Design Director - Books ● **CURTIS KING JR.** Publication Design

BOB HARRAS Senior VP - Editor-in-Chief, DC Comics

DIANE NELSON President ● **DAN DiDIO** Publisher ● **JIM LEE** Publisher ● **GEOFF JOHNS** President & Chief Creative Officer
AMIT DESAI Executive VP – Business & Marketing Strategy, Direct to Consumer & Global Franchise Management
SAM ADES Senior VP – Direct to Consumer ● **BOBBIE CHASE** VP – Talent Development
MARK CHIARELLO Senior VP – Art, Design & Collected Editions ● **JOHN CUNNINGHAM** Senior VP - Sales & Trade Marketing
ANNE DePIES Senior VP – Business Strategy, Finance & Administration ● **DON FALLETTI** VP – Manufacturing Operations
LAWRENCE GANEM VP – Editorial Administration & Talent Relations ● **ALISON GILL** Senior VP – Manufacturing & Operations
HANK KANALZ Senior VP – Editorial Strategy & Administration ● **JAY KOGAN** VP – Legal Affairs
THOMAS LOFTUS VP – Business Affairs ● **JACK MAHAN** VP – Business Affairs
NICK J. NAPOLITANO VP - Manufacturing Administration ● **EDDIE SCANNELL** VP - Consumer Marketing
COURTNEY SIMMONS Senior VP – Publicity & Communications
JIM (SKI) SOKOLOWSKI VP - Comic Book Specialty Sales & Trade Marketing
NANCY SPEARS VP - Mass, Book, Digital Sales & Trade Marketing

BATMAN: NIGHT OF THE MONSTER MEN

Published by DC Comics. Compilation, cover and all new material Copyright © 2017 DC Comics. All Rights Reserved.
Originally published in single magazine form in BATMAN 7-8, NIGHTWING 5-6, DETECTIVE COMICS 941-942.
Copyright © 2016 DC Comics. All Rights Reserved. All characters, their distinctive likenesses and related elements
featured in this publication are trademarks of DC Comics. The stories, characters and incidents featured in this publication are entirely fictional.
DC Comics does not read or accept unsolicited submissions of ideas, stories or artwork.

DC Comics, 2900 West Alameda Ave., Burbank, CA 91505
Printed by LSC Communications, Salem, VA, USA. 1/20/17. First Printing.
ISBN: 978-1-4012-7067-4

Library of Congress Cataloging-in-Publication Data is available.

PEFC Certified

Printed on paper from
sustainably managed
forests, controlled
sources

PEFC/29-31-337   www.pefc.org

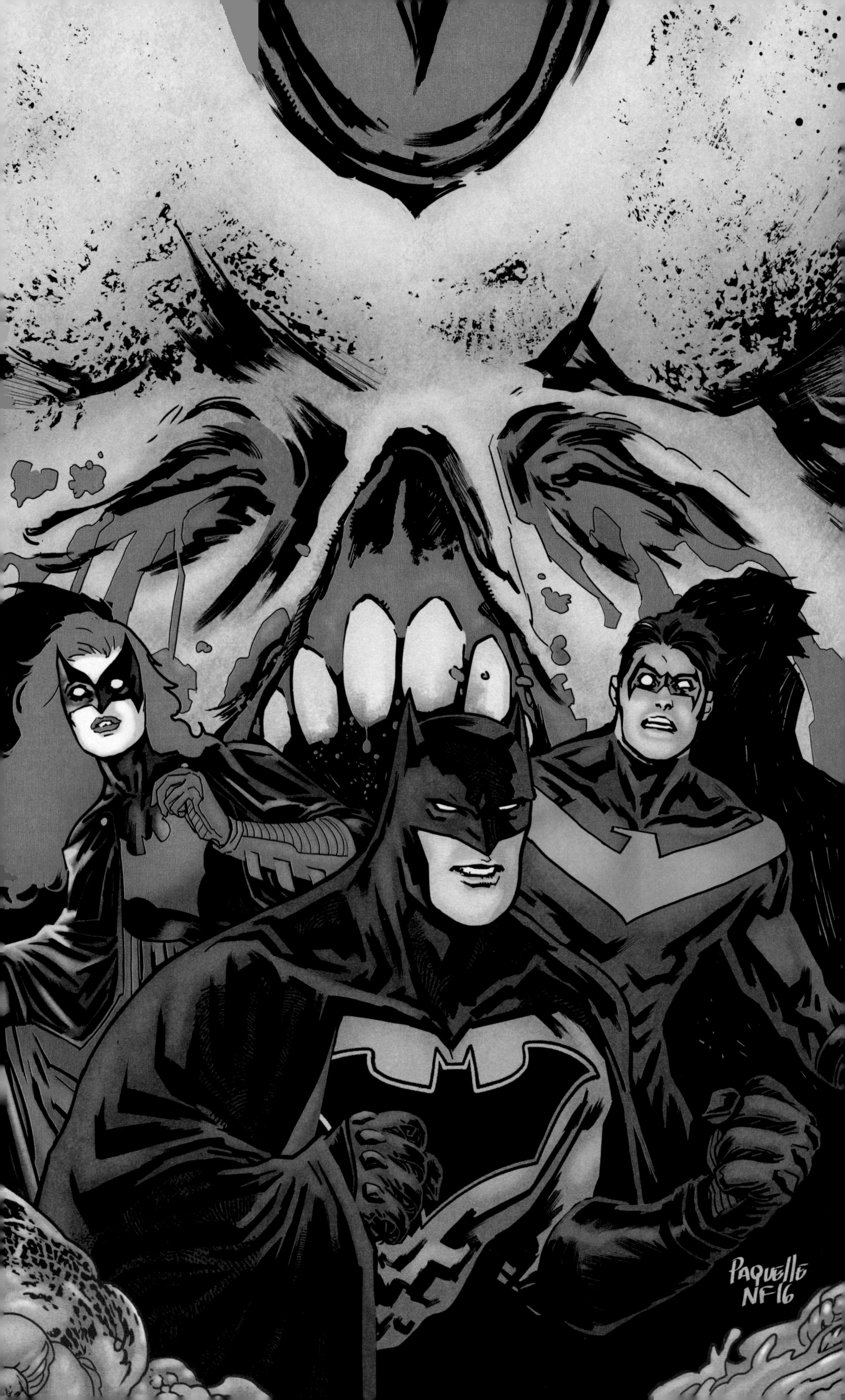
PAQUETTE
NF16

STEVE ORLANDO & TOM KING plot * STEVE ORLANDO script * RILEY ROSSMO art * IVAN PLASCENCIA colors
DERON BENNETT letters * YANICK PAQUETTE & NATHAN FAIRBAIRN cover art

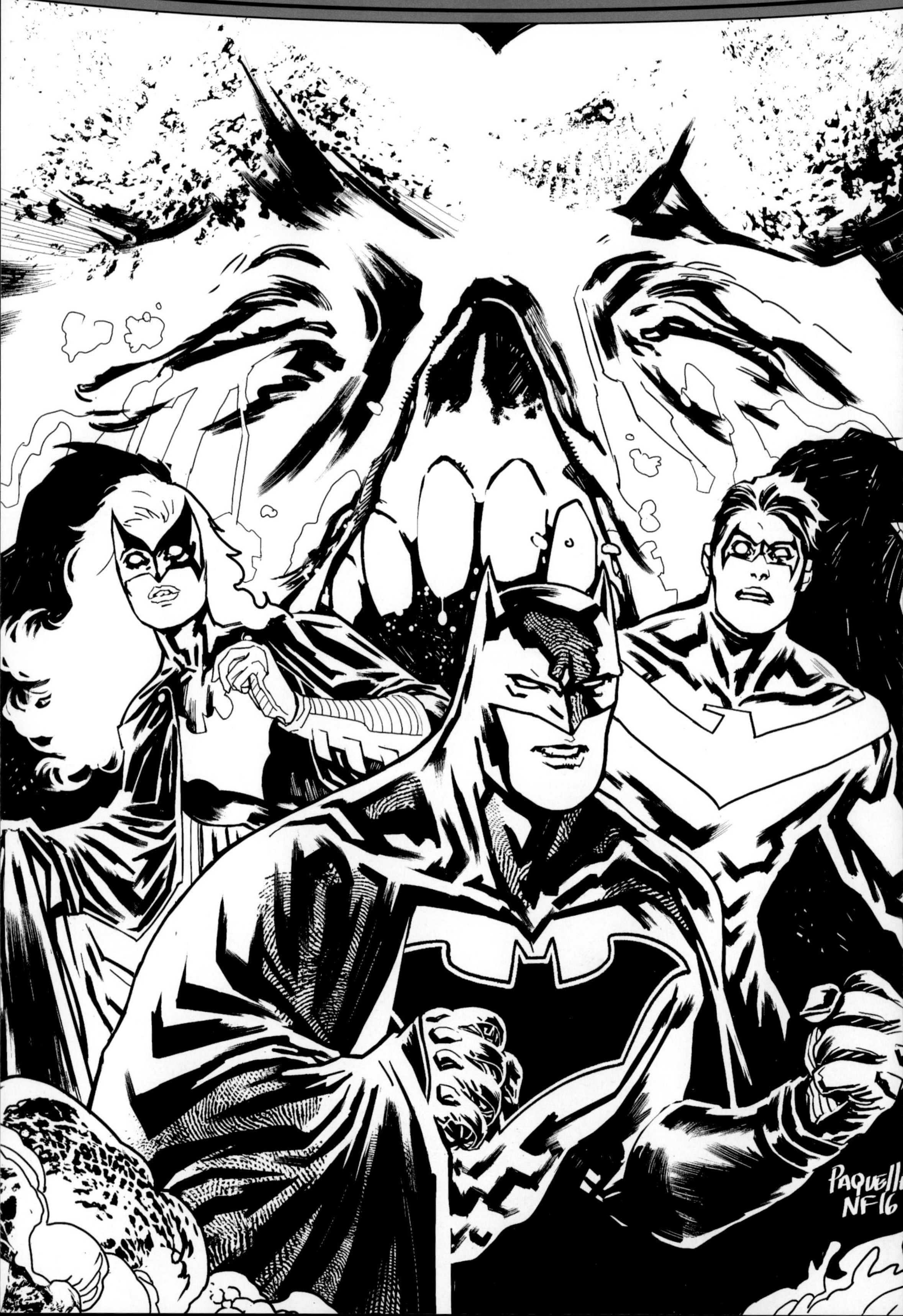
PAQUETTE
NF16

GOTHAM CITY.
TOLLIVER MEMORIAL MORGUE.

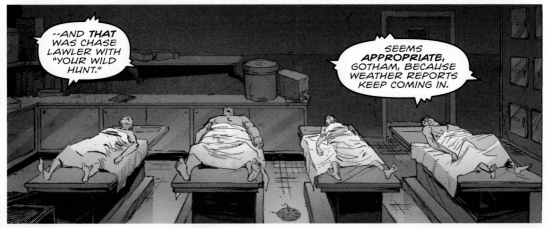

--AND **THAT** WAS CHASE LAWLER WITH "YOUR WILD HUNT."

SEEMS **APPROPRIATE,** GOTHAM, BECAUSE WEATHER REPORTS KEEP COMING IN.

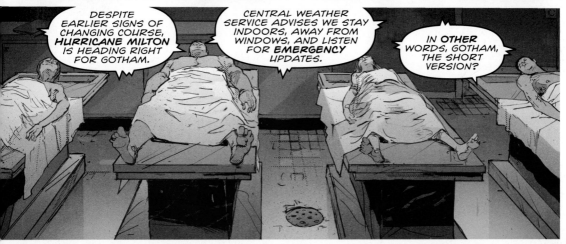

DESPITE EARLIER SIGNS OF CHANGING COURSE, **HURRICANE MILTON** IS HEADING RIGHT FOR GOTHAM.

CENTRAL WEATHER SERVICE ADVISES WE STAY INDOORS, AWAY FROM WINDOWS, AND LISTEN FOR **EMERGENCY** UPDATES.

IN **OTHER** WORDS, GOTHAM, THE SHORT VERSION?

GET READY FOR A **WILD** NIGHT.

FSSS

FSSSS

FSSSS

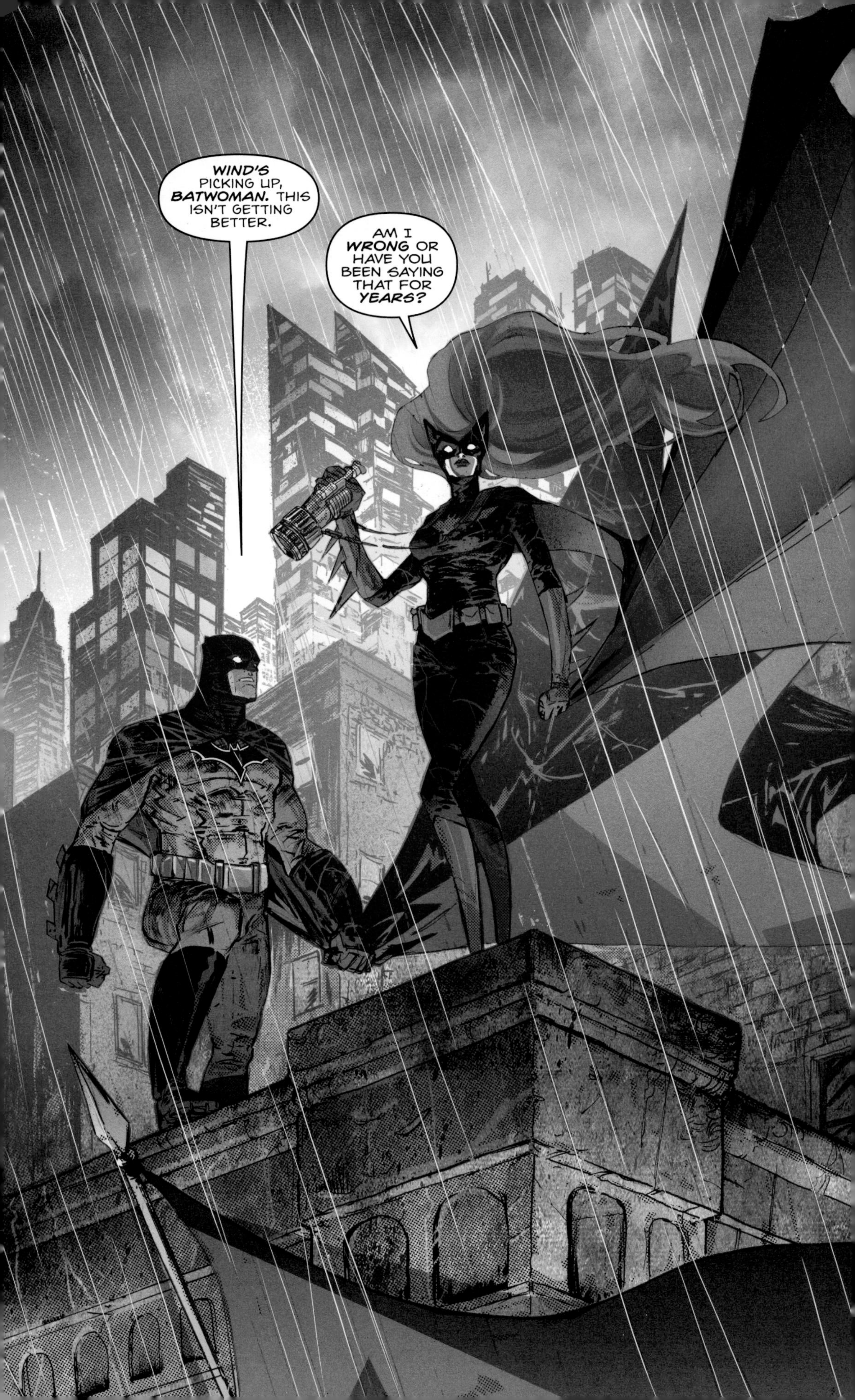
WIND'S PICKING UP, BATWOMAN. THIS ISN'T GETTING BETTER.
AM I WRONG OR HAVE YOU BEEN SAYING THAT FOR YEARS?

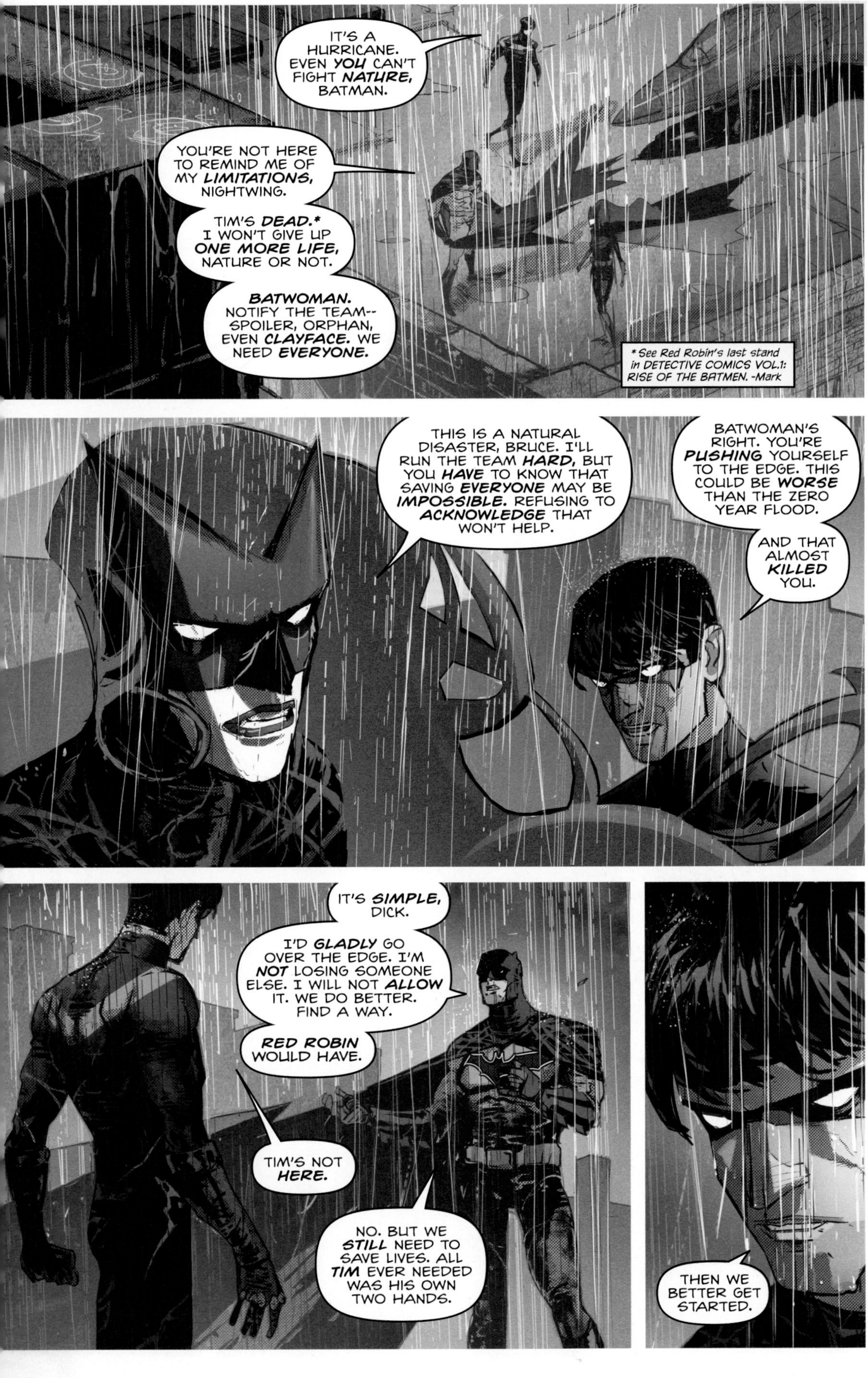

IT'S A HURRICANE. EVEN YOU CAN'T FIGHT NATURE, BATMAN.
YOU'RE NOT HERE TO REMIND ME OF MY LIMITATIONS, NIGHTWING.
TIM'S DEAD.* I WON'T GIVE UP ONE MORE LIFE, NATURE OR NOT.
BATWOMAN. NOTIFY THE TEAM--SPOILER, ORPHAN, EVEN CLAYFACE. WE NEED EVERYONE.
* See Red Robin's last stand in DETECTIVE COMICS VOL.1: RISE OF THE BATMEN. -Mark
THIS IS A NATURAL DISASTER, BRUCE. I'LL RUN THE TEAM HARD, BUT YOU HAVE TO KNOW THAT SAVING EVERYONE MAY BE IMPOSSIBLE. REFUSING TO ACKNOWLEDGE THAT WON'T HELP.
BATWOMAN'S RIGHT. YOU'RE PUSHING YOURSELF TO THE EDGE. THIS COULD BE WORSE THAN THE ZERO YEAR FLOOD.
AND THAT ALMOST KILLED YOU.
IT'S SIMPLE, DICK.
I'D GLADLY GO OVER THE EDGE. I'M NOT LOSING SOMEONE ELSE. I WILL NOT ALLOW IT. WE DO BETTER. FIND A WAY.
RED ROBIN WOULD HAVE.
TIM'S NOT HERE.
NO. BUT WE STILL NEED TO SAVE LIVES. ALL TIM EVER NEEDED WAS HIS OWN TWO HANDS.
THEN WE BETTER GET STARTED.

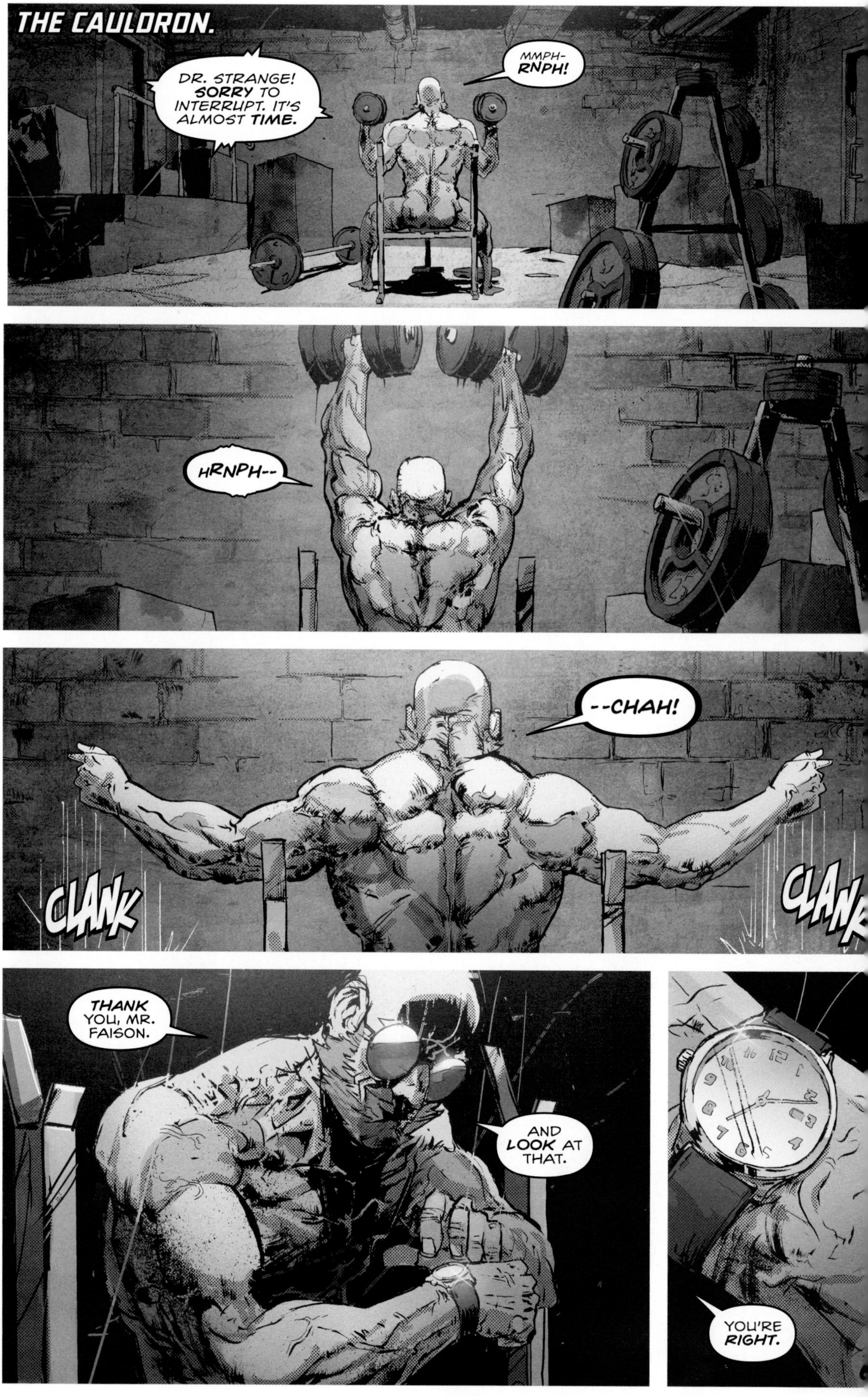
THE CAULDRON.
DR. STRANGE! SORRY TO INTERRUPT. IT'S ALMOST TIME.
MMPH-RNPH!
HRNPH--
--CHAH!
CLANK
CLANK
THANK YOU, MR. FAISON.
AND LOOK AT THAT.
YOU'RE RIGHT.

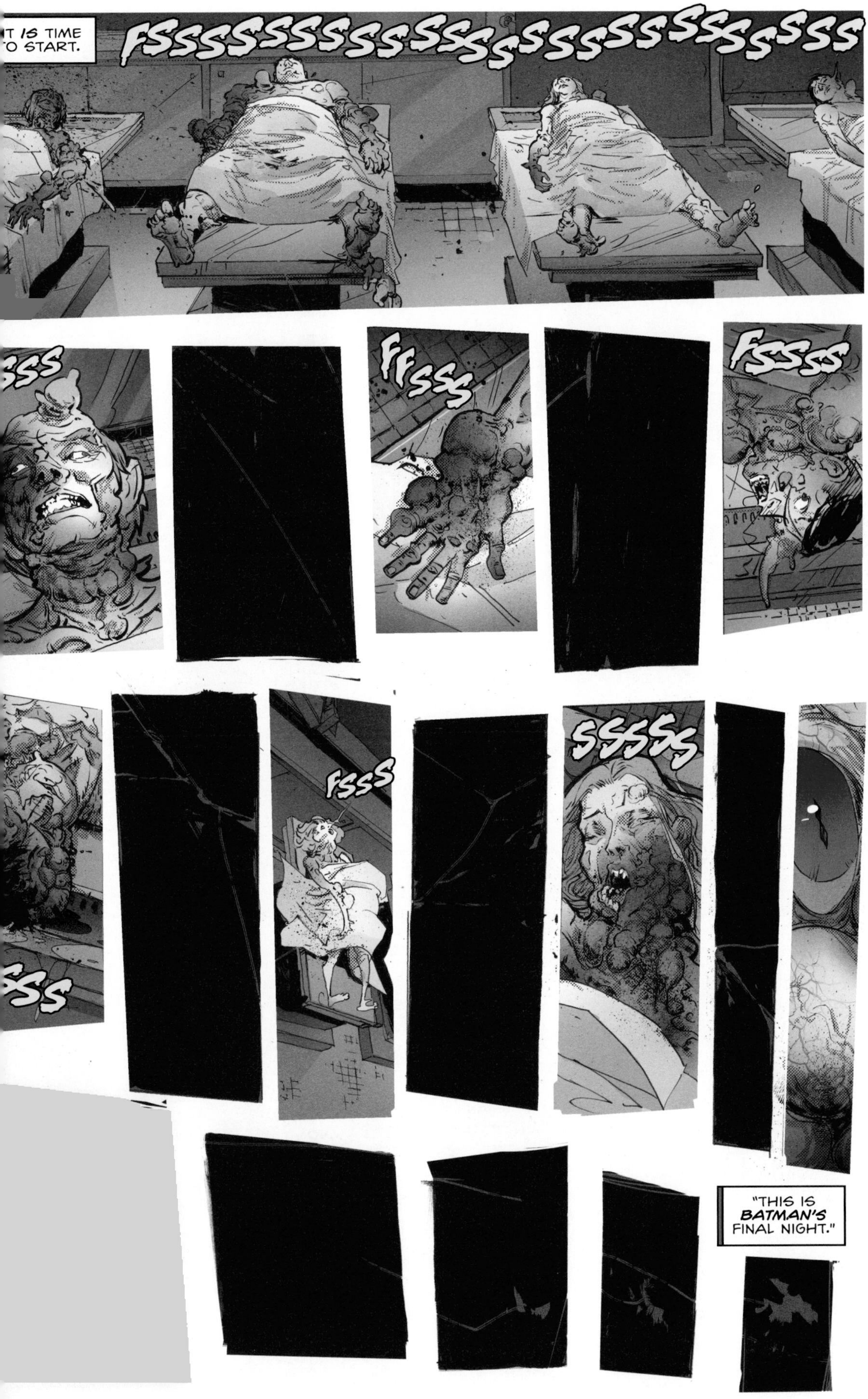
T *IS* TIME
O START.
FSSSSSSSSSSSSSSSSSSSSSSSSSSSS
SSS
FFSSS
FSSSS
SSS
FSSS
SSSSS
"THIS IS *BATMAN'S* FINAL NIGHT."

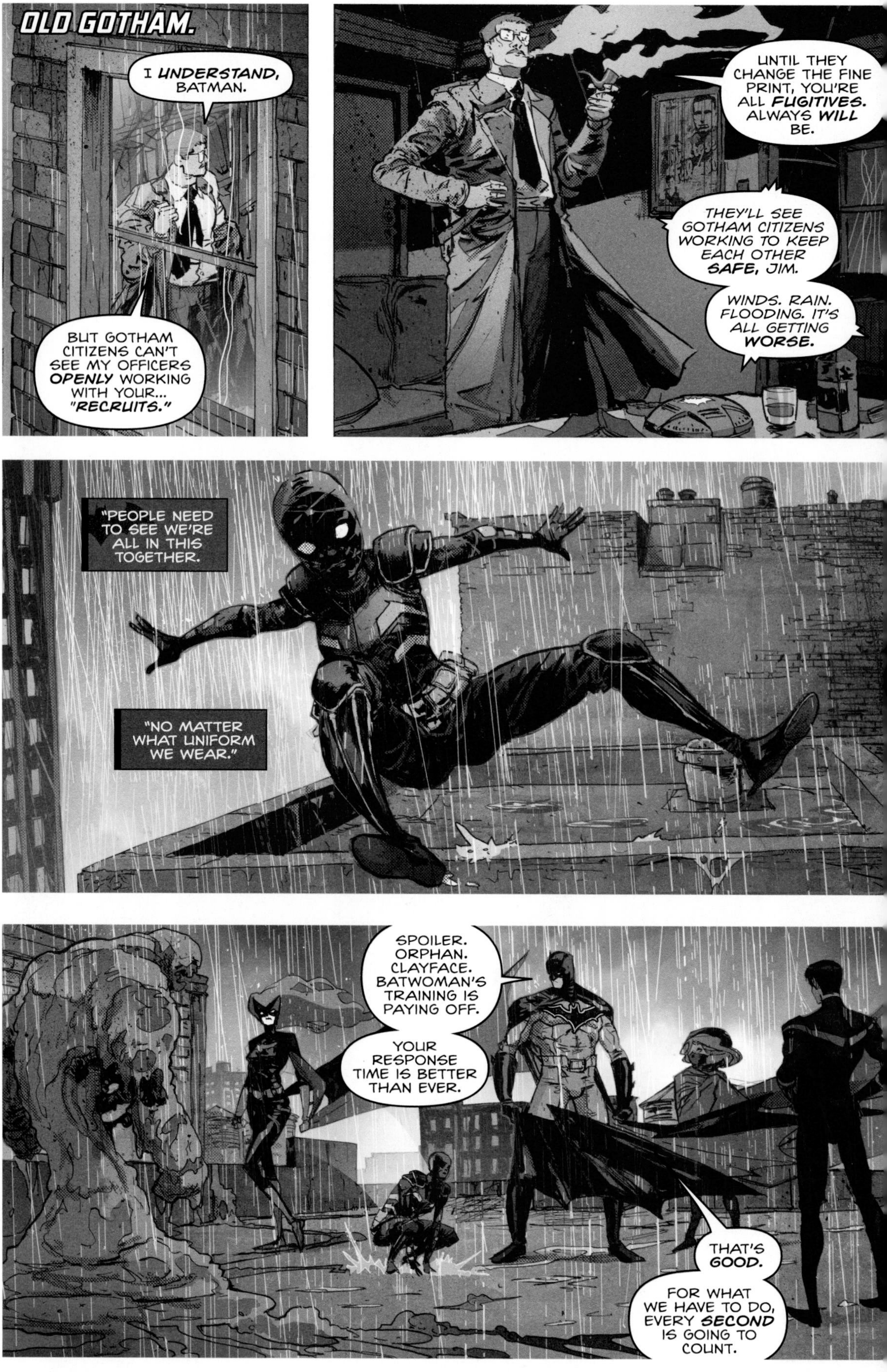
OLD GOTHAM.
I UNDERSTAND, BATMAN.
BUT GOTHAM CITIZENS CAN'T SEE MY OFFICERS OPENLY WORKING WITH YOUR... "RECRUITS."
UNTIL THEY CHANGE THE FINE PRINT, YOU'RE ALL FUGITIVES. ALWAYS WILL BE.
THEY'LL SEE GOTHAM CITIZENS WORKING TO KEEP EACH OTHER SAFE, JIM.
WINDS. RAIN. FLOODING. IT'S ALL GETTING WORSE.
"PEOPLE NEED TO SEE WE'RE ALL IN THIS TOGETHER.
"NO MATTER WHAT UNIFORM WE WEAR."
SPOILER. ORPHAN. CLAYFACE. BATWOMAN'S TRAINING IS PAYING OFF.
YOUR RESPONSE TIME IS BETTER THAN EVER.
THAT'S GOOD.
FOR WHAT WE HAVE TO DO, EVERY SECOND IS GOING TO COUNT.

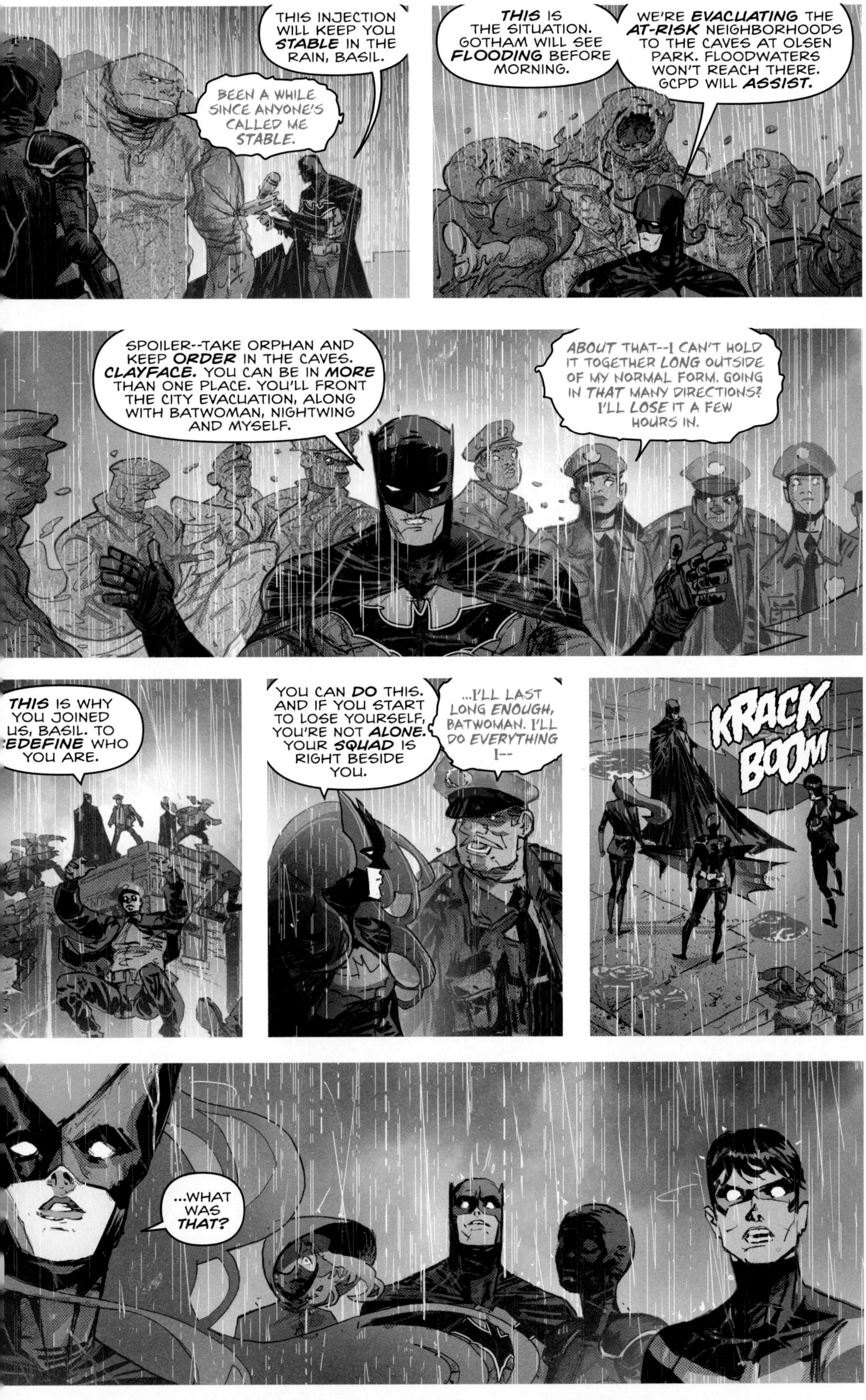
THIS INJECTION WILL KEEP YOU STABLE IN THE RAIN, BASIL.
BEEN A WHILE SINCE ANYONE'S CALLED ME STABLE.
THIS IS THE SITUATION. GOTHAM WILL SEE FLOODING BEFORE MORNING.
WE'RE EVACUATING THE AT-RISK NEIGHBORHOODS TO THE CAVES AT OLSEN PARK. FLOODWATERS WON'T REACH THERE. GCPD WILL ASSIST.
SPOILER--TAKE ORPHAN AND KEEP ORDER IN THE CAVES. CLAYFACE. YOU CAN BE IN MORE THAN ONE PLACE. YOU'LL FRONT THE CITY EVACUATION, ALONG WITH BATWOMAN, NIGHTWING AND MYSELF.
ABOUT THAT--I CAN'T HOLD IT TOGETHER LONG OUTSIDE OF MY NORMAL FORM. GOING IN THAT MANY DIRECTIONS? I'LL LOSE IT A FEW HOURS IN.
THIS IS WHY YOU JOINED US, BASIL. TO EDEFINE WHO YOU ARE.
YOU CAN DO THIS. AND IF YOU START TO LOSE YOURSELF, YOU'RE NOT ALONE. YOUR SQUAD IS RIGHT BESIDE YOU.
...I'LL LAST LONG ENOUGH, BATWOMAN. I'LL DO EVERYTHING I--
KRACK BOOM
...WHAT WAS THAT?

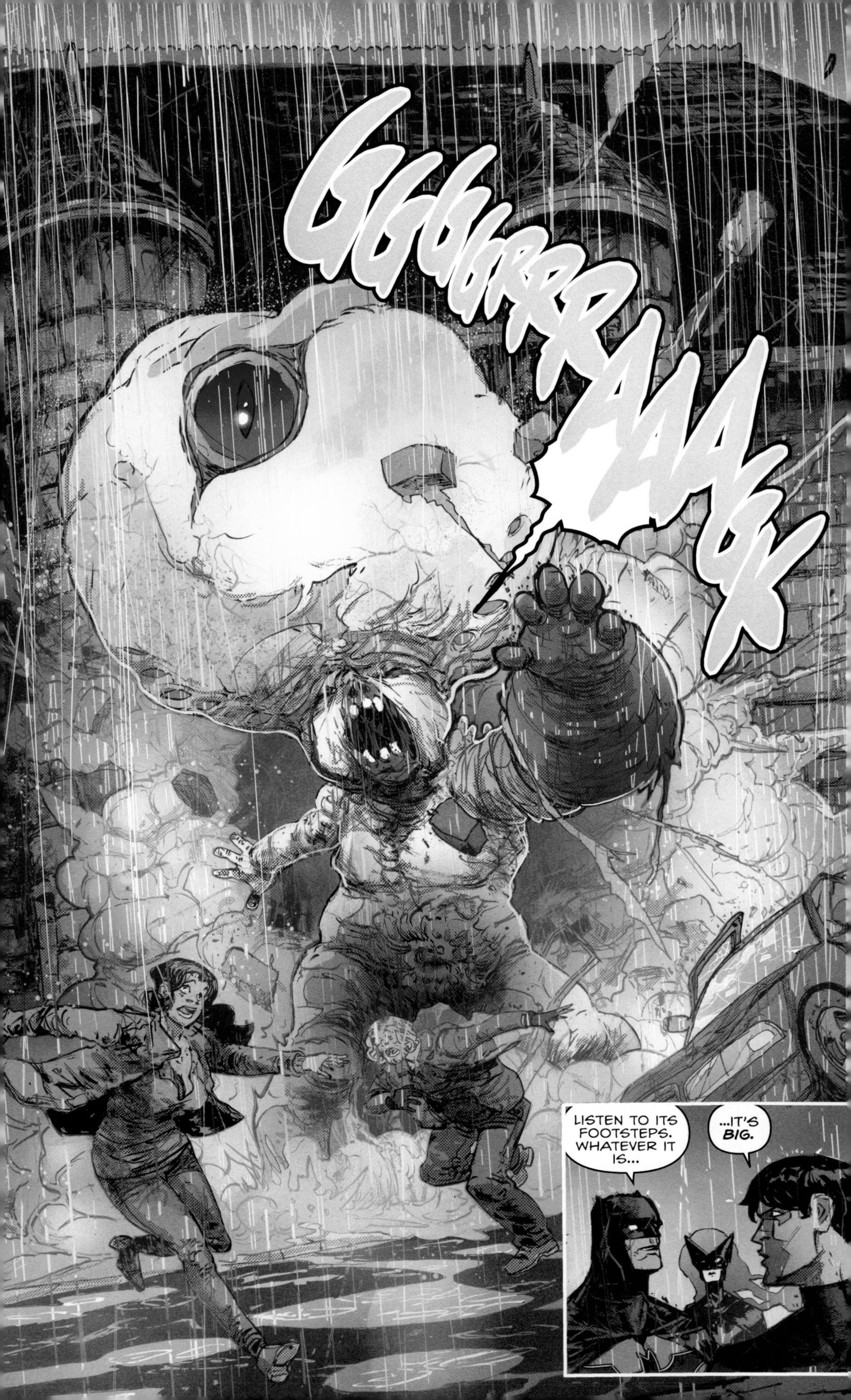
GGGGRRRAAAGK
LISTEN TO ITS FOOTSTEPS. WHATEVER IT IS...
...IT'S *BIG.*

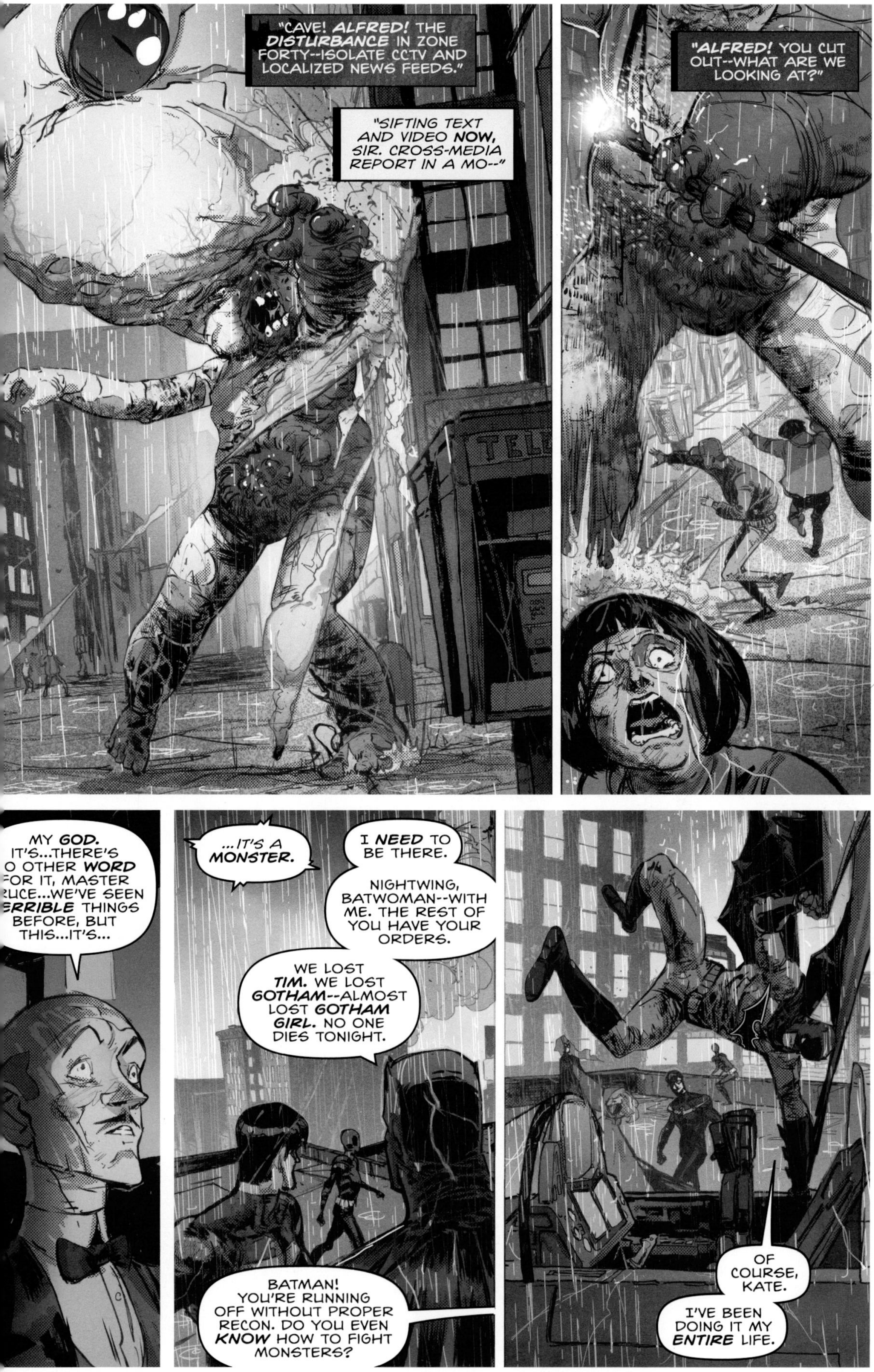
"CAVE! ALFRED! THE DISTURBANCE IN ZONE FORTY--ISOLATE CCTV AND LOCALIZED NEWS FEEDS."
"SIFTING TEXT AND VIDEO NOW, SIR. CROSS-MEDIA REPORT IN A MO--"
"ALFRED! YOU CUT OUT--WHAT ARE WE LOOKING AT?"
MY GOD. IT'S...THERE'S O OTHER WORD FOR IT, MASTER RUCE...WE'VE SEEN ERRIBLE THINGS BEFORE, BUT THIS...IT'S...
...IT'S A MONSTER.
I NEED TO BE THERE.
NIGHTWING, BATWOMAN--WITH ME. THE REST OF YOU HAVE YOUR ORDERS.
WE LOST TIM. WE LOST GOTHAM--ALMOST LOST GOTHAM GIRL. NO ONE DIES TONIGHT.
BATMAN! YOU'RE RUNNING OFF WITHOUT PROPER RECON. DO YOU EVEN KNOW HOW TO FIGHT MONSTERS?
OF COURSE, KATE.
I'VE BEEN DOING IT MY ENTIRE LIFE.

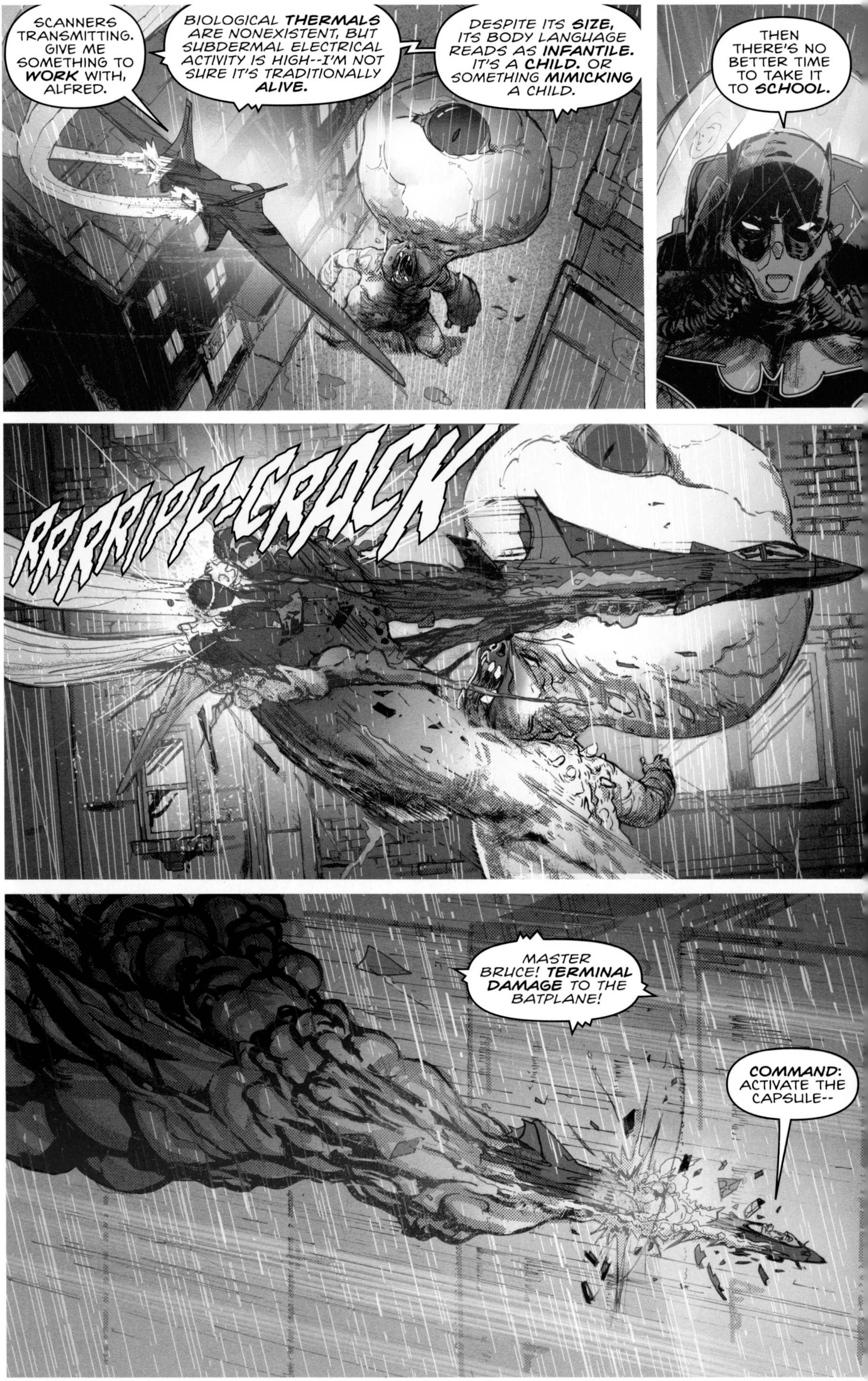
SCANNERS TRANSMITTING. GIVE ME SOMETHING TO **WORK** WITH, ALFRED.
BIOLOGICAL **THERMALS** ARE NONEXISTENT, BUT SUBDERMAL ELECTRICAL ACTIVITY IS HIGH--I'M NOT SURE IT'S TRADITIONALLY **ALIVE.**
DESPITE ITS **SIZE,** ITS BODY LANGUAGE READS AS **INFANTILE.** IT'S A **CHILD.** OR SOMETHING **MIMICKING** A CHILD.
THEN THERE'S NO BETTER TIME TO TAKE IT TO **SCHOOL.**
RRRRIPP-CRACK
MASTER BRUCE! **TERMINAL DAMAGE** TO THE BATPLANE!
COMMAND: ACTIVATE THE CAPSULE--

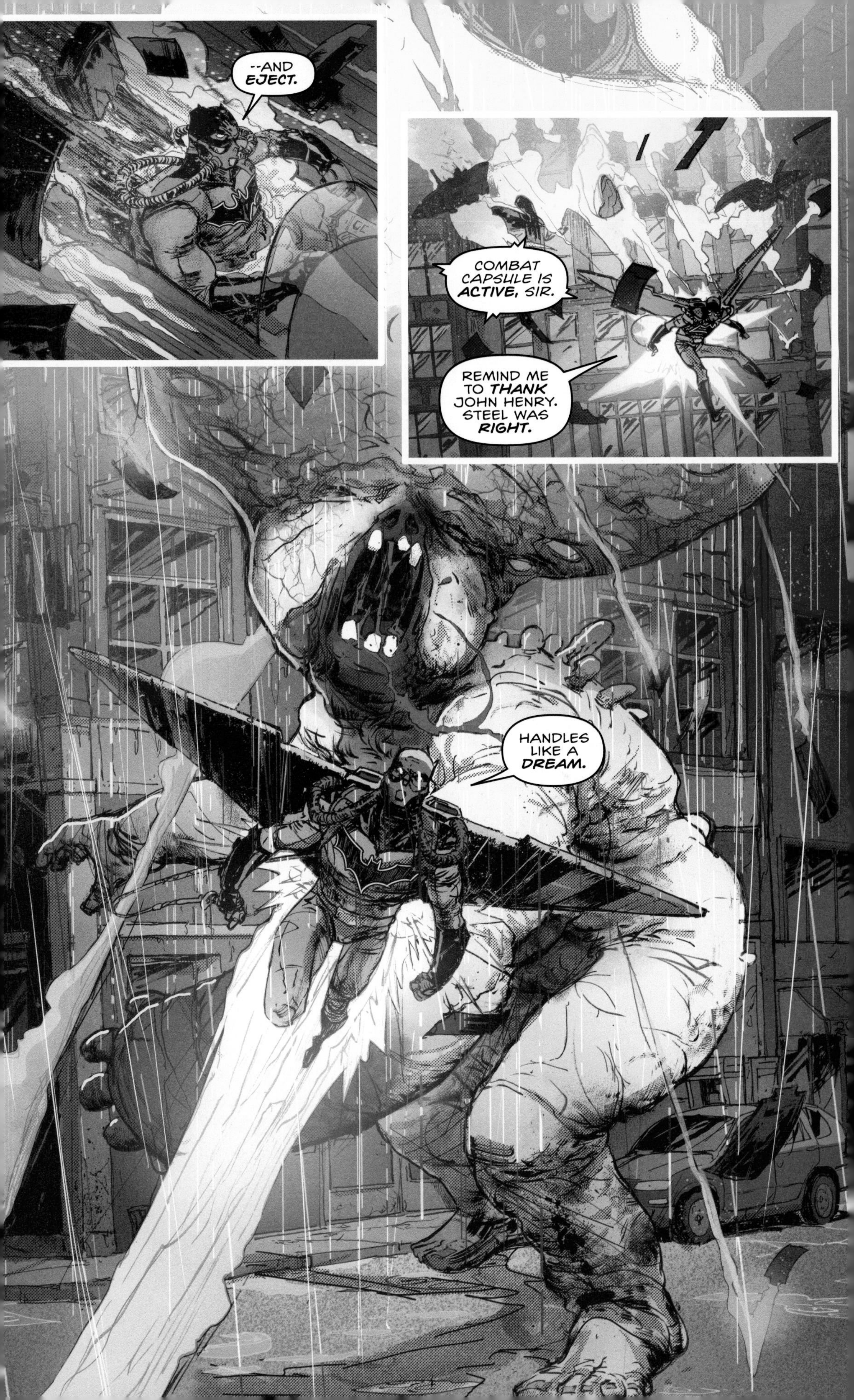
--AND EJECT.
COMBAT CAPSULE IS ACTIVE, SIR.
REMIND ME TO THANK JOHN HENRY. STEEL WAS RIGHT.
HANDLES LIKE A DREAM.

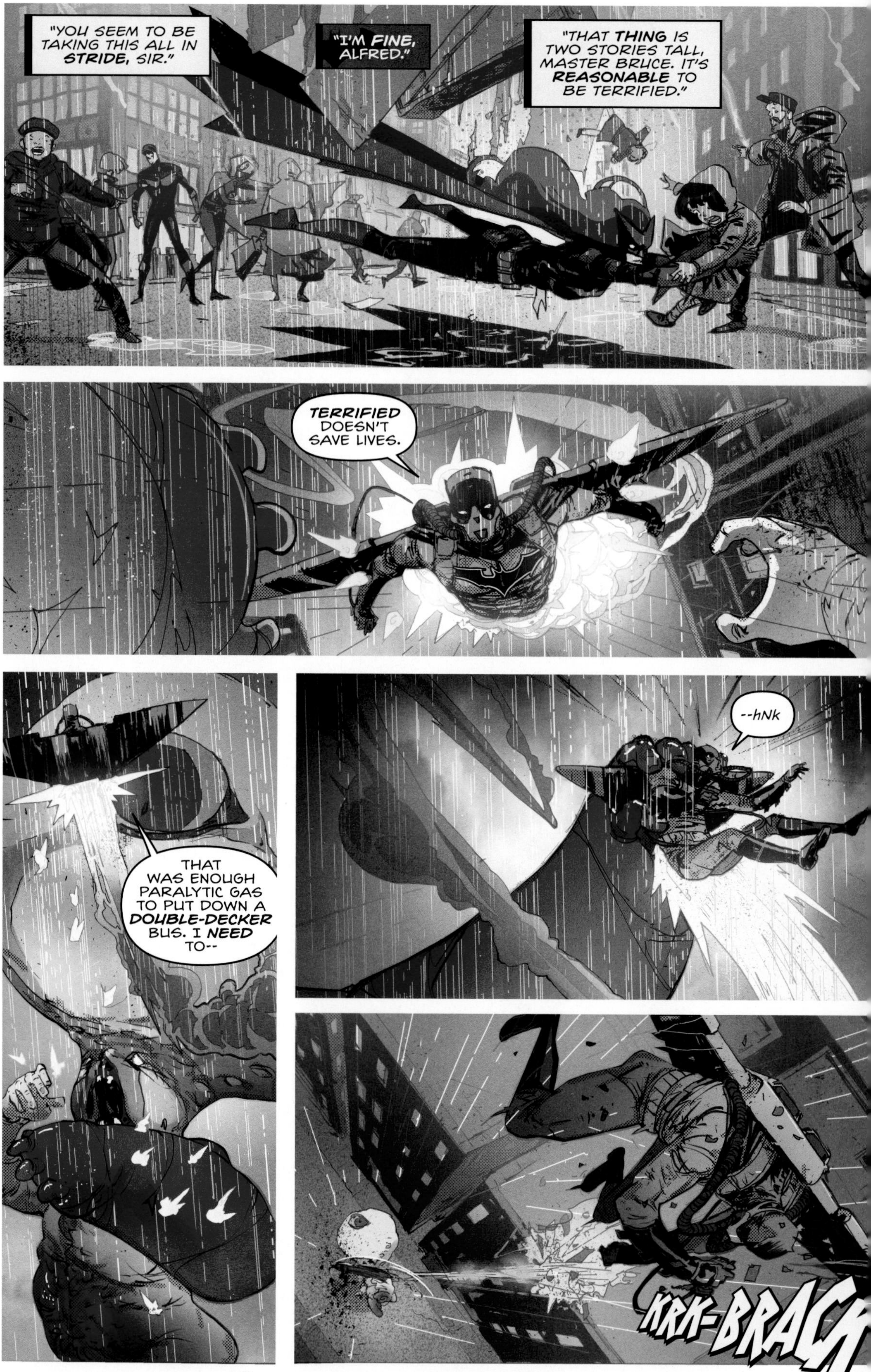
"YOU SEEM TO BE TAKING THIS ALL IN STRIDE, SIR."
"I'M FINE, ALFRED."
"THAT THING IS TWO STORIES TALL, MASTER BRUCE. IT'S REASONABLE TO BE TERRIFIED."
TERRIFIED DOESN'T SAVE LIVES.
THAT WAS ENOUGH PARALYTIC GAS TO PUT DOWN A DOUBLE-DECKER BUS. I NEED TO--
--hNk
KRK-BRACK

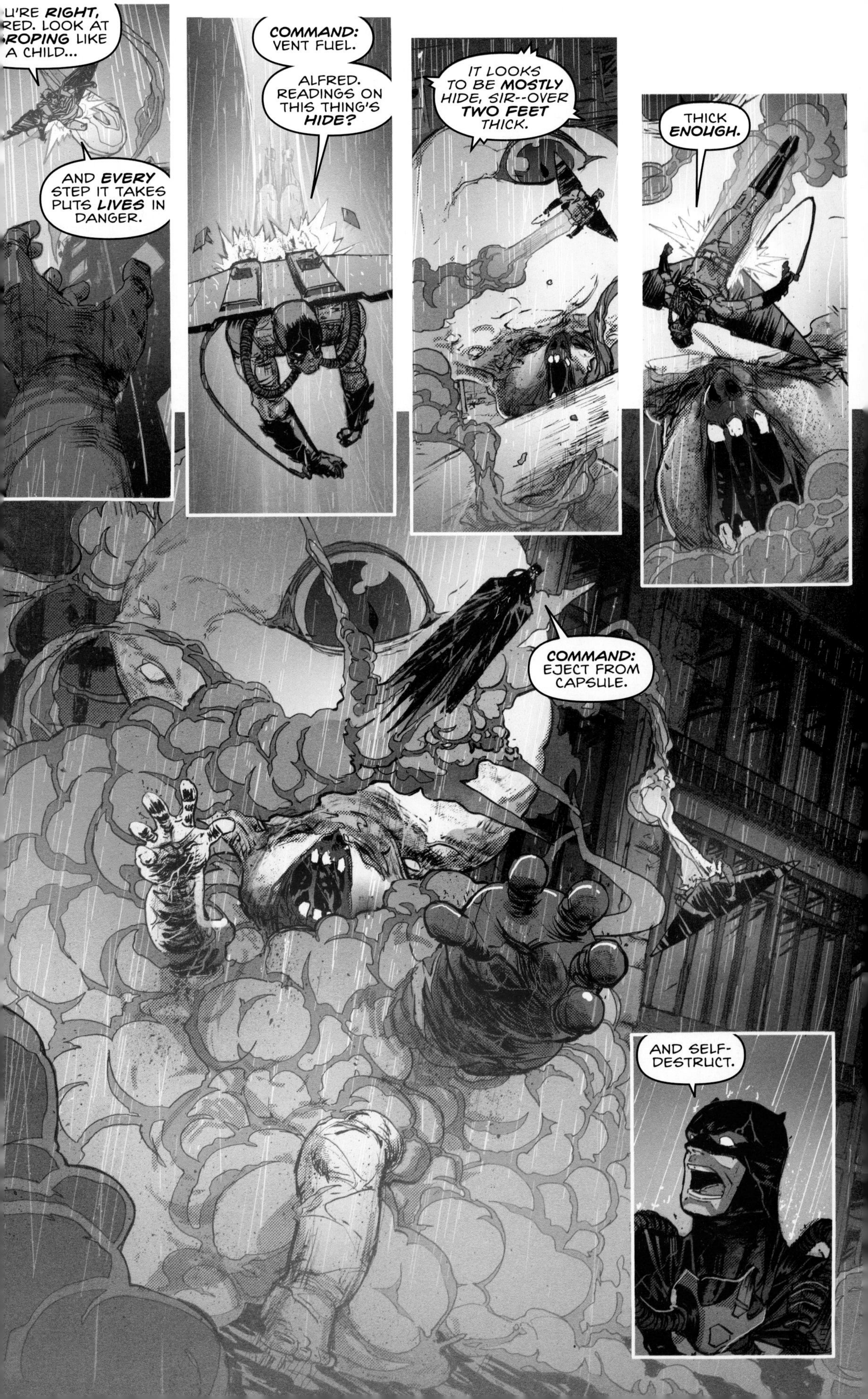

U'RE RIGHT, RED. LOOK AT ROPING LIKE A CHILD...
AND EVERY STEP IT TAKES PUTS LIVES IN DANGER.
COMMAND: VENT FUEL.
ALFRED. READINGS ON THIS THING'S HIDE?
IT LOOKS TO BE MOSTLY HIDE, SIR--OVER TWO FEET THICK.
THICK ENOUGH.
COMMAND: EJECT FROM CAPSULE.
AND SELF-DESTRUCT.

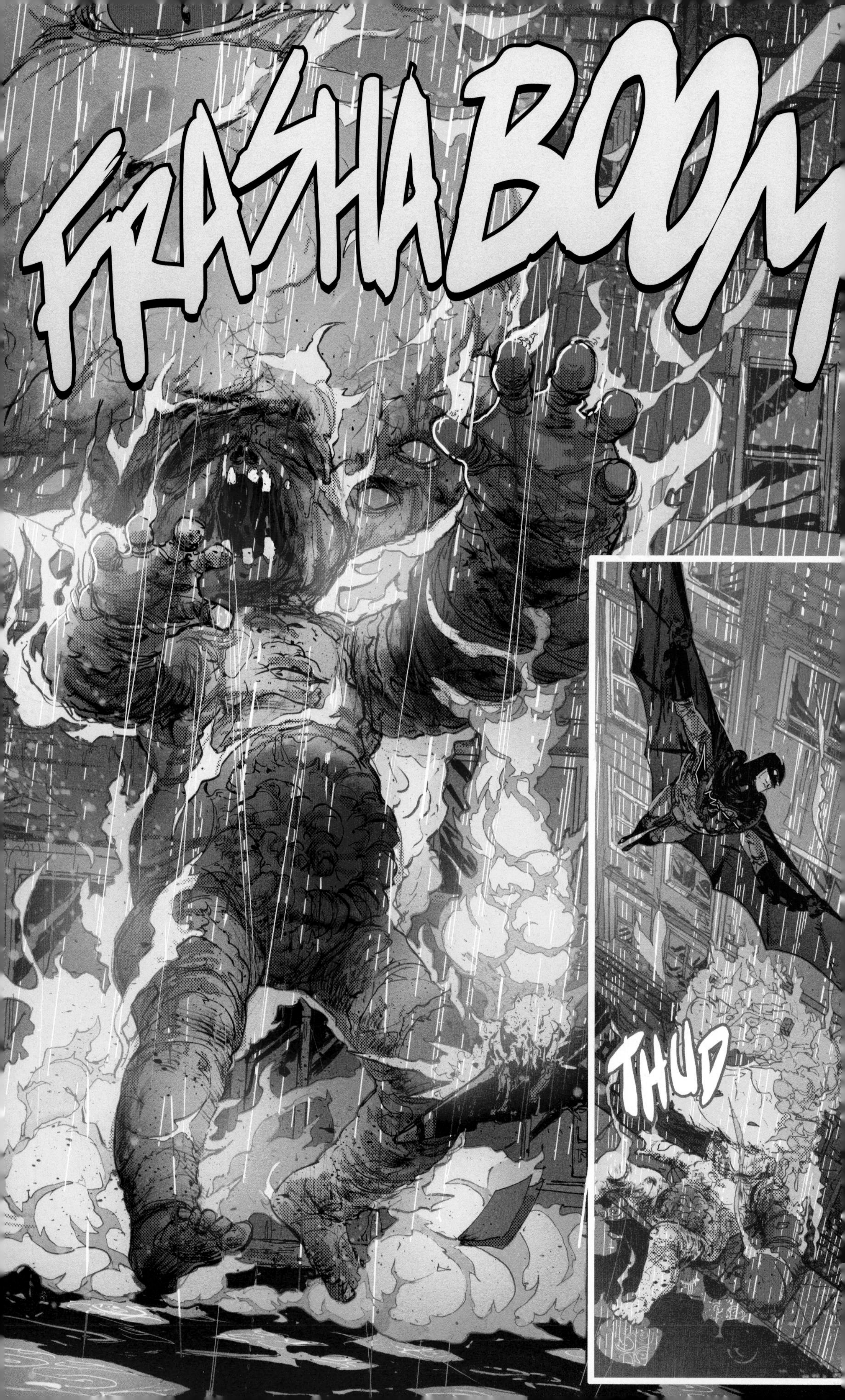
FRASHABOOM
THUD

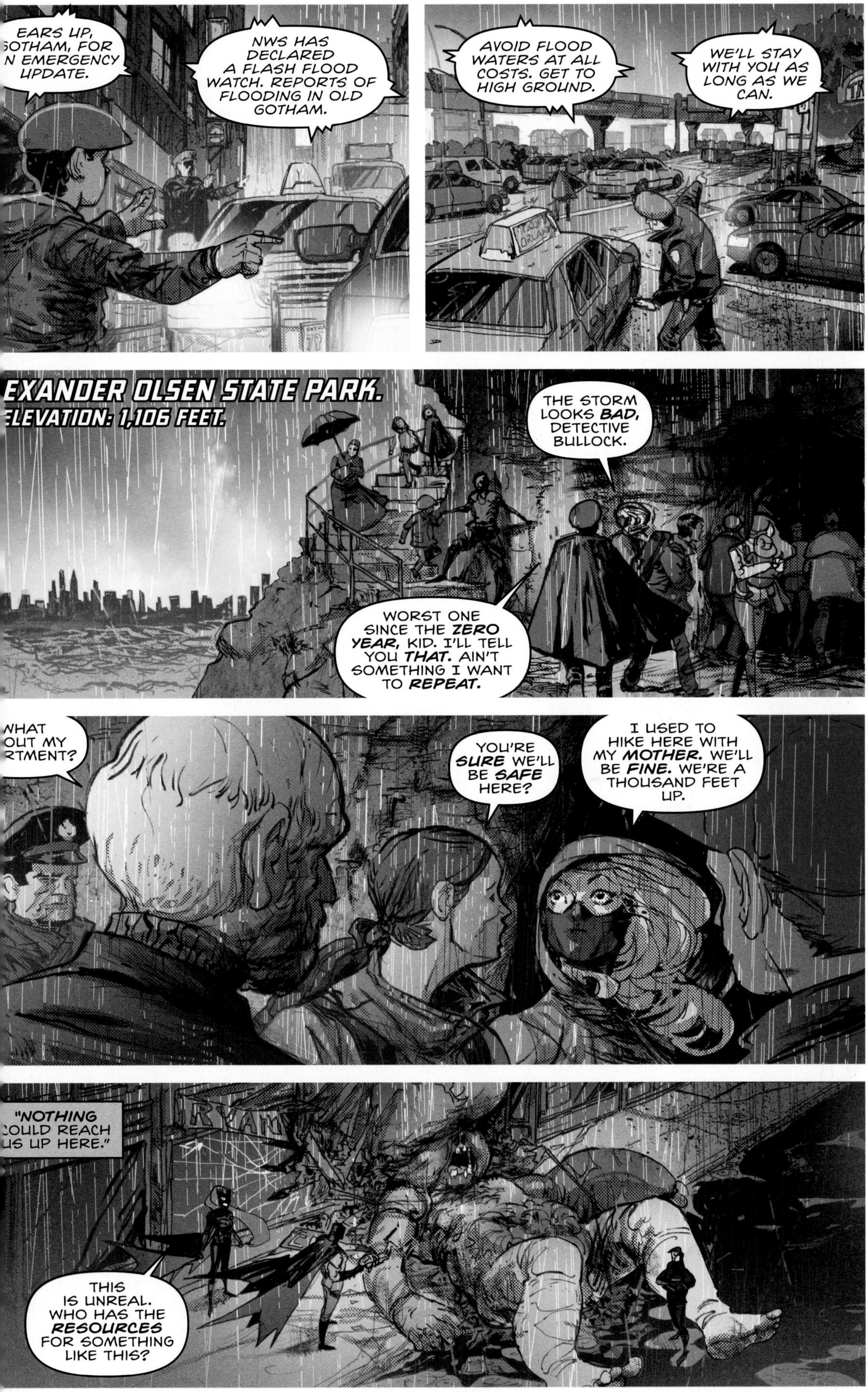
EARS UP, OTHAM, FOR N EMERGENCY UPDATE.
NWS HAS DECLARED A FLASH FLOOD WATCH. REPORTS OF FLOODING IN OLD GOTHAM.
AVOID FLOOD WATERS AT ALL COSTS. GET TO HIGH GROUND.
WE'LL STAY WITH YOU AS LONG AS WE CAN.
EXANDER OLSEN STATE PARK. ELEVATION: 1,106 FEET.
THE STORM LOOKS BAD, DETECTIVE BULLOCK.
WORST ONE SINCE THE ZERO YEAR, KID. I'LL TELL YOU THAT. AIN'T SOMETHING I WANT TO REPEAT.
WHAT OUT MY RTMENT?
YOU'RE SURE WE'LL BE SAFE HERE?
I USED TO HIKE HERE WITH MY MOTHER. WE'LL BE FINE. WE'RE A THOUSAND FEET UP.
"NOTHING COULD REACH US UP HERE."
THIS IS UNREAL. WHO HAS THE RESOURCES FOR SOMETHING LIKE THIS?

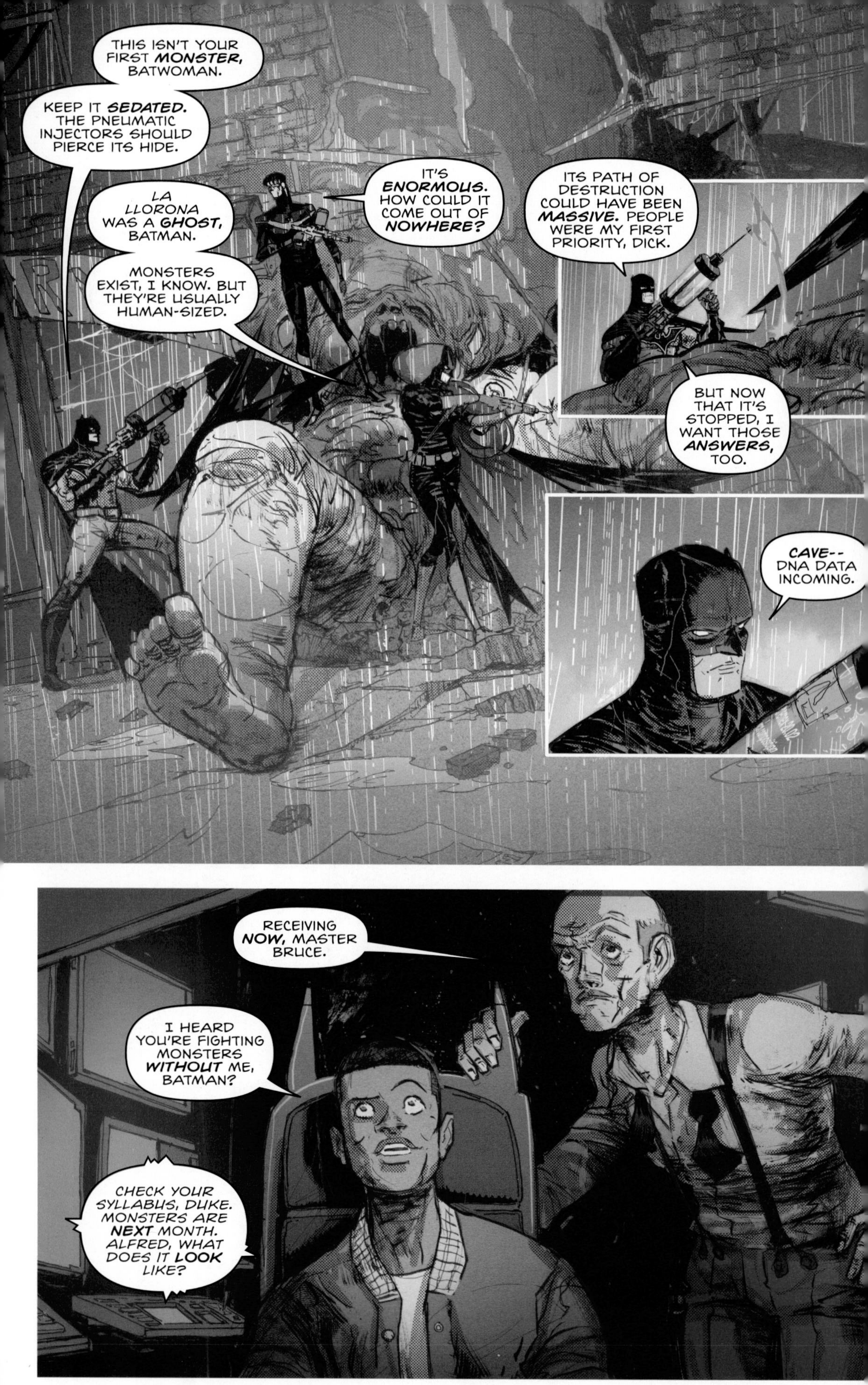
THIS ISN'T YOUR FIRST MONSTER, BATWOMAN.
KEEP IT SEDATED. THE PNEUMATIC INJECTORS SHOULD PIERCE ITS HIDE.
LA LLORONA WAS A GHOST, BATMAN.
MONSTERS EXIST, I KNOW. BUT THEY'RE USUALLY HUMAN-SIZED.
IT'S ENORMOUS. HOW COULD IT COME OUT OF NOWHERE?
ITS PATH OF DESTRUCTION COULD HAVE BEEN MASSIVE. PEOPLE WERE MY FIRST PRIORITY, DICK.
BUT NOW THAT IT'S STOPPED, I WANT THOSE ANSWERS, TOO.
CAVE--DNA DATA INCOMING.
RECEIVING NOW, MASTER BRUCE.
I HEARD YOU'RE FIGHTING MONSTERS WITHOUT ME, BATMAN?
CHECK YOUR SYLLABUS, DUKE. MONSTERS ARE NEXT MONTH. ALFRED, WHAT DOES IT LOOK LIKE?

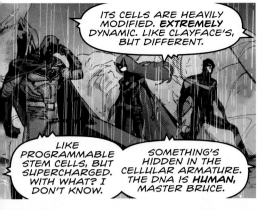

ITS CELLS ARE HEAVILY MODIFIED. **EXTREMELY** DYNAMIC. LIKE CLAYFACE'S, BUT DIFFERENT.

LIKE PROGRAMMABLE STEM CELLS, BUT SUPERCHARGED. WITH WHAT? I DON'T KNOW.

SOMETHING'S HIDDEN IN THE CELLULAR ARMATURE. THE DNA IS **HUMAN**, MASTER BRUCE.

WHAT'S **MORE,** THE BASE DNA PINGS PUBLIC RECORDS. THIS THING WAS LOGGED AT THE TOLLIVER MEMORIAL MORGUE, UNDER THE NAME ROBERT CASTRO.

...CASTRO?

ALFRED? I NEED CRIME SCENE FOOTAGE. GCPD. COMMISSIONER'S OFFICE. THE **D.O.A.** JUST AFTER THE GRUNDY ATTACK.*

FEED IT INTO MY COWL.

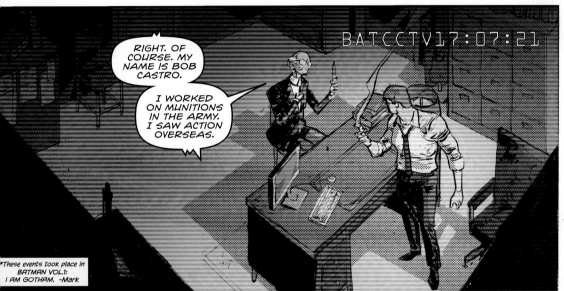

BATCCTV 17:07:21

RIGHT. OF COURSE. MY NAME IS BOB CASTRO.

I WORKED ON MUNITIONS IN THE ARMY. I SAW ACTION OVERSEAS.

*These events took place in BATMAN VOL.1: I AM GOTHAM. -Mark

BATCCTV 17:07:56

BUT THAT'S NOT AN EXCUSE, OR IT'S NOT ANYTHING. FOR WHAT HAPPENED, I MEAN.

IT'S..IT'S JUST, I...I DIDN'T REALLY HAVE A CHOICE, DID I?

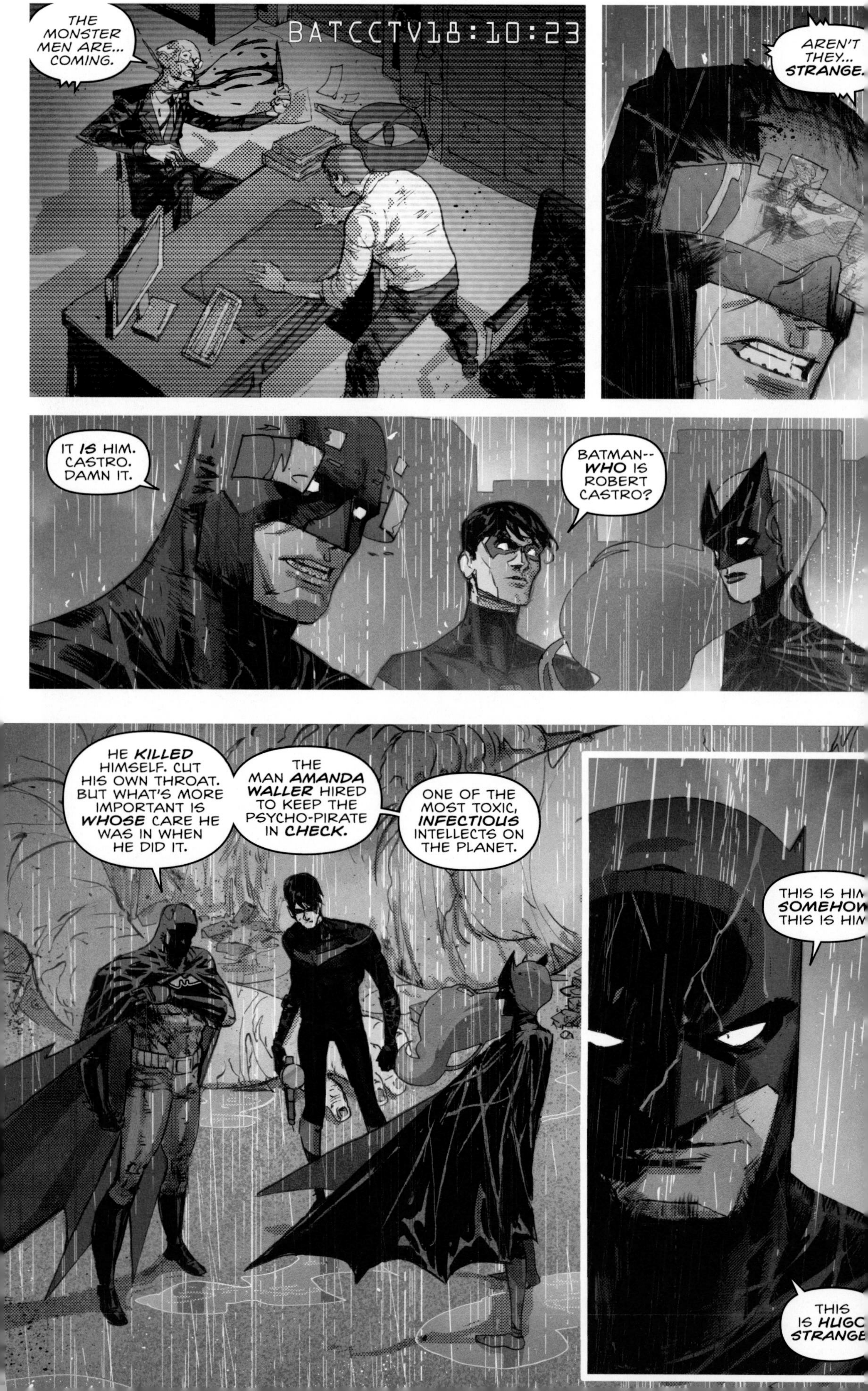
THE MONSTER MEN ARE... COMING.
BATCCTV18:10:23
AREN'T THEY... STRANGE
IT IS HIM. CASTRO. DAMN IT.
BATMAN-- WHO IS ROBERT CASTRO?
HE KILLED HIMSELF. CUT HIS OWN THROAT. BUT WHAT'S MORE IMPORTANT IS WHOSE CARE HE WAS IN WHEN HE DID IT.
THE MAN AMANDA WALLER HIRED TO KEEP THE PSYCHO-PIRATE IN CHECK.
ONE OF THE MOST TOXIC, INFECTIOUS INTELLECTS ON THE PLANET.
THIS IS HI
SOMEHOW
THIS IS HI
THIS IS HUG
STRANGE

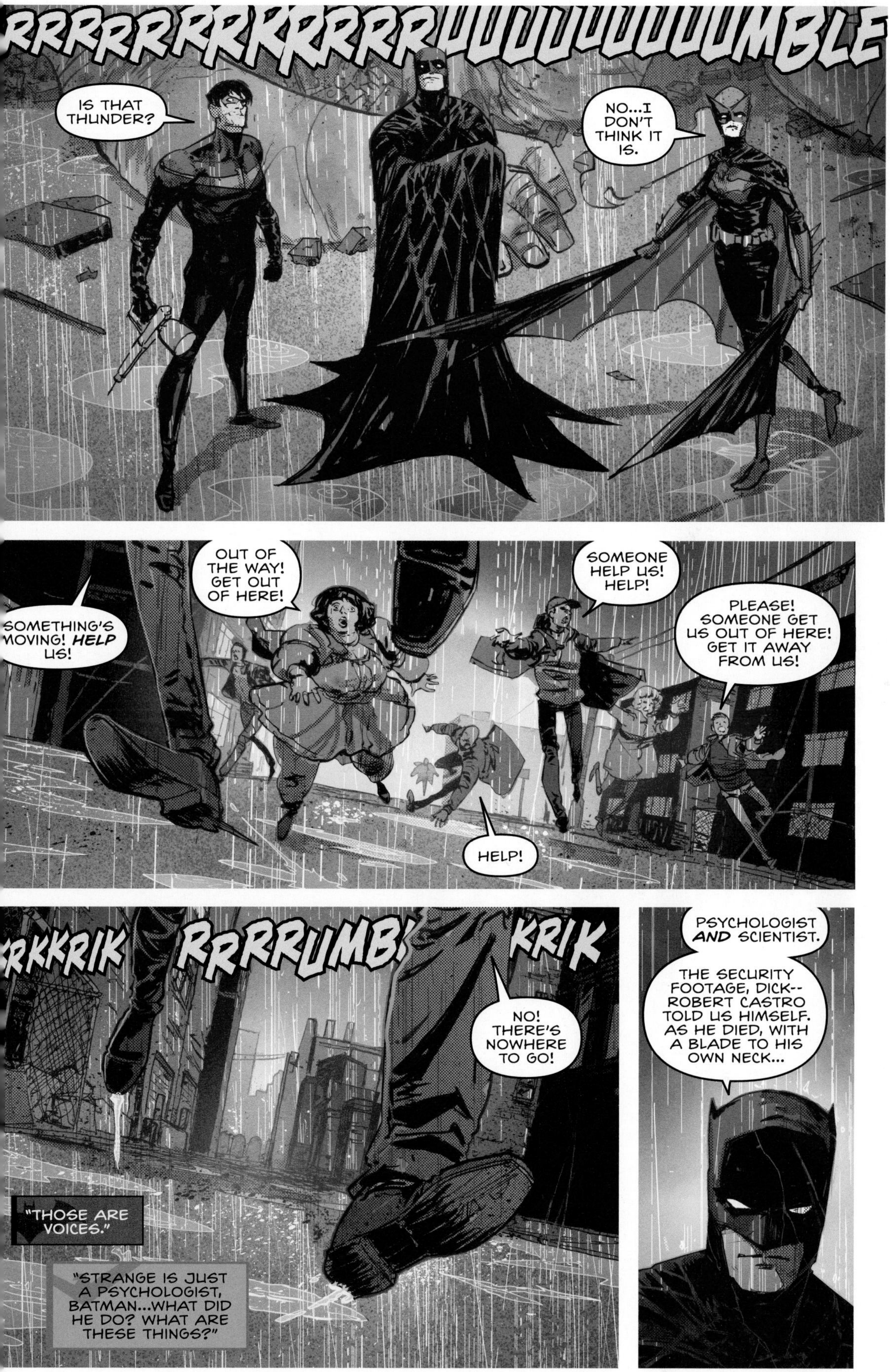
RRRRRRRRRRRRRUUUUUUUUUMBLE
IS THAT THUNDER?
NO...I DON'T THINK IT IS.
SOMETHING'S MOVING! HELP US!
OUT OF THE WAY! GET OUT OF HERE!
SOMEONE HELP US! HELP!
PLEASE! SOMEONE GET US OUT OF HERE! GET IT AWAY FROM US!
HELP!
KKKRIK
RRRRUMB
KRIK
NO! THERE'S NOWHERE TO GO!
"THOSE ARE VOICES."
"STRANGE IS JUST A PSYCHOLOGIST, BATMAN...WHAT DID HE DO? WHAT ARE THESE THINGS?"
PSYCHOLOGIST AND SCIENTIST.
THE SECURITY FOOTAGE, DICK-- ROBERT CASTRO TOLD US HIMSELF. AS HE DIED, WITH A BLADE TO HIS OWN NECK...

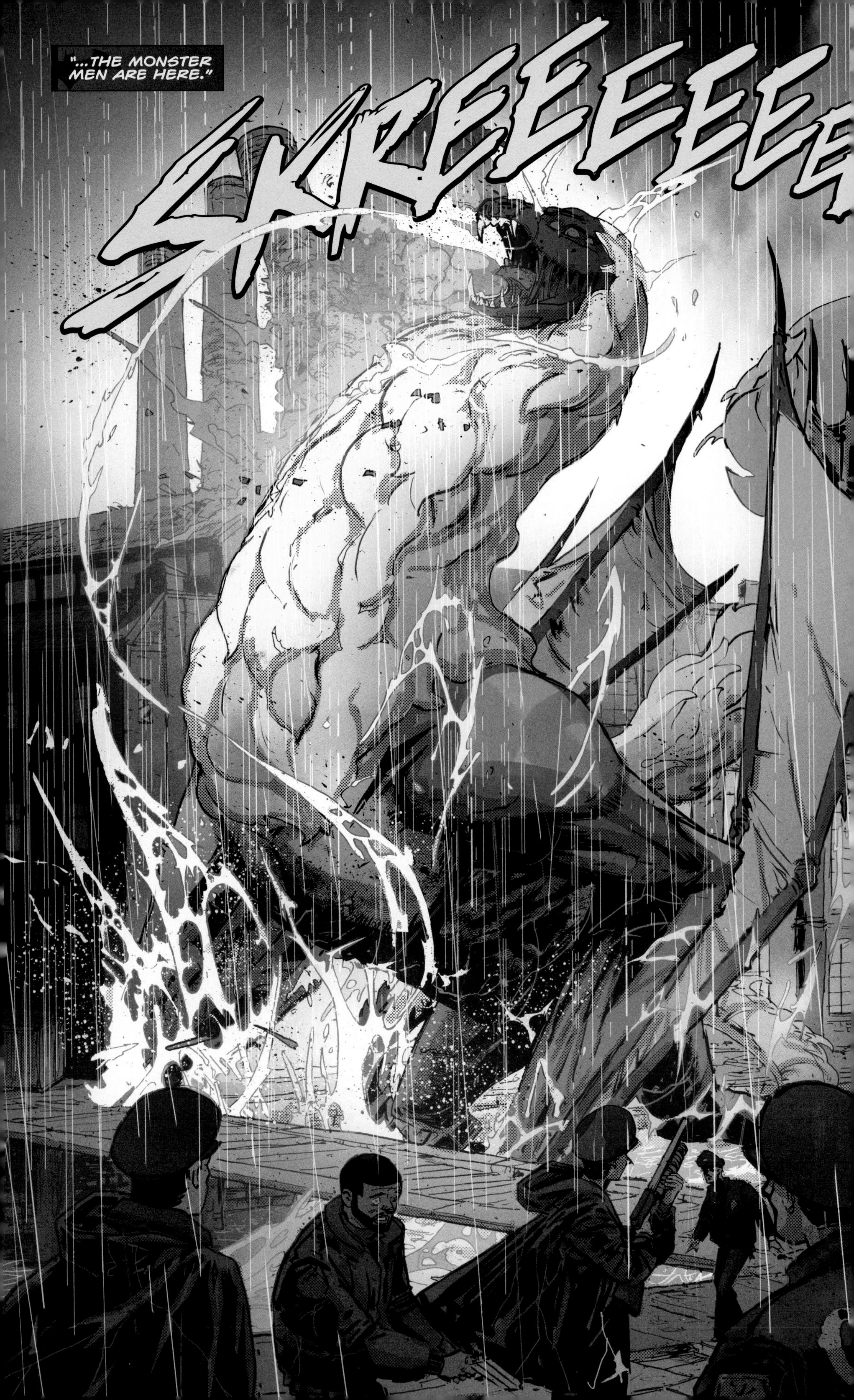
"...THE MONSTER MEN ARE HERE."
SKREEEEEE

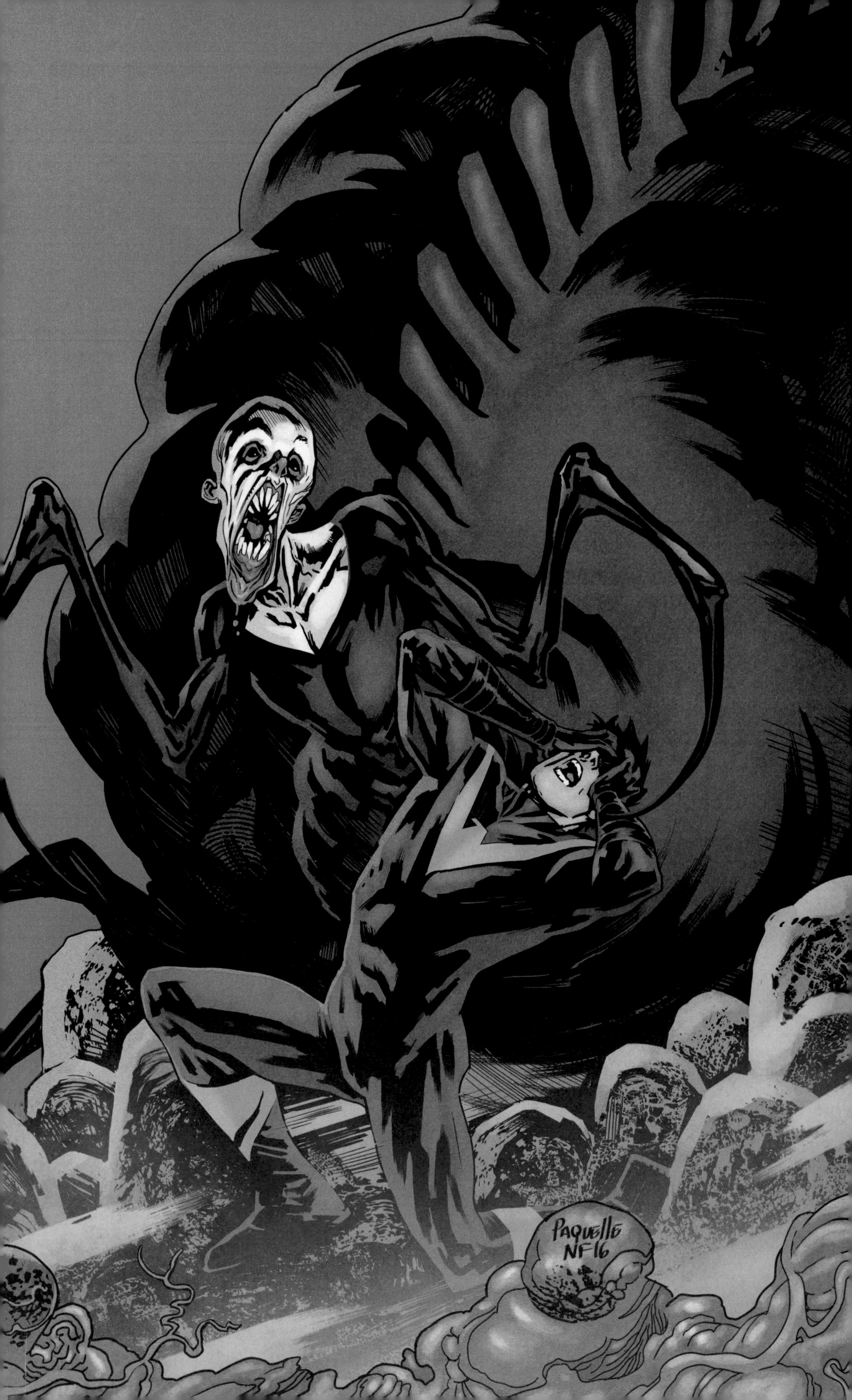
PAQUETTE
NF16

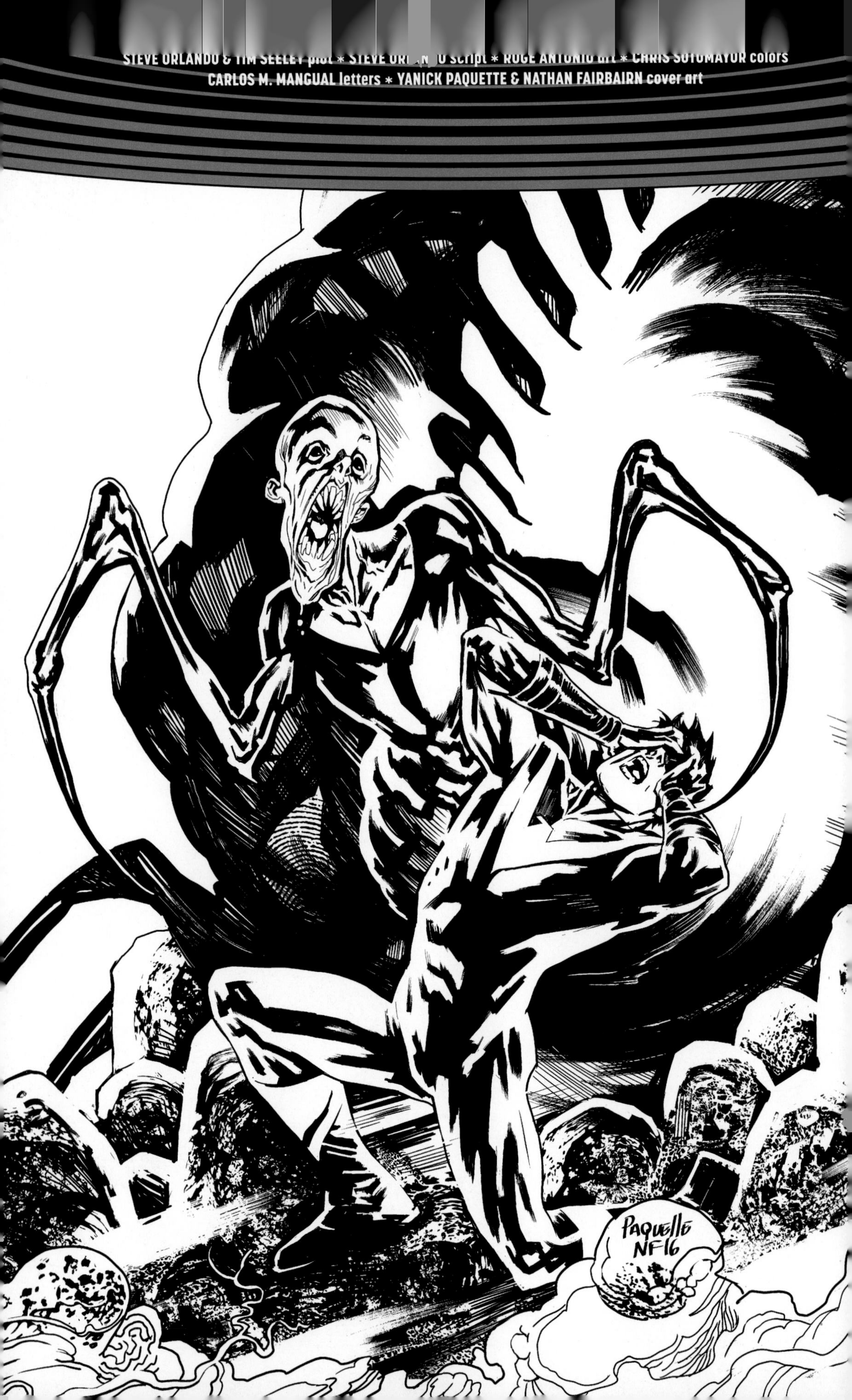
STEVE ORLANDO & TIM SEELEY plot * STEVE ORLANDO script * ROGE ANTONIO art * CHRIS SOTOMAYOR colors
CARLOS M. MANGUAL letters * YANICK PAQUETTE & NATHAN FAIRBAIRN cover art
PAQUETTE NF16

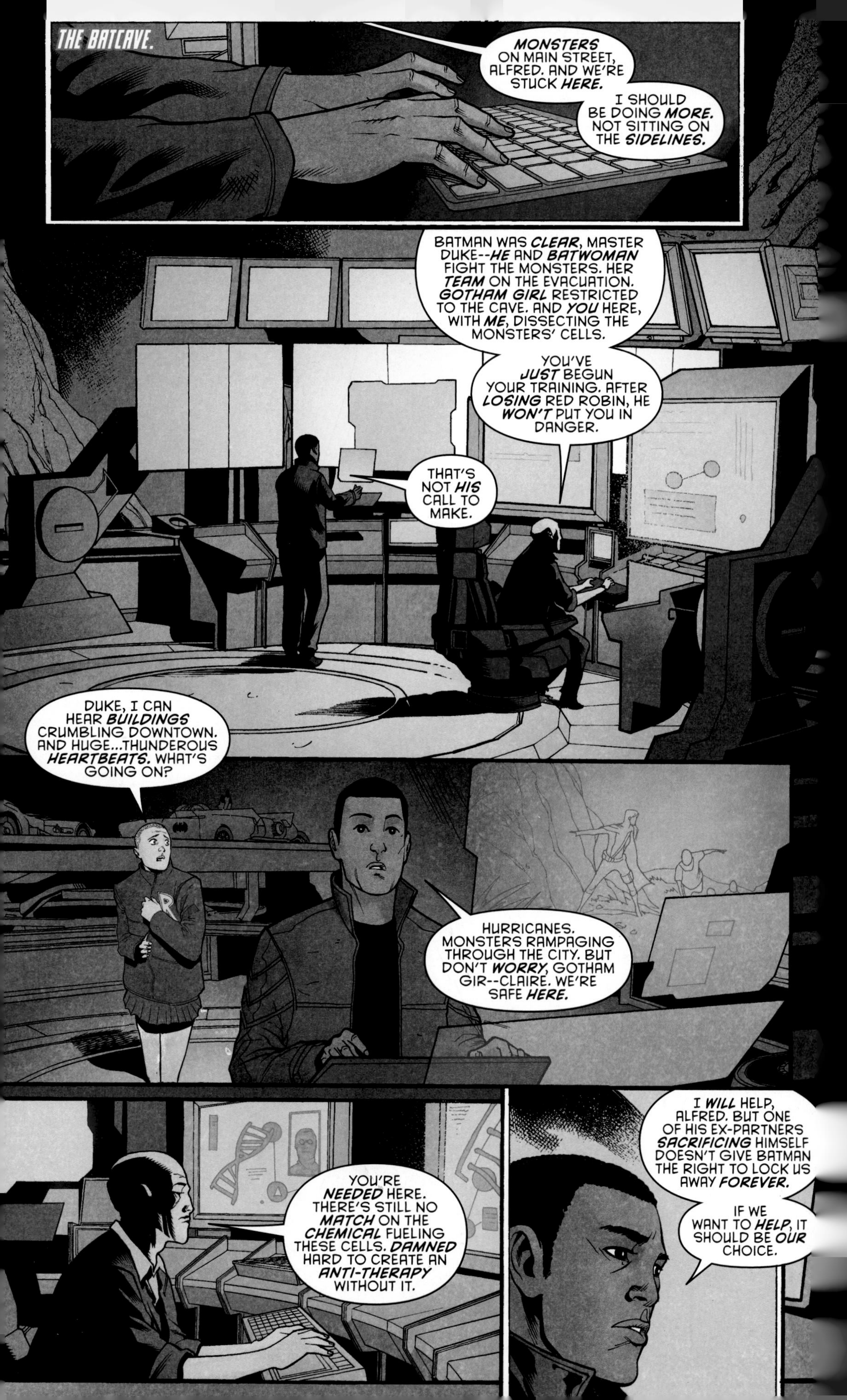
THE BATCAVE.
MONSTERS ON MAIN STREET, ALFRED. AND WE'RE STUCK HERE.
I SHOULD BE DOING MORE. NOT SITTING ON THE SIDELINES.
BATMAN WAS CLEAR, MASTER DUKE--HE AND BATWOMAN FIGHT THE MONSTERS. HER TEAM ON THE EVACUATION. GOTHAM GIRL RESTRICTED TO THE CAVE. AND YOU HERE, WITH ME, DISSECTING THE MONSTERS' CELLS.
YOU'VE JUST BEGUN YOUR TRAINING. AFTER LOSING RED ROBIN, HE WON'T PUT YOU IN DANGER.
THAT'S NOT HIS CALL TO MAKE.
DUKE, I CAN HEAR BUILDINGS CRUMBLING DOWNTOWN. AND HUGE...THUNDEROUS HEARTBEATS. WHAT'S GOING ON?
HURRICANES. MONSTERS RAMPAGING THROUGH THE CITY. BUT DON'T WORRY, GOTHAM GIR--CLAIRE. WE'RE SAFE HERE.
YOU'RE NEEDED HERE. THERE'S STILL NO MATCH ON THE CHEMICAL FUELING THESE CELLS. DAMNED HARD TO CREATE AN ANTI-THERAPY WITHOUT IT.
I WILL HELP, ALFRED. BUT ONE OF HIS EX-PARTNERS SACRIFICING HIMSELF DOESN'T GIVE BATMAN THE RIGHT TO LOCK US AWAY FOREVER.
IF WE WANT TO HELP, IT SHOULD BE OUR CHOICE.

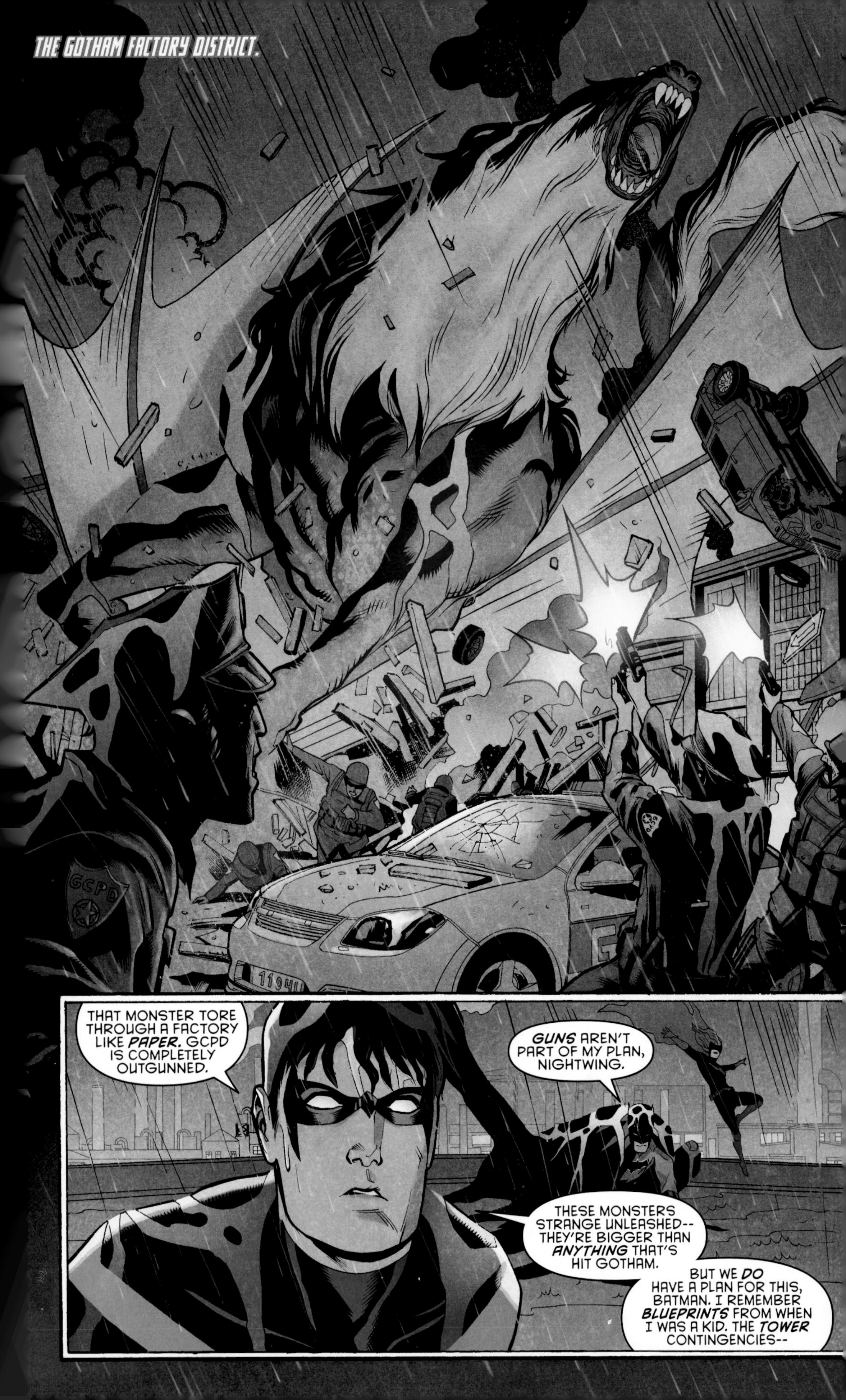
THE GOTHAM FACTORY DISTRICT.
THAT MONSTER TORE THROUGH A FACTORY LIKE *PAPER.* GCPD IS COMPLETELY OUTGUNNED.
GUNS AREN'T PART OF MY PLAN, NIGHTWING.
THESE MONSTERS STRANGE UNLEASHED-- THEY'RE BIGGER THAN *ANYTHING* THAT'S HIT GOTHAM.
BUT WE *DO* HAVE A PLAN FOR THIS, BATMAN. I REMEMBER *BLUEPRINTS* FROM WHEN I WAS A KID. THE *TOWER* CONTINGENCIES--

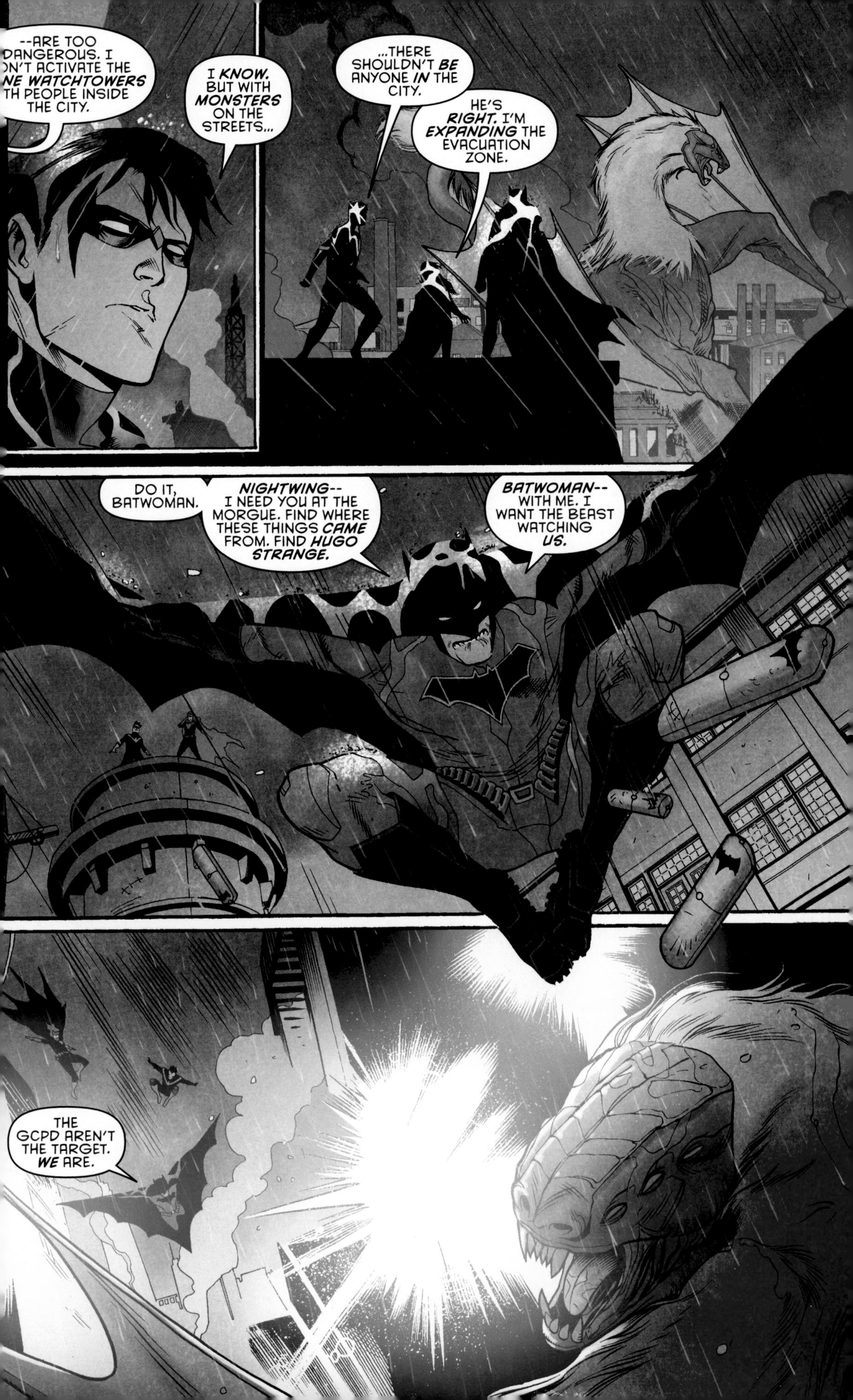
--ARE TOO DANGEROUS. I ON'T ACTIVATE THE NE WATCHTOWERS TH PEOPLE INSIDE THE CITY.
I KNOW. BUT WITH MONSTERS ON THE STREETS...
...THERE SHOULDN'T BE ANYONE IN THE CITY.
HE'S RIGHT. I'M EXPANDING THE EVACUATION ZONE.
DO IT, BATWOMAN.
NIGHTWING-- I NEED YOU AT THE MORGUE. FIND WHERE THESE THINGS CAME FROM. FIND HUGO STRANGE.
BATWOMAN-- WITH ME. I WANT THE BEAST WATCHING US.
THE GCPD AREN'T THE TARGET. WE ARE.

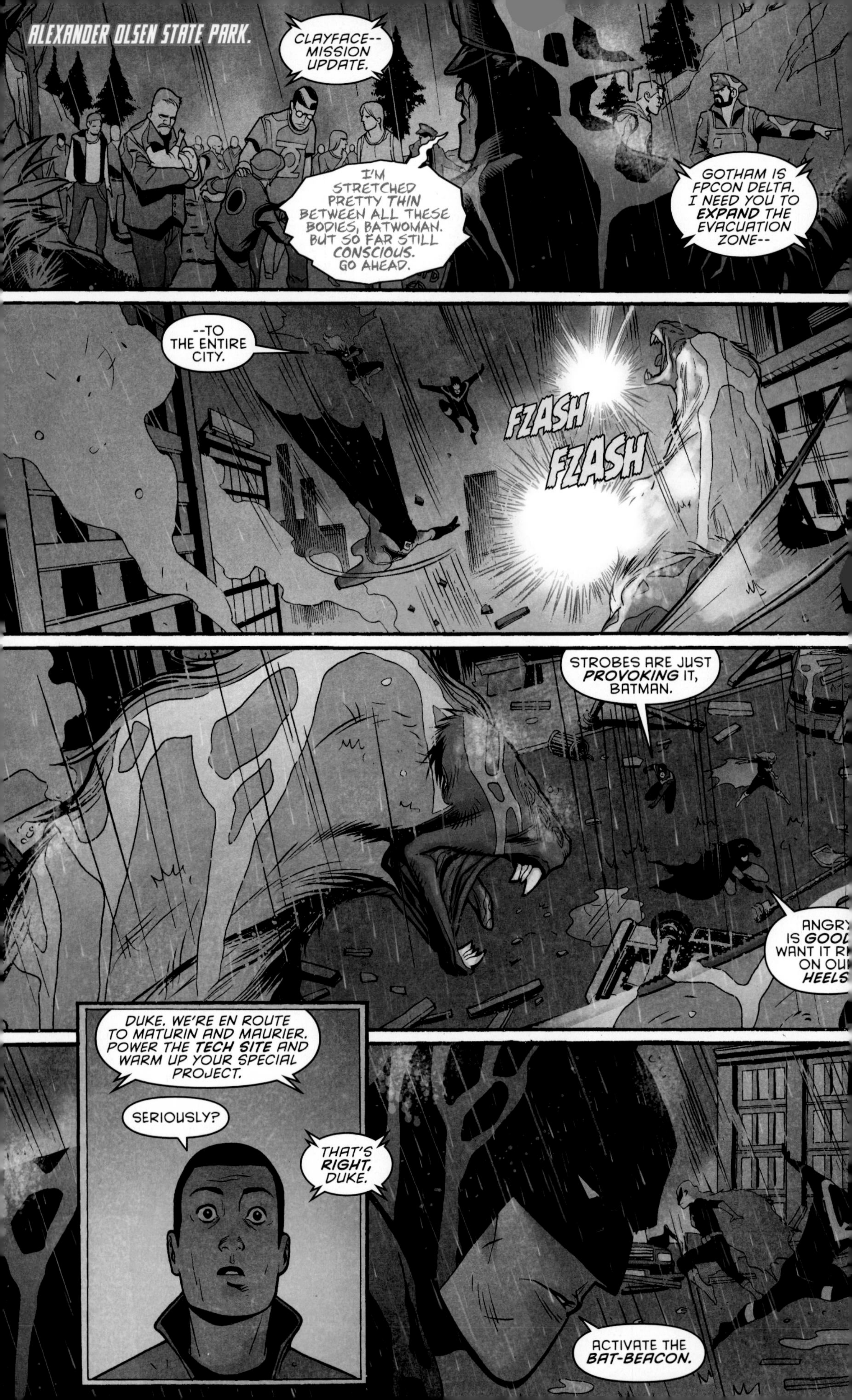
ALEXANDER OLSEN STATE PARK.
CLAYFACE-- MISSION UPDATE.
I'M STRETCHED PRETTY THIN BETWEEN ALL THESE BODIES, BATWOMAN. BUT SO FAR STILL CONSCIOUS. GO AHEAD.
GOTHAM IS FPCON DELTA. I NEED YOU TO EXPAND THE EVACUATION ZONE--
--TO THE ENTIRE CITY.
FZASH
FZASH
STROBES ARE JUST PROVOKING IT, BATMAN.
DUKE. WE'RE EN ROUTE TO MATURIN AND MAURIER. POWER THE TECH SITE AND WARM UP YOUR SPECIAL PROJECT.
SERIOUSLY?
THAT'S RIGHT, DUKE.
ACTIVATE THE BAT-BEACON.

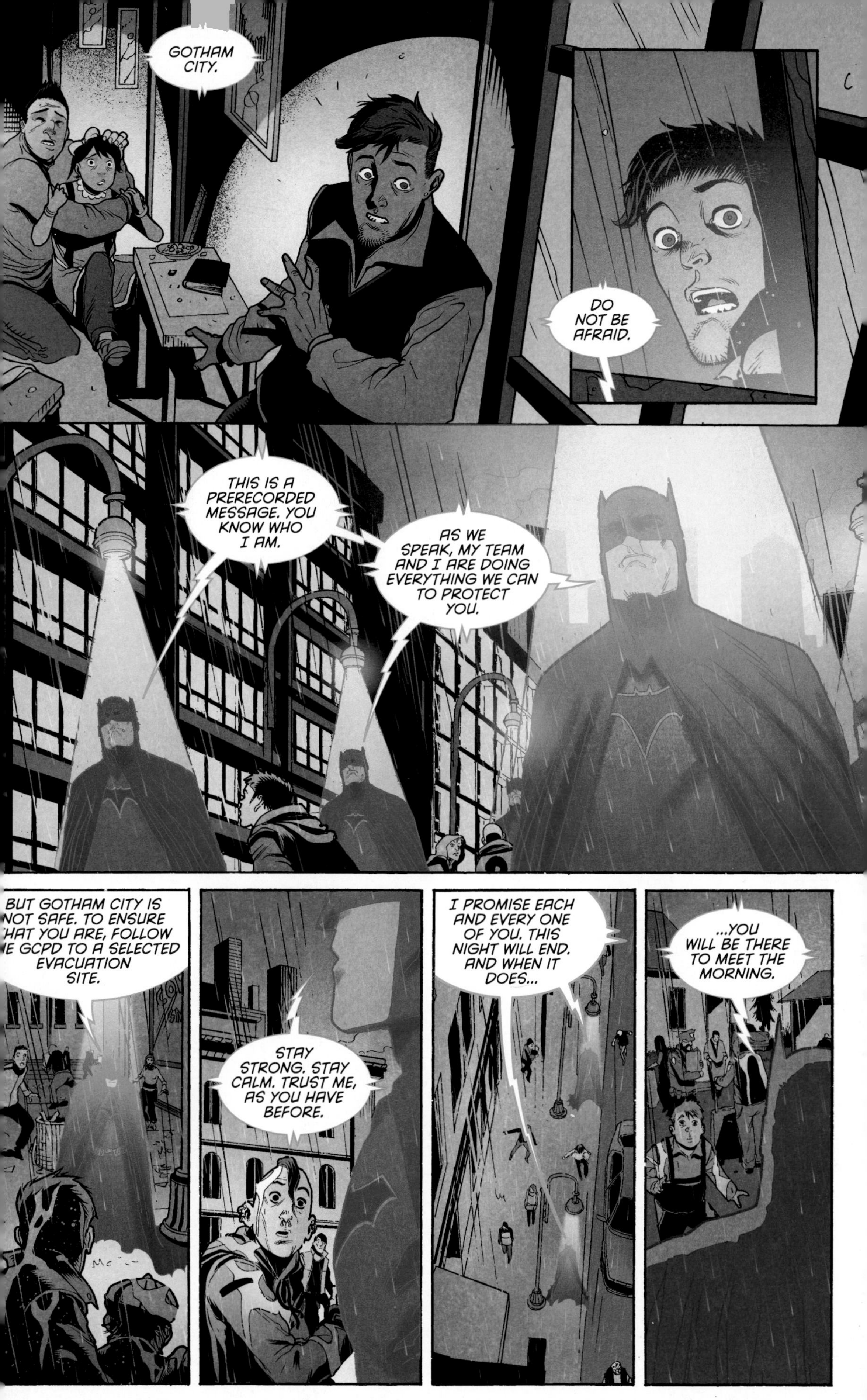
GOTHAM CITY.
DO NOT BE AFRAID.
THIS IS A PRERECORDED MESSAGE. YOU KNOW WHO I AM.
AS WE SPEAK, MY TEAM AND I ARE DOING EVERYTHING WE CAN TO PROTECT YOU.
BUT GOTHAM CITY IS NOT SAFE. TO ENSURE THAT YOU ARE, FOLLOW THE GCPD TO A SELECTED EVACUATION SITE.
STAY STRONG. STAY CALM. TRUST ME, AS YOU HAVE BEFORE.
I PROMISE EACH AND EVERY ONE OF YOU. THIS NIGHT WILL END. AND WHEN IT DOES...
...YOU WILL BE THERE TO MEET THE MORNING.

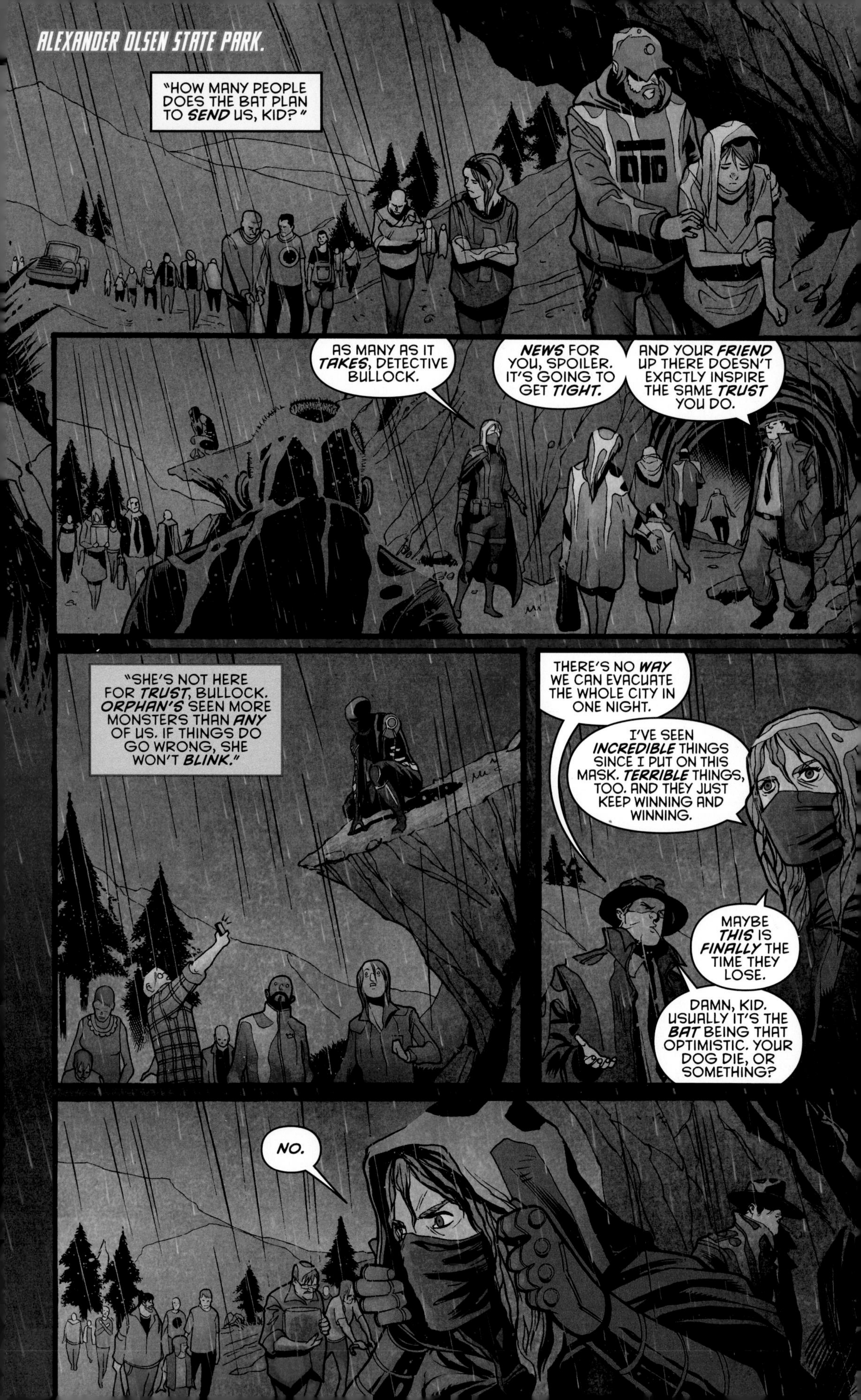
ALEXANDER OLSEN STATE PARK.
"HOW MANY PEOPLE DOES THE BAT PLAN TO SEND US, KID?"
AS MANY AS IT TAKES, DETECTIVE BULLOCK.
NEWS FOR YOU, SPOILER. IT'S GOING TO GET TIGHT.
AND YOUR FRIEND UP THERE DOESN'T EXACTLY INSPIRE THE SAME TRUST YOU DO.
"SHE'S NOT HERE FOR TRUST, BULLOCK. ORPHAN'S SEEN MORE MONSTERS THAN ANY OF US. IF THINGS DO GO WRONG, SHE WON'T BLINK."
THERE'S NO WAY WE CAN EVACUATE THE WHOLE CITY IN ONE NIGHT.
I'VE SEEN INCREDIBLE THINGS SINCE I PUT ON THIS MASK. TERRIBLE THINGS, TOO. AND THEY JUST KEEP WINNING AND WINNING.
MAYBE THIS IS FINALLY THE TIME THEY LOSE.
DAMN, KID. USUALLY IT'S THE BAT BEING THAT OPTIMISTIC. YOUR DOG DIE, OR SOMETHING?
NO.

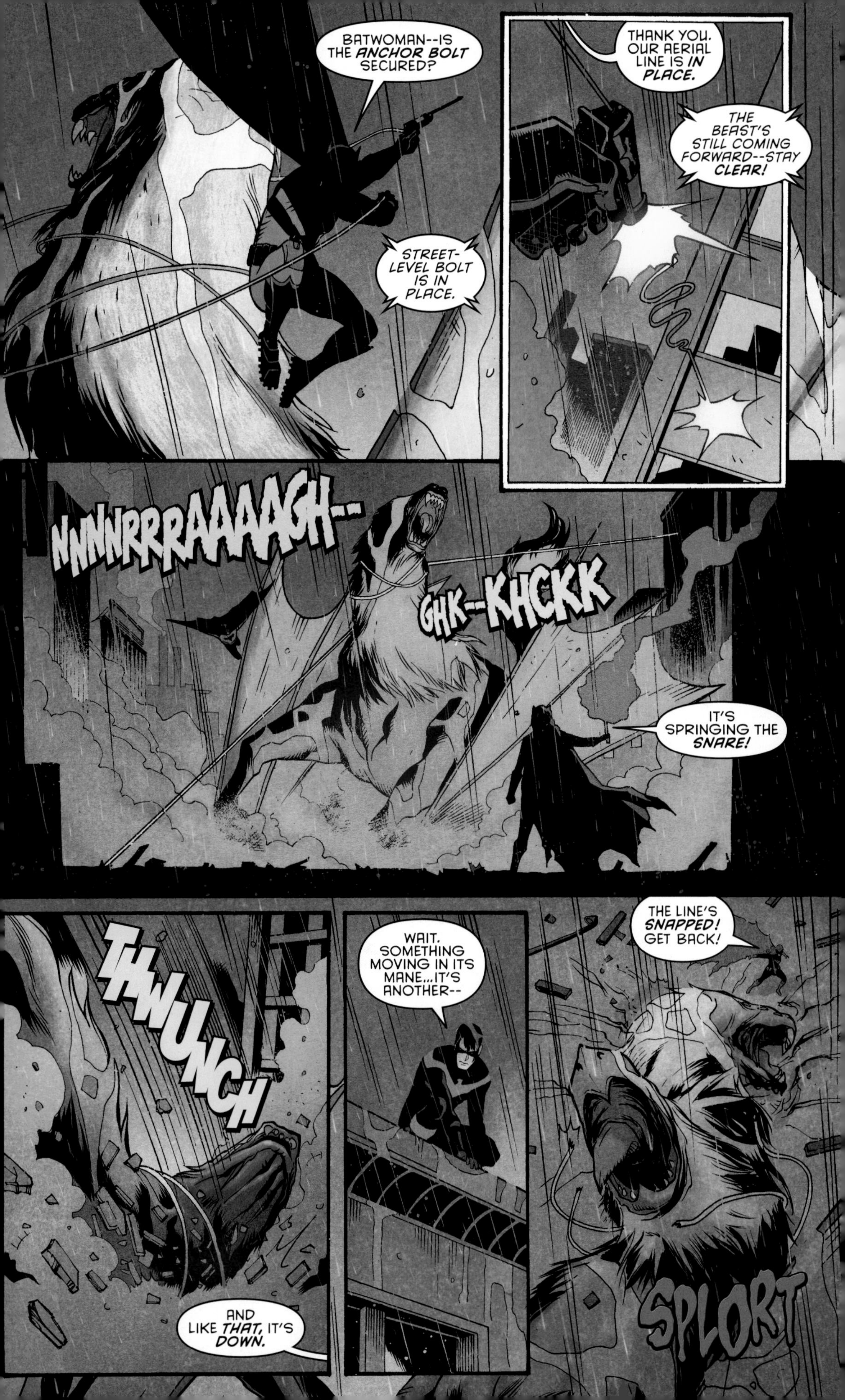
BATWOMAN--IS THE ANCHOR BOLT SECURED?
STREET-LEVEL BOLT IS IN PLACE.
THANK YOU. OUR AERIAL LINE IS IN PLACE.
THE BEAST'S STILL COMING FORWARD--STAY CLEAR!
NNNNRRRAAAAGH--
GHK--KHCKK
IT'S SPRINGING THE SNARE!
THWUNCH
AND LIKE THAT, IT'S DOWN.
WAIT. SOMETHING MOVING IN ITS MANE...IT'S ANOTHER--
THE LINE'S SNAPPED! GET BACK!
SPLORT

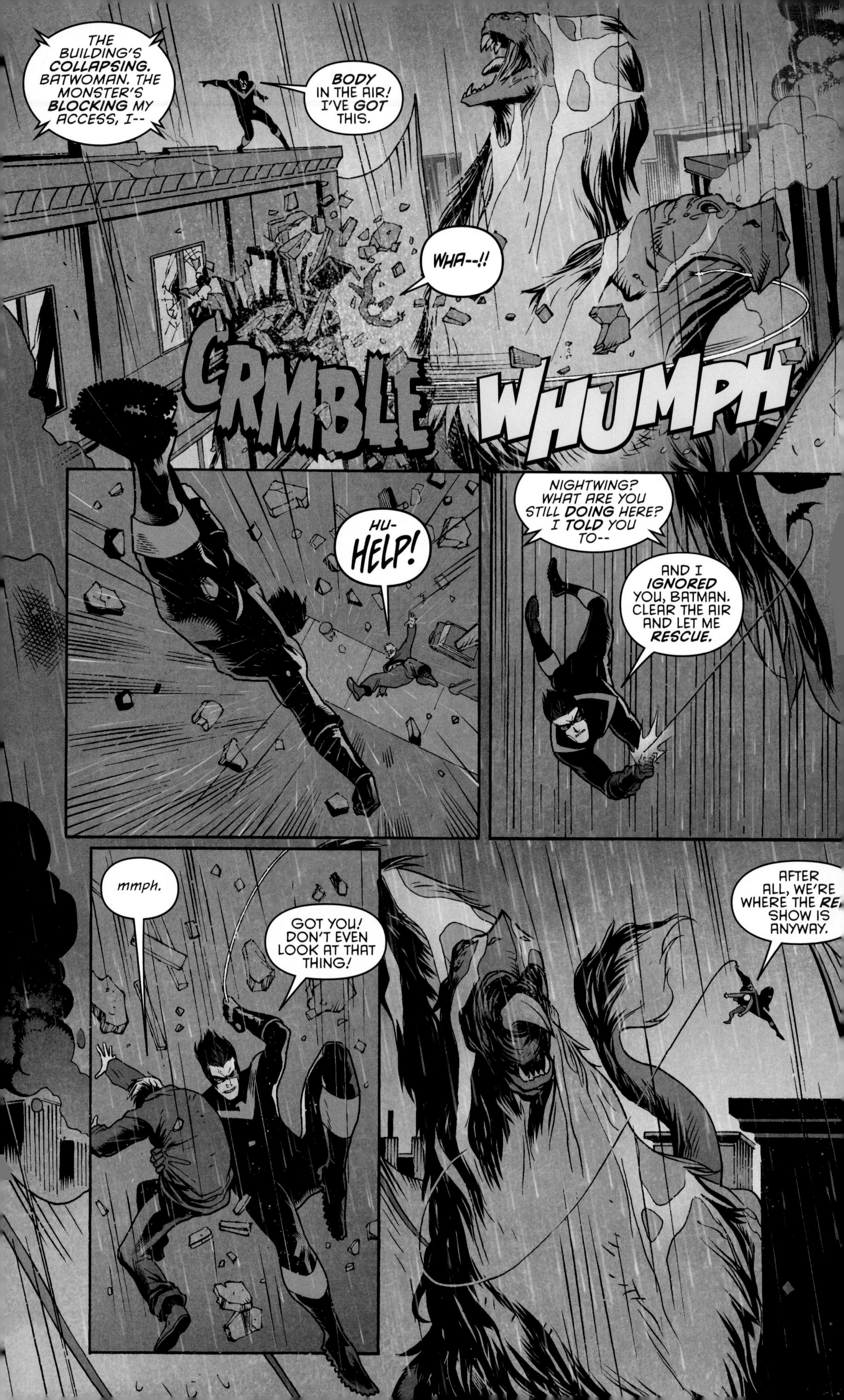
THE BUILDING'S COLLAPSING. BATWOMAN. THE MONSTER'S BLOCKING MY ACCESS, I--
BODY IN THE AIR! I'VE GOT THIS.
WHA--!!
CRMBLE
WHUMPH
HU-HELP!
NIGHTWING? WHAT ARE YOU STILL DOING HERE? I TOLD YOU TO--
AND I IGNORED YOU, BATMAN. CLEAR THE AIR AND LET ME RESCUE.
mmph.
GOT YOU! DON'T EVEN LOOK AT THAT THING!
AFTER ALL, WE'RE WHERE THE RE SHOW IS ANYWAY.

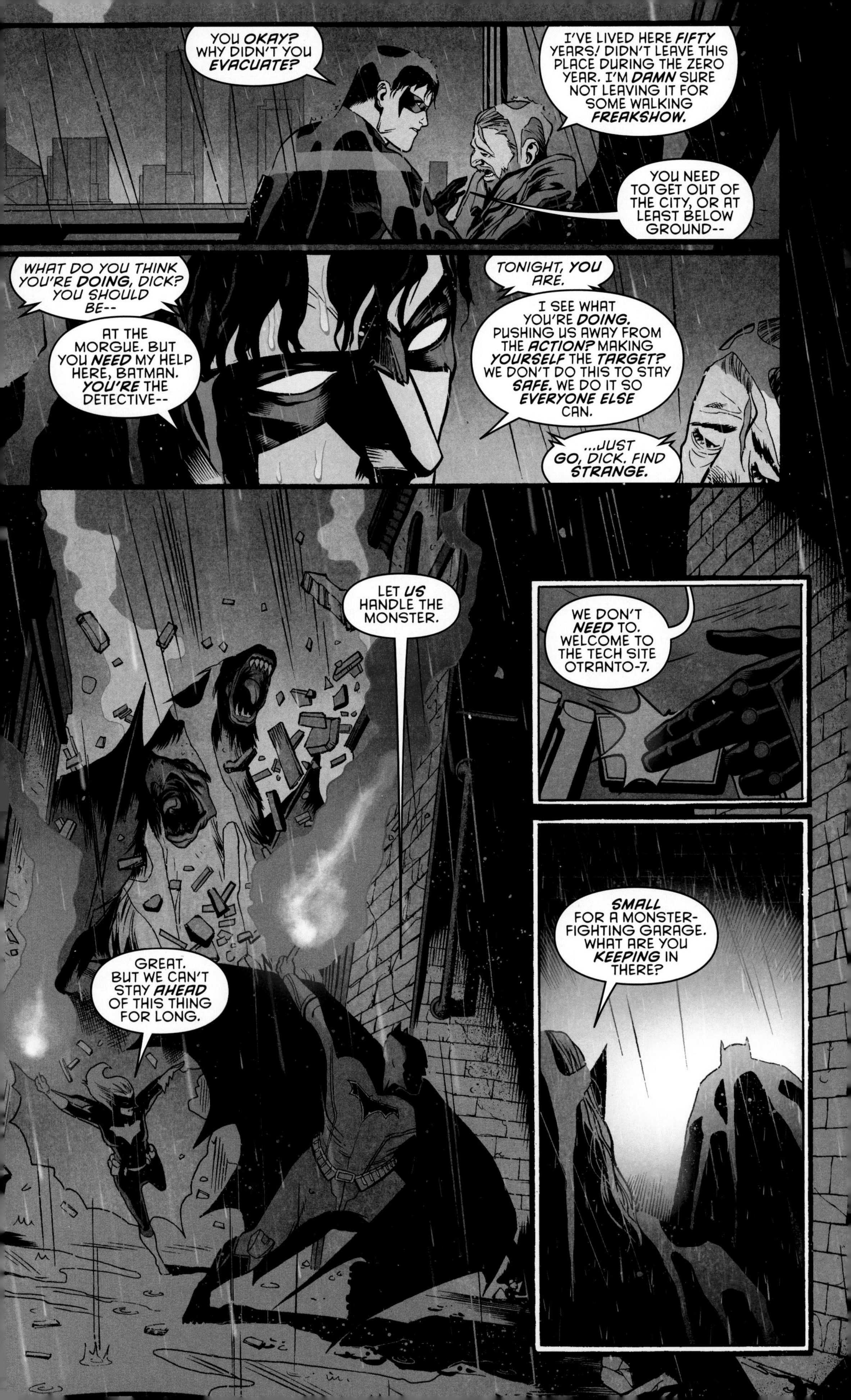

YOU OKAY? WHY DIDN'T YOU EVACUATE?
I'VE LIVED HERE FIFTY YEARS! DIDN'T LEAVE THIS PLACE DURING THE ZERO YEAR. I'M DAMN SURE NOT LEAVING IT FOR SOME WALKING FREAKSHOW.
YOU NEED TO GET OUT OF THE CITY, OR AT LEAST BELOW GROUND--
WHAT DO YOU THINK YOU'RE DOING, DICK? YOU SHOULD BE--
AT THE MORGUE. BUT YOU NEED MY HELP HERE, BATMAN. YOU'RE THE DETECTIVE--
TONIGHT, YOU ARE.
I SEE WHAT YOU'RE DOING. PUSHING US AWAY FROM THE ACTION? MAKING YOURSELF THE TARGET? WE DON'T DO THIS TO STAY SAFE. WE DO IT SO EVERYONE ELSE CAN.
...JUST GO, DICK. FIND STRANGE.
LET US HANDLE THE MONSTER.
GREAT. BUT WE CAN'T STAY AHEAD OF THIS THING FOR LONG.
WE DON'T NEED TO. WELCOME TO THE TECH SITE OTRANTO-7.
SMALL FOR A MONSTER-FIGHTING GARAGE. WHAT ARE YOU KEEPING IN THERE?

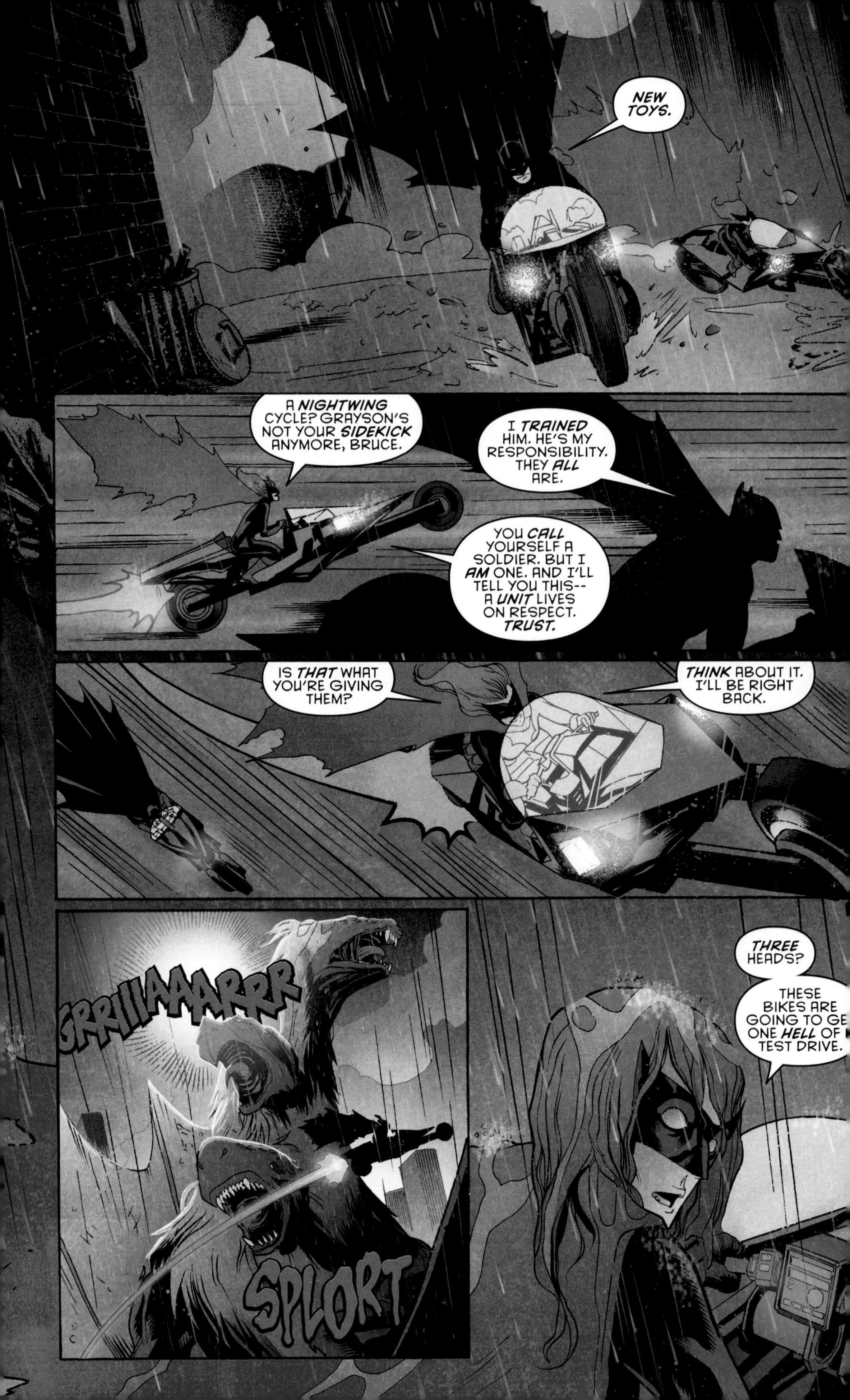
NEW TOYS.
A NIGHTWING CYCLE? GRAYSON'S NOT YOUR SIDEKICK ANYMORE, BRUCE.
I TRAINED HIM. HE'S MY RESPONSIBILITY. THEY ALL ARE.
YOU CALL YOURSELF A SOLDIER. BUT I AM ONE. AND I'LL TELL YOU THIS-- A UNIT LIVES ON RESPECT. TRUST.
IS THAT WHAT YOU'RE GIVING THEM?
THINK ABOUT IT. I'LL BE RIGHT BACK.
GRRIIIAAAARRR
SPLORT
THREE HEADS?
THESE BIKES ARE GOING TO GE ONE HELL OF TEST DRIVE.

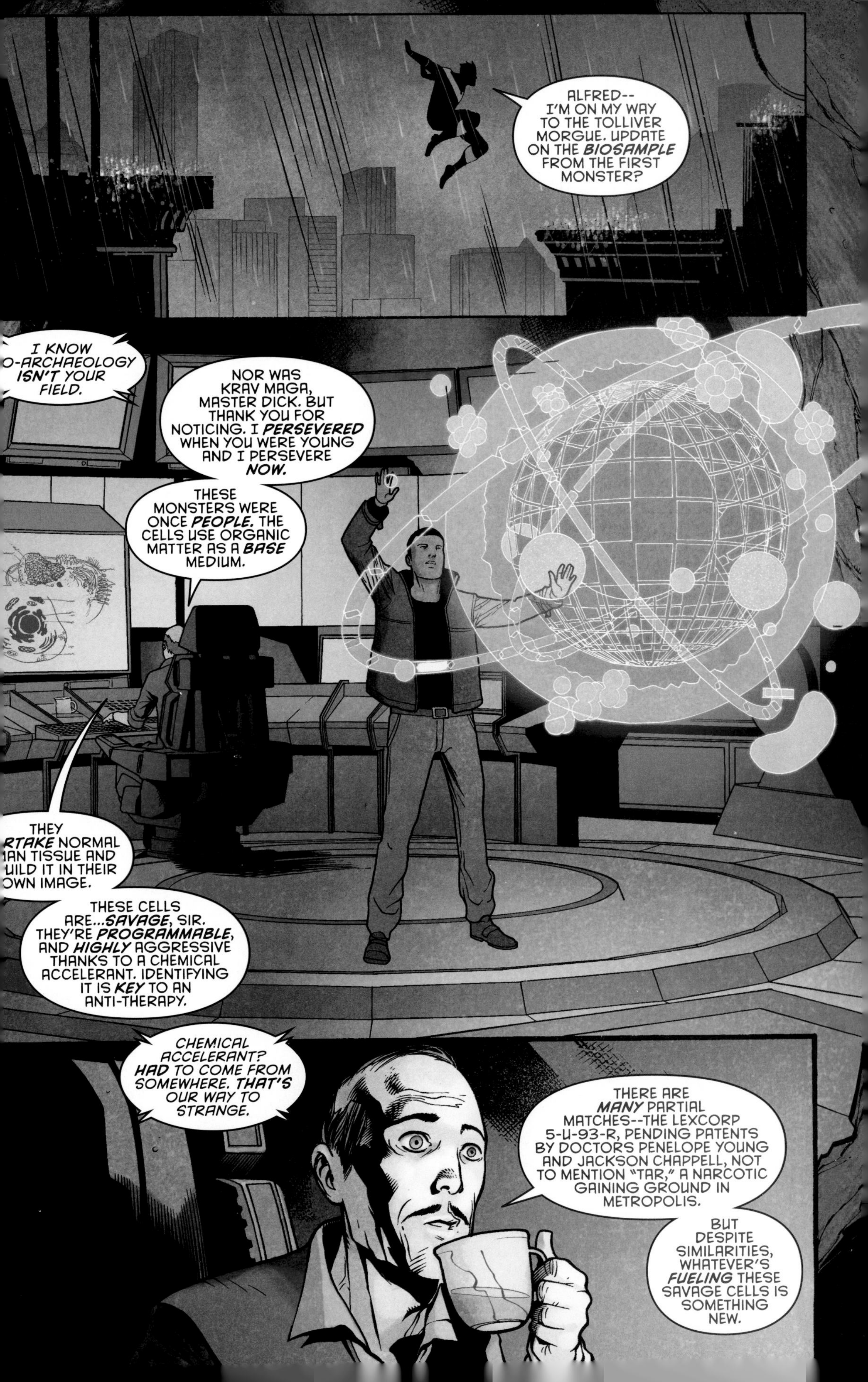
ALFRED-- I'M ON MY WAY TO THE TOLLIVER MORGUE. UPDATE ON THE BIOSAMPLE FROM THE FIRST MONSTER?
I KNOW O-ARCHAEOLOGY ISN'T YOUR FIELD.
NOR WAS KRAV MAGA, MASTER DICK. BUT THANK YOU FOR NOTICING. I PERSEVERED WHEN YOU WERE YOUNG AND I PERSEVERE NOW.
THESE MONSTERS WERE ONCE PEOPLE. THE CELLS USE ORGANIC MATTER AS A BASE MEDIUM.
THEY RTAKE NORMAL IAN TISSUE AND UILD IT IN THEIR OWN IMAGE.
THESE CELLS ARE...SAVAGE, SIR. THEY'RE PROGRAMMABLE, AND HIGHLY AGGRESSIVE THANKS TO A CHEMICAL ACCELERANT. IDENTIFYING IT IS KEY TO AN ANTI-THERAPY.
CHEMICAL ACCELERANT? HAD TO COME FROM SOMEWHERE. THAT'S OUR WAY TO STRANGE.
THERE ARE MANY PARTIAL MATCHES--THE LEXCORP 5-U-93-R, PENDING PATENTS BY DOCTORS PENELOPE YOUNG AND JACKSON CHAPPELL, NOT TO MENTION "TAR," A NARCOTIC GAINING GROUND IN METROPOLIS.
BUT DESPITE SIMILARITIES, WHATEVER'S FUELING THESE SAVAGE CELLS IS SOMETHING NEW.

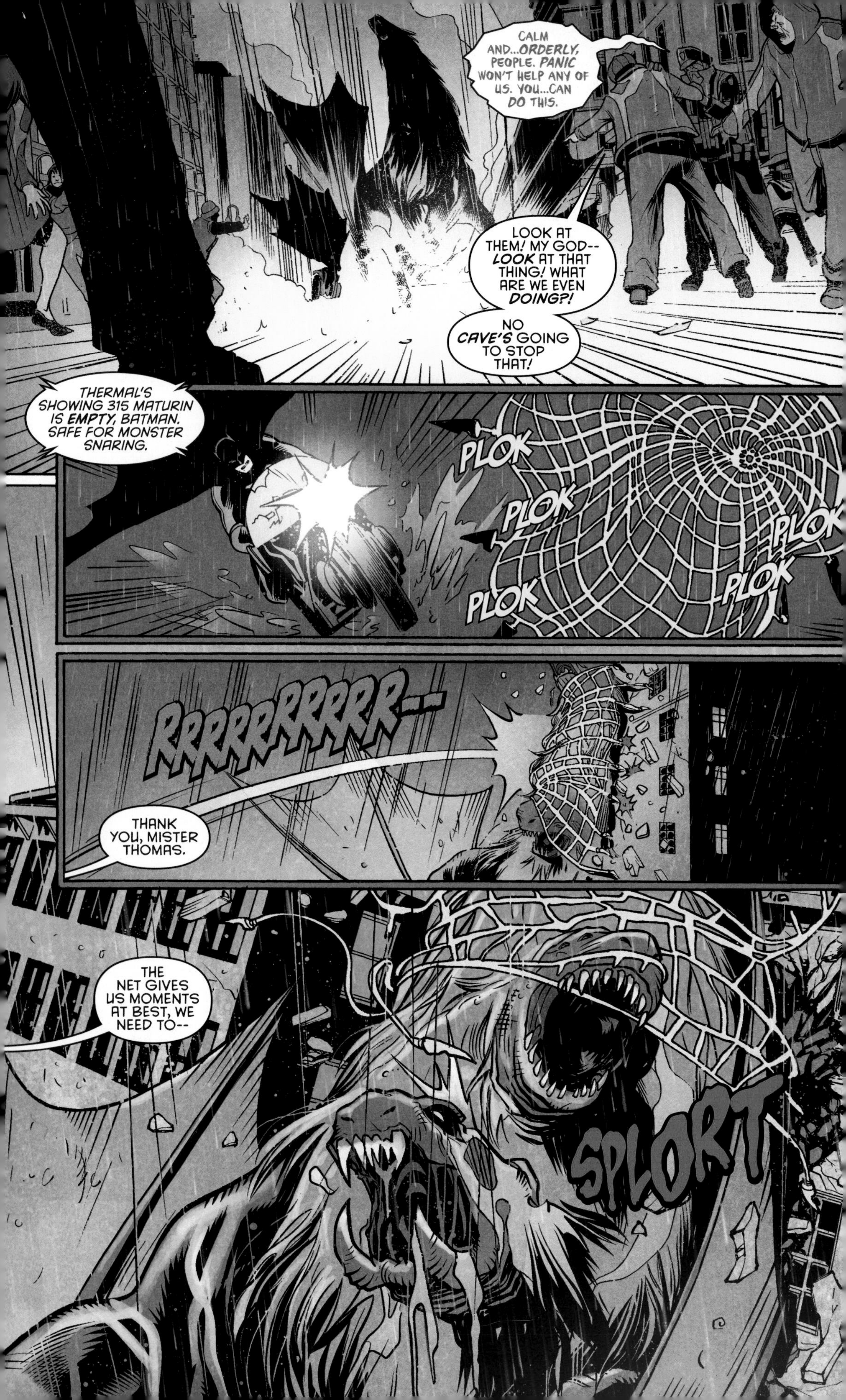

CALM AND...ORDERLY, PEOPLE. PANIC WON'T HELP ANY OF US. YOU...CAN DO THIS.
LOOK AT THEM! MY GOD-- LOOK AT THAT THING! WHAT ARE WE EVEN DOING?!
NO CAVE'S GOING TO STOP THAT!
THERMAL'S SHOWING 315 MATURIN IS EMPTY, BATMAN. SAFE FOR MONSTER SNARING.
PLOK
PLOK
PLOK
PLOK
PLOK
RRRRRRRRRR--
THANK YOU, MISTER THOMAS.
THE NET GIVES US MOMENTS AT BEST, WE NEED TO--
SPLORT

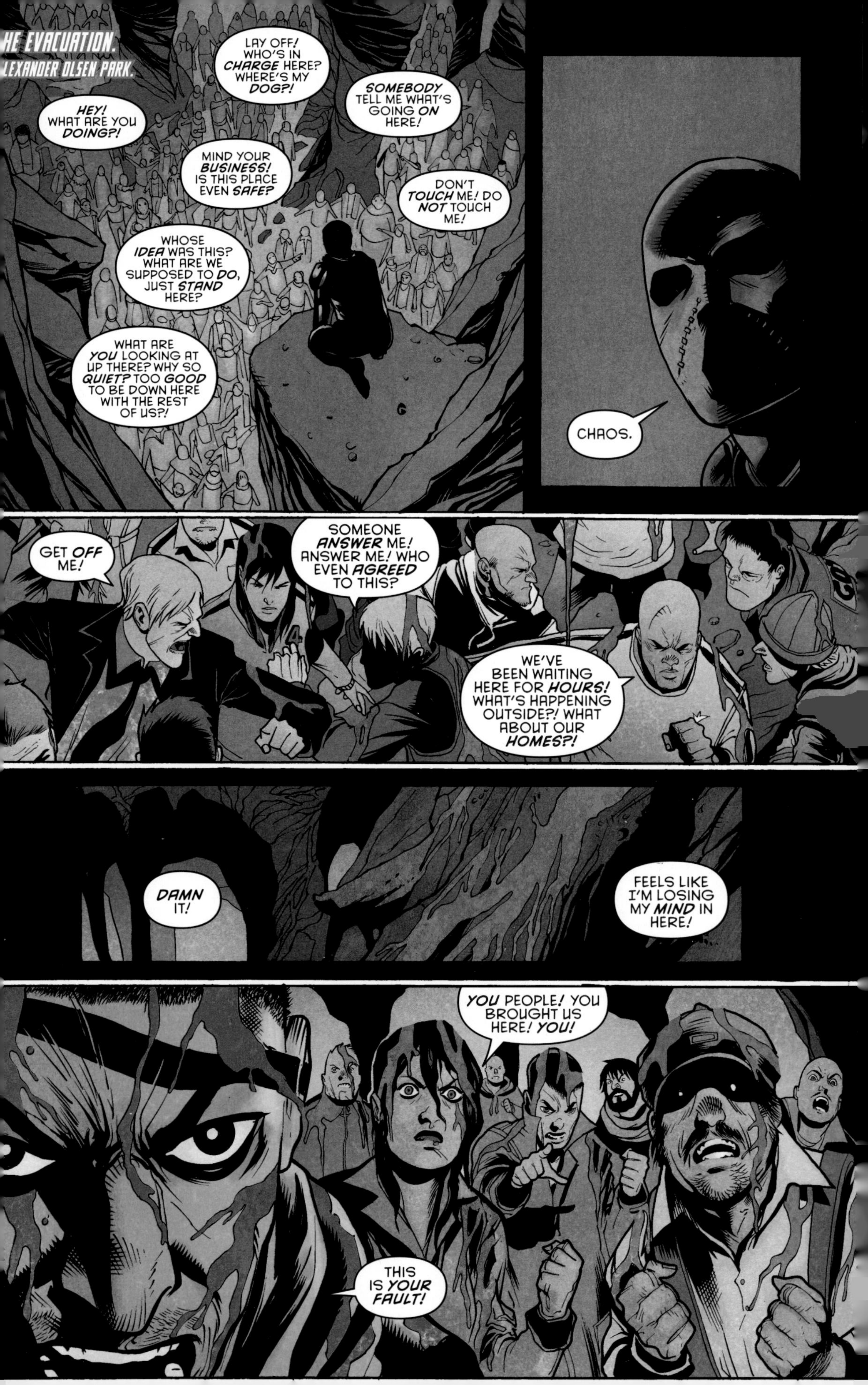
HE EVACUATION.
LEXANDER OLSEN PARK.
HEY! WHAT ARE YOU DOING?!
LAY OFF! WHO'S IN CHARGE HERE? WHERE'S MY DOG?!
MIND YOUR BUSINESS! IS THIS PLACE EVEN SAFE?
SOMEBODY TELL ME WHAT'S GOING ON HERE!
DON'T TOUCH ME! DO NOT TOUCH ME!
WHOSE IDEA WAS THIS? WHAT ARE WE SUPPOSED TO DO, JUST STAND HERE?
WHAT ARE YOU LOOKING AT UP THERE? WHY SO QUIET? TOO GOOD TO BE DOWN HERE WITH THE REST OF US?!
CHAOS.
GET OFF ME!
SOMEONE ANSWER ME! ANSWER ME! WHO EVEN AGREED TO THIS?
WE'VE BEEN WAITING HERE FOR HOURS! WHAT'S HAPPENING OUTSIDE?! WHAT ABOUT OUR HOMES?!
DAMN IT!
FEELS LIKE I'M LOSING MY MIND IN HERE!
YOU PEOPLE! YOU BROUGHT US HERE! YOU!
THIS IS YOUR FAULT!

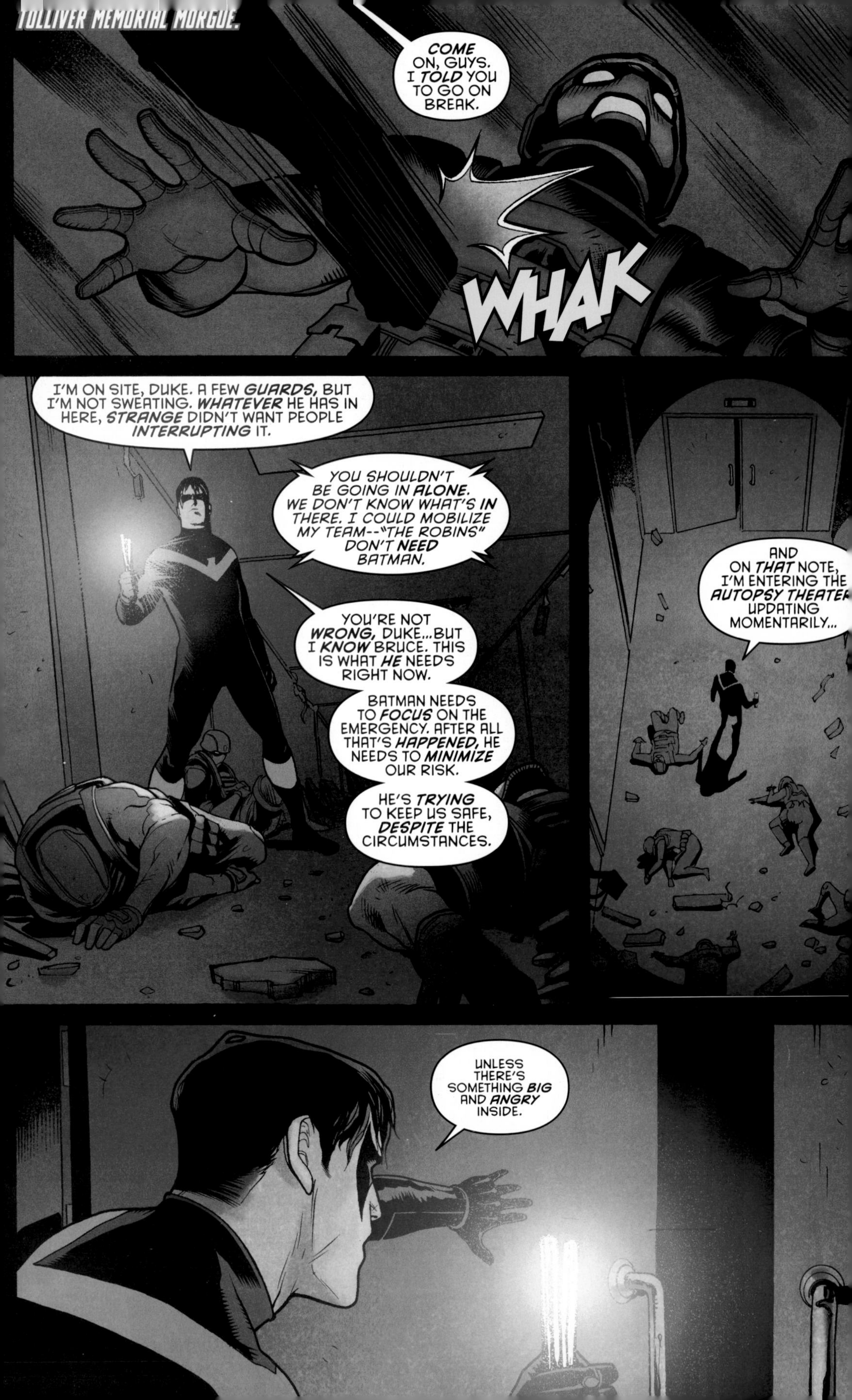
TOLLIVER MEMORIAL MORGUE.
COME ON, GUYS. I TOLD YOU TO GO ON BREAK.
WHAK
I'M ON SITE, DUKE. A FEW GUARDS, BUT I'M NOT SWEATING. WHATEVER HE HAS IN HERE, STRANGE DIDN'T WANT PEOPLE INTERRUPTING IT.
YOU SHOULDN'T BE GOING IN ALONE. WE DON'T KNOW WHAT'S IN THERE. I COULD MOBILIZE MY TEAM--"THE ROBINS" DON'T NEED BATMAN.
YOU'RE NOT WRONG, DUKE...BUT I KNOW BRUCE. THIS IS WHAT HE NEEDS RIGHT NOW.
BATMAN NEEDS TO FOCUS ON THE EMERGENCY. AFTER ALL THAT'S HAPPENED, HE NEEDS TO MINIMIZE OUR RISK.
HE'S TRYING TO KEEP US SAFE, DESPITE THE CIRCUMSTANCES.
AND ON THAT NOTE, I'M ENTERING THE AUTOPSY THEATER UPDATING MOMENTARILY...
UNLESS THERE'S SOMETHING BIG AND ANGRY INSIDE.

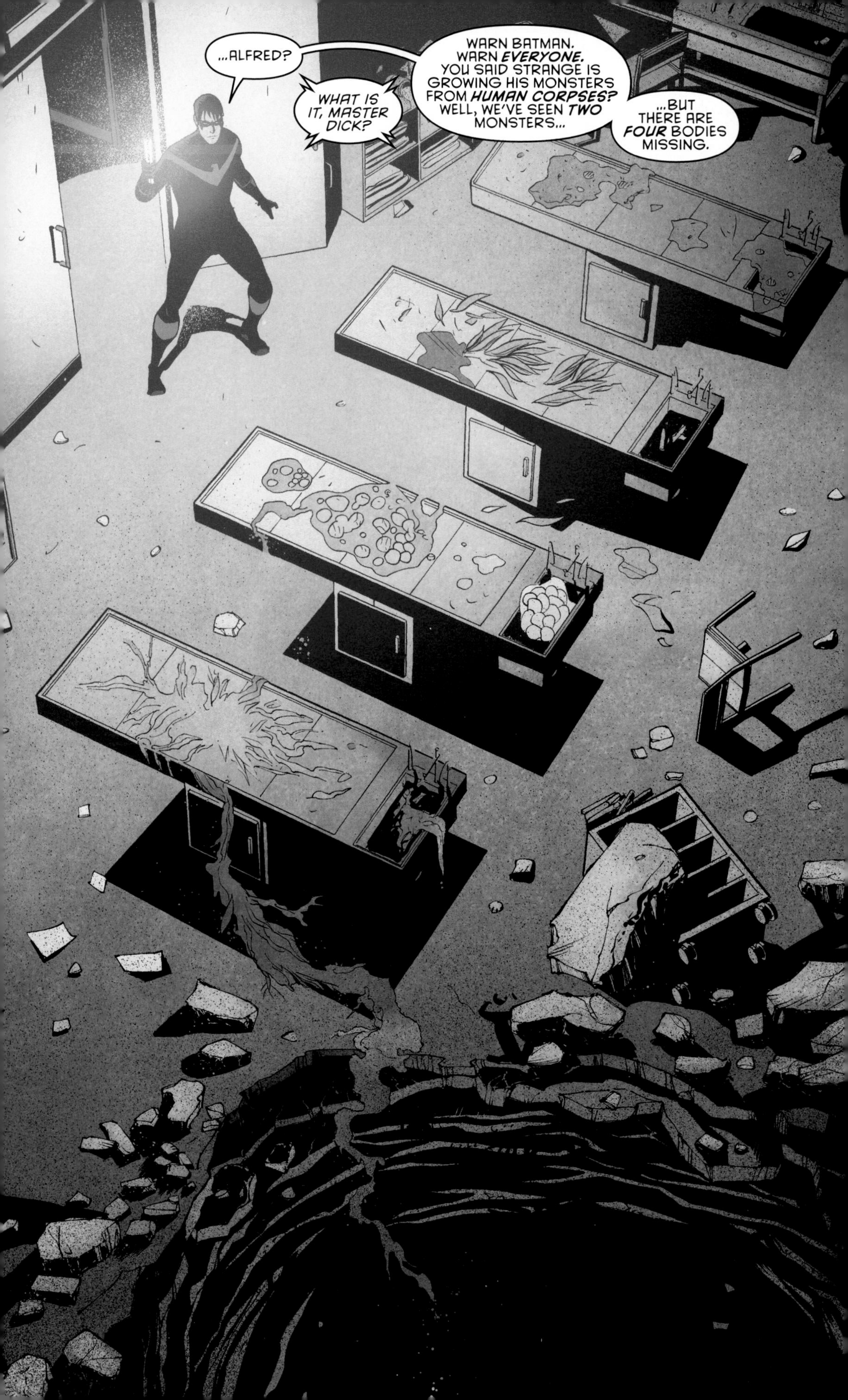
...ALFRED?
WHAT IS IT, MASTER DICK?
WARN BATMAN. WARN *EVERYONE.* YOU SAID STRANGE IS GROWING HIS MONSTERS FROM *HUMAN CORPSES?* WELL, WE'VE SEEN *TWO* MONSTERS...
...BUT THERE ARE *FOUR* BODIES MISSING.

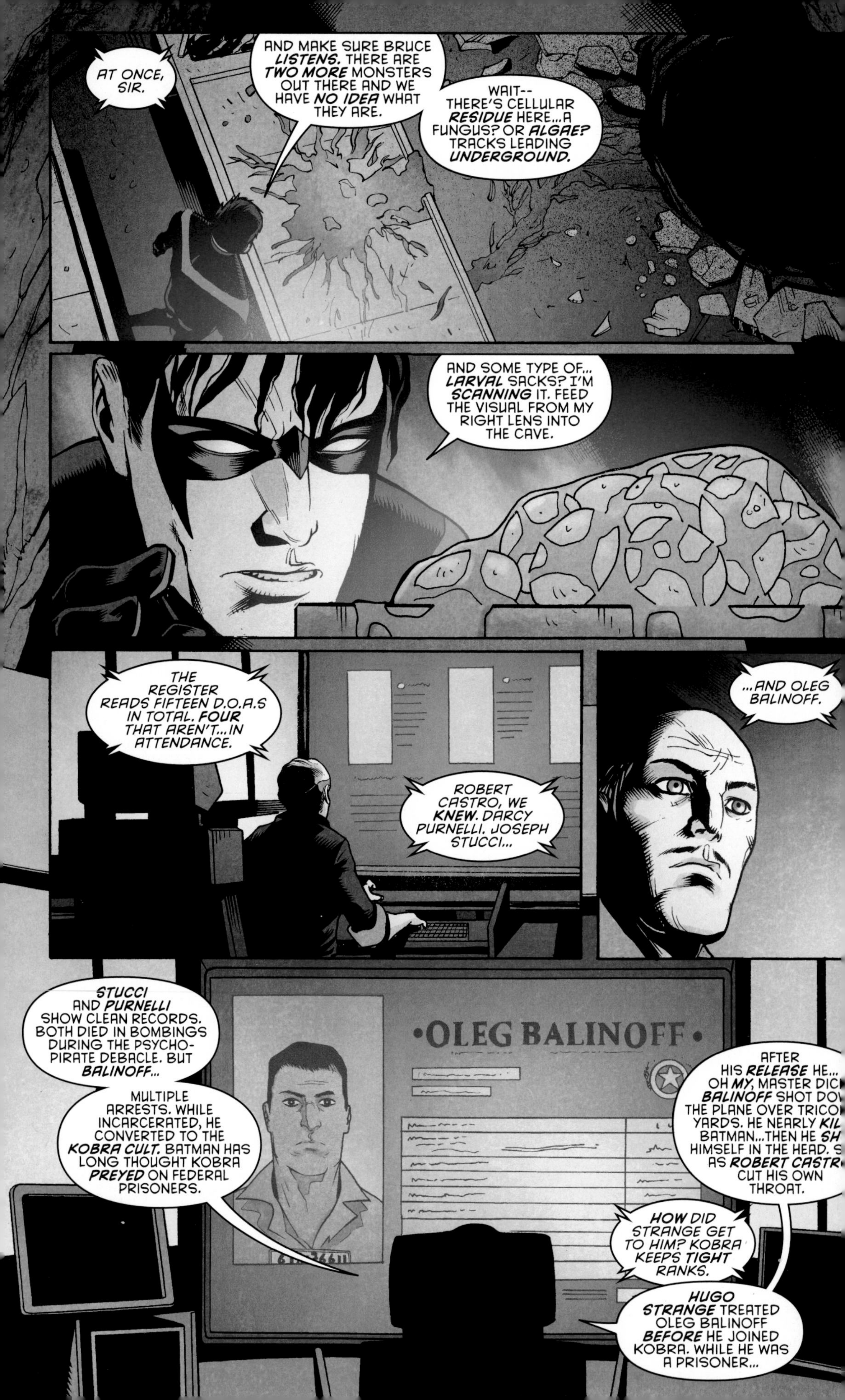

AT ONCE, SIR.
AND MAKE SURE BRUCE LISTENS. THERE ARE TWO MORE MONSTERS OUT THERE AND WE HAVE NO IDEA WHAT THEY ARE.
WAIT-- THERE'S CELLULAR RESIDUE HERE...A FUNGUS? OR ALGAE? TRACKS LEADING UNDERGROUND.
AND SOME TYPE OF... LARVAL SACKS? I'M SCANNING IT. FEED THE VISUAL FROM MY RIGHT LENS INTO THE CAVE.
THE REGISTER READS FIFTEEN D.O.A.S IN TOTAL. FOUR THAT AREN'T...IN ATTENDANCE.
ROBERT CASTRO, WE KNEW. DARCY PURNELLI. JOSEPH STUCCI...
...AND OLEG BALINOFF.
STUCCI AND PURNELLI SHOW CLEAN RECORDS. BOTH DIED IN BOMBINGS DURING THE PSYCHO-PIRATE DEBACLE. BUT BALINOFF...
MULTIPLE ARRESTS. WHILE INCARCERATED, HE CONVERTED TO THE KOBRA CULT. BATMAN HAS LONG THOUGHT KOBRA PREYED ON FEDERAL PRISONERS.
•OLEG BALINOFF•
AFTER HIS RELEASE HE... OH MY, MASTER DIC BALINOFF SHOT DOW THE PLANE OVER TRICO YARDS. HE NEARLY KIL BATMAN...THEN HE SH HIMSELF IN THE HEAD. S AS ROBERT CASTR CUT HIS OWN THROAT.
HOW DID STRANGE GET TO HIM? KOBRA KEEPS TIGHT RANKS.
HUGO STRANGE TREATED OLEG BALINOFF BEFORE HE JOINED KOBRA. WHILE HE WAS A PRISONER...

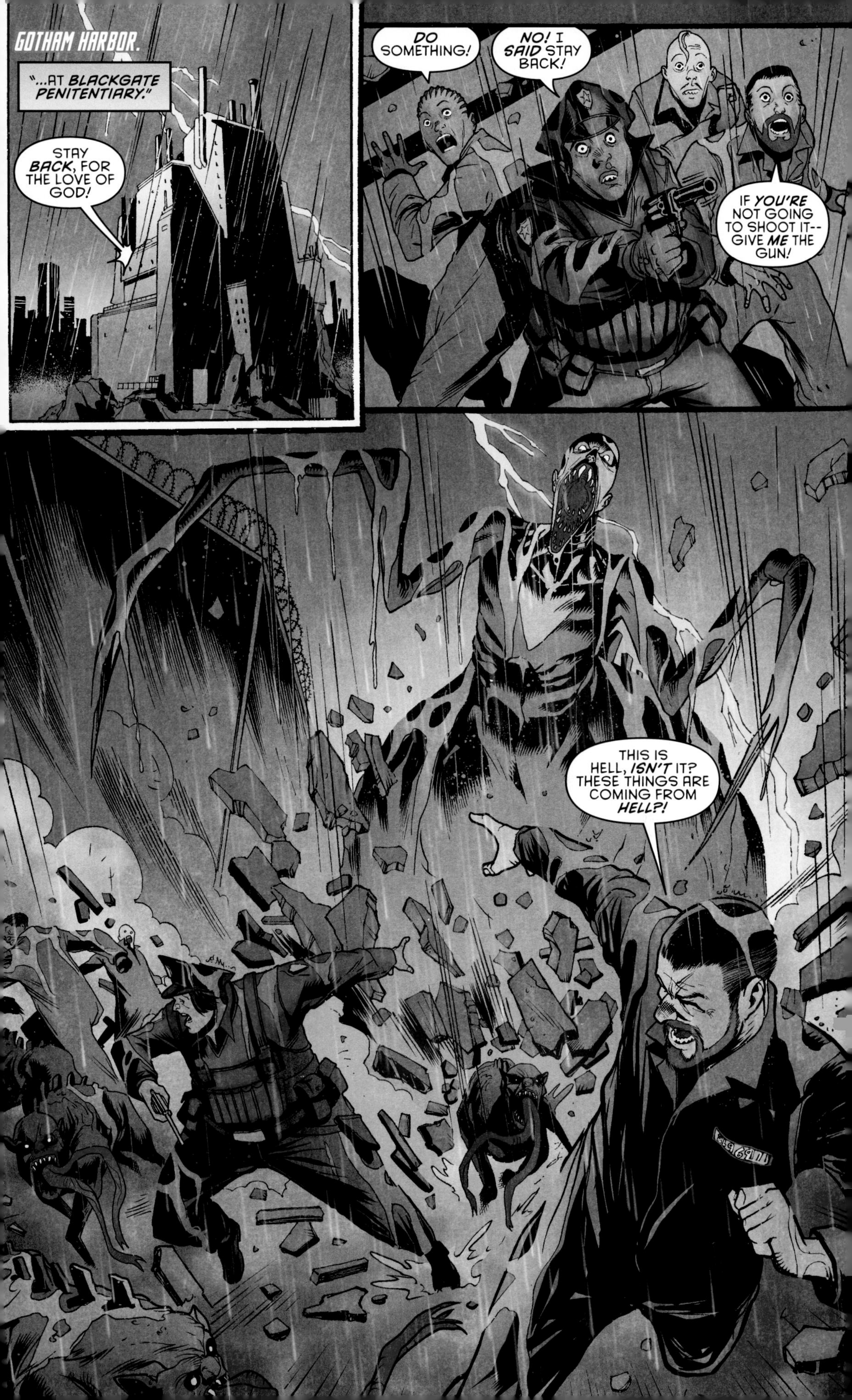
GOTHAM HARBOR.
"...AT BLACKGATE PENITENTIARY."
STAY BACK, FOR THE LOVE OF GOD!
DO SOMETHING!
NO! I SAID STAY BACK!
IF YOU'RE NOT GOING TO SHOOT IT--GIVE ME THE GUN!
THIS IS HELL, ISN'T IT? THESE THINGS ARE COMING FROM HELL?!

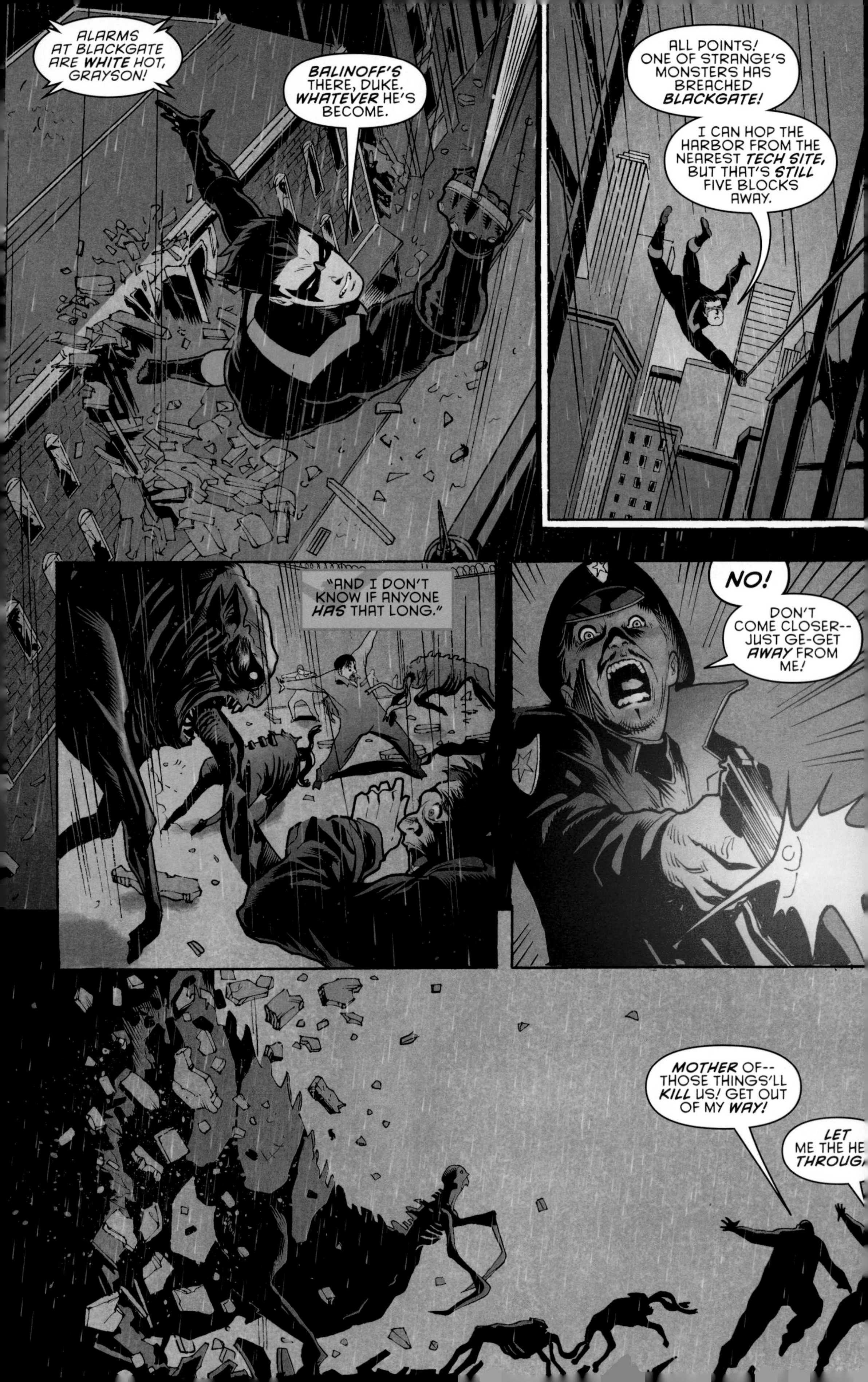
ALARMS AT BLACKGATE ARE WHITE HOT, GRAYSON!
BALINOFF'S THERE, DUKE. WHATEVER HE'S BECOME.
ALL POINTS! ONE OF STRANGE'S MONSTERS HAS BREACHED BLACKGATE!
I CAN HOP THE HARBOR FROM THE NEAREST TECH SITE, BUT THAT'S STILL FIVE BLOCKS AWAY.
"AND I DON'T KNOW IF ANYONE HAS THAT LONG."
NO!
DON'T COME CLOSER-- JUST GE-GET AWAY FROM ME!
MOTHER OF-- THOSE THINGS'LL KILL US! GET OUT OF MY WAY!

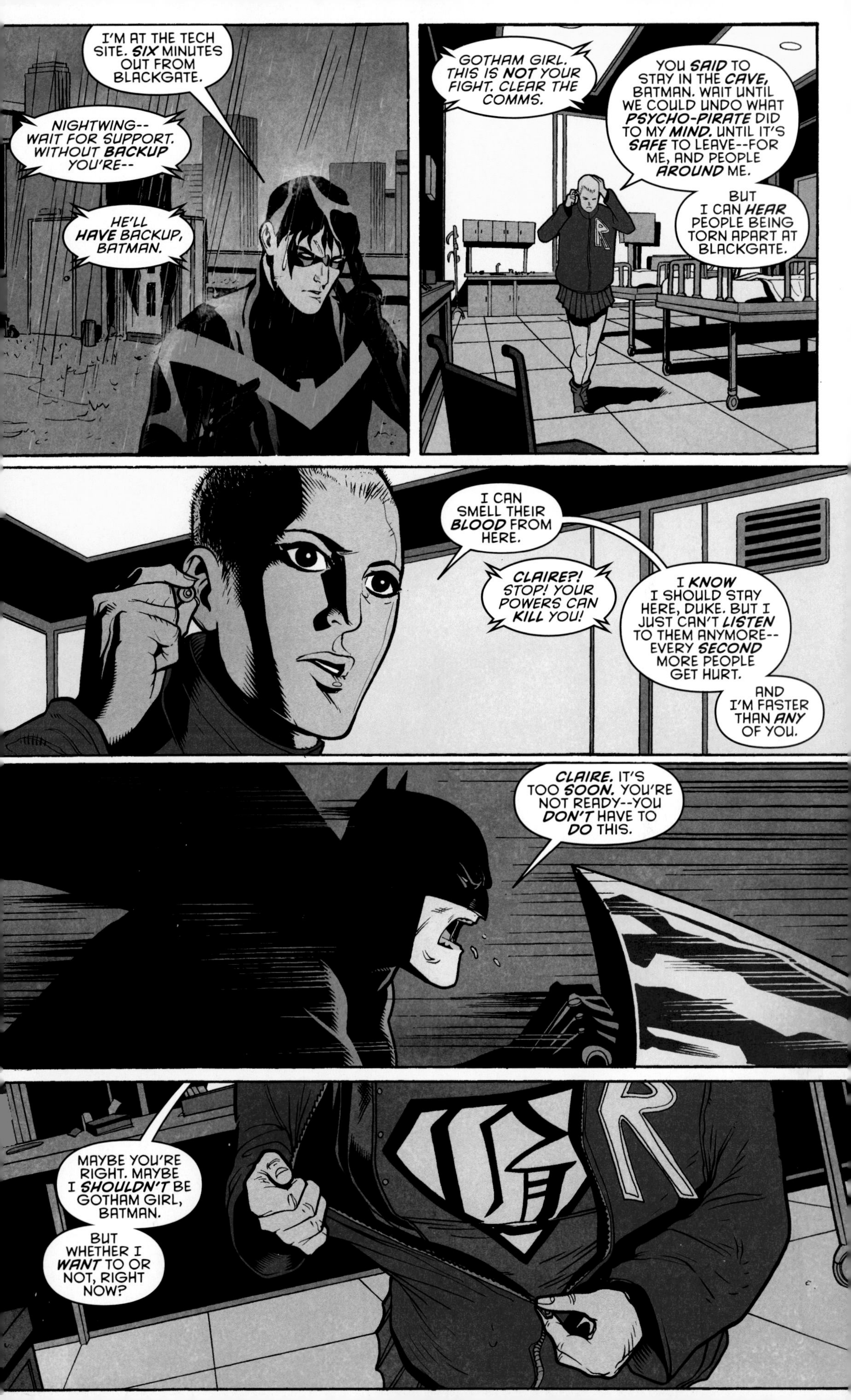
I'M AT THE TECH SITE. SIX MINUTES OUT FROM BLACKGATE.
NIGHTWING-- WAIT FOR SUPPORT. WITHOUT BACKUP YOU'RE--
HE'LL HAVE BACKUP, BATMAN.
GOTHAM GIRL. THIS IS NOT YOUR FIGHT. CLEAR THE COMMS.
YOU SAID TO STAY IN THE CAVE, BATMAN. WAIT UNTIL WE COULD UNDO WHAT PSYCHO-PIRATE DID TO MY MIND. UNTIL IT'S SAFE TO LEAVE--FOR ME, AND PEOPLE AROUND ME.
BUT I CAN HEAR PEOPLE BEING TORN APART AT BLACKGATE.
I CAN SMELL THEIR BLOOD FROM HERE.
CLAIRE?! STOP! YOUR POWERS CAN KILL YOU!
I KNOW I SHOULD STAY HERE, DUKE. BUT I JUST CAN'T LISTEN TO THEM ANYMORE-- EVERY SECOND MORE PEOPLE GET HURT.
AND I'M FASTER THAN ANY OF YOU.
CLAIRE. IT'S TOO SOON. YOU'RE NOT READY--YOU DON'T HAVE TO DO THIS.
MAYBE YOU'RE RIGHT. MAYBE I SHOULDN'T BE GOTHAM GIRL, BATMAN.
BUT WHETHER I WANT TO OR NOT, RIGHT NOW?

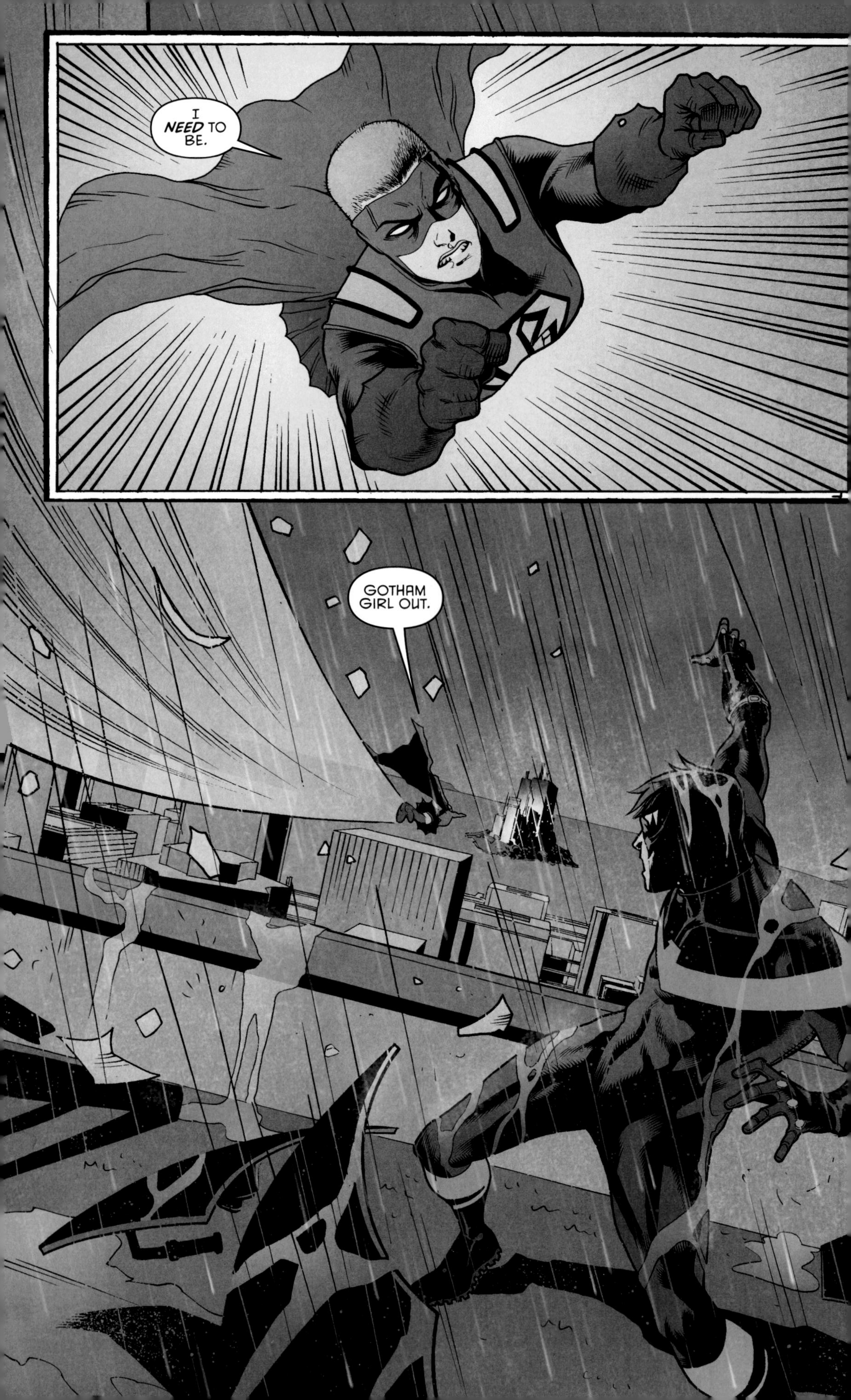
I NEED TO BE.
GOTHAM GIRL OUT.

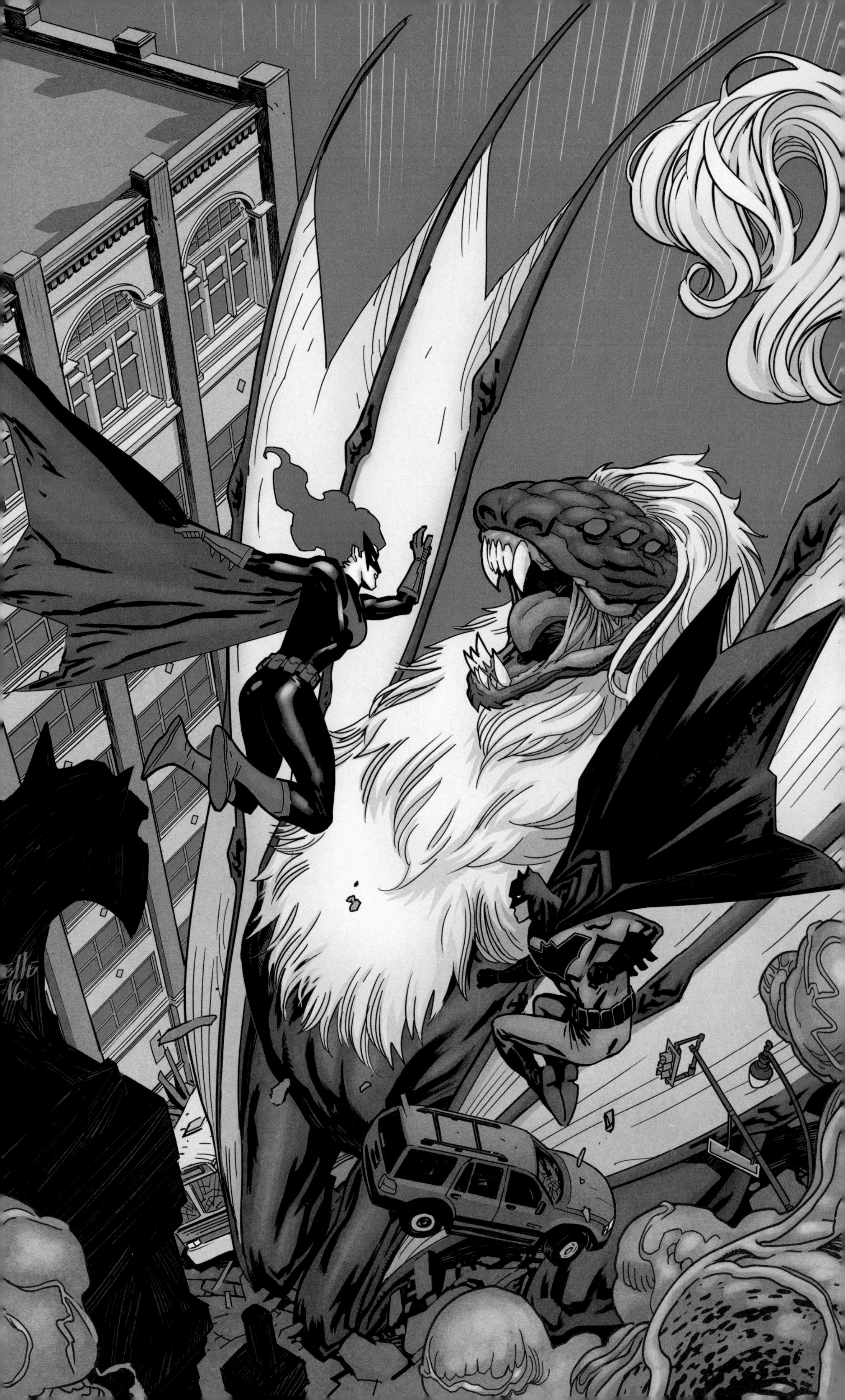

STEVE ORLANDO & JAMES TYNION IV plot ✱ STEVE ORLANDO script ✱ ANDY MacDONALD art ✱ JOHN RAUCH colors
MARILYN PATRIZIO letters ✱ YANICK PAQUETTE & NATHAN FAIRBAIRN cover art

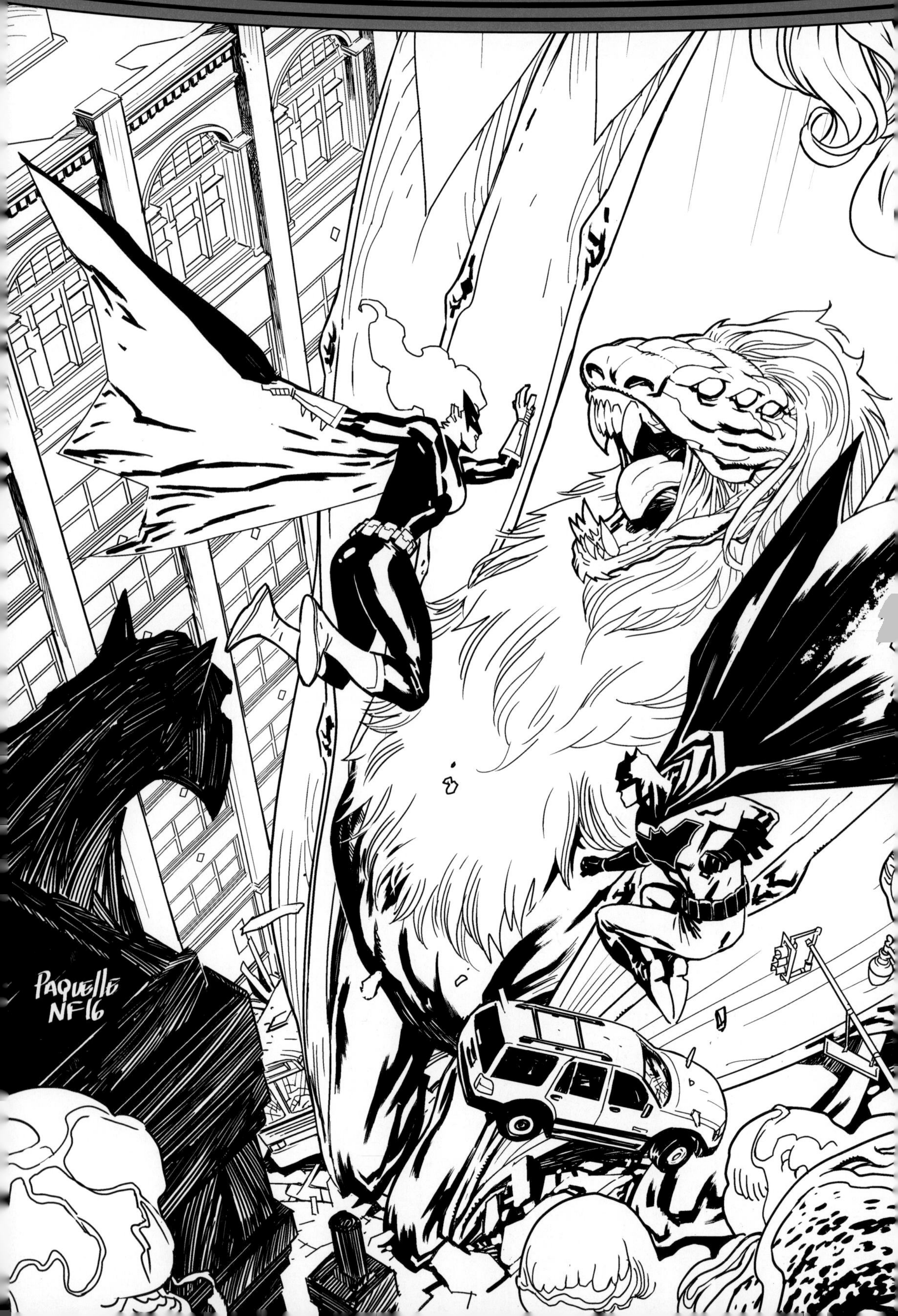
PAQUETTE
NF16

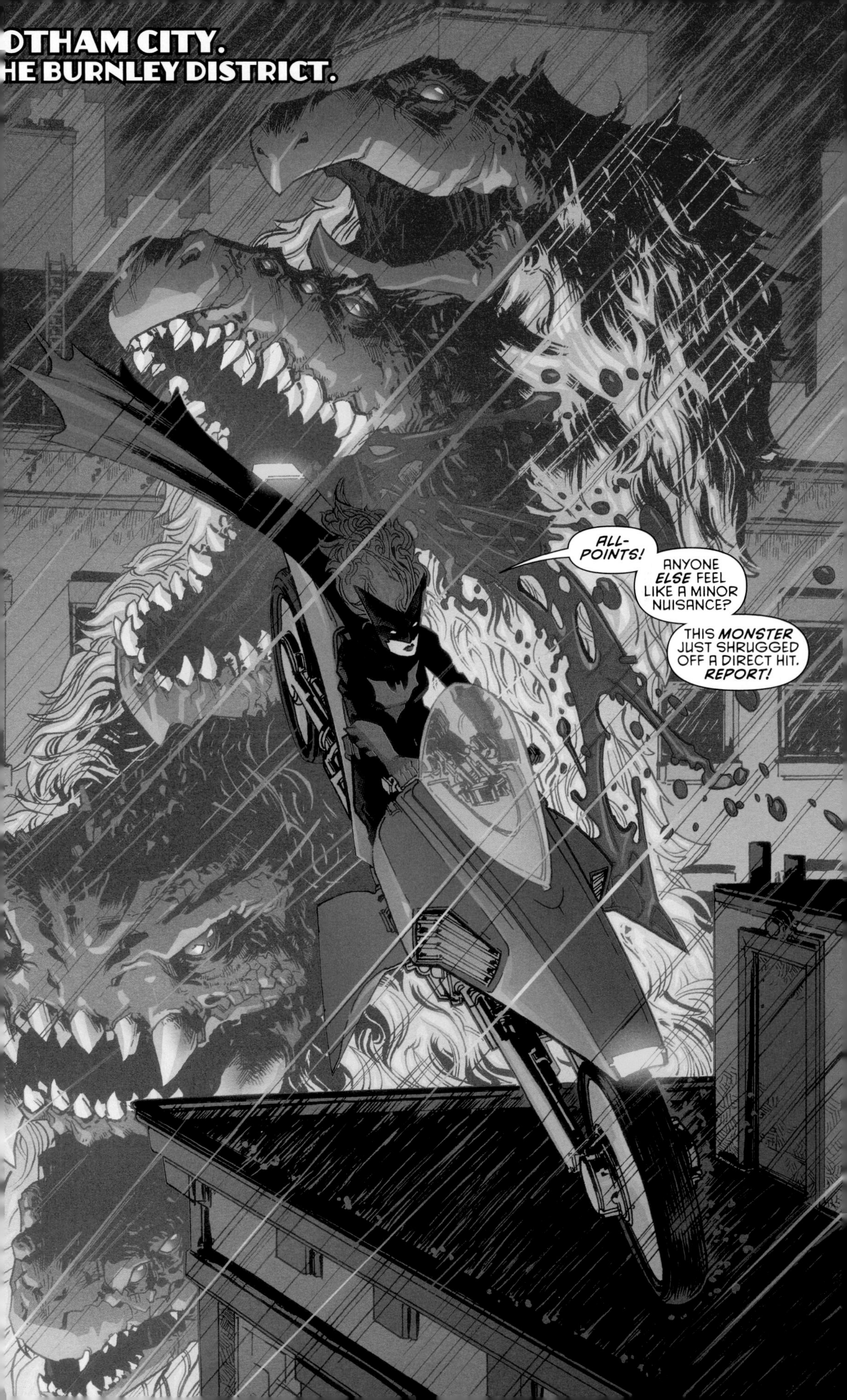
OTHAM CITY.
HE BURNLEY DISTRICT.
ALL-POINTS!
ANYONE ELSE FEEL LIKE A MINOR NUISANCE?
THIS MONSTER JUST SHRUGGED OFF A DIRECT HIT. REPORT!

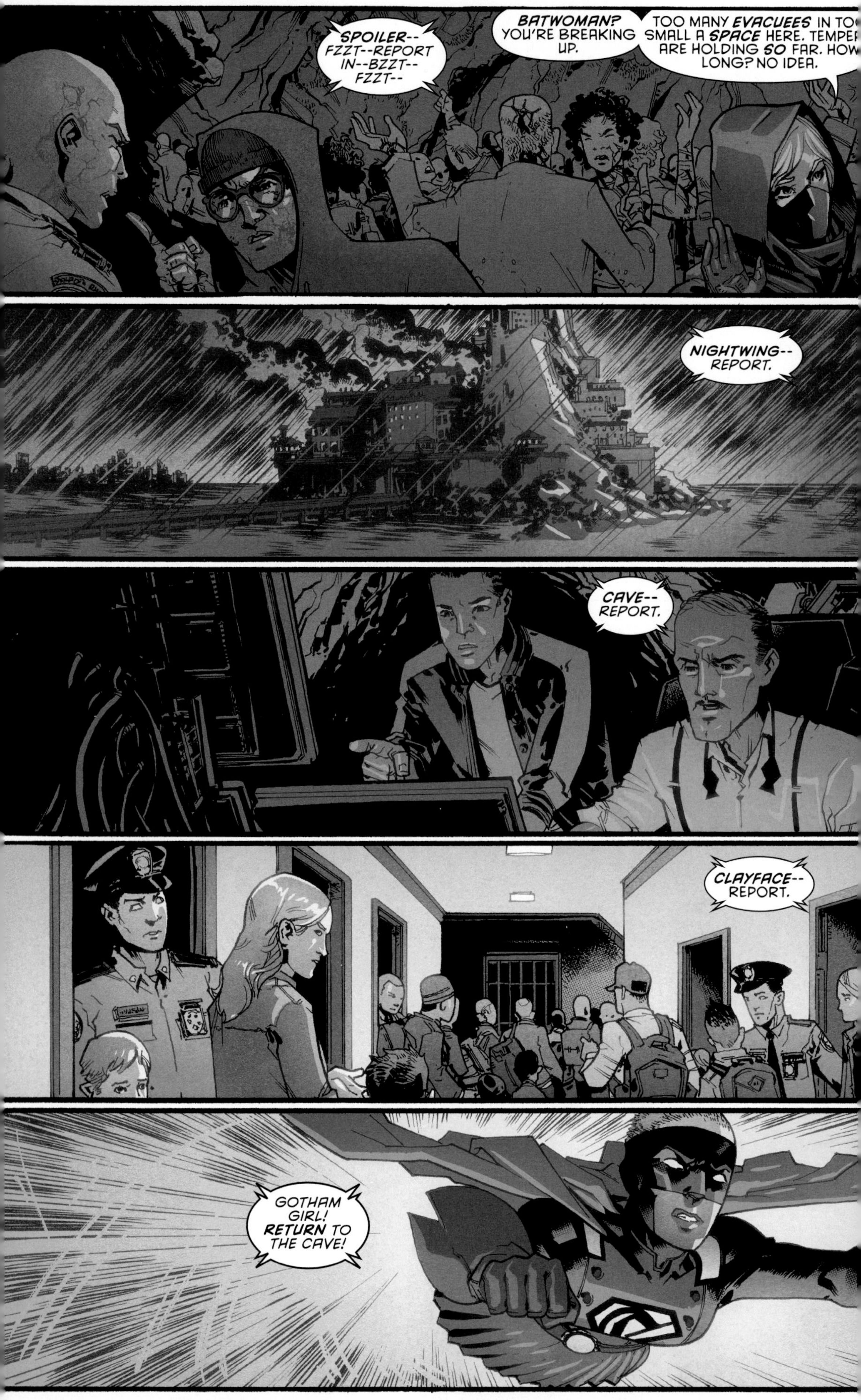
SPOILER--
FZZT--REPORT IN--BZZT--FZZT--
BATWOMAN? YOU'RE BREAKING UP.
TOO MANY EVACUEES IN TOO SMALL A SPACE HERE. TEMPERS ARE HOLDING SO FAR. HOW LONG? NO IDEA.
NIGHTWING--REPORT.
CAVE--REPORT.
CLAYFACE--REPORT.
GOTHAM GIRL! RETURN TO THE CAVE!

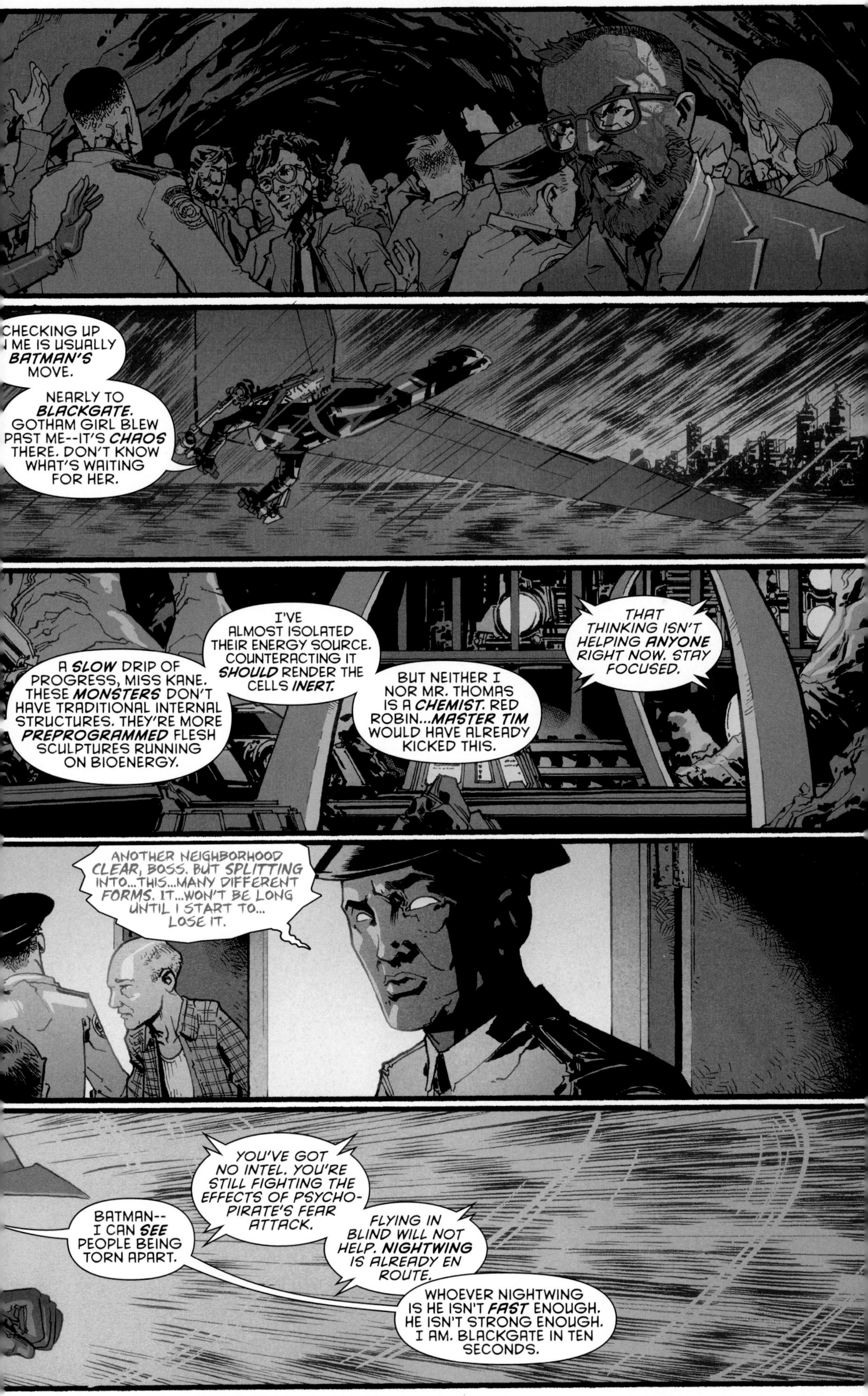
CHECKING UP ON ME IS USUALLY BATMAN'S MOVE.
NEARLY TO BLACKGATE. GOTHAM GIRL BLEW PAST ME--IT'S CHAOS THERE. DON'T KNOW WHAT'S WAITING FOR HER.
A SLOW DRIP OF PROGRESS, MISS KANE. THESE MONSTERS DON'T HAVE TRADITIONAL INTERNAL STRUCTURES. THEY'RE MORE PREPROGRAMMED FLESH SCULPTURES RUNNING ON BIOENERGY.
I'VE ALMOST ISOLATED THEIR ENERGY SOURCE. COUNTERACTING IT SHOULD RENDER THE CELLS INERT.
BUT NEITHER I NOR MR. THOMAS IS A CHEMIST. RED ROBIN...MASTER TIM WOULD HAVE ALREADY KICKED THIS.
THAT THINKING ISN'T HELPING ANYONE RIGHT NOW. STAY FOCUSED.
ANOTHER NEIGHBORHOOD CLEAR, BOSS. BUT SPLITTING INTO...THIS...MANY DIFFERENT FORMS. IT...WON'T BE LONG UNTIL I START TO... LOSE IT.
BATMAN-- I CAN SEE PEOPLE BEING TORN APART.
YOU'VE GOT NO INTEL. YOU'RE STILL FIGHTING THE EFFECTS OF PSYCHO-PIRATE'S FEAR ATTACK.
FLYING IN BLIND WILL NOT HELP. NIGHTWING IS ALREADY EN ROUTE.
WHOEVER NIGHTWING IS HE ISN'T FAST ENOUGH. HE ISN'T STRONG ENOUGH. I AM. BLACKGATE IN TEN SECONDS.

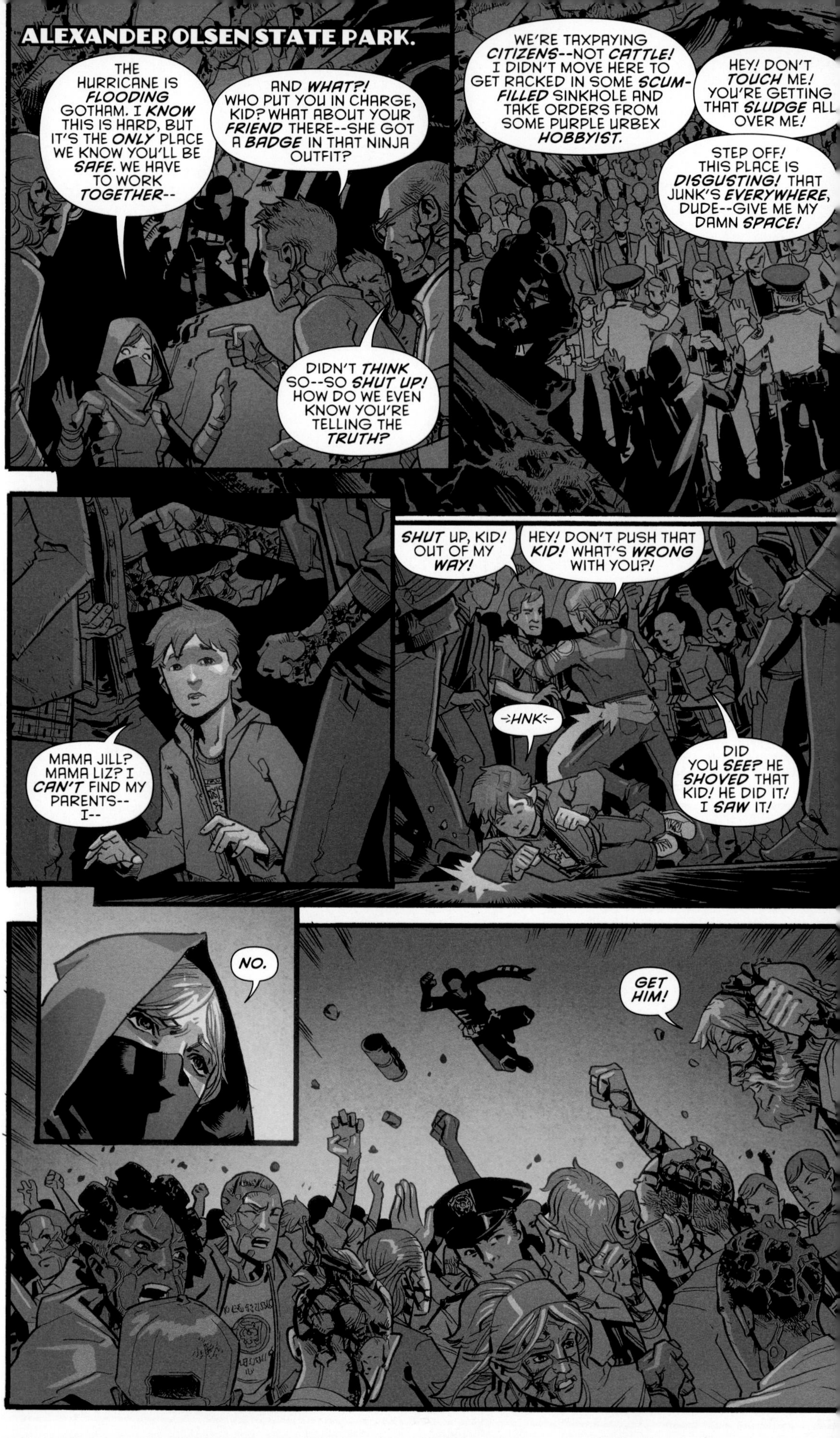
ALEXANDER OLSEN STATE PARK.
THE HURRICANE IS FLOODING GOTHAM. I KNOW THIS IS HARD, BUT IT'S THE ONLY PLACE WE KNOW YOU'LL BE SAFE. WE HAVE TO WORK TOGETHER--
AND WHAT?! WHO PUT YOU IN CHARGE, KID? WHAT ABOUT YOUR FRIEND THERE--SHE GOT A BADGE IN THAT NINJA OUTFIT?
DIDN'T THINK SO--SO SHUT UP! HOW DO WE EVEN KNOW YOU'RE TELLING THE TRUTH?
WE'RE TAXPAYING CITIZENS--NOT CATTLE! I DIDN'T MOVE HERE TO GET RACKED IN SOME SCUM-FILLED SINKHOLE AND TAKE ORDERS FROM SOME PURPLE URBEX HOBBYIST.
HEY! DON'T TOUCH ME! YOU'RE GETTING THAT SLUDGE ALL OVER ME!
STEP OFF! THIS PLACE IS DISGUSTING! THAT JUNK'S EVERYWHERE, DUDE--GIVE ME MY DAMN SPACE!
MAMA JILL? MAMA LIZ? I CAN'T FIND MY PARENTS-- I--
SHUT UP, KID! OUT OF MY WAY!
HEY! DON'T PUSH THAT KID! WHAT'S WRONG WITH YOU?!
HNK
DID YOU SEE? HE SHOVED THAT KID! HE DID IT! I SAW IT!
NO.
GET HIM!

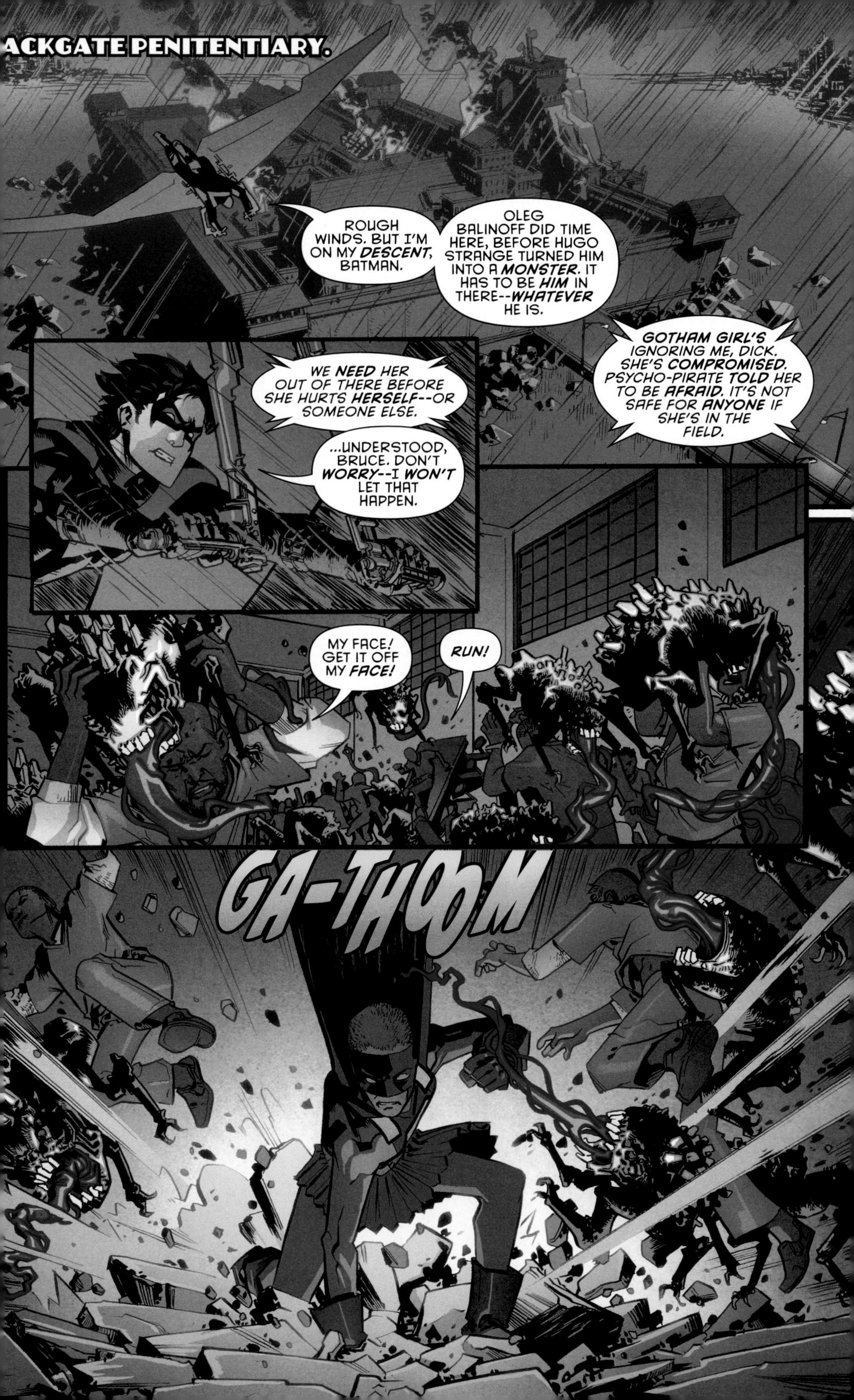

ACKGATE PENITENTIARY.
ROUGH WINDS. BUT I'M ON MY DESCENT, BATMAN.
OLEG BALINOFF DID TIME HERE, BEFORE HUGO STRANGE TURNED HIM INTO A MONSTER. IT HAS TO BE HIM IN THERE--WHATEVER HE IS.
GOTHAM GIRL'S IGNORING ME, DICK. SHE'S COMPROMISED. PSYCHO-PIRATE TOLD HER TO BE AFRAID. IT'S NOT SAFE FOR ANYONE IF SHE'S IN THE FIELD.
WE NEED HER OUT OF THERE BEFORE SHE HURTS HERSELF--OR SOMEONE ELSE.
...UNDERSTOOD, BRUCE. DON'T WORRY--I WON'T LET THAT HAPPEN.
MY FACE! GET IT OFF MY FACE!
RUN!
GA-THOOM

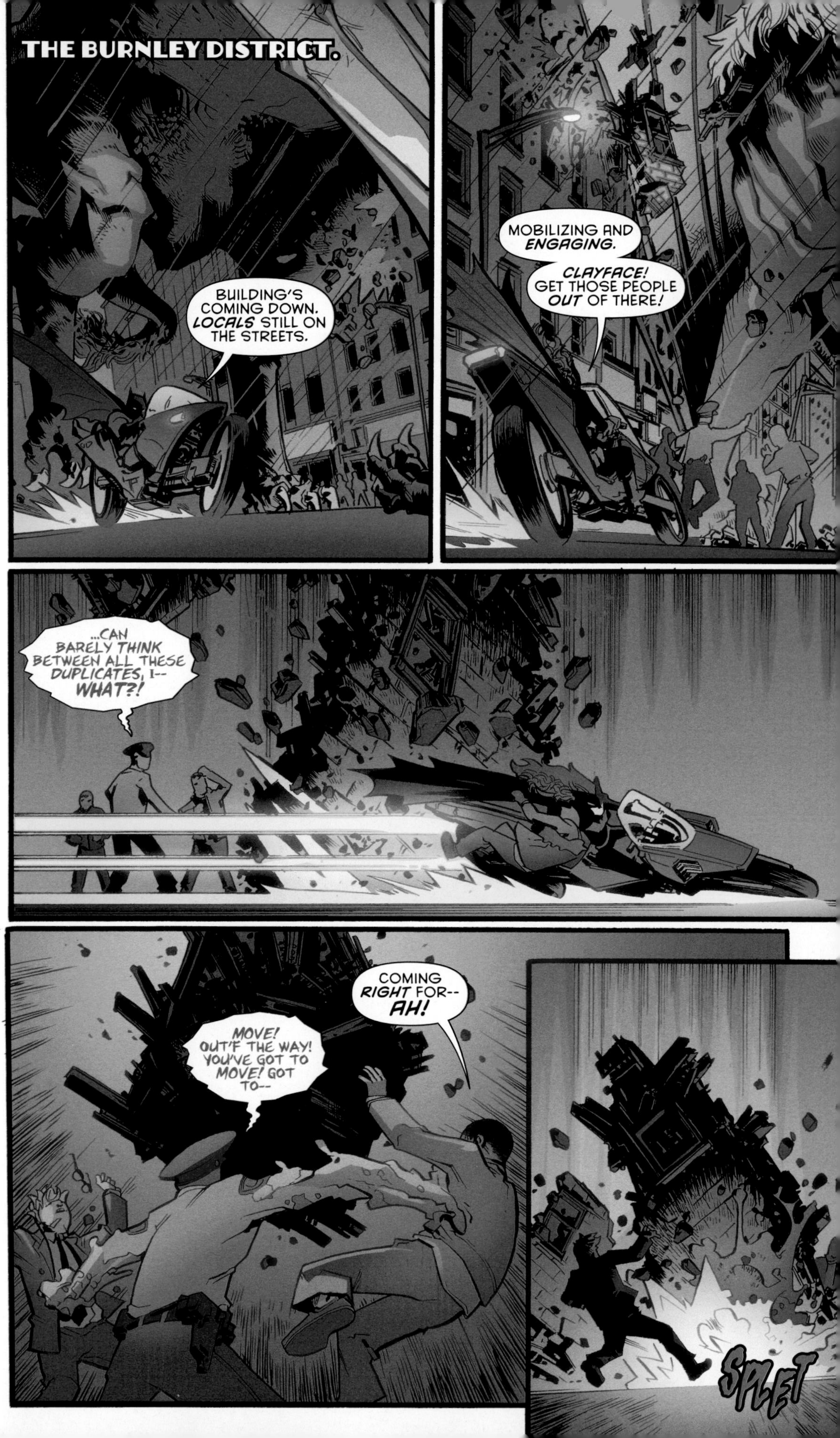
THE BURNLEY DISTRICT.
BUILDING'S COMING DOWN. LOCALS STILL ON THE STREETS.
MOBILIZING AND ENGAGING.
CLAYFACE! GET THOSE PEOPLE OUT OF THERE!
...CAN BARELY THINK BETWEEN ALL THESE DUPLICATES, I-- WHAT?!
MOVE! OUT'F THE WAY! YOU'VE GOT TO MOVE! GOT TO--
COMING RIGHT FOR-- AH!
SPLET

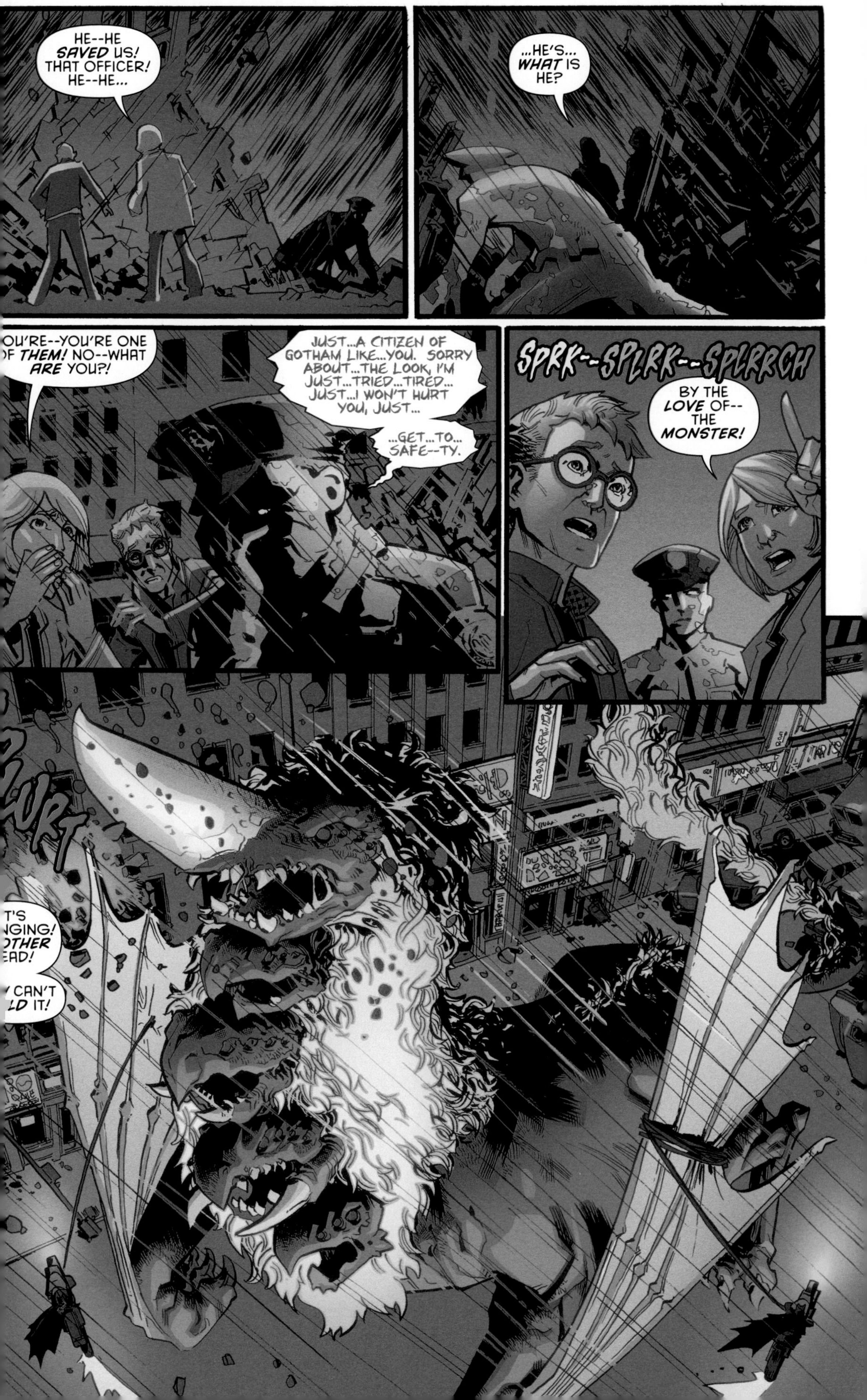
HE--HE SAVED US! THAT OFFICER! HE--HE...
...HE'S... WHAT IS HE?
OU'RE--YOU'RE ONE F THEM! NO--WHAT ARE YOU?!
JUST...A CITIZEN OF GOTHAM LIKE...YOU. SORRY ABOUT...THE LOOK, I'M JUST...TRIED...TIRED... JUST...I WON'T HURT YOU, JUST...
...GET...TO... SAFE--TY.
SPRK--SPLRK--SPLRRCH
BY THE LOVE OF-- THE MONSTER!
T'S NGING! OTHER EAD!
Y CAN'T LD IT!

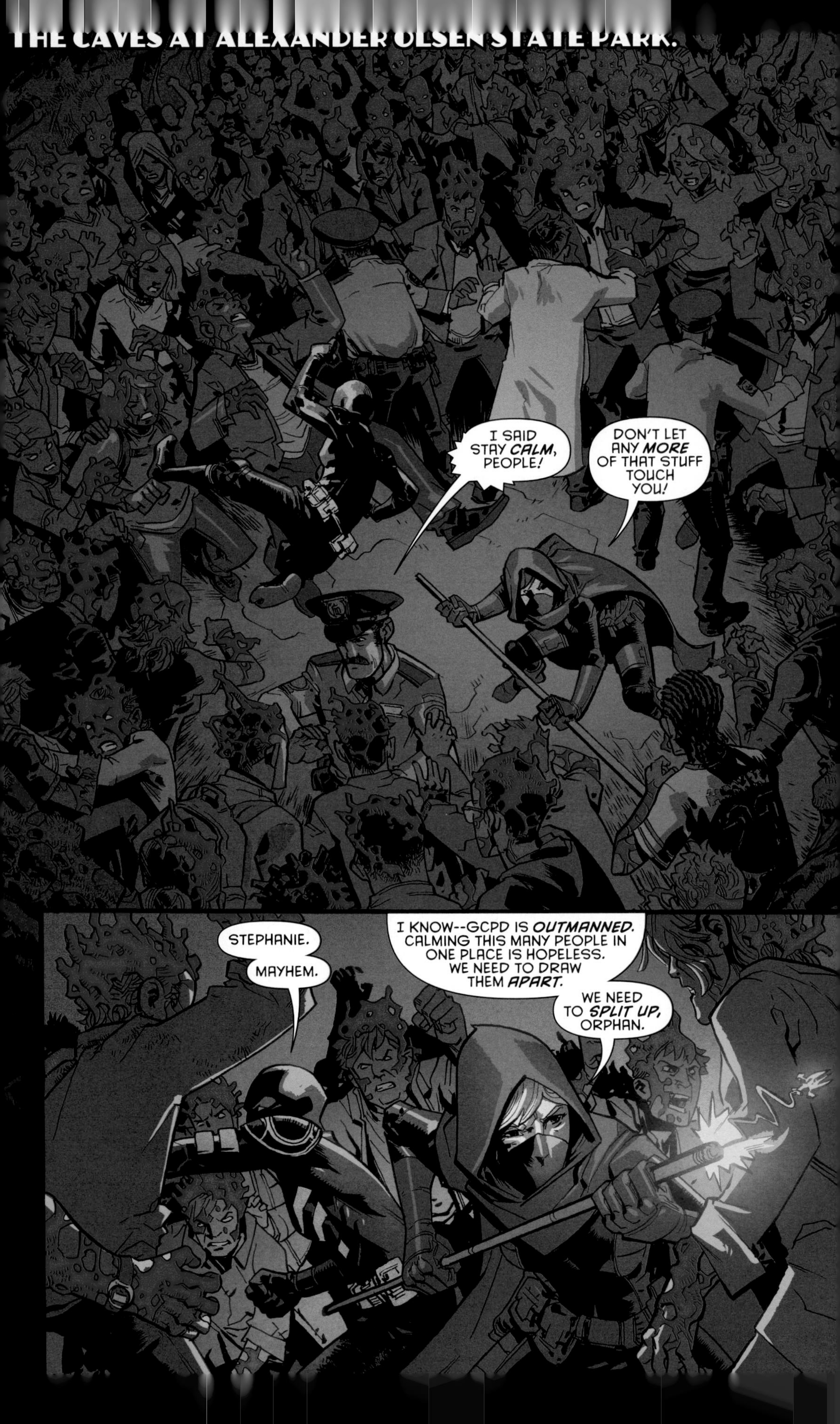
THE CAVES AT ALEXANDER OLSEN STATE PARK.
I SAID STAY CALM, PEOPLE!
DON'T LET ANY MORE OF THAT STUFF TOUCH YOU!
STEPHANIE.
MAYHEM.
I KNOW--GCPD IS OUTMANNED. CALMING THIS MANY PEOPLE IN ONE PLACE IS HOPELESS. WE NEED TO DRAW THEM APART.
WE NEED TO SPLIT UP, ORPHAN.

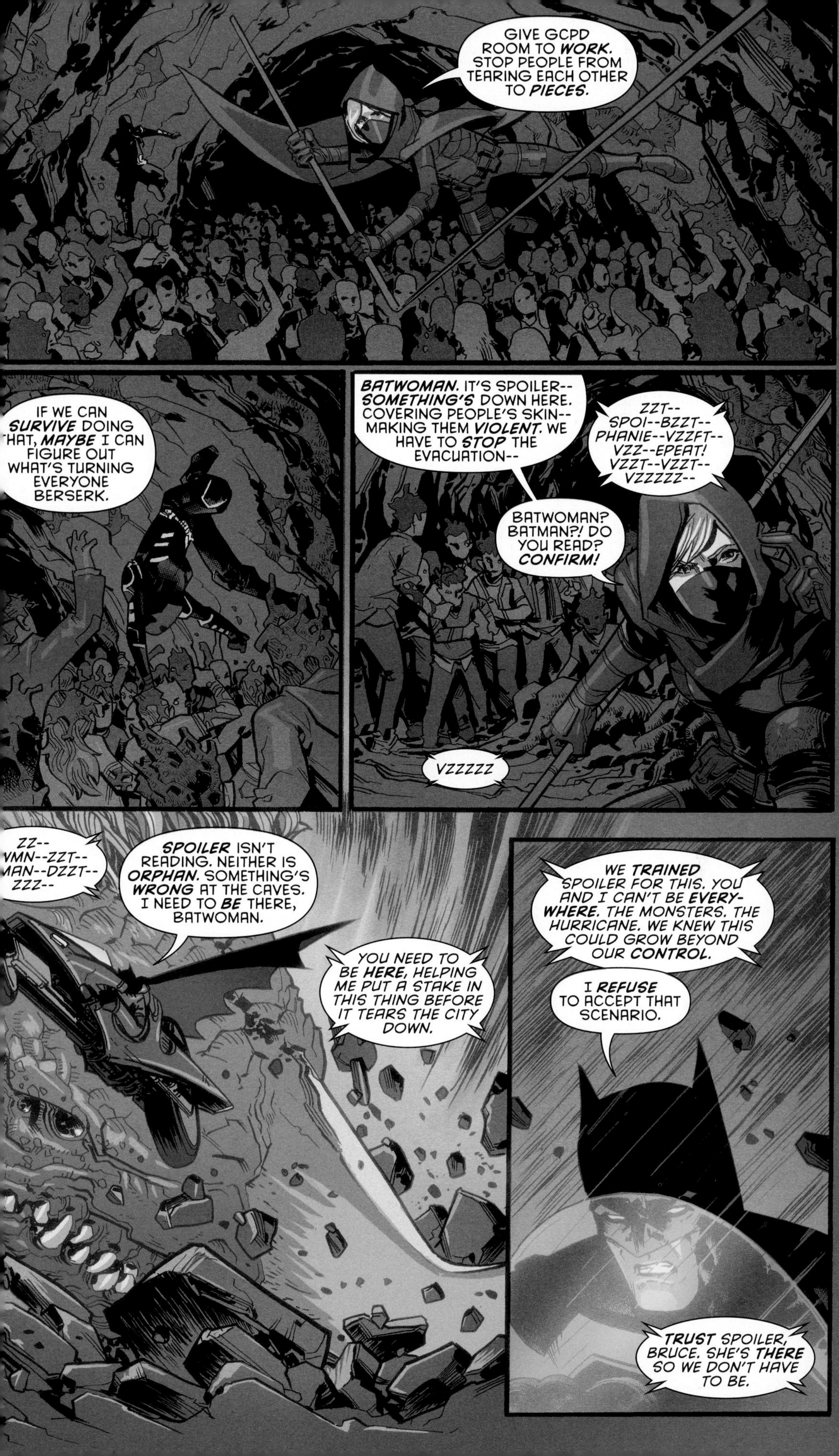
GIVE GCPD ROOM TO WORK. STOP PEOPLE FROM TEARING EACH OTHER TO PIECES.
IF WE CAN SURVIVE DOING THAT, MAYBE I CAN FIGURE OUT WHAT'S TURNING EVERYONE BERSERK.
BATWOMAN. IT'S SPOILER-- SOMETHING'S DOWN HERE. COVERING PEOPLE'S SKIN-- MAKING THEM VIOLENT. WE HAVE TO STOP THE EVACUATION--
ZZT-- SPOI--BZZT-- PHANIE--VZZFT-- VZZ--EPEAT! VZZT--VZZT-- VZZZZZ--
BATWOMAN? BATMAN?! DO YOU READ? CONFIRM!
VZZZZZ
ZZ-- WMN--ZZT-- MAN--DZZT-- ZZZ--
SPOILER ISN'T READING. NEITHER IS ORPHAN. SOMETHING'S WRONG AT THE CAVES. I NEED TO BE THERE, BATWOMAN.
YOU NEED TO BE HERE, HELPING ME PUT A STAKE IN THIS THING BEFORE IT TEARS THE CITY DOWN.
WE TRAINED SPOILER FOR THIS. YOU AND I CAN'T BE EVERY-WHERE. THE MONSTERS. THE HURRICANE. WE KNEW THIS COULD GROW BEYOND OUR CONTROL.
I REFUSE TO ACCEPT THAT SCENARIO.
TRUST SPOILER, BRUCE. SHE'S THERE SO WE DON'T HAVE TO BE.

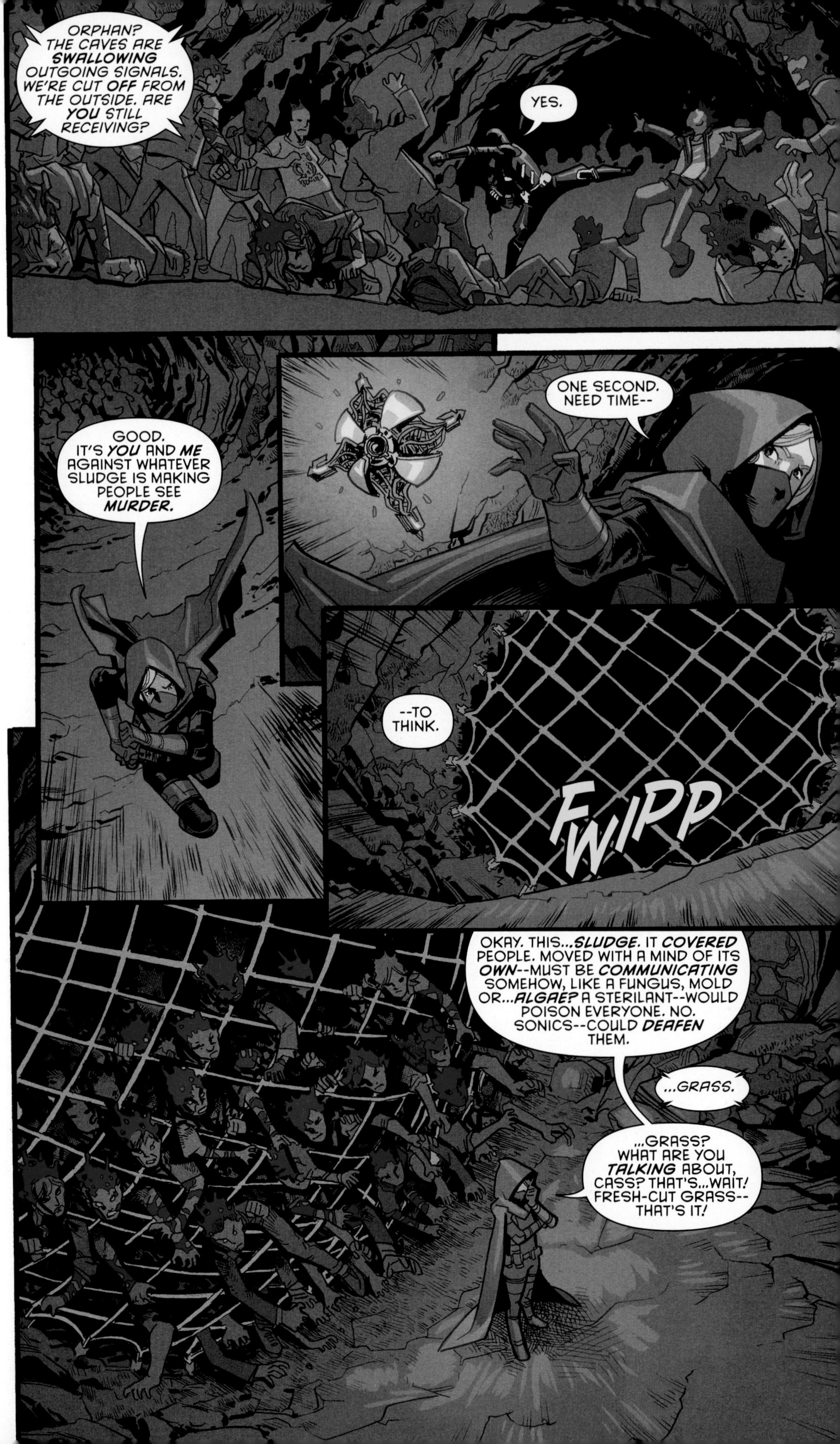

ORPHAN? THE CAVES ARE SWALLOWING OUTGOING SIGNALS. WE'RE CUT OFF FROM THE OUTSIDE. ARE YOU STILL RECEIVING?
YES.
GOOD. IT'S YOU AND ME AGAINST WHATEVER SLUDGE IS MAKING PEOPLE SEE MURDER.
ONE SECOND. NEED TIME--
--TO THINK.
FWIPP
OKAY. THIS...SLUDGE. IT COVERED PEOPLE. MOVED WITH A MIND OF ITS OWN--MUST BE COMMUNICATING SOMEHOW, LIKE A FUNGUS, MOLD OR...ALGAE? A STERILANT--WOULD POISON EVERYONE. NO. SONICS--COULD DEAFEN THEM.
...GRASS.
...GRASS? WHAT ARE YOU TALKING ABOUT, CASS? THAT'S...WAIT! FRESH-CUT GRASS--THAT'S IT!

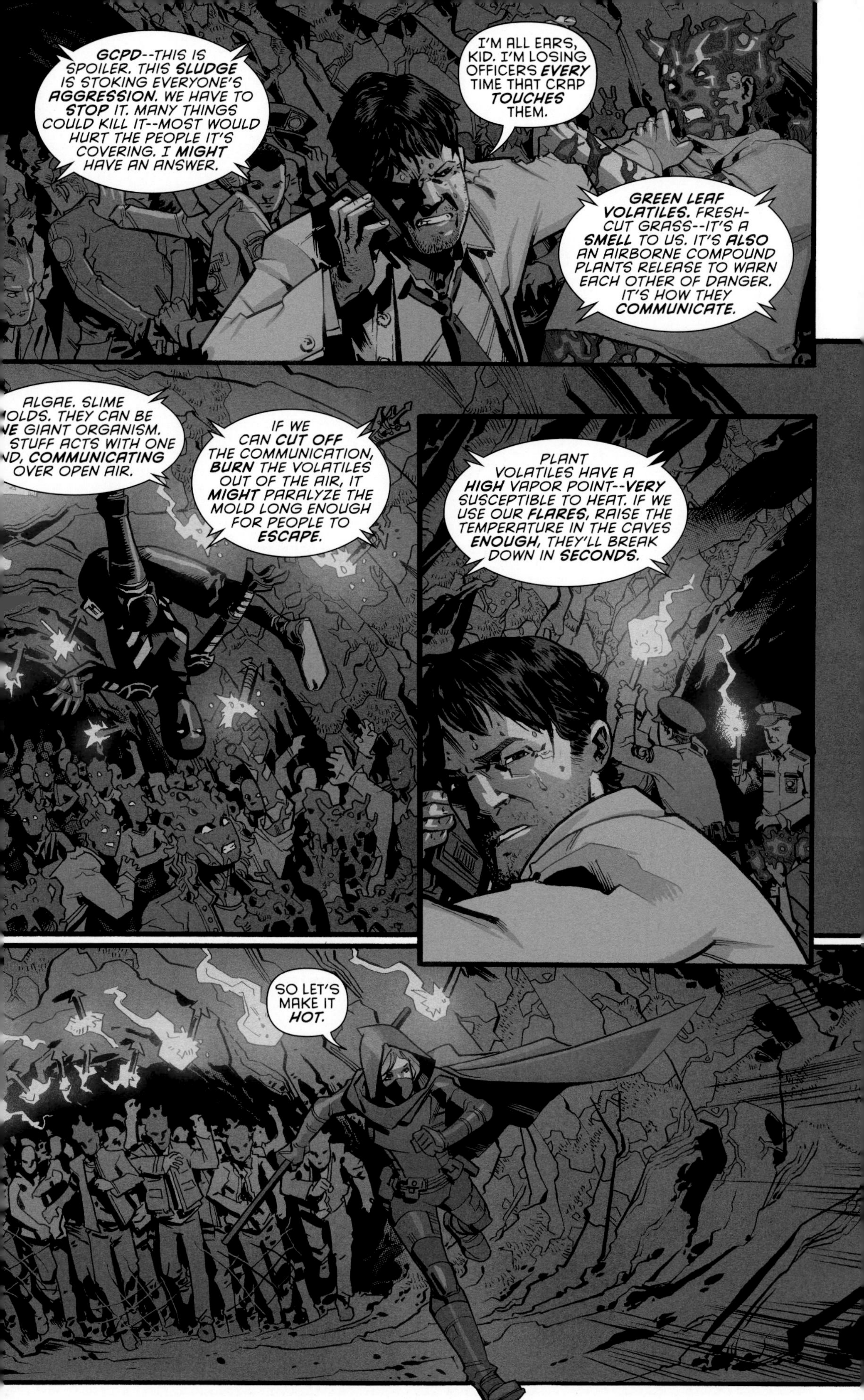
GCPD--THIS IS SPOILER. THIS SLUDGE IS STOKING EVERYONE'S AGGRESSION. WE HAVE TO STOP IT. MANY THINGS COULD KILL IT--MOST WOULD HURT THE PEOPLE IT'S COVERING. I MIGHT HAVE AN ANSWER.
I'M ALL EARS, KID. I'M LOSING OFFICERS EVERY TIME THAT CRAP TOUCHES THEM.
GREEN LEAF VOLATILES. FRESH-CUT GRASS--IT'S A SMELL TO US. IT'S ALSO AN AIRBORNE COMPOUND PLANTS RELEASE TO WARN EACH OTHER OF DANGER. IT'S HOW THEY COMMUNICATE.
ALGAE. SLIME OLDS. THEY CAN BE E GIANT ORGANISM. STUFF ACTS WITH ONE ND, COMMUNICATING OVER OPEN AIR.
IF WE CAN CUT OFF THE COMMUNICATION, BURN THE VOLATILES OUT OF THE AIR, IT MIGHT PARALYZE THE MOLD LONG ENOUGH FOR PEOPLE TO ESCAPE.
PLANT VOLATILES HAVE A HIGH VAPOR POINT--VERY SUSCEPTIBLE TO HEAT. IF WE USE OUR FLARES, RAISE THE TEMPERATURE IN THE CAVES ENOUGH, THEY'LL BREAK DOWN IN SECONDS.
SO LET'S MAKE IT HOT.

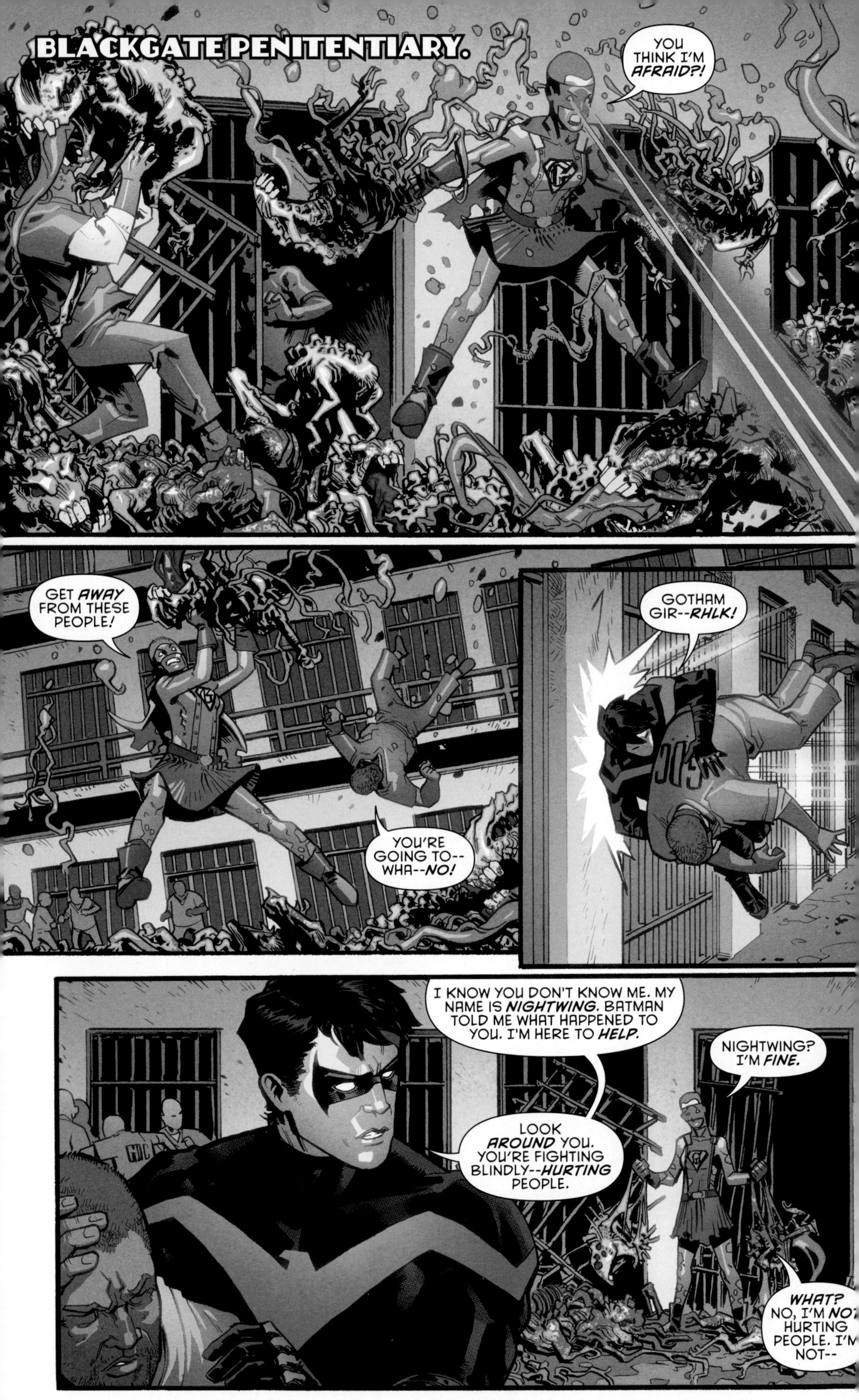

BLACKGATE PENITENTIARY.
YOU THINK I'M AFRAID?!
GET AWAY FROM THESE PEOPLE!
YOU'RE GOING TO-- WHA--NO!
GOTHAM GIR--RHLK!
I KNOW YOU DON'T KNOW ME. MY NAME IS NIGHTWING. BATMAN TOLD ME WHAT HAPPENED TO YOU. I'M HERE TO HELP.
NIGHTWING? I'M FINE.
LOOK AROUND YOU. YOU'RE FIGHTING BLINDLY--HURTING PEOPLE.
WHAT? NO, I'M NOT HURTING PEOPLE. I'M NOT--

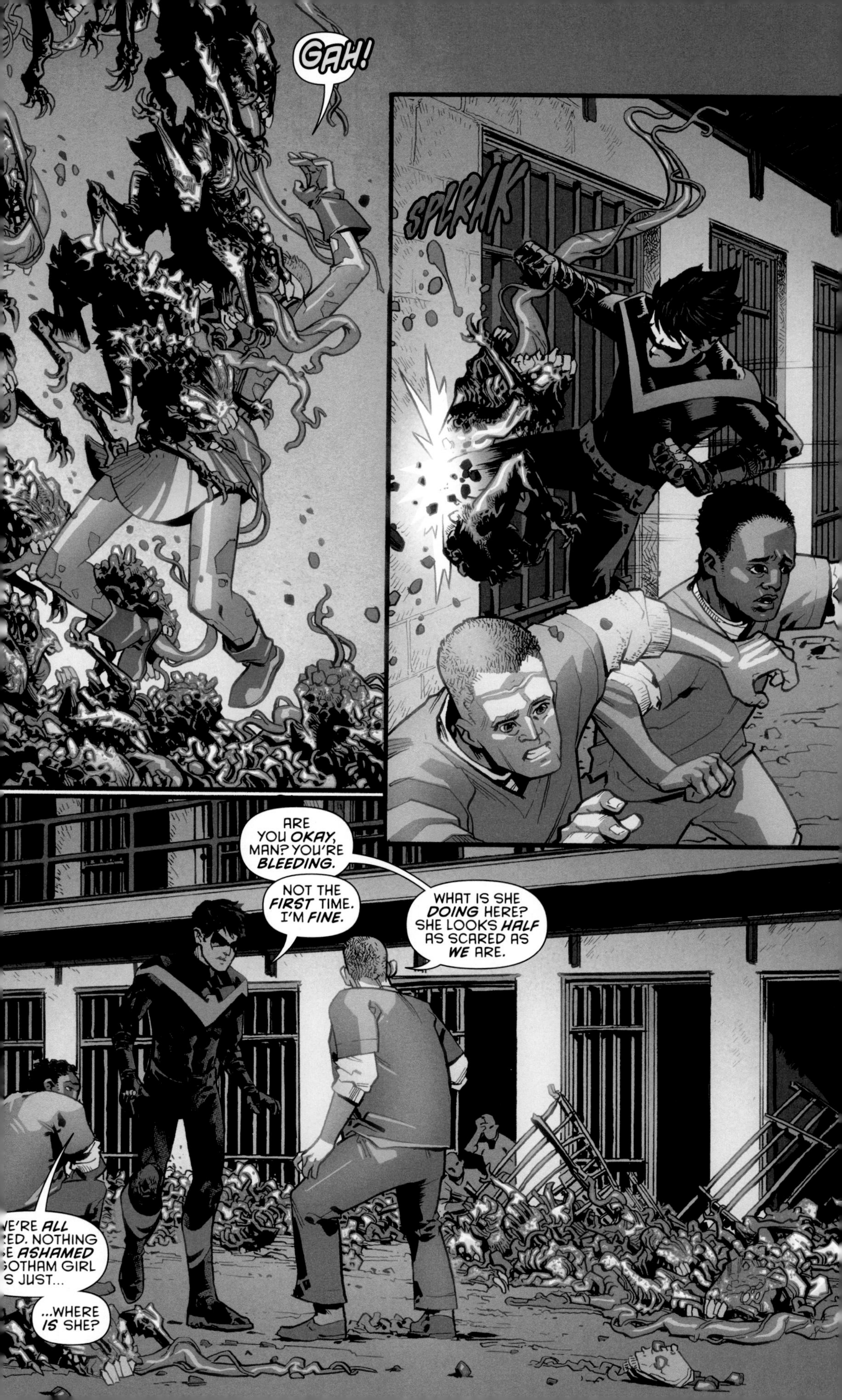
GAH!
SPLRAK
ARE YOU OKAY, MAN? YOU'RE BLEEDING.
NOT THE FIRST TIME. I'M FINE.
WHAT IS SHE DOING HERE? SHE LOOKS HALF AS SCARED AS WE ARE.
...WHERE IS SHE?

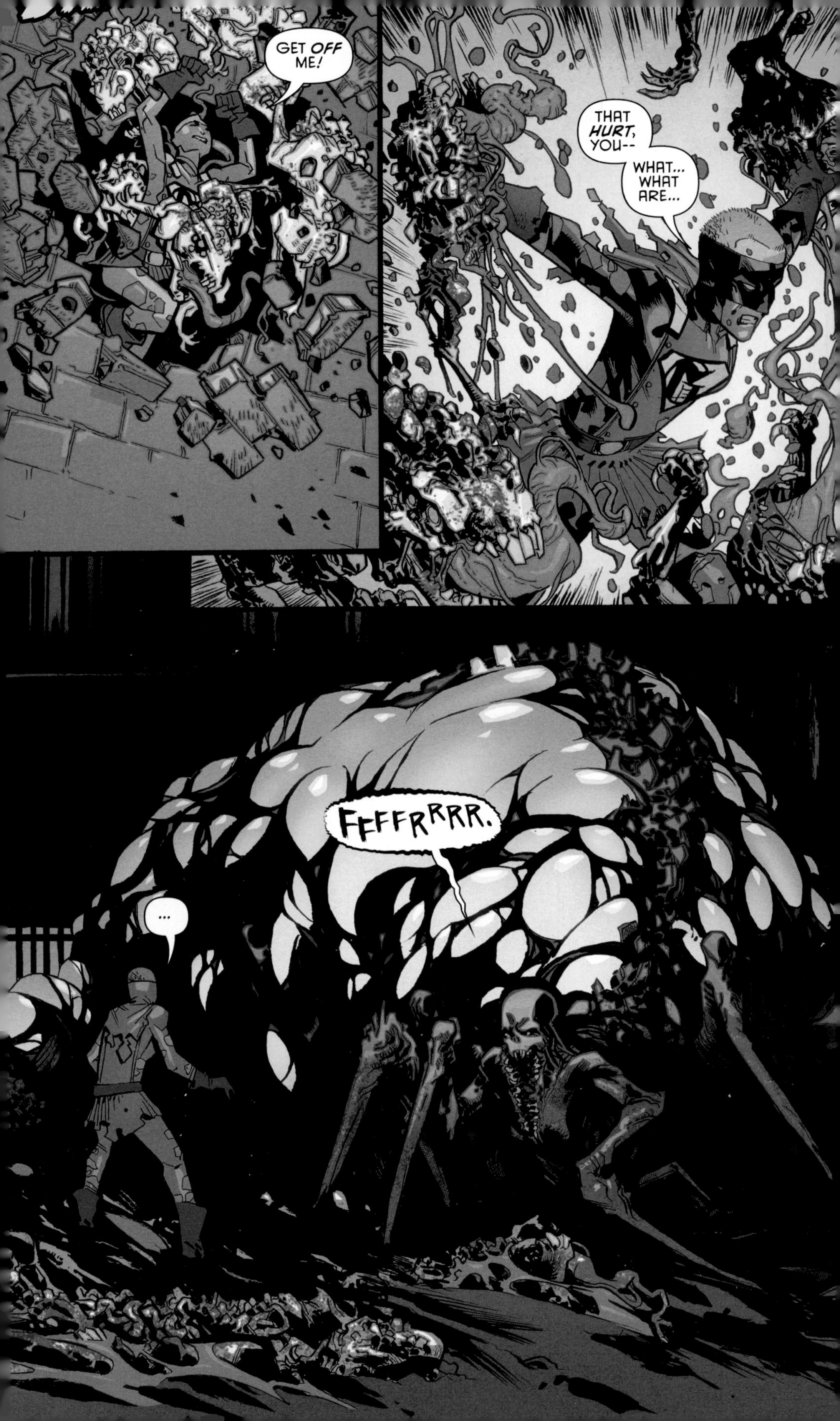
GET OFF ME!
THAT HURT, YOU--
WHAT... WHAT ARE...
FFFFRRRR.
...

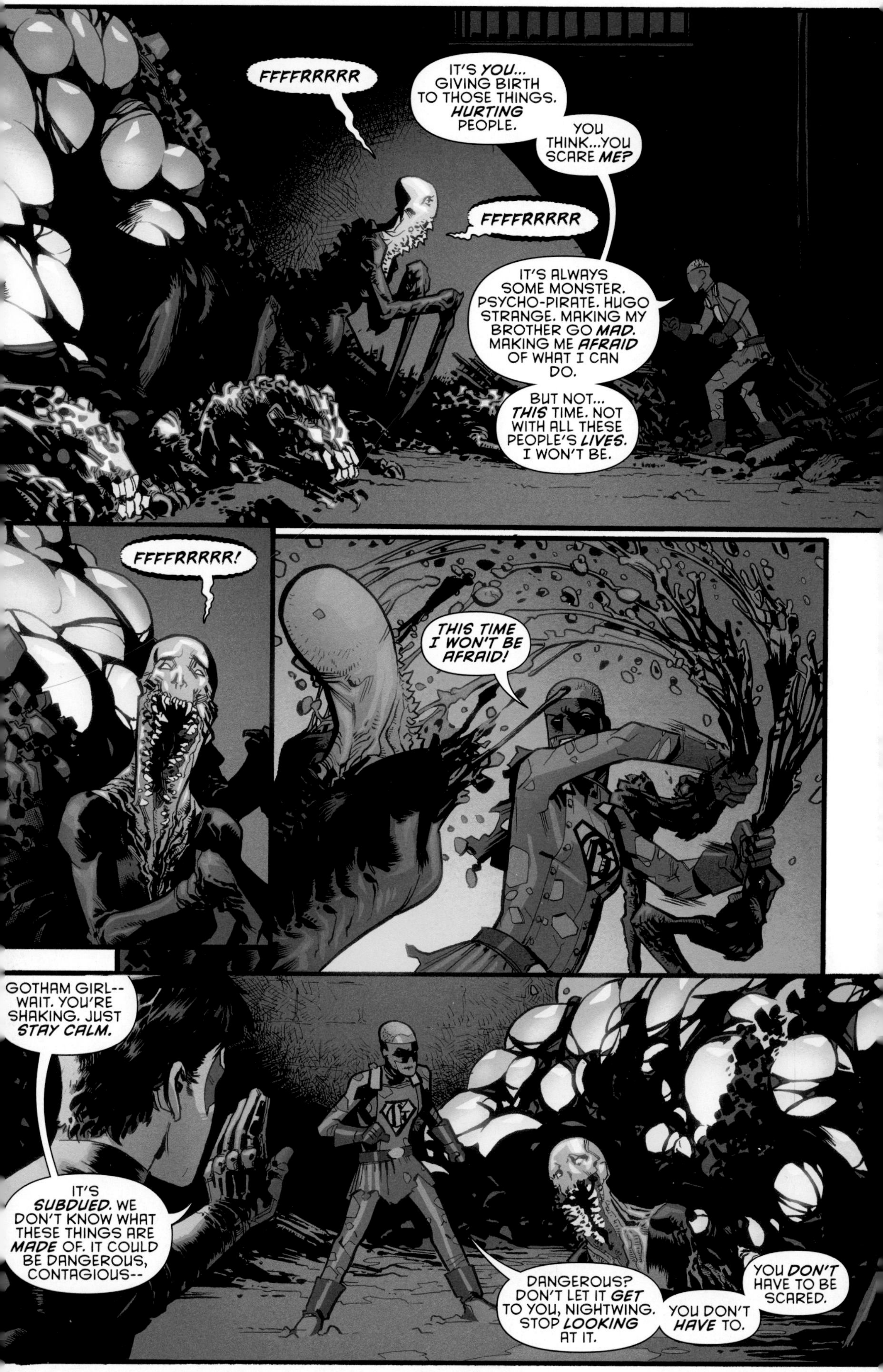
FFFFRRRRR
IT'S YOU... GIVING BIRTH TO THOSE THINGS. HURTING PEOPLE.
YOU THINK...YOU SCARE ME?
FFFFRRRRR
IT'S ALWAYS SOME MONSTER. PSYCHO-PIRATE. HUGO STRANGE. MAKING MY BROTHER GO MAD. MAKING ME AFRAID OF WHAT I CAN DO.
BUT NOT... THIS TIME. NOT WITH ALL THESE PEOPLE'S LIVES. I WON'T BE.
FFFFRRRRR!
THIS TIME I WON'T BE AFRAID!
GOTHAM GIRL-- WAIT. YOU'RE SHAKING. JUST STAY CALM.
IT'S SUBDUED. WE DON'T KNOW WHAT THESE THINGS ARE MADE OF. IT COULD BE DANGEROUS, CONTAGIOUS--
DANGEROUS? DON'T LET IT GET TO YOU, NIGHTWING. STOP LOOKING AT IT.
YOU DON'T HAVE TO.
YOU DON'T HAVE TO BE SCARED.

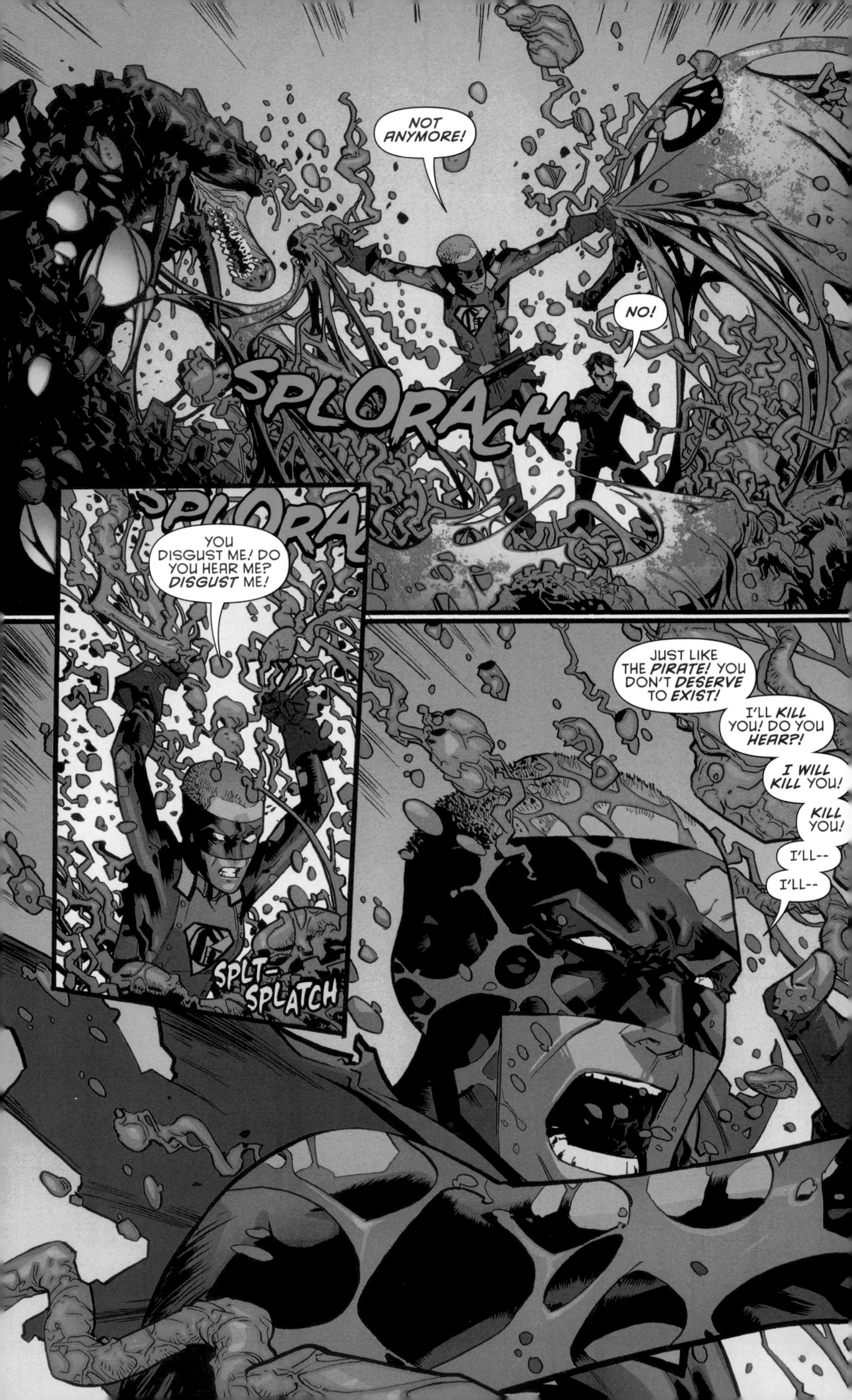
NOT ANYMORE!
NO!
SPLORACH
SPLORA
YOU DISGUST ME! DO YOU HEAR ME? *DISGUST* ME!
SPLT-SPLATCH
JUST LIKE THE *PIRATE!* YOU DON'T *DESERVE* TO *EXIST!*
I'LL *KILL* YOU! DO YOU *HEAR?!*
I WILL KILL YOU!
KILL YOU!
I'LL--
I'LL--

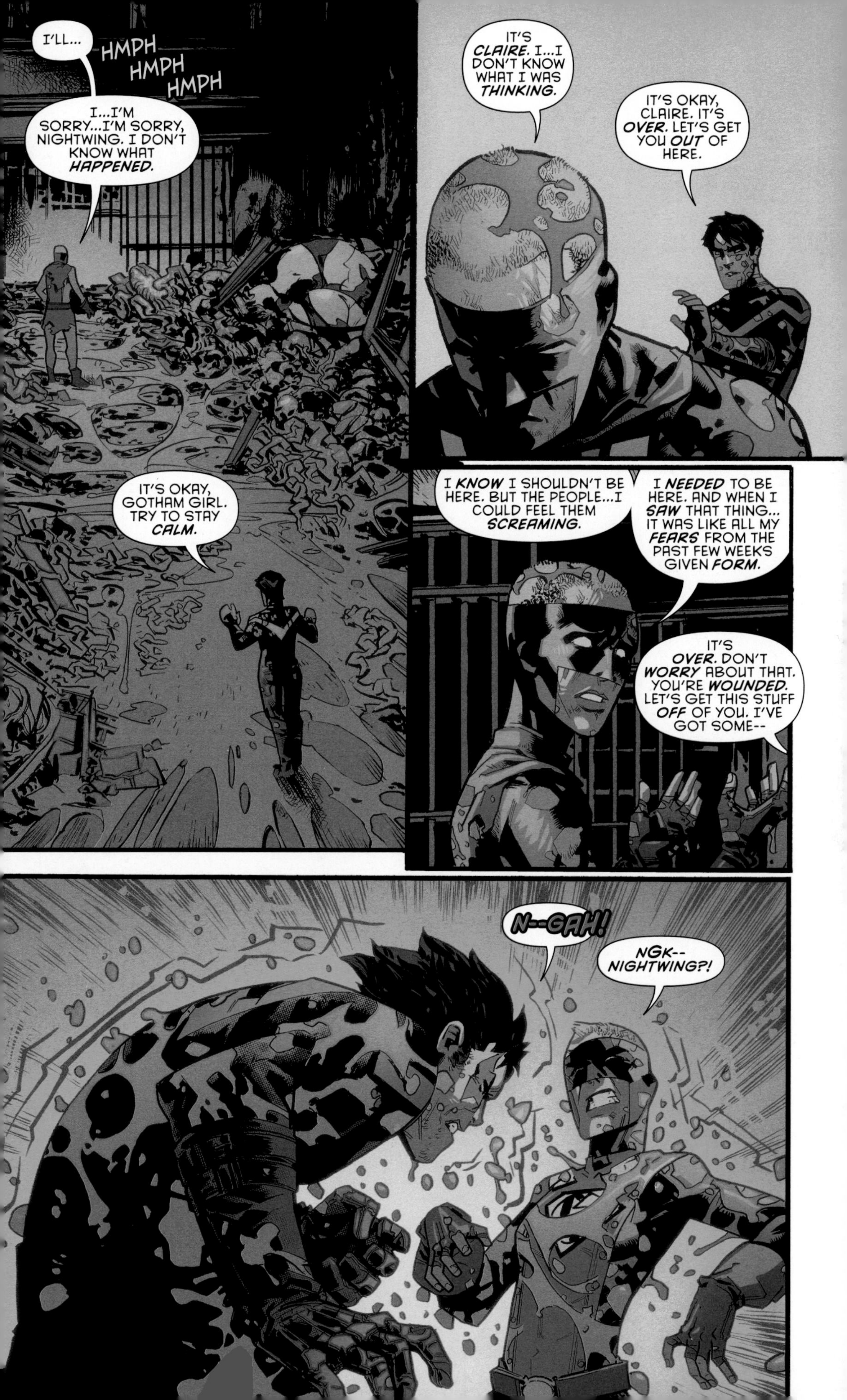
I'LL...
HMPH HMPH HMPH
I...I'M SORRY...I'M SORRY, NIGHTWING. I DON'T KNOW WHAT HAPPENED.
IT'S OKAY, GOTHAM GIRL. TRY TO STAY CALM.
IT'S CLAIRE. I...I DON'T KNOW WHAT I WAS THINKING.
IT'S OKAY, CLAIRE. IT'S OVER. LET'S GET YOU OUT OF HERE.
I KNOW I SHOULDN'T BE HERE. BUT THE PEOPLE...I COULD FEEL THEM SCREAMING.
I NEEDED TO BE HERE. AND WHEN I SAW THAT THING... IT WAS LIKE ALL MY FEARS FROM THE PAST FEW WEEKS GIVEN FORM.
IT'S OVER. DON'T WORRY ABOUT THAT. YOU'RE WOUNDED. LET'S GET THIS STUFF OFF OF YOU. I'VE GOT SOME--
N--GAH!
NGK-- NIGHTWING?!

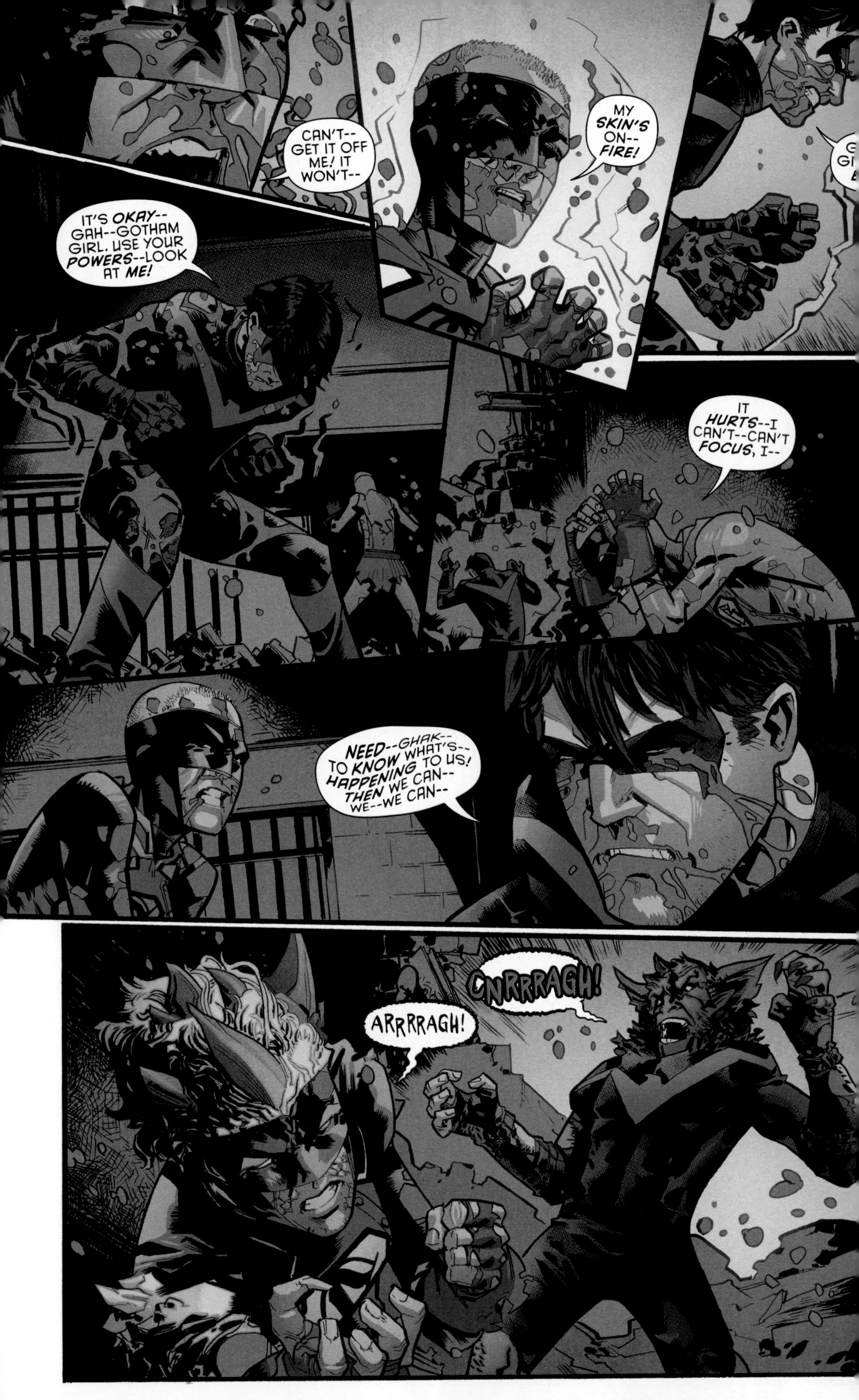
CAN'T-- GET IT OFF ME! IT WON'T--
MY SKIN'S ON-- FIRE!
IT'S OKAY-- GAH--GOTHAM GIRL. USE YOUR POWERS--LOOK AT ME!
IT HURTS--I CAN'T--CAN'T FOCUS, I--
NEED--GHAK--TO KNOW WHAT'S--HAPPENING TO US! THEN WE CAN-- WE--WE CAN--
CNRRRAGH!
ARRRRAGH!

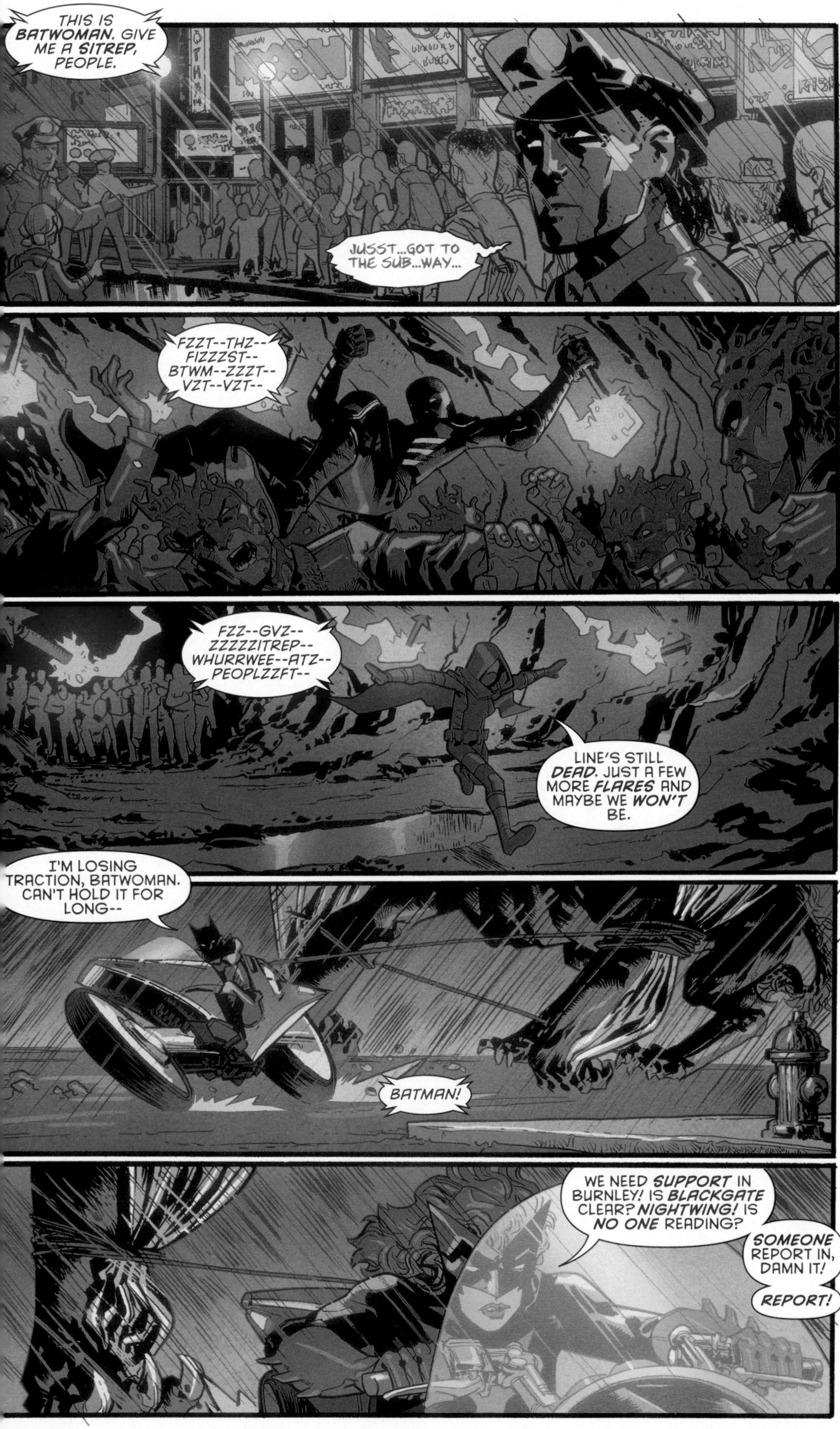
THIS IS BATWOMAN. GIVE ME A SITREP, PEOPLE.
JUSST...GOT TO THE SUB...WAY...
FZZT--THZ--FIZZZST--BTWM--ZZZT--VZT--VZT--
FZZ--GVZ--ZZZZZITREP--WHURRWEE--ATZ--PEOPLZZFT--
LINE'S STILL DEAD. JUST A FEW MORE FLARES AND MAYBE WE WON'T BE.
I'M LOSING TRACTION, BATWOMAN. CAN'T HOLD IT FOR LONG--
BATMAN!
WE NEED SUPPORT IN BURNLEY! IS BLACKGATE CLEAR? NIGHTWING! IS NO ONE READING?
SOMEONE REPORT IN, DAMN IT!
REPORT!

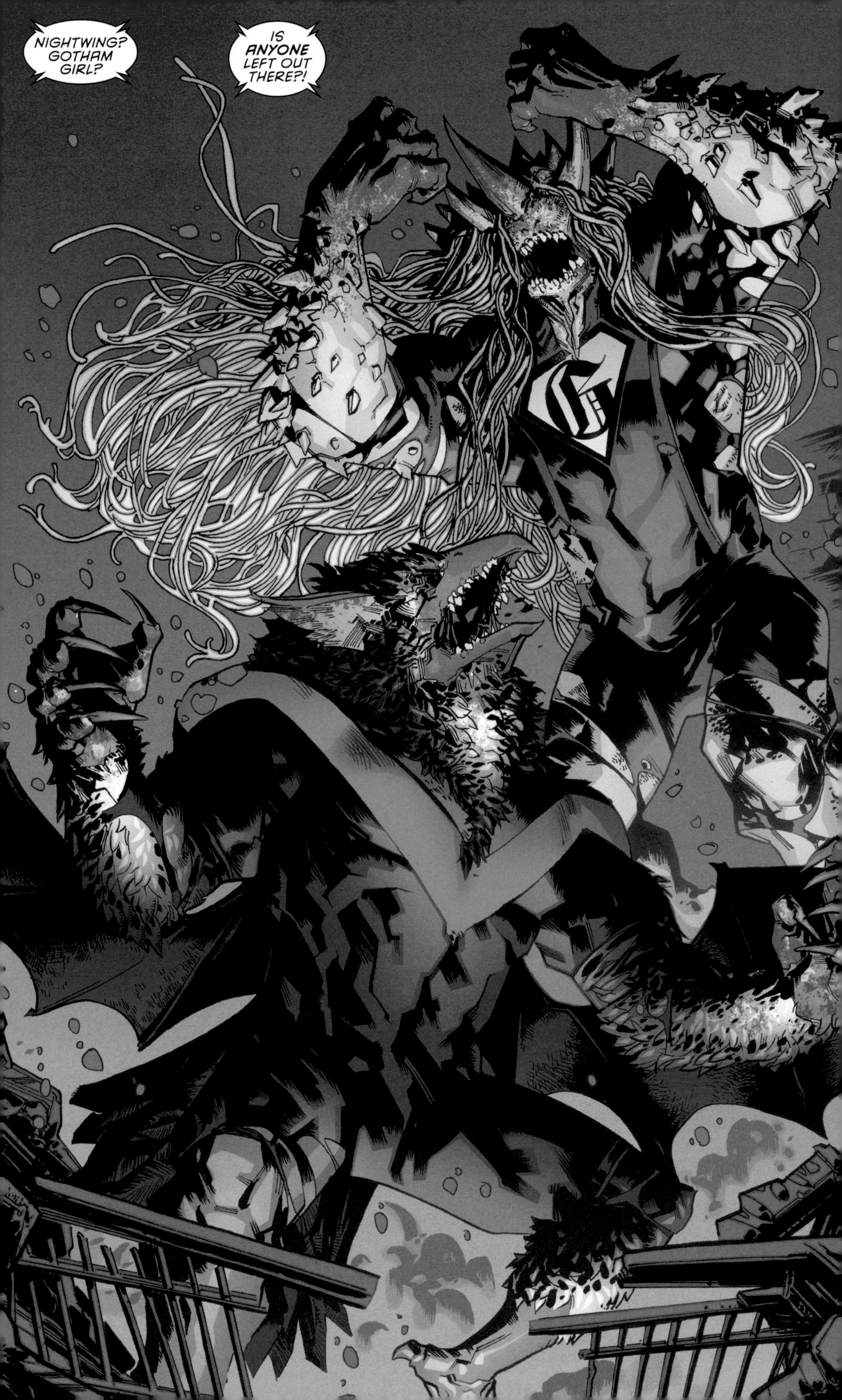
NIGHTWING? GOTHAM GIRL?
IS ANYONE LEFT OUT THERE?!

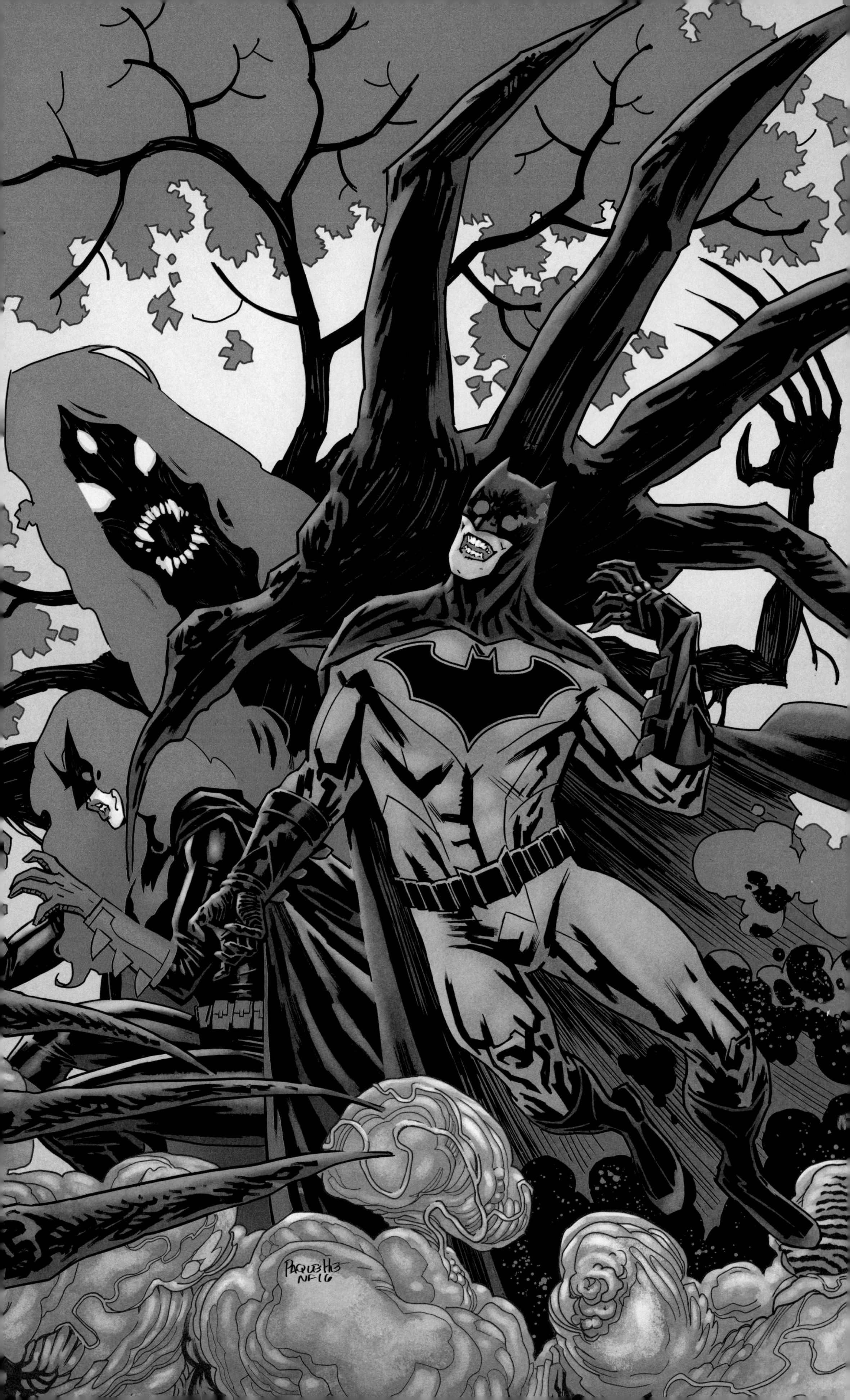

TOM KING & STEVE ORLANDO plot * STEVE ORLANDO script * RILEY ROSSMO art * IVAN PLASCENCIA colors
DERON BENNETT letters * YANICK PAQUETTE & NATHAN FAIRBAIRN cover art

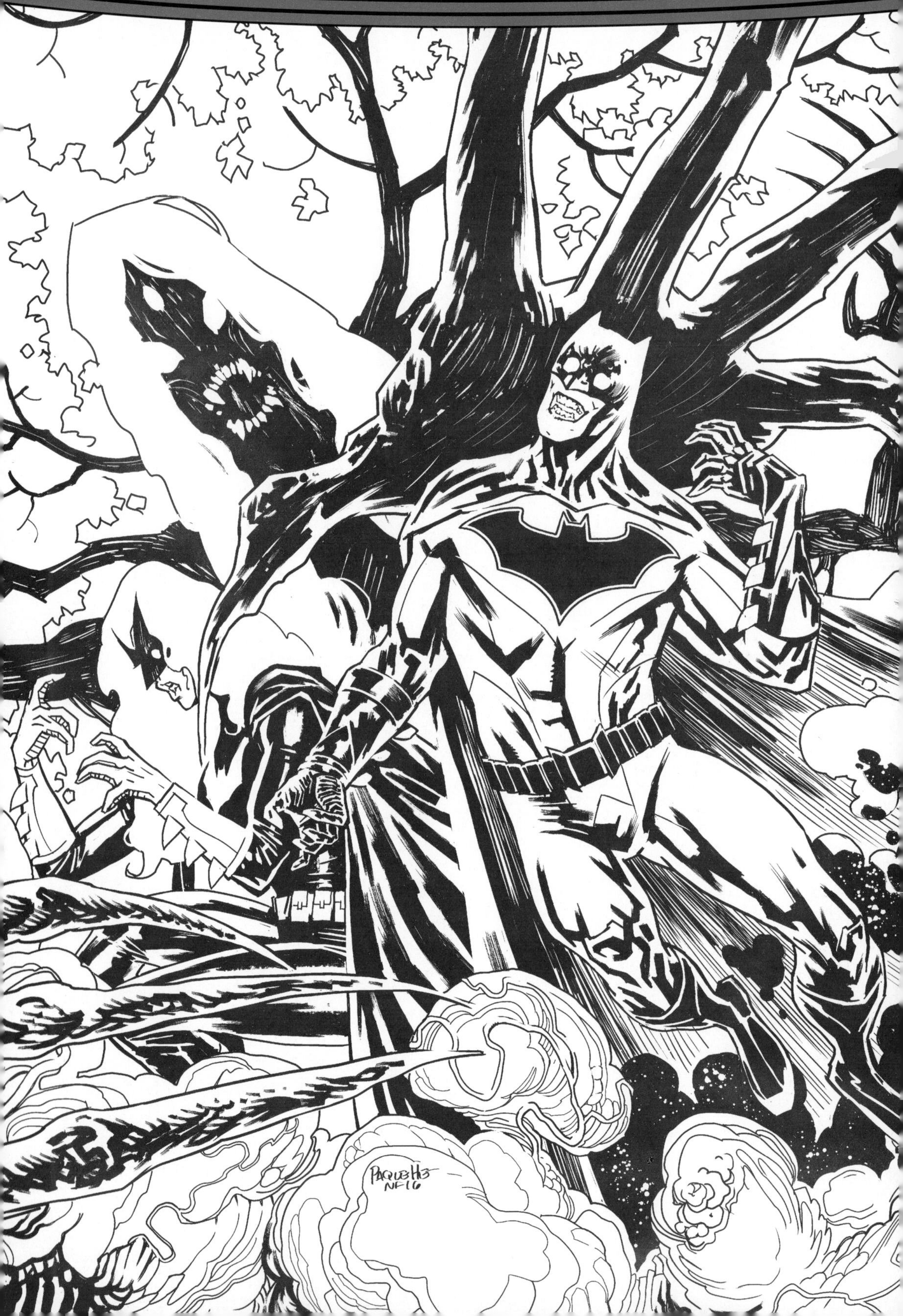

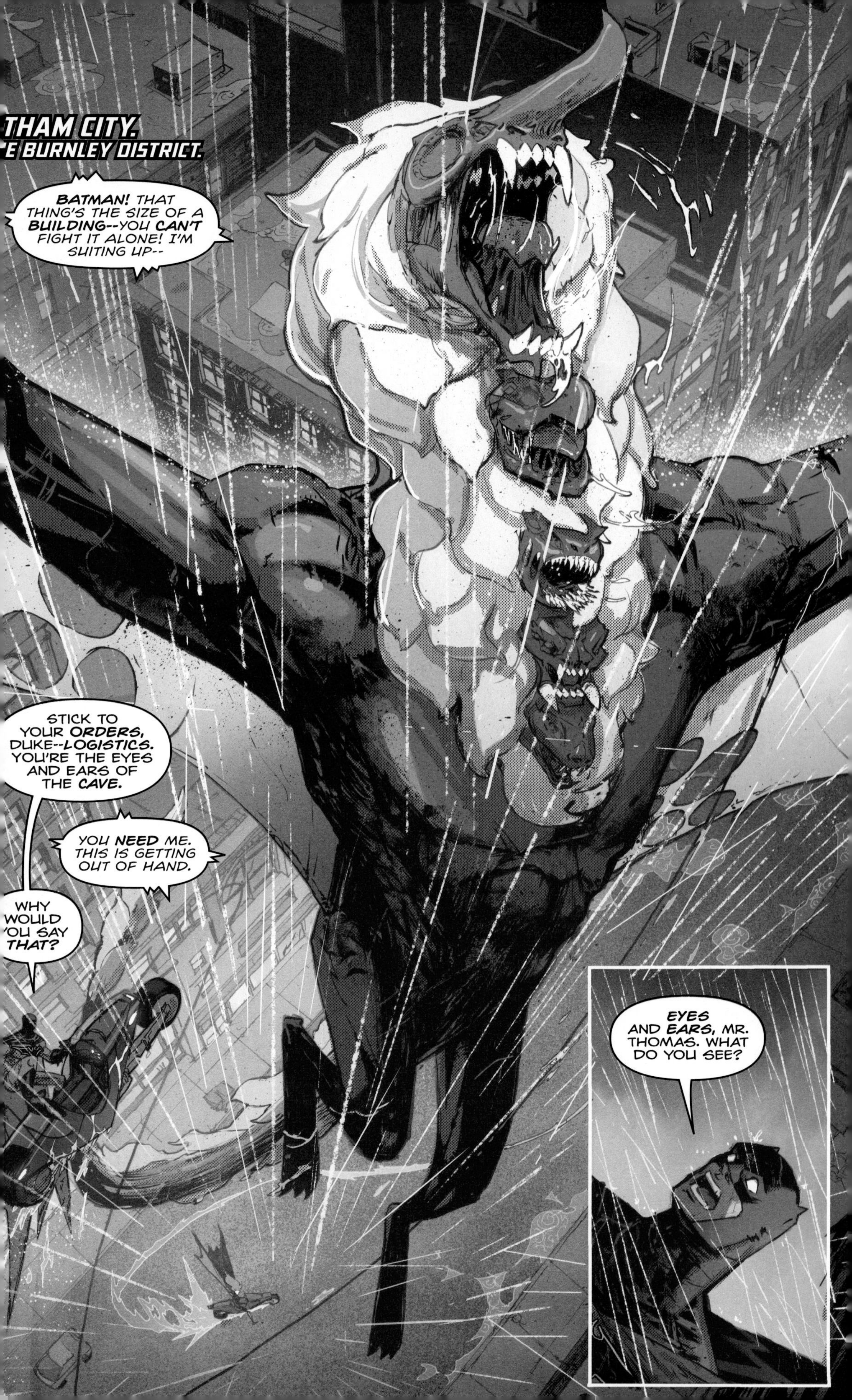
THAM CITY.
E BURNLEY DISTRICT.
BATMAN! THAT THING'S THE SIZE OF A BUILDING--YOU CAN'T FIGHT IT ALONE! I'M SUITING UP--
STICK TO YOUR ORDERS, DUKE--LOGISTICS. YOU'RE THE EYES AND EARS OF THE CAVE.
YOU NEED ME. THIS IS GETTING OUT OF HAND.
WHY WOULD YOU SAY THAT?
EYES AND EARS, MR. THOMAS. WHAT DO YOU SEE?

BATWOMAN EYEING YOUR TRAJECTORY, FOR ONE.

BATMAN'S SWINGING A HUNDRED FEET UP, EASY. THAT COMBAT CYCLE DOESN'T *FLY*.

IT JUST HASN'T *TRIED*, DUKE. FIELD EXPEDIENCY.

BATMAN'S NOT ALONE WHILE *I'M* HERE. HOW ARE WE DOING IN THE FIELD?

THE CAVES AT ALEXANDER OLSEN STATE PARK.

"COMMS STILL DEAD ON *SPOILER* AND *ORPHAN*."

KEEP PLANTING FLARES!

SCREAMING'S STOPPED AT *BLACKGATE*, BUT NIGHTWING AND GOTHAM GIRL ARE NON-RESPONSIVE.

NIGHTWING'S *BIOMETRY*-- HIS HEART RATE'S *SPIKING*. SOMETHING'S *WRONG* WITH THEM, BATMAN.

I *NEED* MORE THAN THAT, DUKE. NOW.

THE BATCAVE.

STRANGE'S *MONSTER CELLS* ARE DRIVEN BY A *SUPER-STEROID*. IT CAUSES *MASSIVE* BIOELECTRIC SURGES...I'M GETTING THE SAME READINGS OFF NIGHTWING.

ALFRED AND I DON'T HAVE RED ROBIN'S MIND FOR SCIENCE, BUT WE'RE TRYING. WE *FINALLY* STRIPPED THE STEROID TO ITS ROOT FORMULA. NOT A *COMPLETE* MATCH, BUT IT HAS *NOTABLE* SIMILARITIES..

...TO VENOM.

BIOSAMPLE: active volta

7600amps; C4.exe)

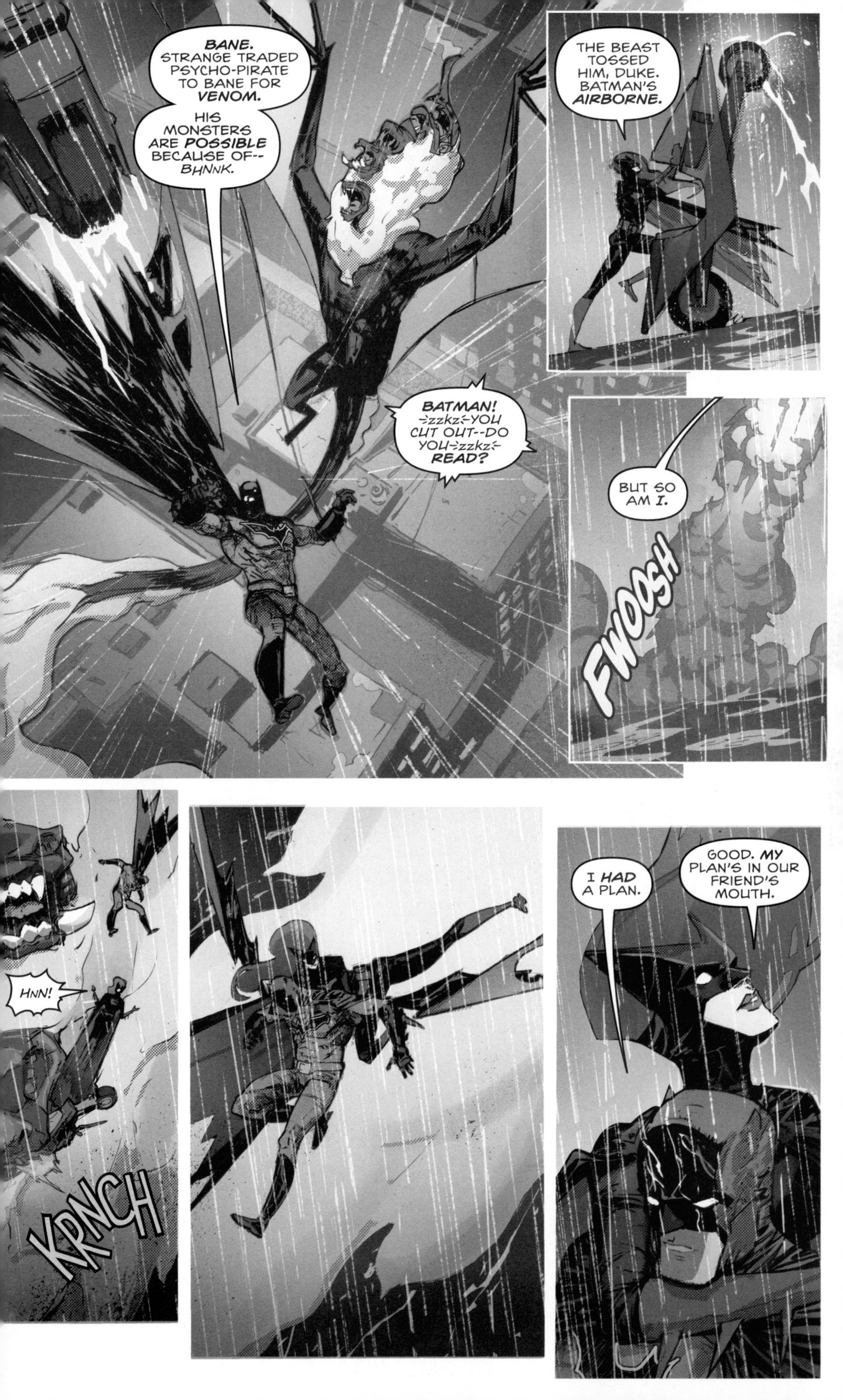
BANE. STRANGE TRADED PSYCHO-PIRATE TO BANE FOR VENOM.
HIS MONSTERS ARE POSSIBLE BECAUSE OF-- BHNNK.
THE BEAST TOSSED HIM, DUKE. BATMAN'S AIRBORNE.
BATMAN! -zzkz- YOU CUT OUT--DO YOU -zzkz- READ?
BUT SO AM I.
FWOOSH
HNN!
KRNCH
I HAD A PLAN.
GOOD. MY PLAN'S IN OUR FRIEND'S MOUTH.

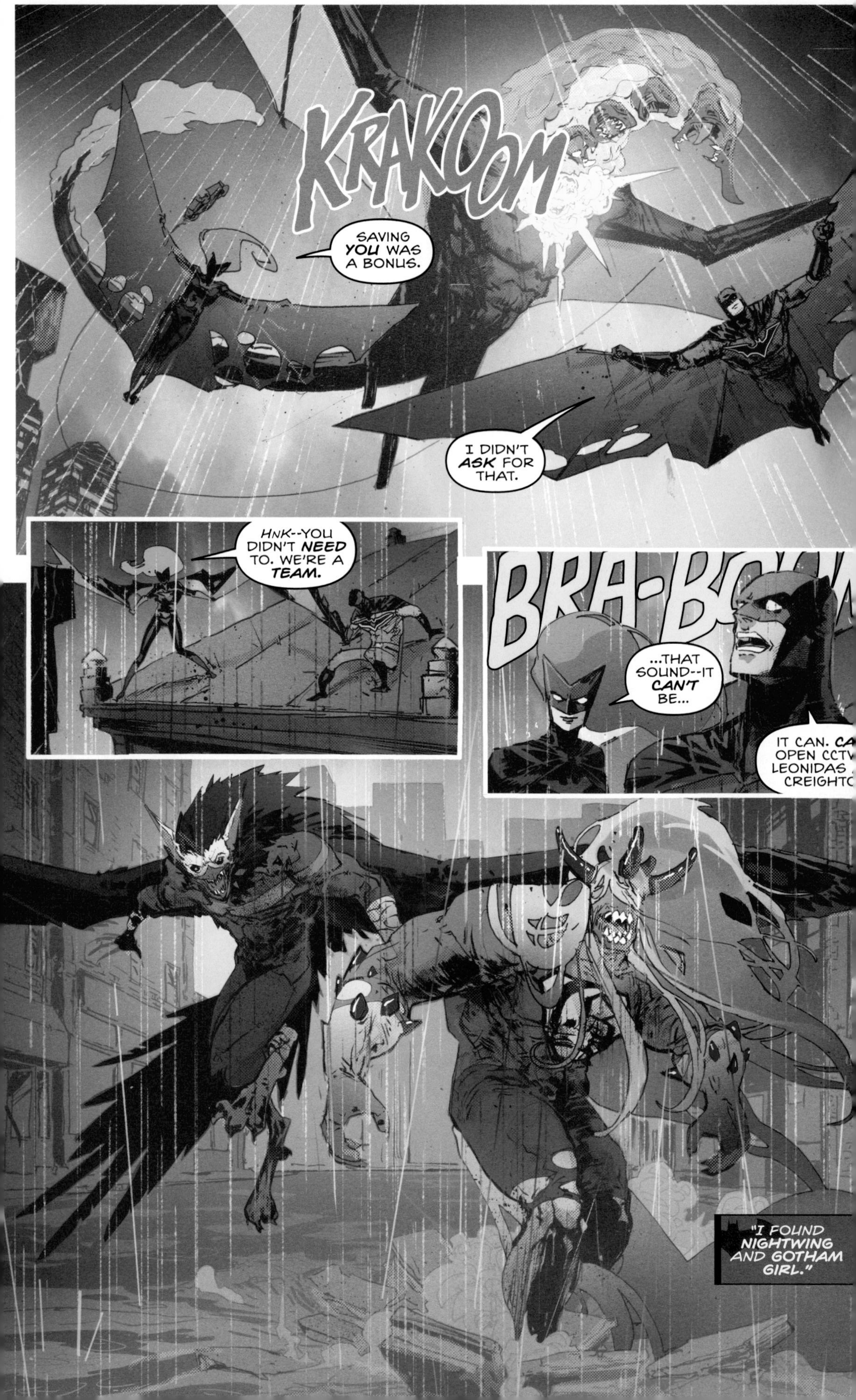
KRAKOOM
SAVING YOU WAS A BONUS.
I DIDN'T ASK FOR THAT.
HNK--YOU DIDN'T NEED TO. WE'RE A TEAM.
BRA-BO
...THAT SOUND--IT CAN'T BE...
"I FOUND NIGHTWING AND GOTHAM GIRL."

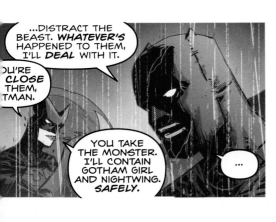

...DISTRACT THE BEAST. **WHATEVER'S** HAPPENED TO THEM, I'LL **DEAL** WITH IT.

OU'RE **CLOSE** THEM, TMAN.

YOU TAKE THE MONSTER. I'LL CONTAIN GOTHAM GIRL AND NIGHTWING. **SAFELY.**

...

CYCLE-- DETACH BAT-LINE.

STROBES.

AUTOPILOT.

SO. I'VE BEEN WHIPPING THE **REST** OF THE FAMILY INTO SHAPE, BUT YOU'VE **BOTH** BEEN MISSING CLASS.

SHUK

...TIME FOR A LESSON.

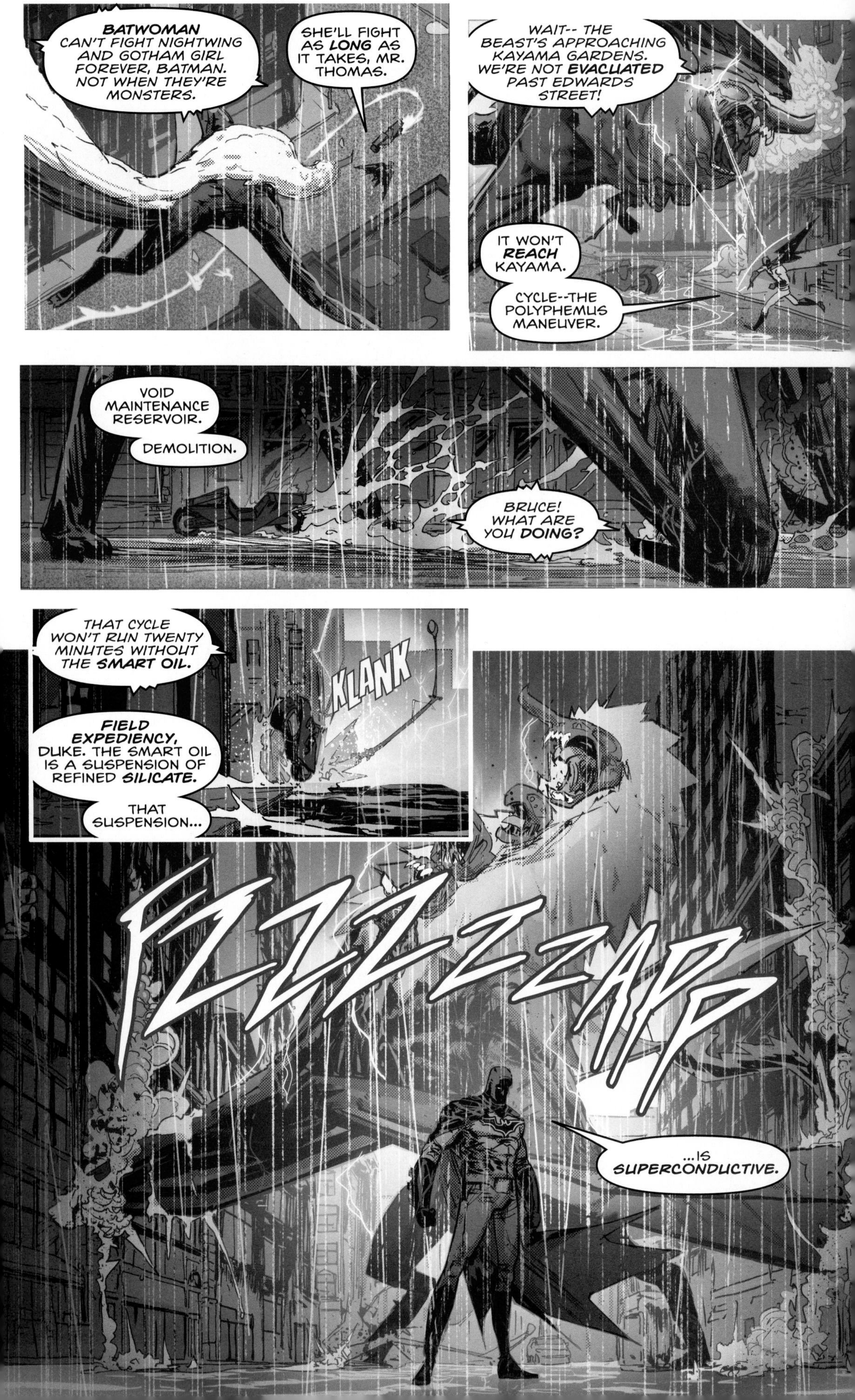
BATWOMAN CAN'T FIGHT NIGHTWING AND GOTHAM GIRL FOREVER, BATMAN. NOT WHEN THEY'RE MONSTERS.
SHE'LL FIGHT AS LONG AS IT TAKES, MR. THOMAS.
WAIT-- THE BEAST'S APPROACHING KAYAMA GARDENS. WE'RE NOT EVACUATED PAST EDWARDS STREET!
IT WON'T REACH KAYAMA.
CYCLE--THE POLYPHEMUS MANEUVER.
VOID MAINTENANCE RESERVOIR.
DEMOLITION.
BRUCE! WHAT ARE YOU DOING?
THAT CYCLE WON'T RUN TWENTY MINUTES WITHOUT THE SMART OIL.
KLANK
FIELD EXPEDIENCY, DUKE. THE SMART OIL IS A SUSPENSION OF REFINED SILICATE.
THAT SUSPENSION...
FZZZZZAPP
...IS SUPERCONDUCTIVE.

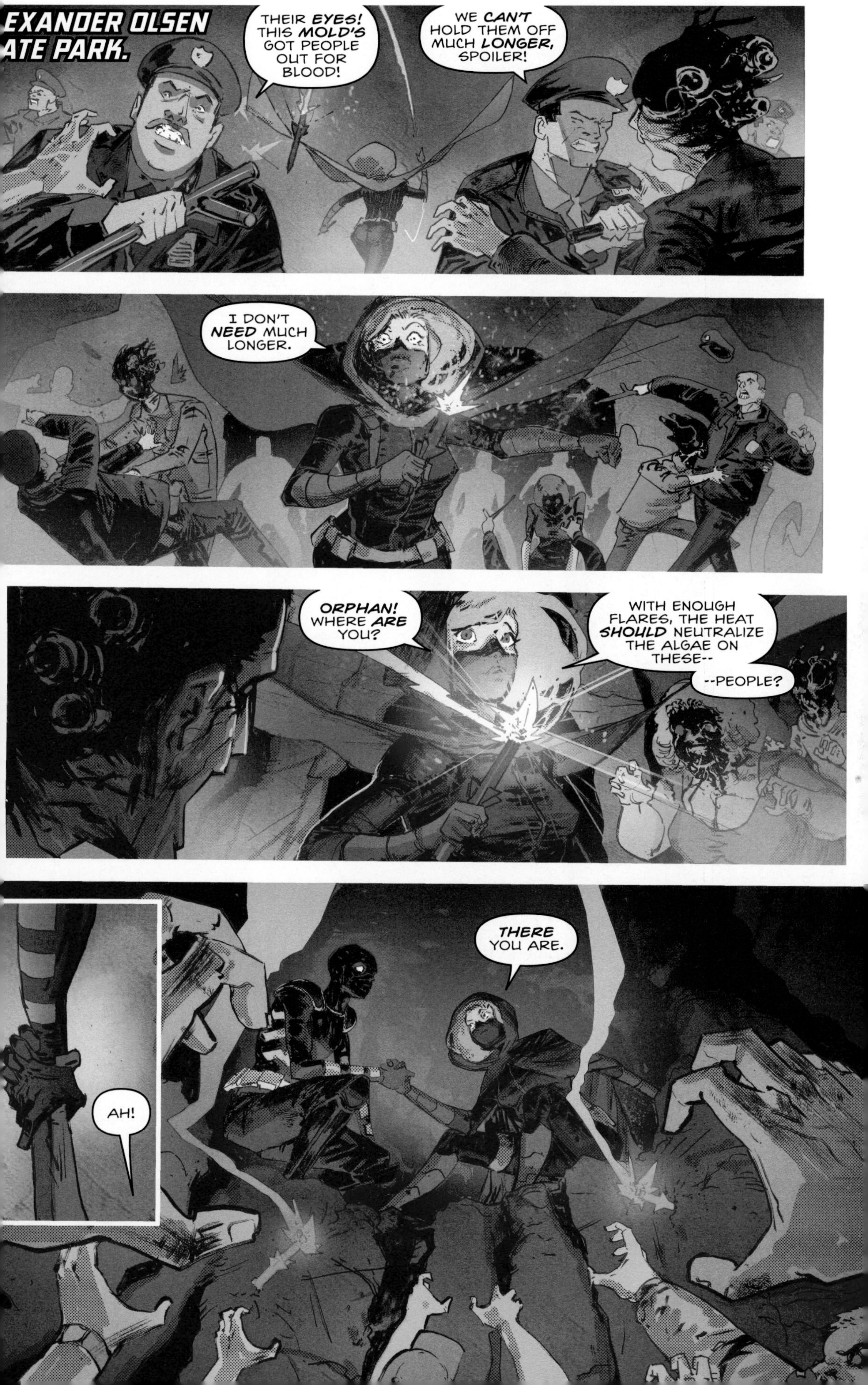
EXANDER OLSEN
ATE PARK.
THEIR EYES! THIS MOLD'S GOT PEOPLE OUT FOR BLOOD!
WE CAN'T HOLD THEM OFF MUCH LONGER, SPOILER!
I DON'T NEED MUCH LONGER.
ORPHAN! WHERE ARE YOU?
WITH ENOUGH FLARES, THE HEAT SHOULD NEUTRALIZE THE ALGAE ON THESE--
--PEOPLE?
AH!
THERE YOU ARE.

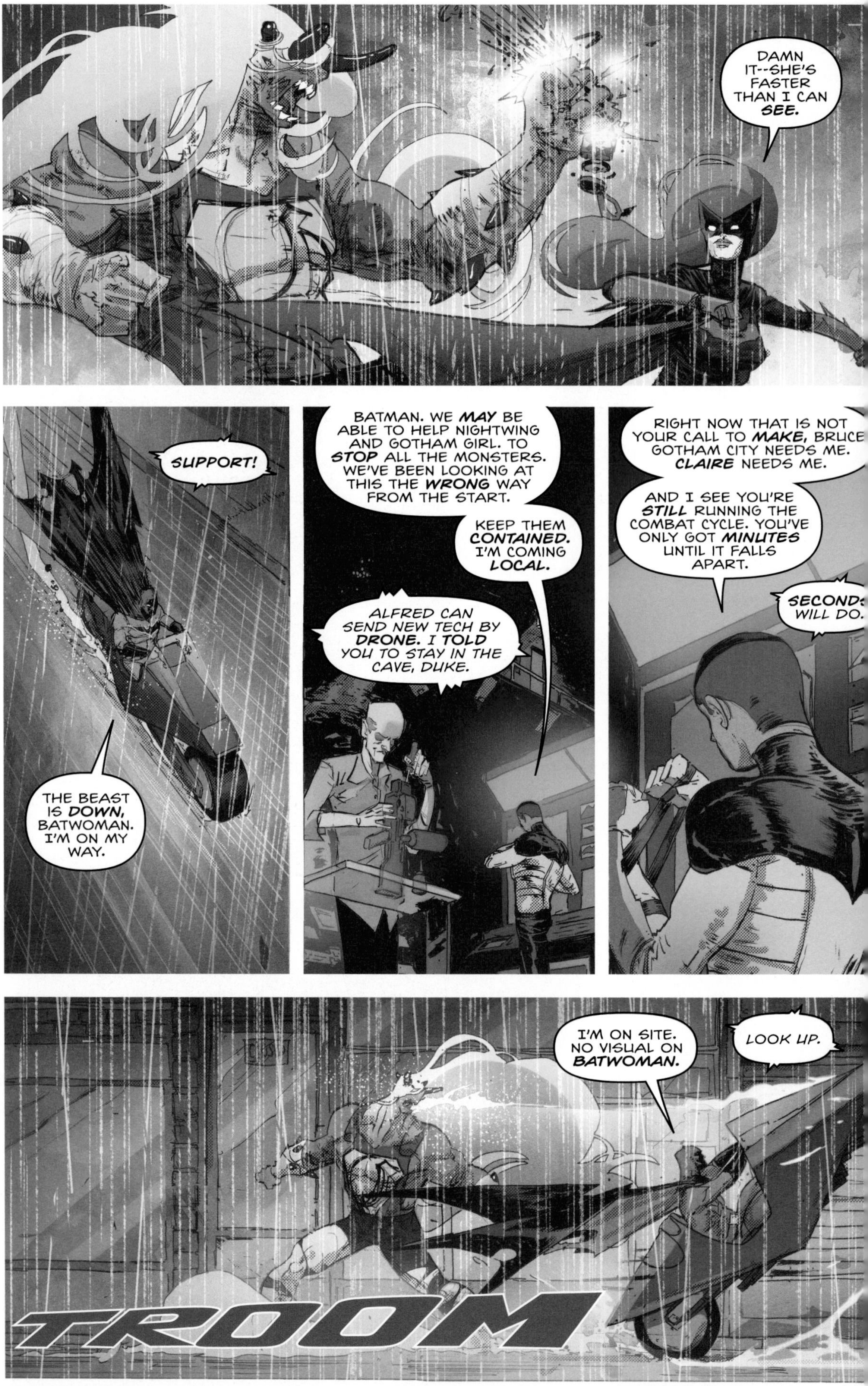
DAMN IT--SHE'S FASTER THAN I CAN **SEE.**
SUPPORT!
THE BEAST IS **DOWN,** BATWOMAN. I'M ON MY WAY.
BATMAN. WE **MAY** BE ABLE TO HELP NIGHTWING AND GOTHAM GIRL. TO **STOP** ALL THE MONSTERS. WE'VE BEEN LOOKING AT THIS THE **WRONG** WAY FROM THE START.
KEEP THEM **CONTAINED.** I'M COMING **LOCAL.**
ALFRED CAN SEND NEW TECH BY **DRONE.** **I TOLD** YOU TO STAY IN THE CAVE, DUKE.
RIGHT NOW THAT IS NOT YOUR CALL TO **MAKE,** BRUCE. GOTHAM CITY NEEDS ME. **CLAIRE** NEEDS ME.
AND I SEE YOU'RE **STILL** RUNNING THE COMBAT CYCLE. YOU'VE ONLY GOT **MINUTES** UNTIL IT FALLS APART.
SECONDS WILL DO.
I'M ON SITE. NO VISUAL ON **BATWOMAN.**
LOOK UP.
TROOM

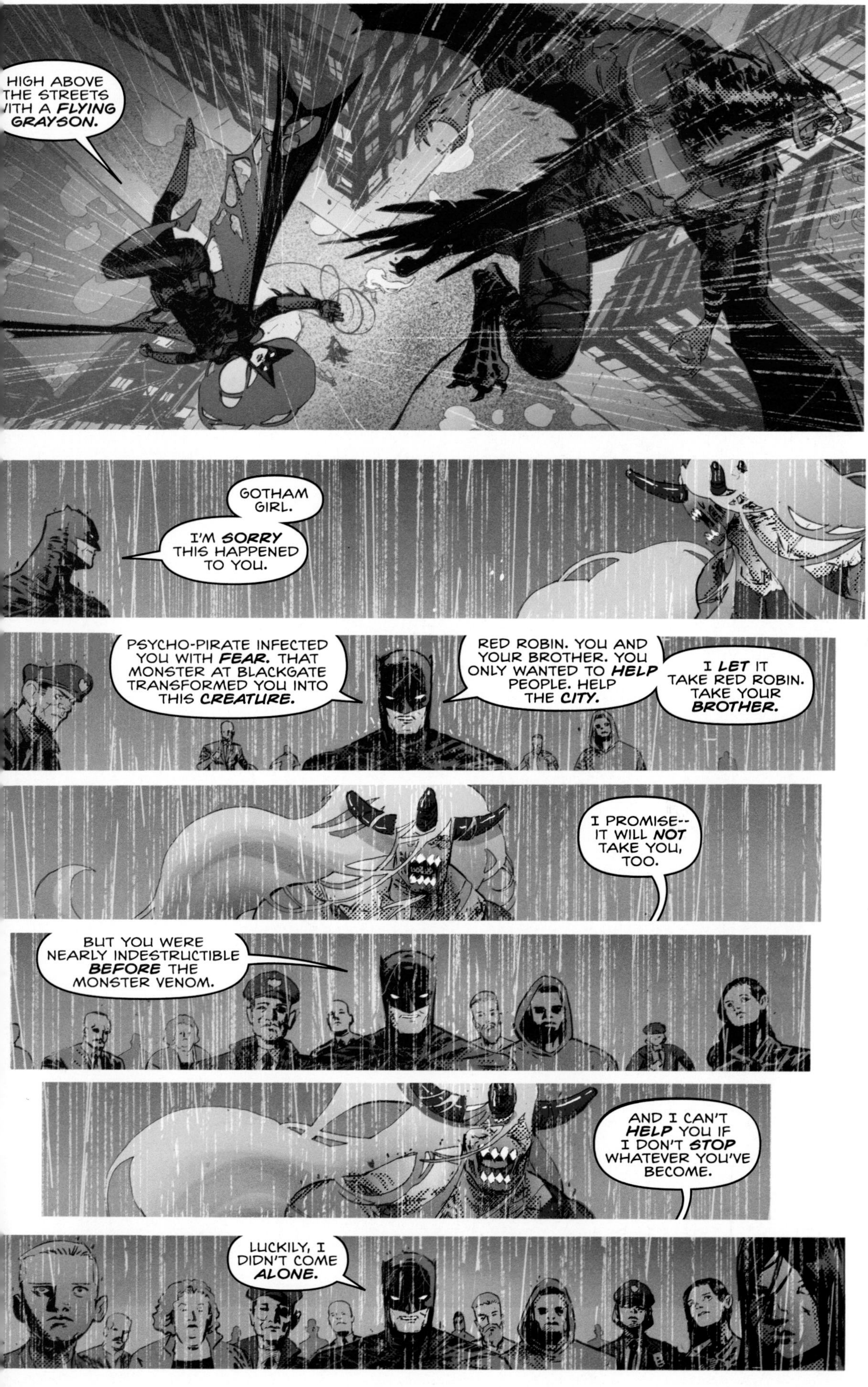
HIGH ABOVE THE STREETS WITH A FLYING GRAYSON.
GOTHAM GIRL.
I'M SORRY THIS HAPPENED TO YOU.
PSYCHO-PIRATE INFECTED YOU WITH FEAR. THAT MONSTER AT BLACKGATE TRANSFORMED YOU INTO THIS CREATURE.
RED ROBIN. YOU AND YOUR BROTHER. YOU ONLY WANTED TO HELP PEOPLE. HELP THE CITY.
I LET IT TAKE RED ROBIN. TAKE YOUR BROTHER.
I PROMISE-- IT WILL NOT TAKE YOU, TOO.
BUT YOU WERE NEARLY INDESTRUCTIBLE BEFORE THE MONSTER VENOM.
AND I CAN'T HELP YOU IF I DON'T STOP WHATEVER YOU'VE BECOME.
LUCKILY, I DIDN'T COME ALONE.

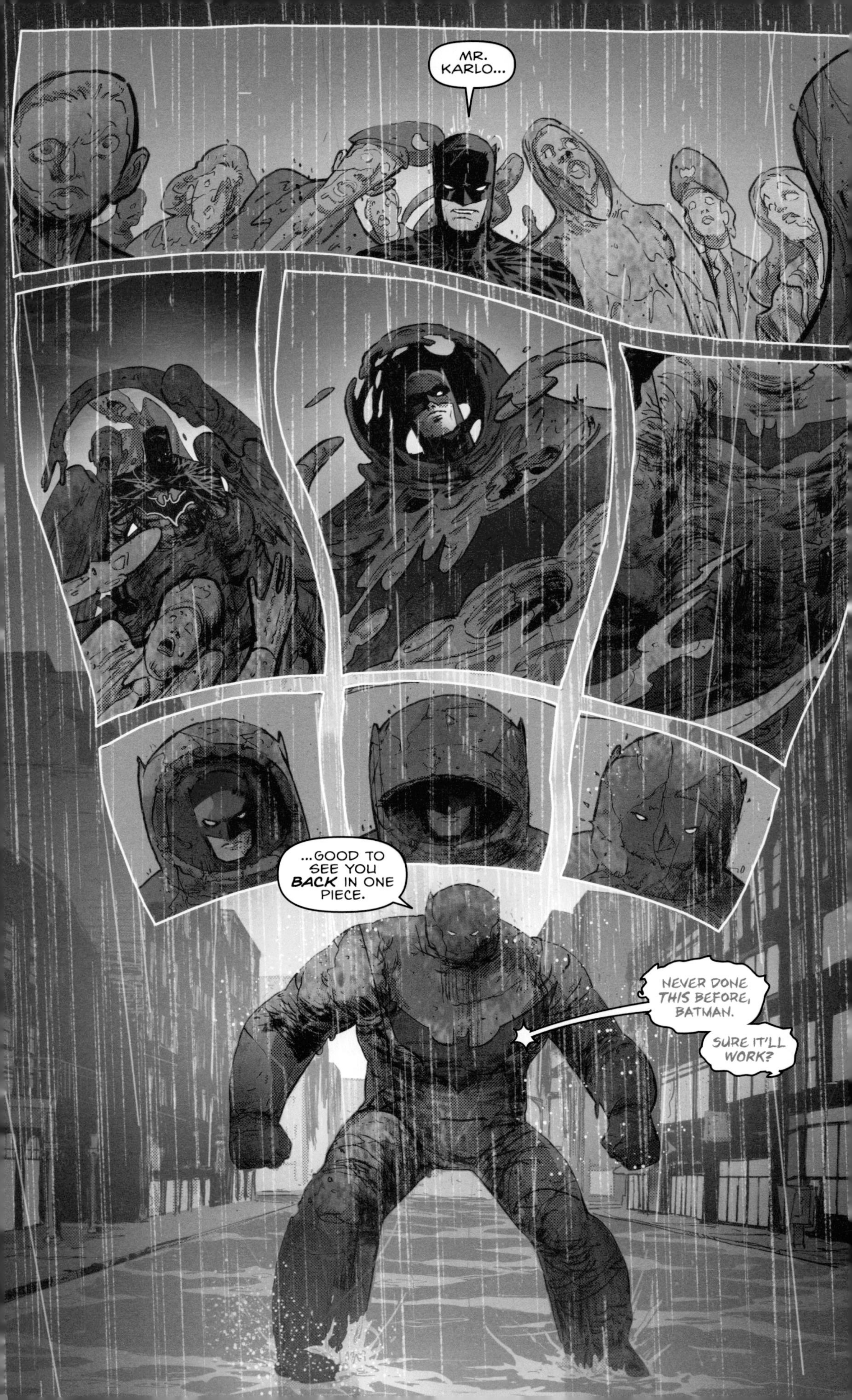
MR. KARLO...
...GOOD TO SEE YOU BACK IN ONE PIECE.
NEVER DONE THIS BEFORE, BATMAN.
SURE IT'LL WORK?

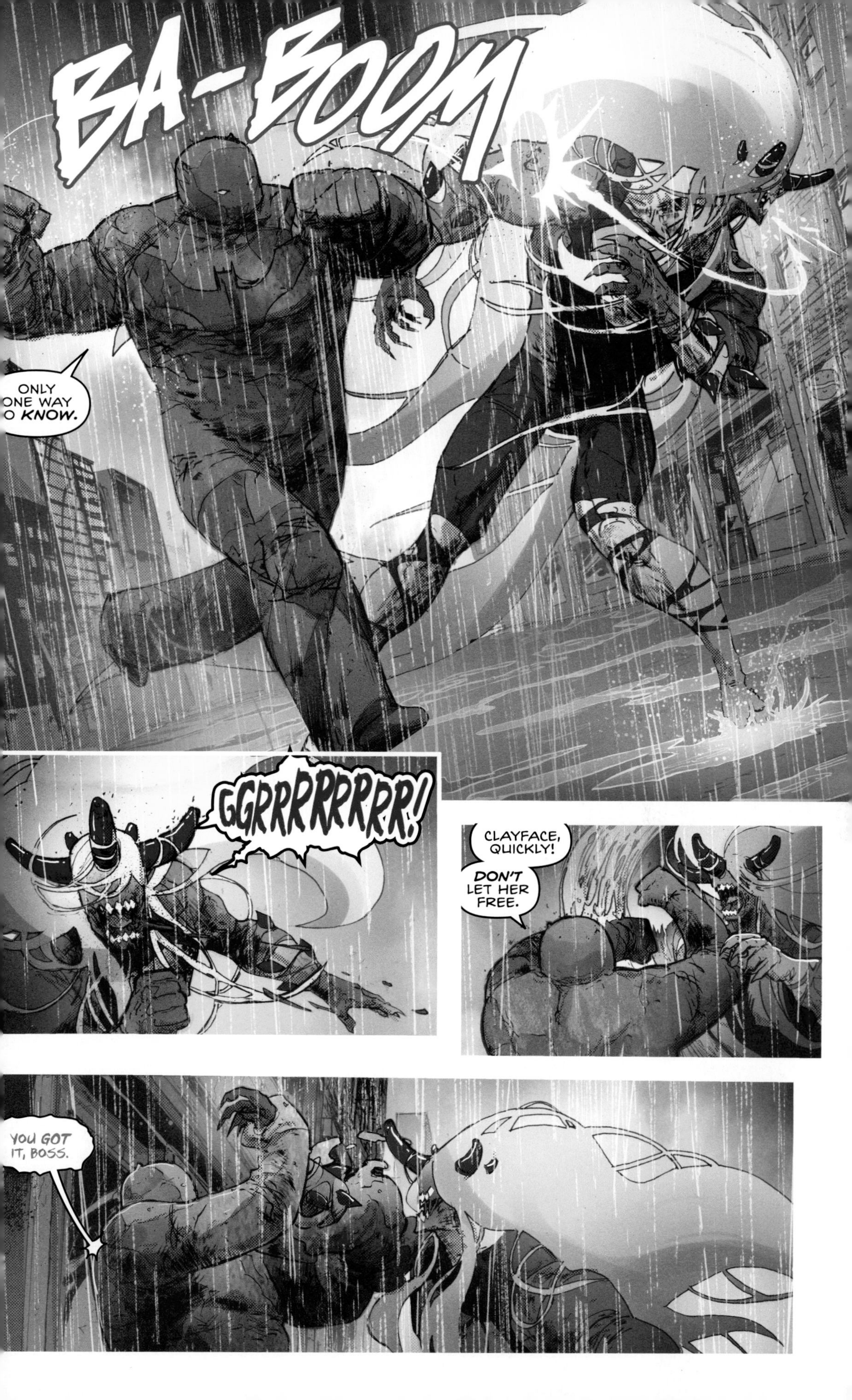
BA-BOOM
ONLY ONE WAY O KNOW.
GGRRRRRRRR!
CLAYFACE, QUICKLY!
DON'T LET HER FREE.
YOU GOT IT, BOSS.

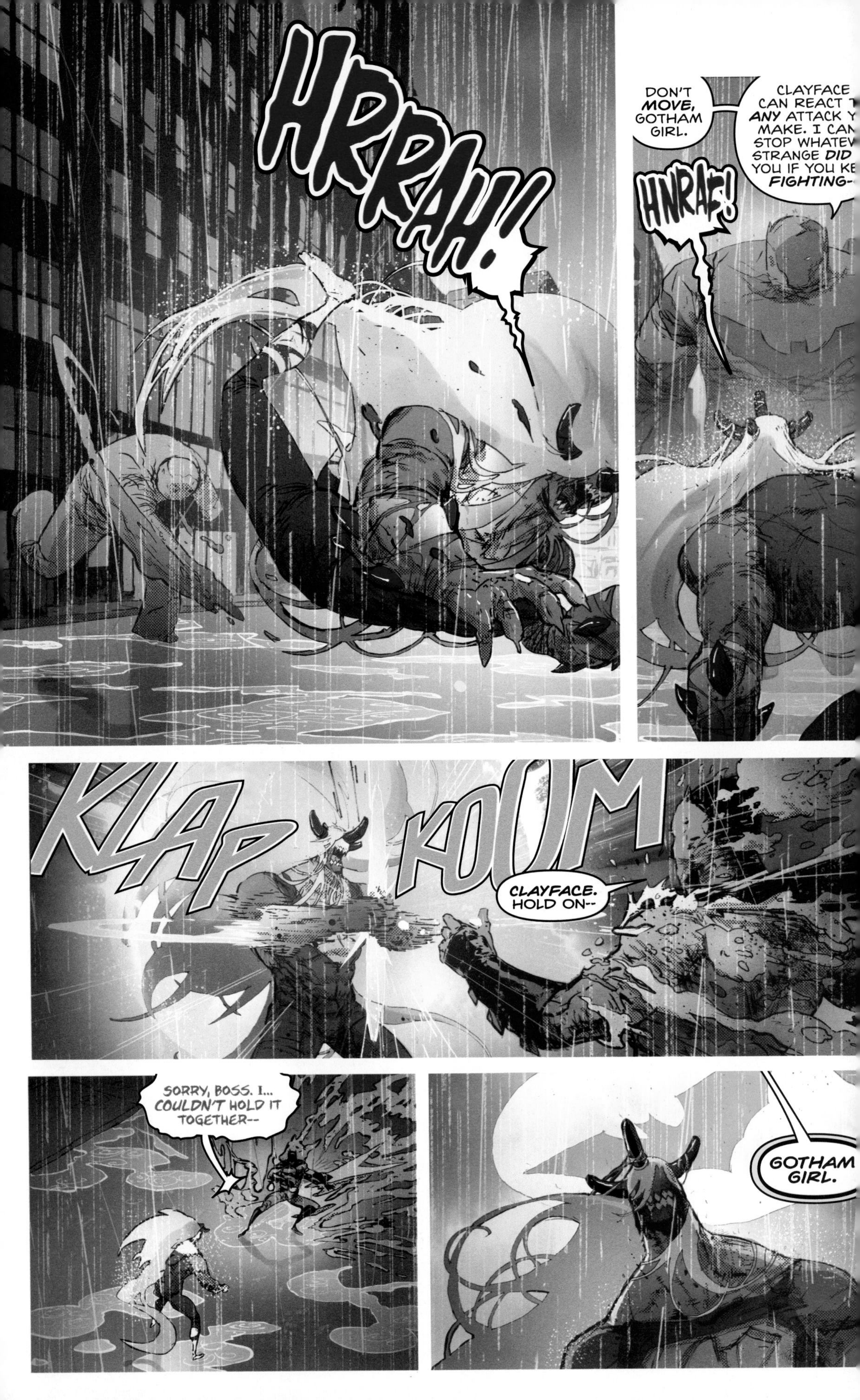
HRRAH!!
DON'T MOVE, GOTHAM GIRL.
CLAYFACE CAN REACT T ANY ATTACK Y MAKE. I CAN STOP WHATEV STRANGE DID YOU IF YOU KE FIGHTING--
HNRAF!
KLAP KOOM
CLAYFACE. HOLD ON--
SORRY, BOSS. I... COULDN'T HOLD IT TOGETHER--
GOTHAM GIRL.

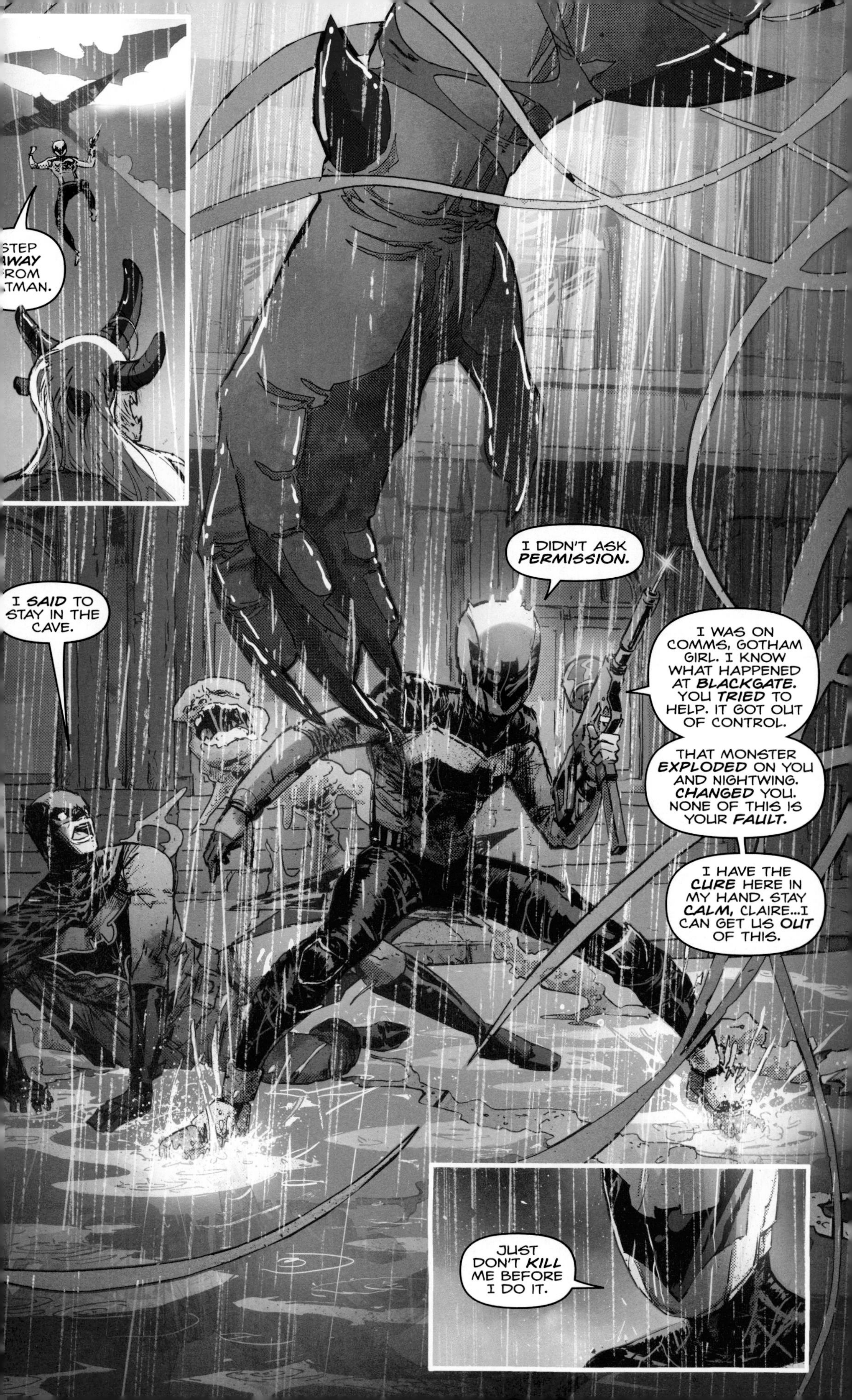

STEP AWAY ROM TMAN.
I SAID TO STAY IN THE CAVE.
I DIDN'T ASK PERMISSION.
I WAS ON COMMS, GOTHAM GIRL. I KNOW WHAT HAPPENED AT BLACKGATE. YOU TRIED TO HELP. IT GOT OUT OF CONTROL.
THAT MONSTER EXPLODED ON YOU AND NIGHTWING. CHANGED YOU. NONE OF THIS IS YOUR FAULT.
I HAVE THE CURE HERE IN MY HAND. STAY CALM, CLAIRE...I CAN GET US OUT OF THIS.
JUST DON'T KILL ME BEFORE I DO IT.

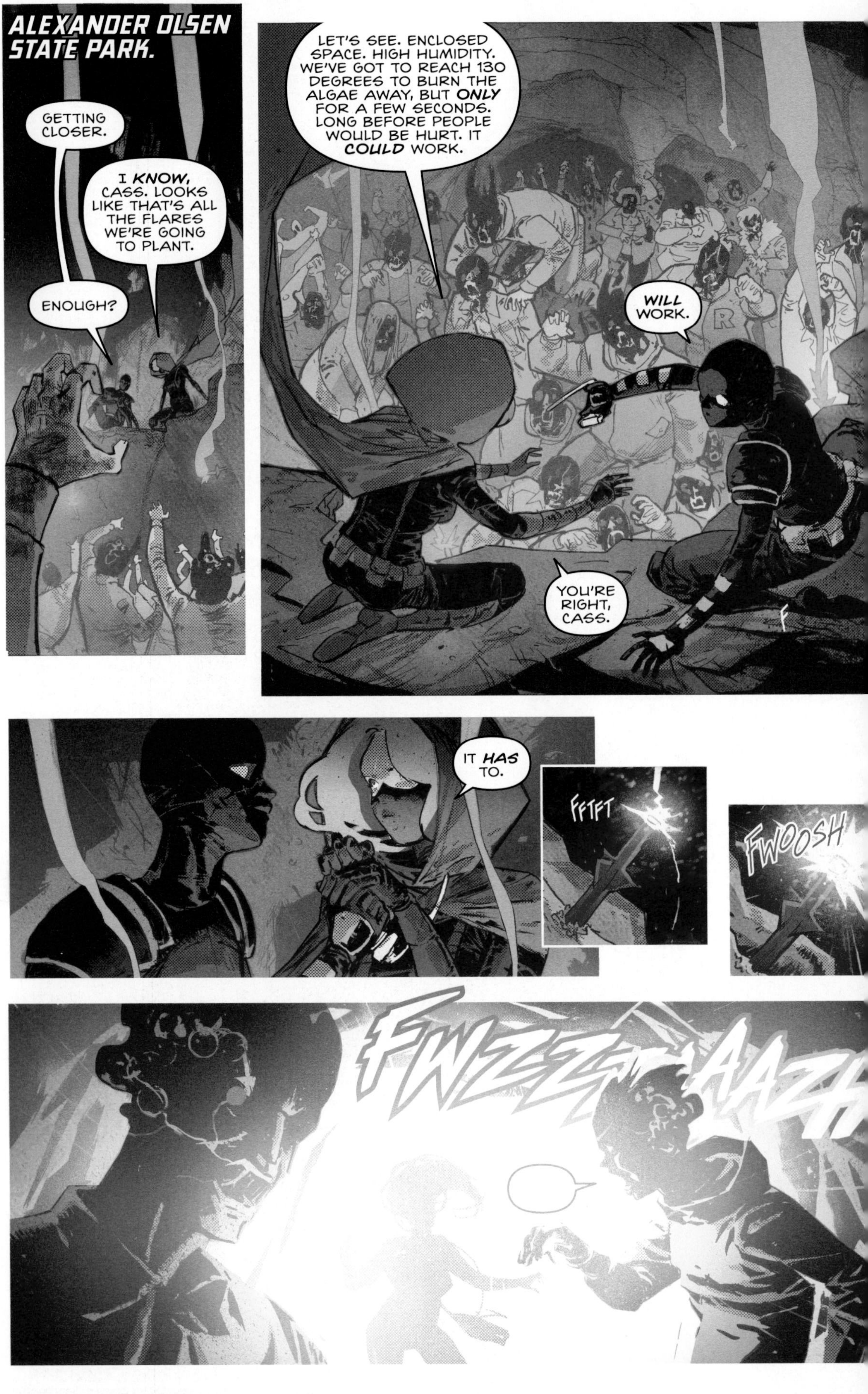
ALEXANDER OLSEN STATE PARK.
GETTING CLOSER.
I KNOW, CASS. LOOKS LIKE THAT'S ALL THE FLARES WE'RE GOING TO PLANT.
ENOUGH?
LET'S SEE. ENCLOSED SPACE. HIGH HUMIDITY. WE'VE GOT TO REACH 130 DEGREES TO BURN THE ALGAE AWAY, BUT ONLY FOR A FEW SECONDS. LONG BEFORE PEOPLE WOULD BE HURT. IT COULD WORK.
WILL WORK.
YOU'RE RIGHT, CASS.
IT HAS TO.
FFTFT
FWOOSH
FWZZT
AAZH

? WHAT
PENED?
IS ALL
HIS?

WHERE ARE WE? I BARELY *REMEMBER* GETTING HERE.

HEY! SOMEONE'S *UP* THERE.

HELP THEM DOWN!

...THANK YOU. YOU'VE *ALL* BEEN THROUGH A LOT.

HOW DO YOU *FEEL?*

GOOD *ENOUGH,* I GUESS. WHAT *WAS* THAT STUFF?

WHERE'S IT GOING?

A LIVING SLIME MOLD PUSHING YOUR *BASE* URGES. MONSTERS HAVE *MANY* FACES. GOTHAM IS UNDER ATTACK.

WE'RE UNDER ATTACK.

RRRUMMMBLE

BUT YOU TOOK *CARE* OF IT. *BURNT* IT OFF US. IT'S *OVER* NOW, RIGHT?

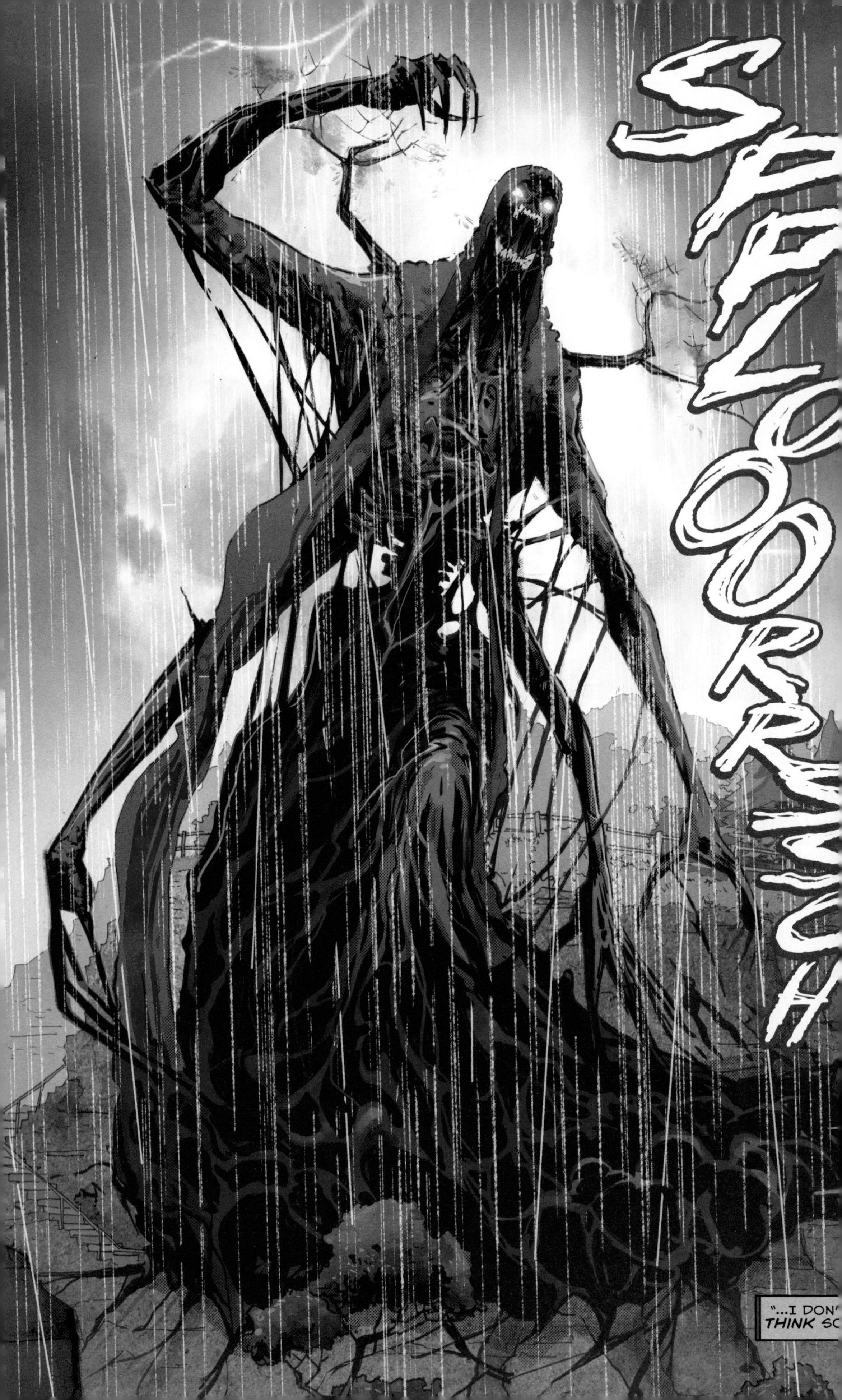
"...I DON'
THINK

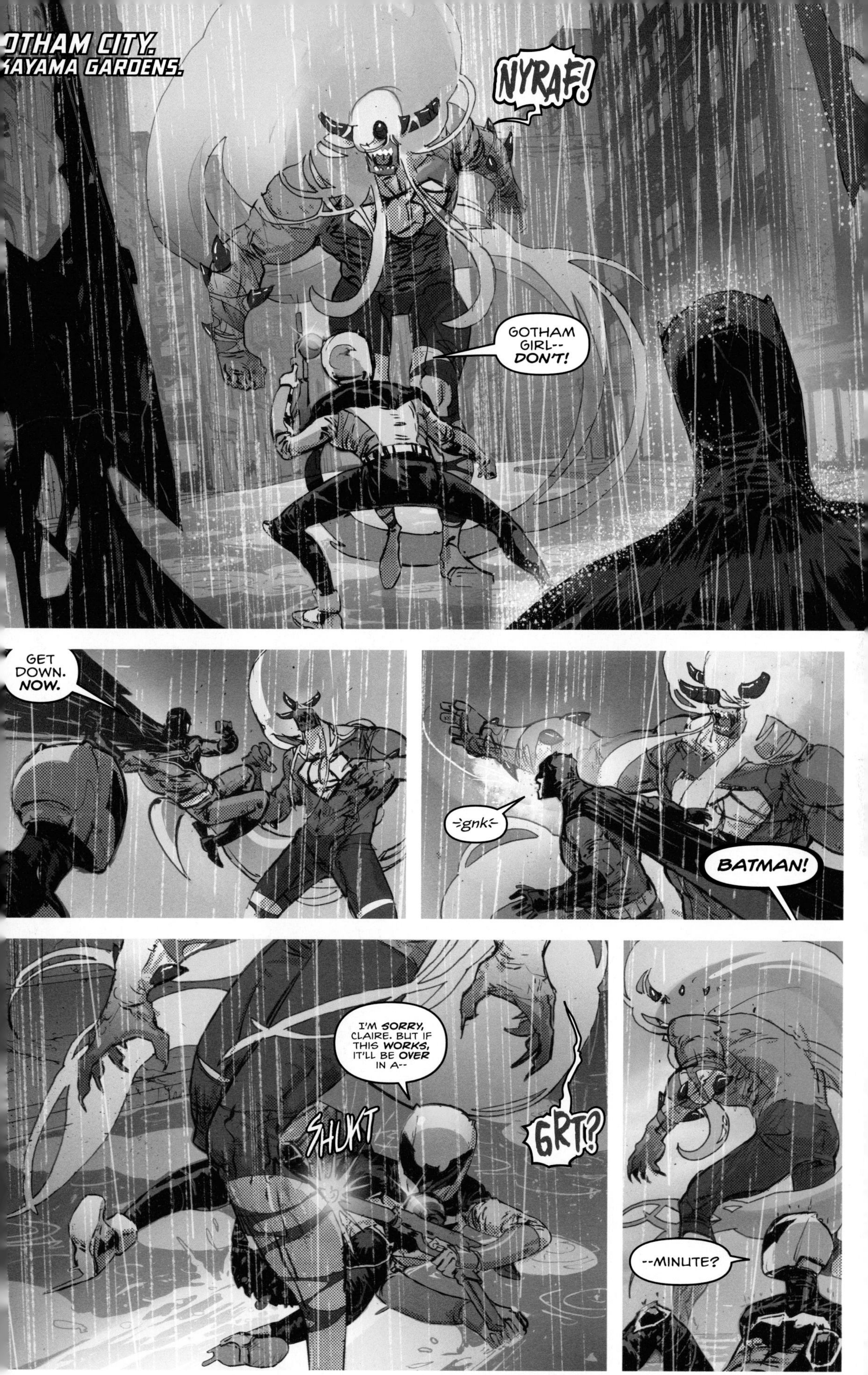
OTHAM CITY.
AYAMA GARDENS.
NYRAF!
GOTHAM GIRL-- DON'T!
GET DOWN. NOW.
gnk
BATMAN!
I'M SORRY, CLAIRE. BUT IF THIS WORKS, IT'LL BE OVER IN A--
SHUKT
GRT?
--MINUTE?

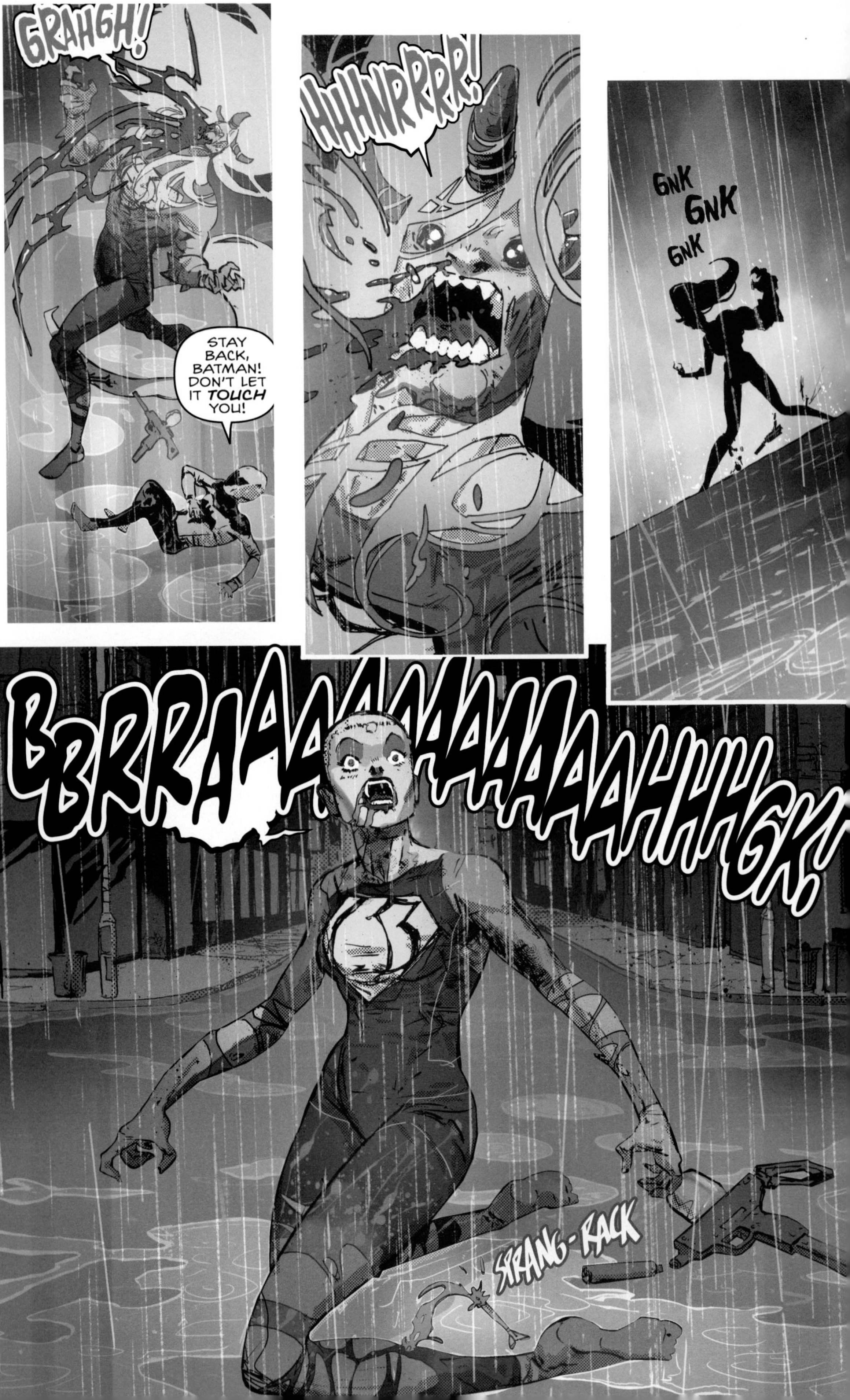
GRAHGH!
STAY BACK, BATMAN! DON'T LET IT TOUCH YOU!
HHHNRRRR!
GNK
GNK
GNK
BBRRAAAAAAAAAAHHHGK!
SPRANG-RACK

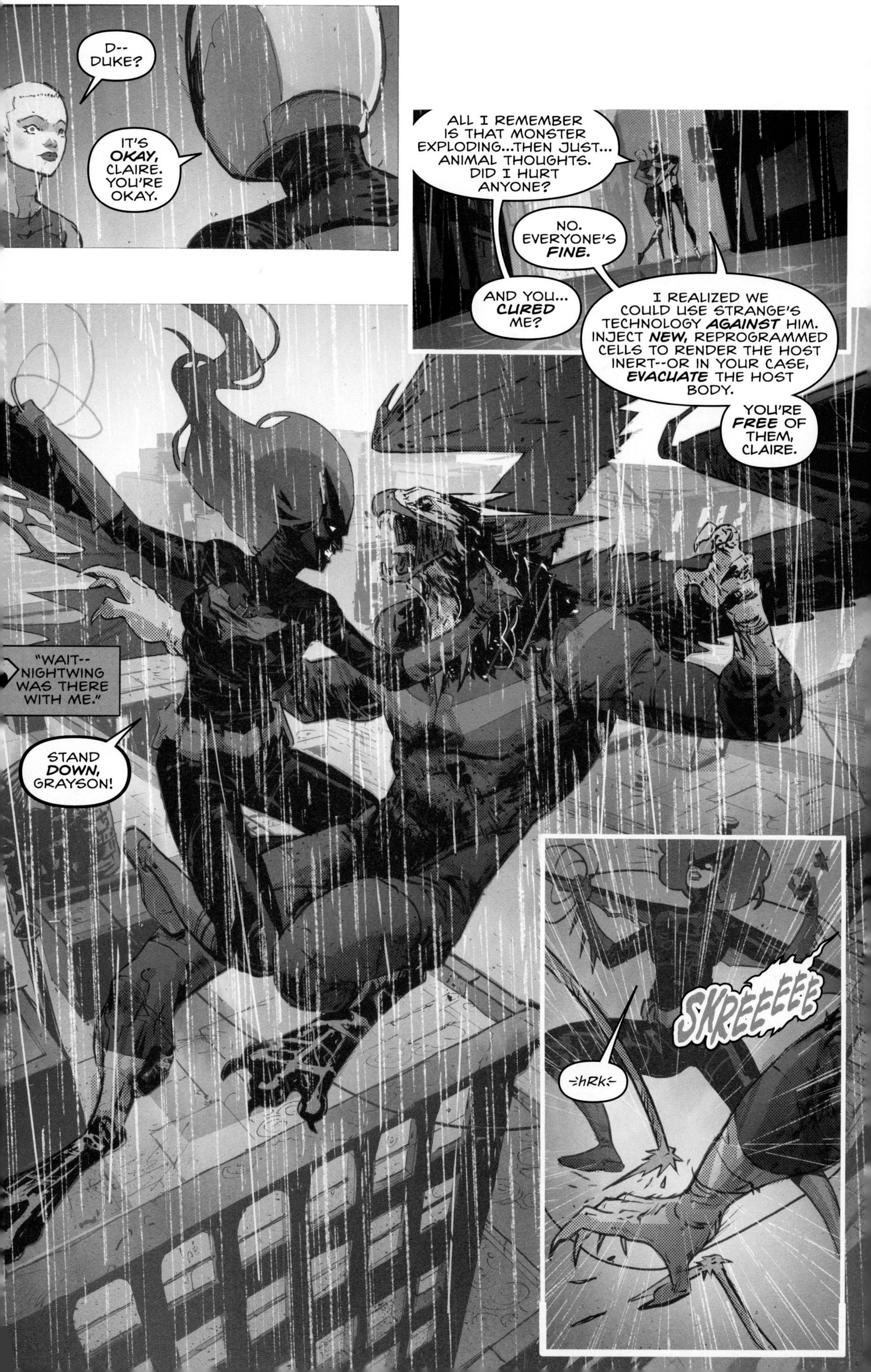
D--
DUKE?
IT'S OKAY, CLAIRE. YOU'RE OKAY.
ALL I REMEMBER IS THAT MONSTER EXPLODING...THEN JUST... ANIMAL THOUGHTS. DID I HURT ANYONE?
NO. EVERYONE'S FINE.
AND YOU... CURED ME?
I REALIZED WE COULD USE STRANGE'S TECHNOLOGY AGAINST HIM. INJECT NEW, REPROGRAMMED CELLS TO RENDER THE HOST INERT--OR IN YOUR CASE, EVACUATE THE HOST BODY.
YOU'RE FREE OF THEM, CLAIRE.
"WAIT-- NIGHTWING WAS THERE WITH ME."
STAND DOWN, GRAYSON!
SKREEEEE
hRk

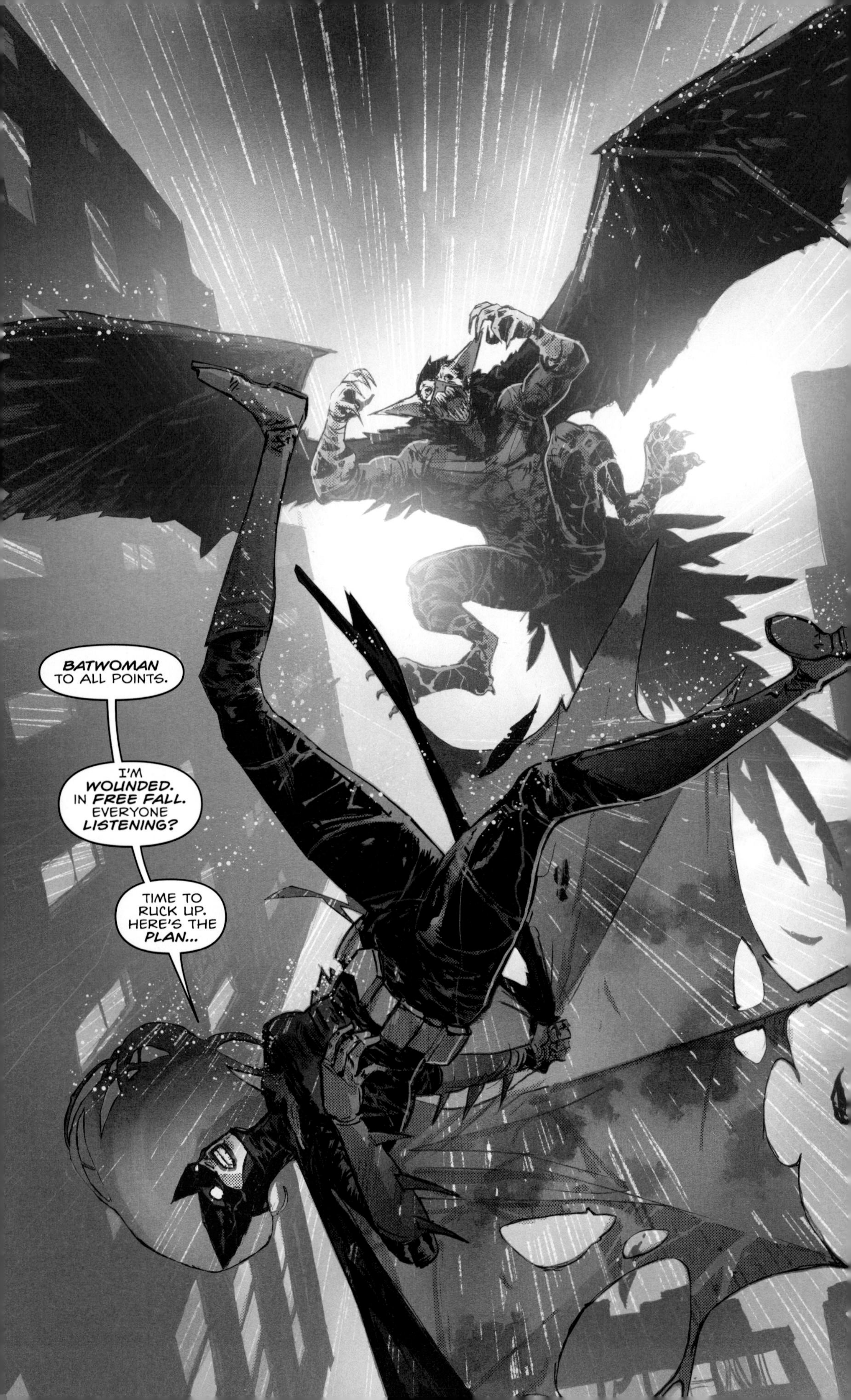

BATWOMAN TO ALL POINTS.
I'M WOUNDED. IN FREE FALL. EVERYONE LISTENING?
TIME TO RUCK UP. HERE'S THE PLAN...

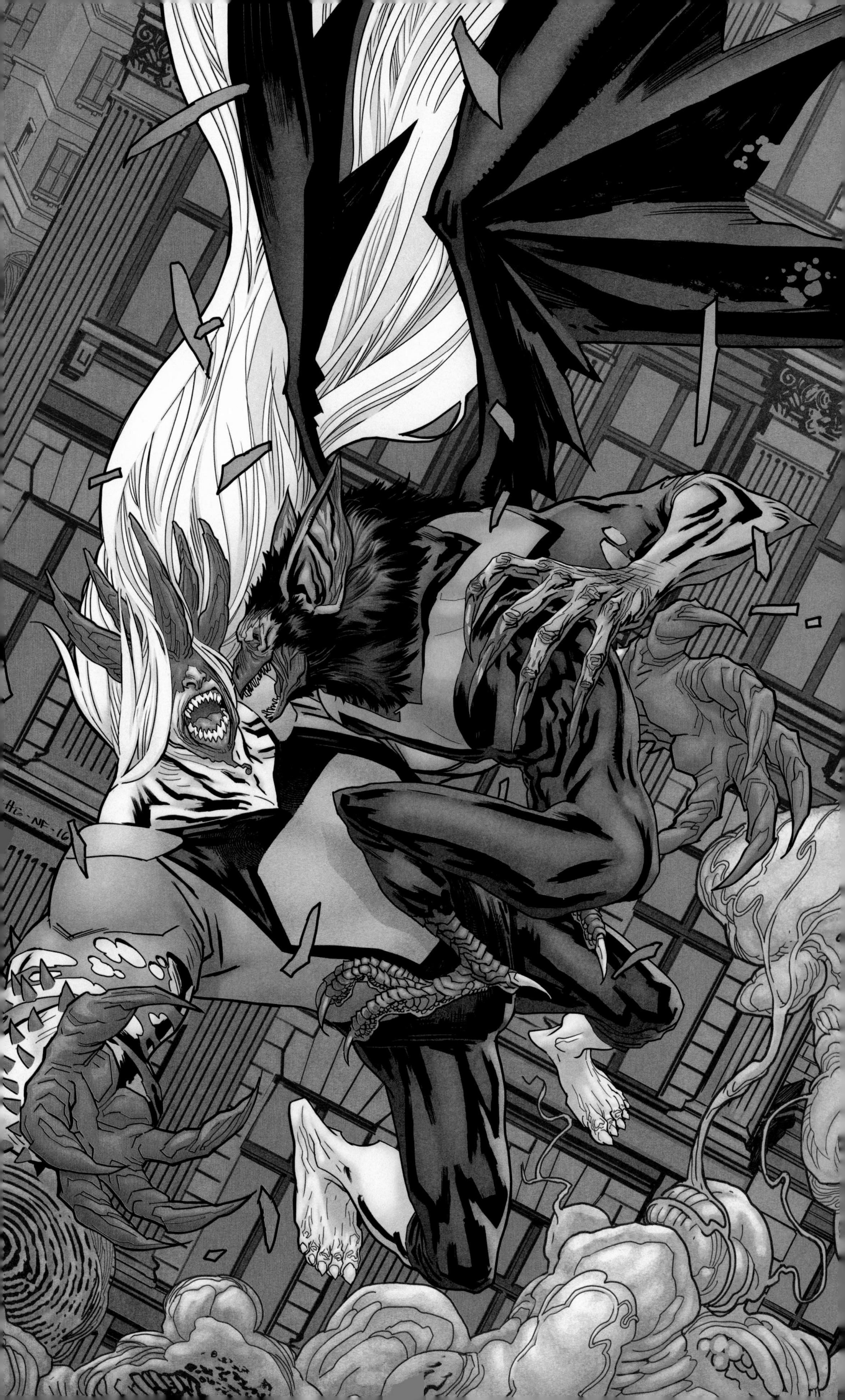

STEVE ORLANDO & TIM SEELEY plot * STEVE ORLANDO script * ROGE ANTONIO art * CHRIS SOTOMAYOR colors
CARLOS M. MANGUAL letters * YANICK PAQUETTE & NATHAN FAIRBAIRN cover art

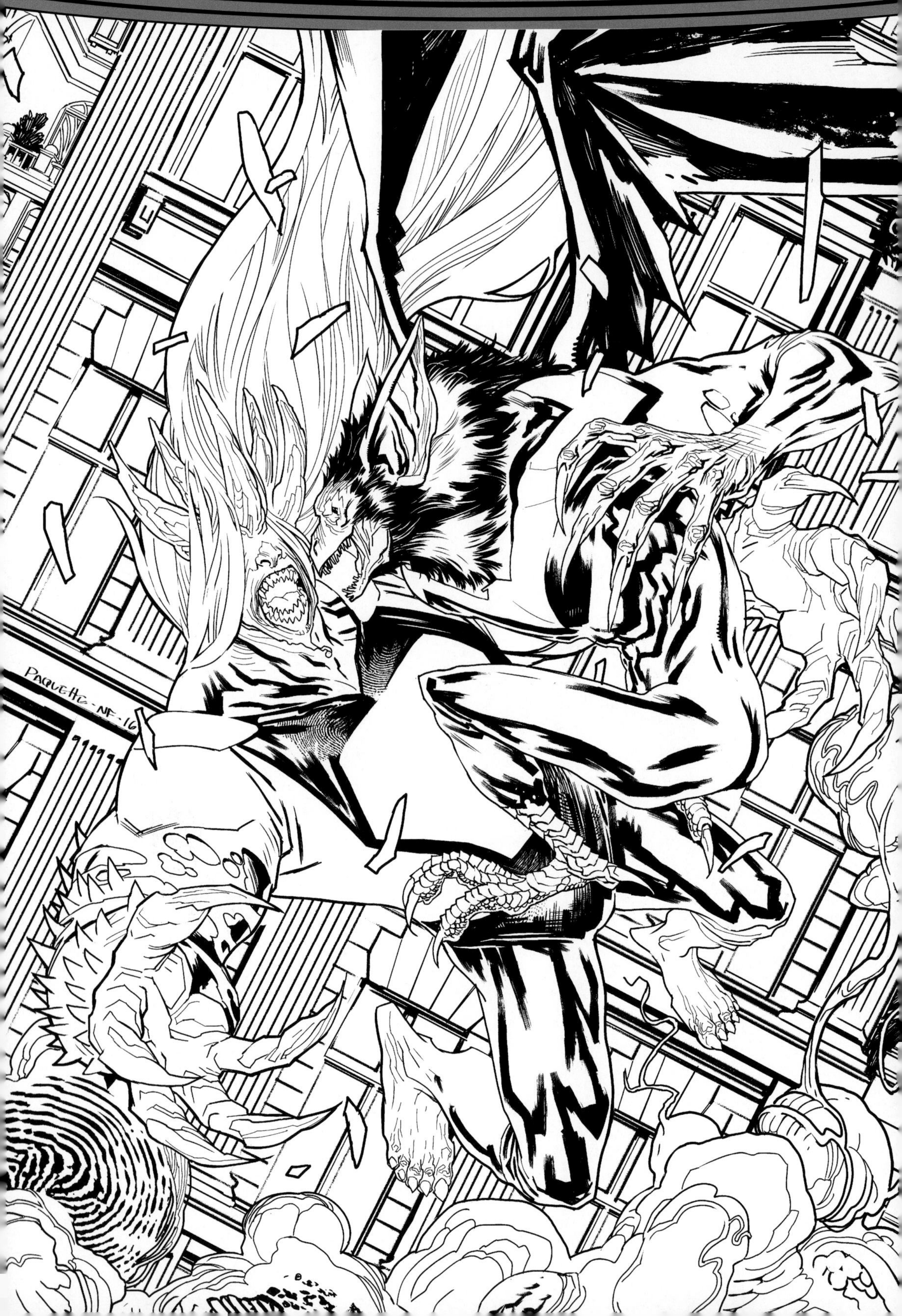

PAQUETTE-NF-16

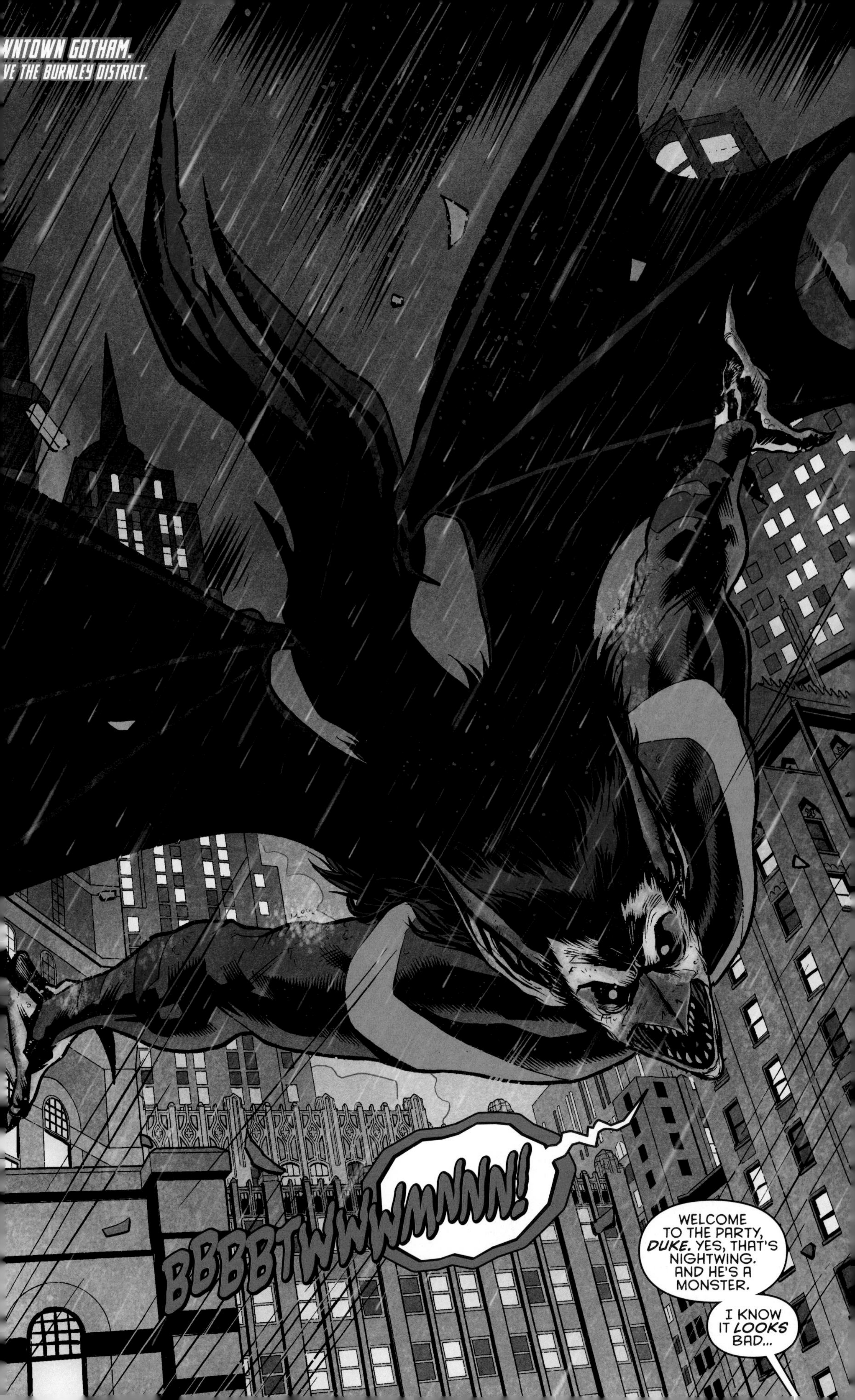

WNTOWN GOTHAM.
VE THE BURNLEY DISTRICT.
BBBBTWWWMNNN!
WELCOME TO THE PARTY, DUKE. YES, THAT'S NIGHTWING. AND HE'S A MONSTER.
I KNOW IT LOOKS BAD...

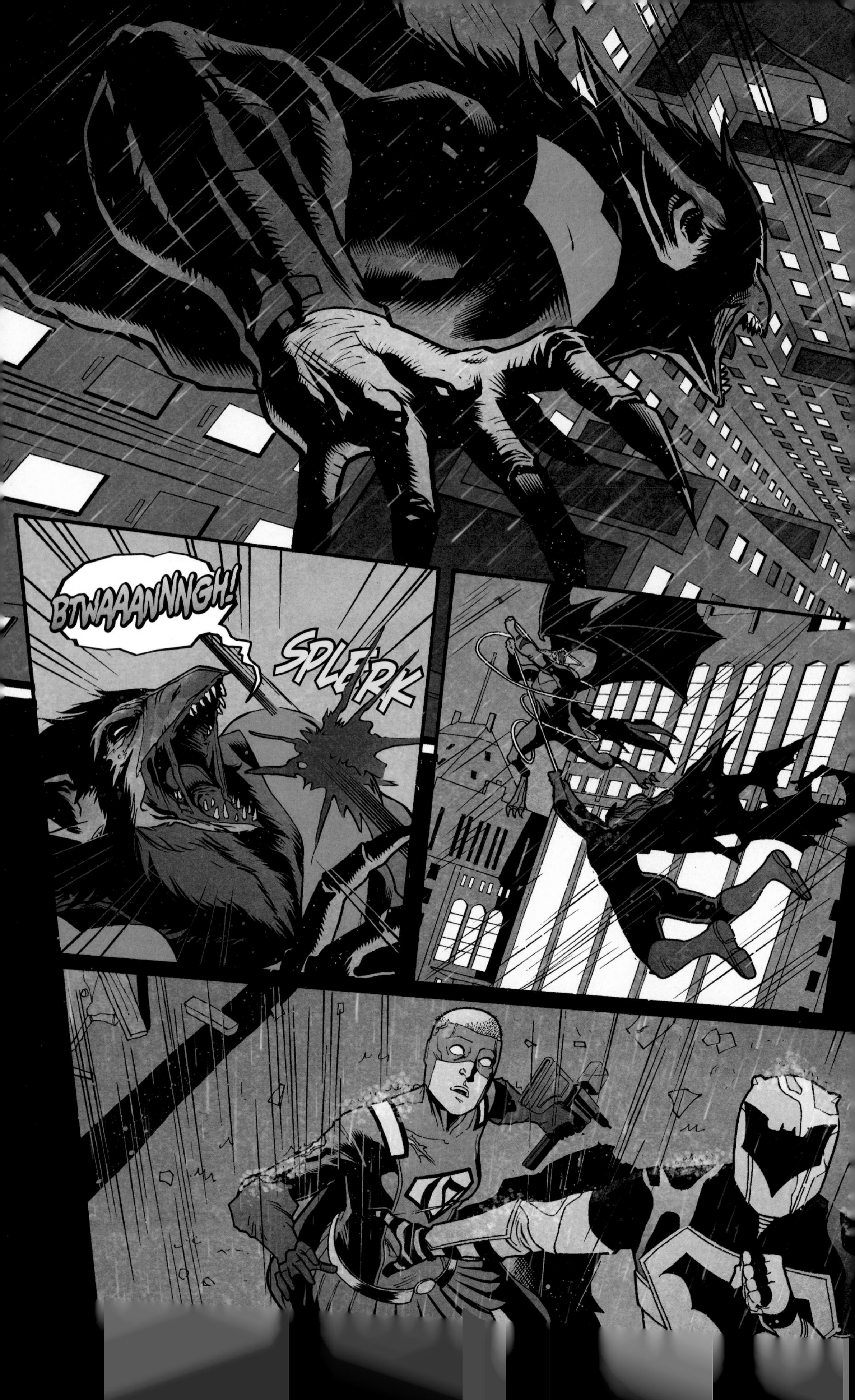
BTWAAANNNGH!
SPLERK

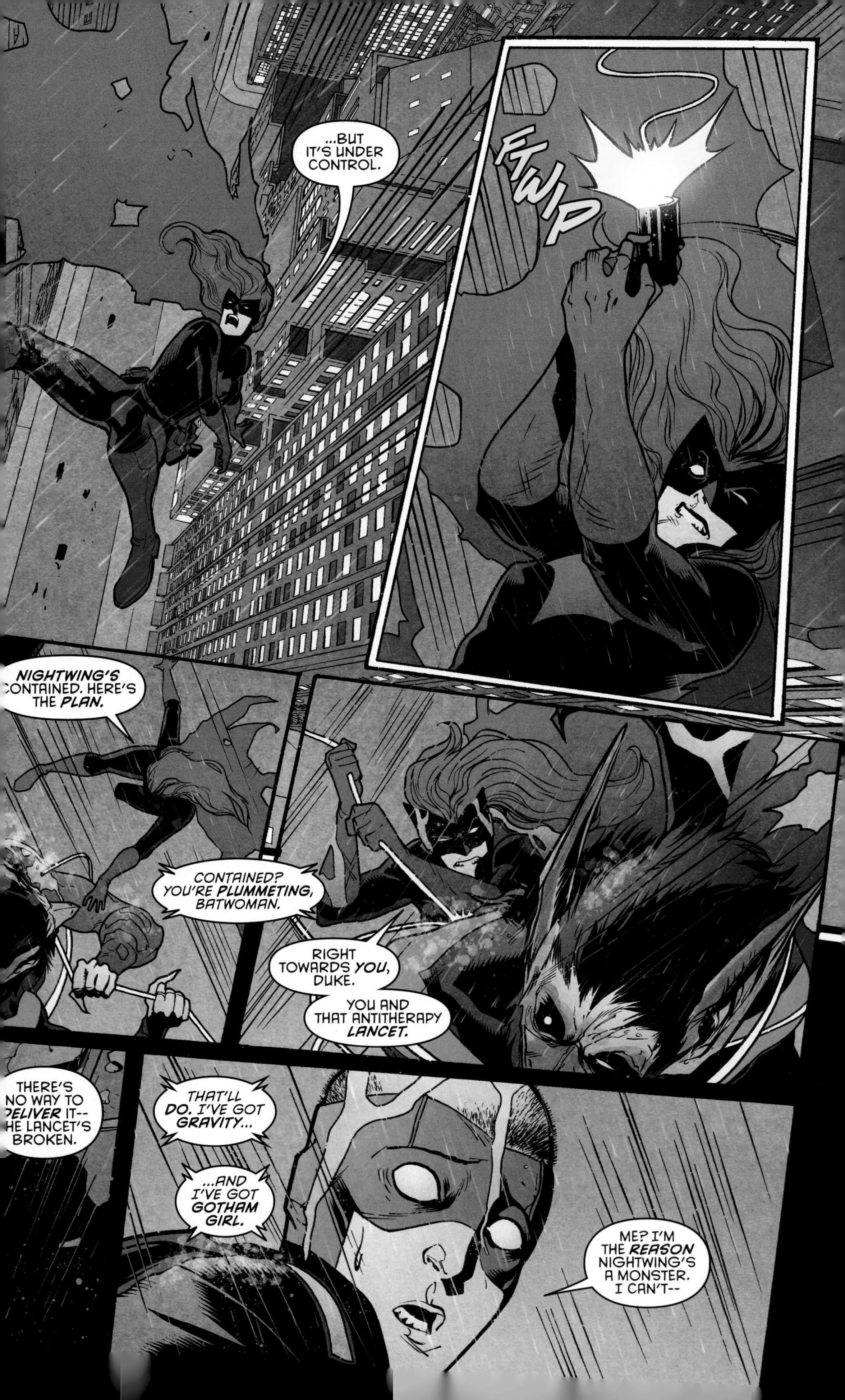
...BUT IT'S UNDER CONTROL.
FFWIP
NIGHTWING'S CONTAINED. HERE'S THE PLAN.
CONTAINED? YOU'RE PLUMMETING, BATWOMAN.
RIGHT TOWARDS YOU, DUKE.
YOU AND THAT ANTITHERAPY LANCET.
THERE'S NO WAY TO DELIVER IT-- THE LANCET'S BROKEN.
THAT'LL DO. I'VE GOT GRAVITY...
...AND I'VE GOT GOTHAM GIRL.
ME? I'M THE REASON NIGHTWING'S A MONSTER. I CAN'T--

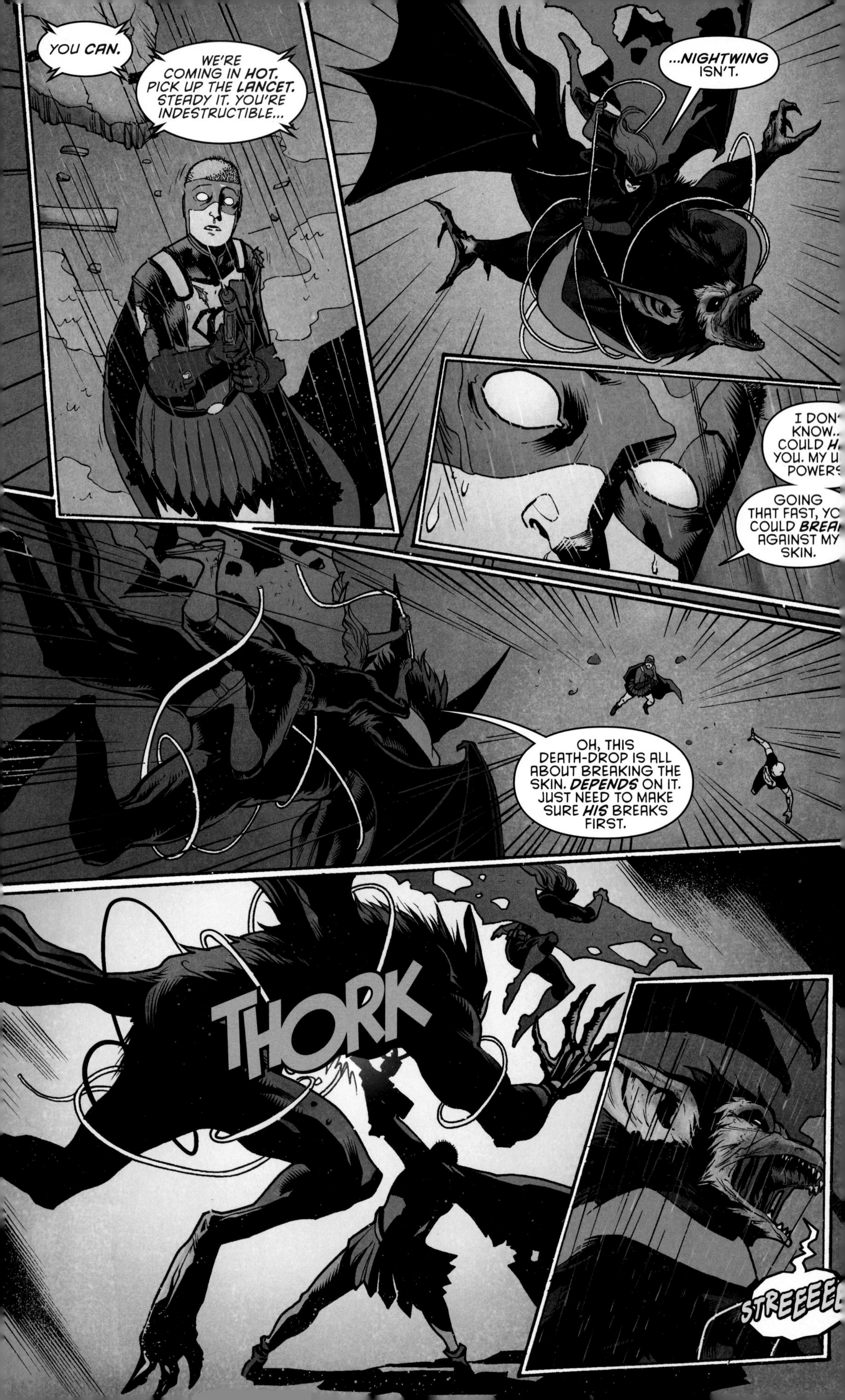
YOU CAN.
WE'RE COMING IN HOT. PICK UP THE LANCET. STEADY IT. YOU'RE INDESTRUCTIBLE...
...NIGHTWING ISN'T.
I DON KNOW.. COULD H YOU. MY U POWERS
GOING THAT FAST, YO COULD BREA AGAINST MY SKIN.
OH, THIS DEATH-DROP IS ALL ABOUT BREAKING THE SKIN. DEPENDS ON IT. JUST NEED TO MAKE SURE HIS BREAKS FIRST.
THORK
STREEEE

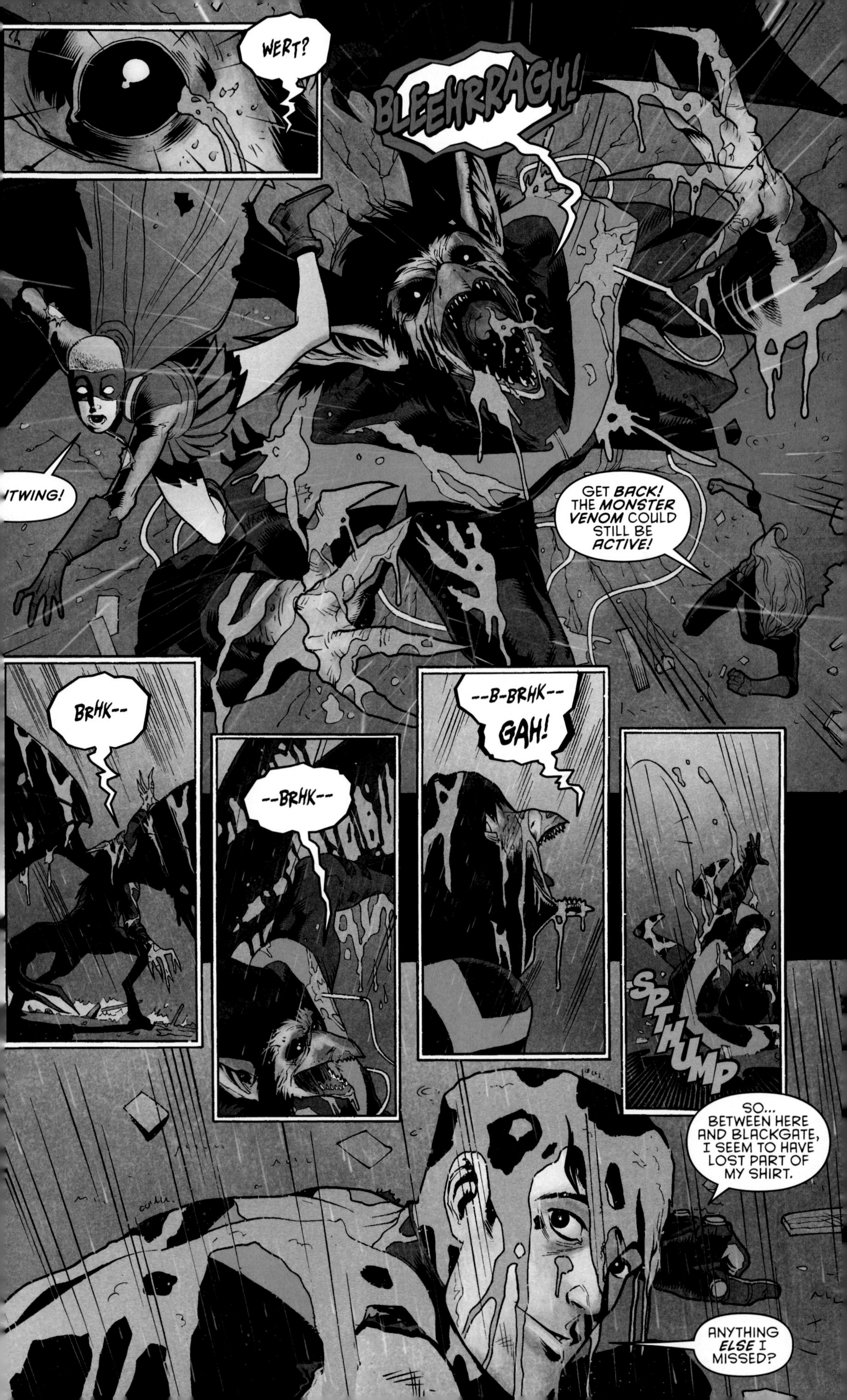

WERT?
BLEEHRRAGH!
...TWING!
GET BACK! THE MONSTER VENOM COULD STILL BE ACTIVE!
BRHK--
--BRHK--
--B-BRHK--
GAH!
SPTHUMP
SO... BETWEEN HERE AND BLACKGATE, I SEEM TO HAVE LOST PART OF MY SHIRT.
ANYTHING ELSE I MISSED?

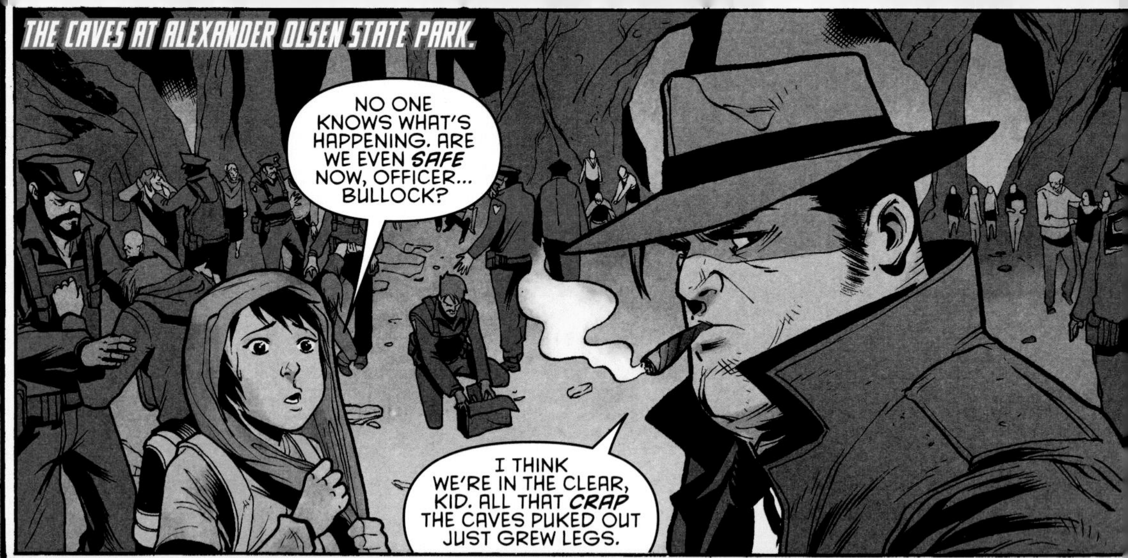
THE CAVES AT ALEXANDER OLSEN STATE PARK.
NO ONE KNOWS WHAT'S HAPPENING. ARE WE EVEN SAFE NOW, OFFICER... BULLOCK?
I THINK WE'RE IN THE CLEAR, KID. ALL THAT CRAP THE CAVES PUKED OUT JUST GREW LEGS.

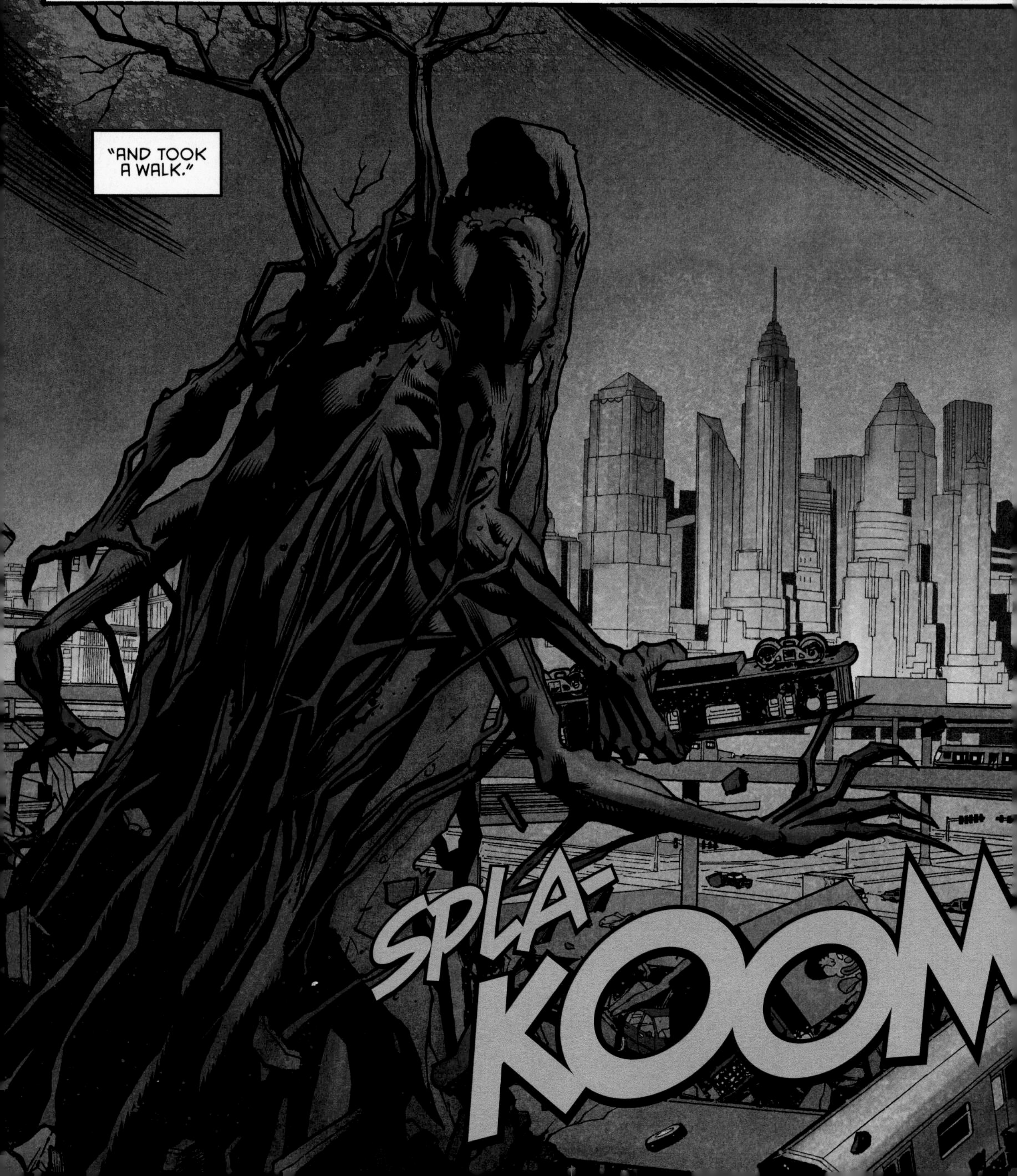
"AND TOOK A WALK."
SPLA-
KOOM

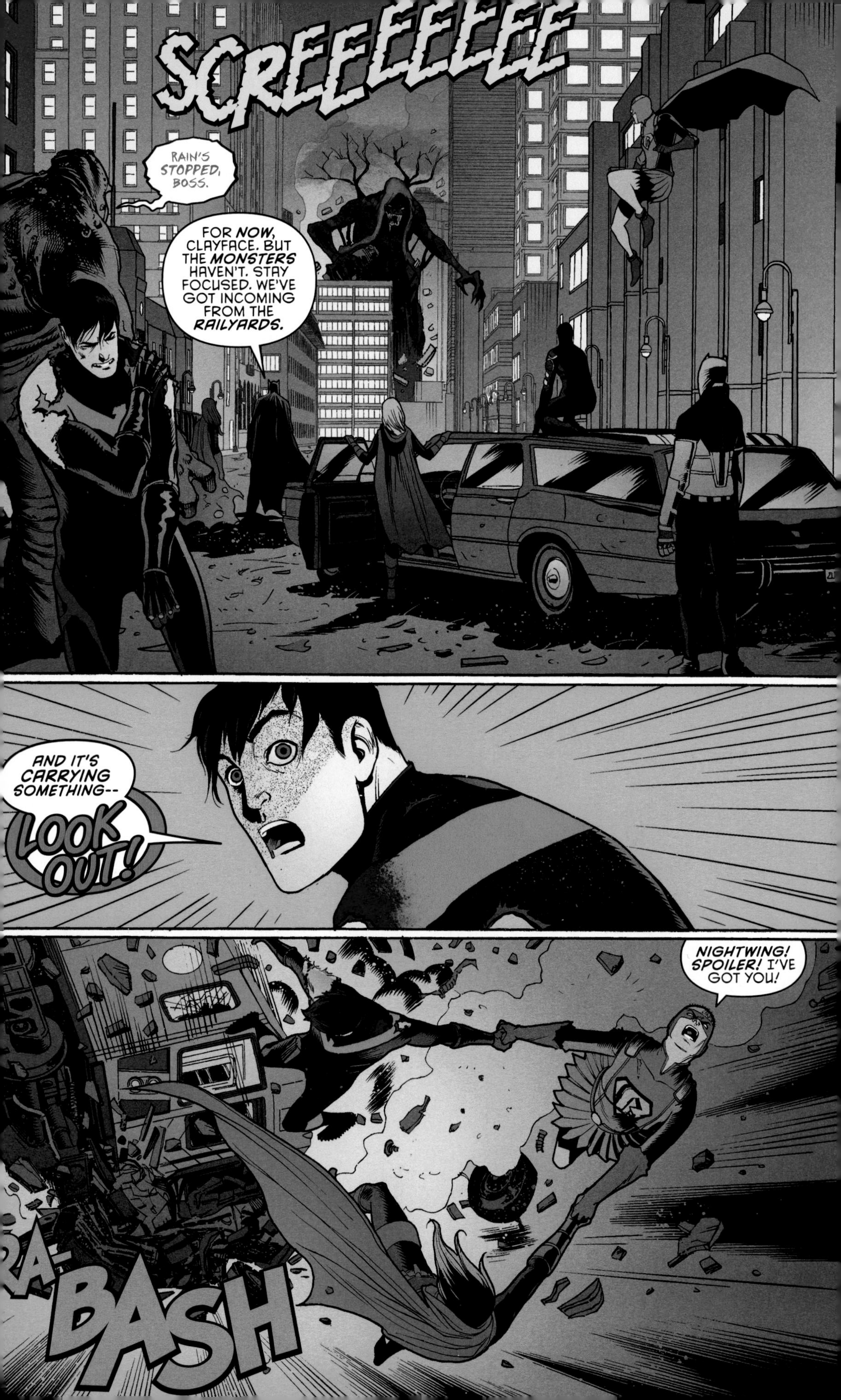

SCREEEEEEE
RAIN'S STOPPED, BOSS.
FOR NOW, CLAYFACE. BUT THE MONSTERS HAVEN'T. STAY FOCUSED. WE'VE GOT INCOMING FROM THE RAILYARDS.
AND IT'S CARRYING SOMETHING--
LOOK OUT!
NIGHTWING! SPOILER! I'VE GOT YOU!
KRA-BASH

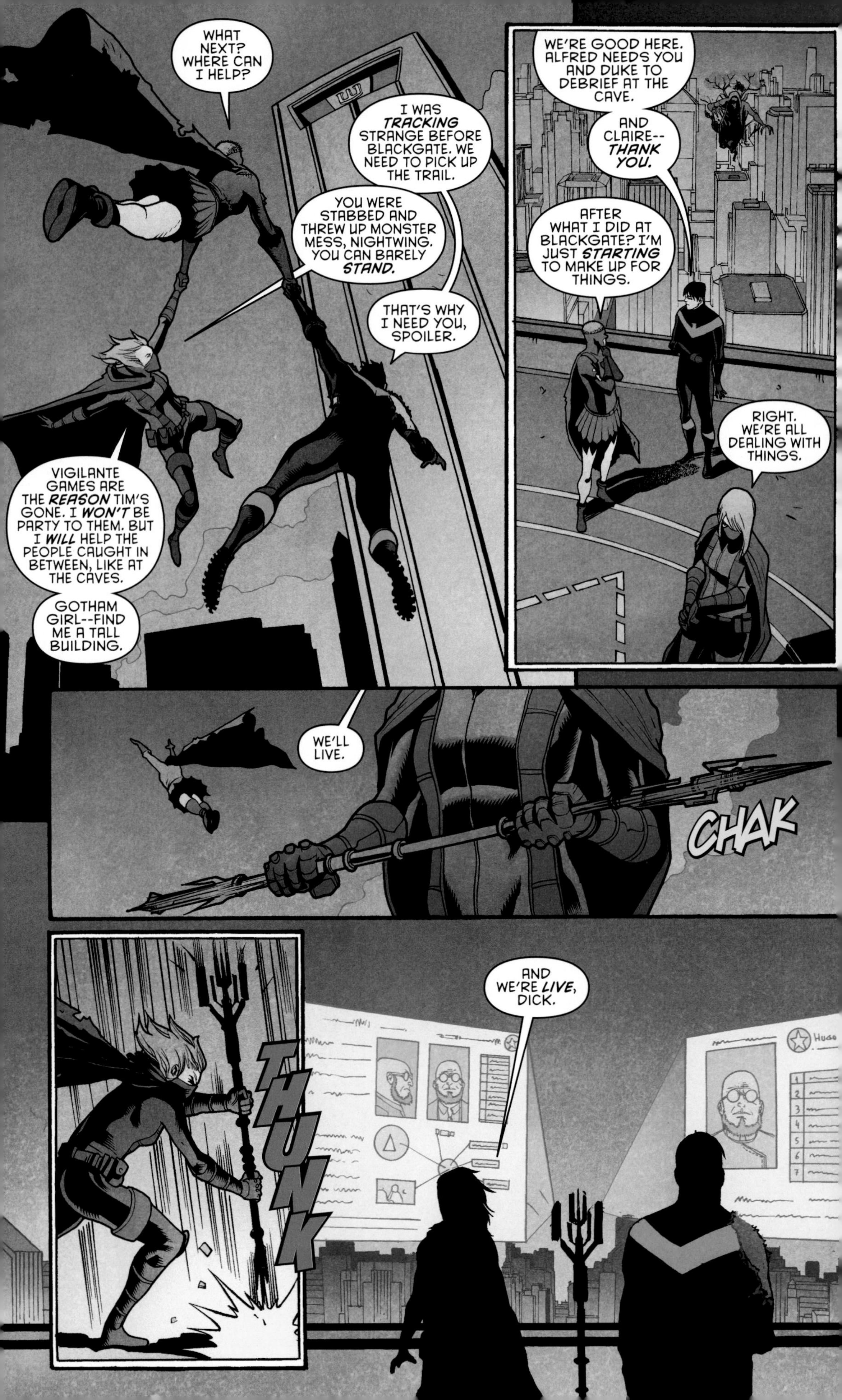
WHAT NEXT? WHERE CAN I HELP?
I WAS TRACKING STRANGE BEFORE BLACKGATE. WE NEED TO PICK UP THE TRAIL.
YOU WERE STABBED AND THREW UP MONSTER MESS, NIGHTWING. YOU CAN BARELY STAND.
THAT'S WHY I NEED YOU, SPOILER.
VIGILANTE GAMES ARE THE REASON TIM'S GONE. I WON'T BE PARTY TO THEM. BUT I WILL HELP THE PEOPLE CAUGHT IN BETWEEN, LIKE AT THE CAVES.
GOTHAM GIRL--FIND ME A TALL BUILDING.
WE'RE GOOD HERE. ALFRED NEEDS YOU AND DUKE TO DEBRIEF AT THE CAVE.
AND CLAIRE-- THANK YOU.
AFTER WHAT I DID AT BLACKGATE? I'M JUST STARTING TO MAKE UP FOR THINGS.
RIGHT. WE'RE ALL DEALING WITH THINGS.
WE'LL LIVE.
CHAK
THUNK
AND WE'RE LIVE, DICK.
HUGO

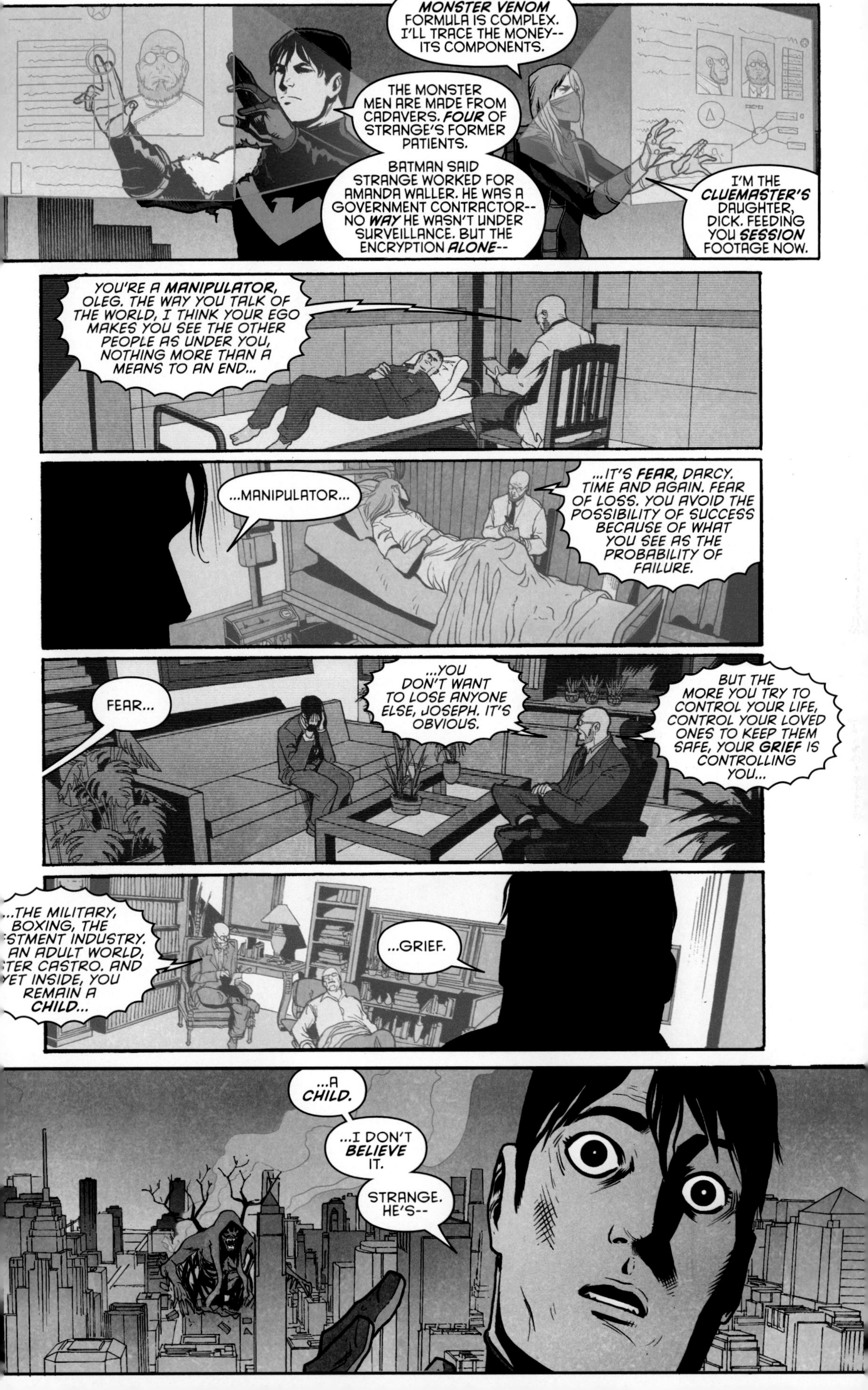
STRANGE'S MONSTER VENOM FORMULA IS COMPLEX. I'LL TRACE THE MONEY-- ITS COMPONENTS.
THE MONSTER MEN ARE MADE FROM CADAVERS. FOUR OF STRANGE'S FORMER PATIENTS.
BATMAN SAID STRANGE WORKED FOR AMANDA WALLER. HE WAS A GOVERNMENT CONTRACTOR-- NO WAY HE WASN'T UNDER SURVEILLANCE. BUT THE ENCRYPTION ALONE--
I'M THE CLUEMASTER'S DAUGHTER, DICK. FEEDING YOU SESSION FOOTAGE NOW.
YOU'RE A MANIPULATOR, OLEG. THE WAY YOU TALK OF THE WORLD, I THINK YOUR EGO MAKES YOU SEE THE OTHER PEOPLE AS UNDER YOU, NOTHING MORE THAN A MEANS TO AN END...
...MANIPULATOR...
...IT'S FEAR, DARCY. TIME AND AGAIN. FEAR OF LOSS. YOU AVOID THE POSSIBILITY OF SUCCESS BECAUSE OF WHAT YOU SEE AS THE PROBABILITY OF FAILURE.
FEAR...
...YOU DON'T WANT TO LOSE ANYONE ELSE, JOSEPH. IT'S OBVIOUS.
BUT THE MORE YOU TRY TO CONTROL YOUR LIFE, CONTROL YOUR LOVED ONES TO KEEP THEM SAFE, YOUR GRIEF IS CONTROLLING YOU...
...THE MILITARY, BOXING, THE STMENT INDUSTRY. AN ADULT WORLD, TER CASTRO. AND YET INSIDE, YOU REMAIN A CHILD...
...GRIEF.
...A CHILD.
...I DON'T BELIEVE IT.
STRANGE. HE'S--

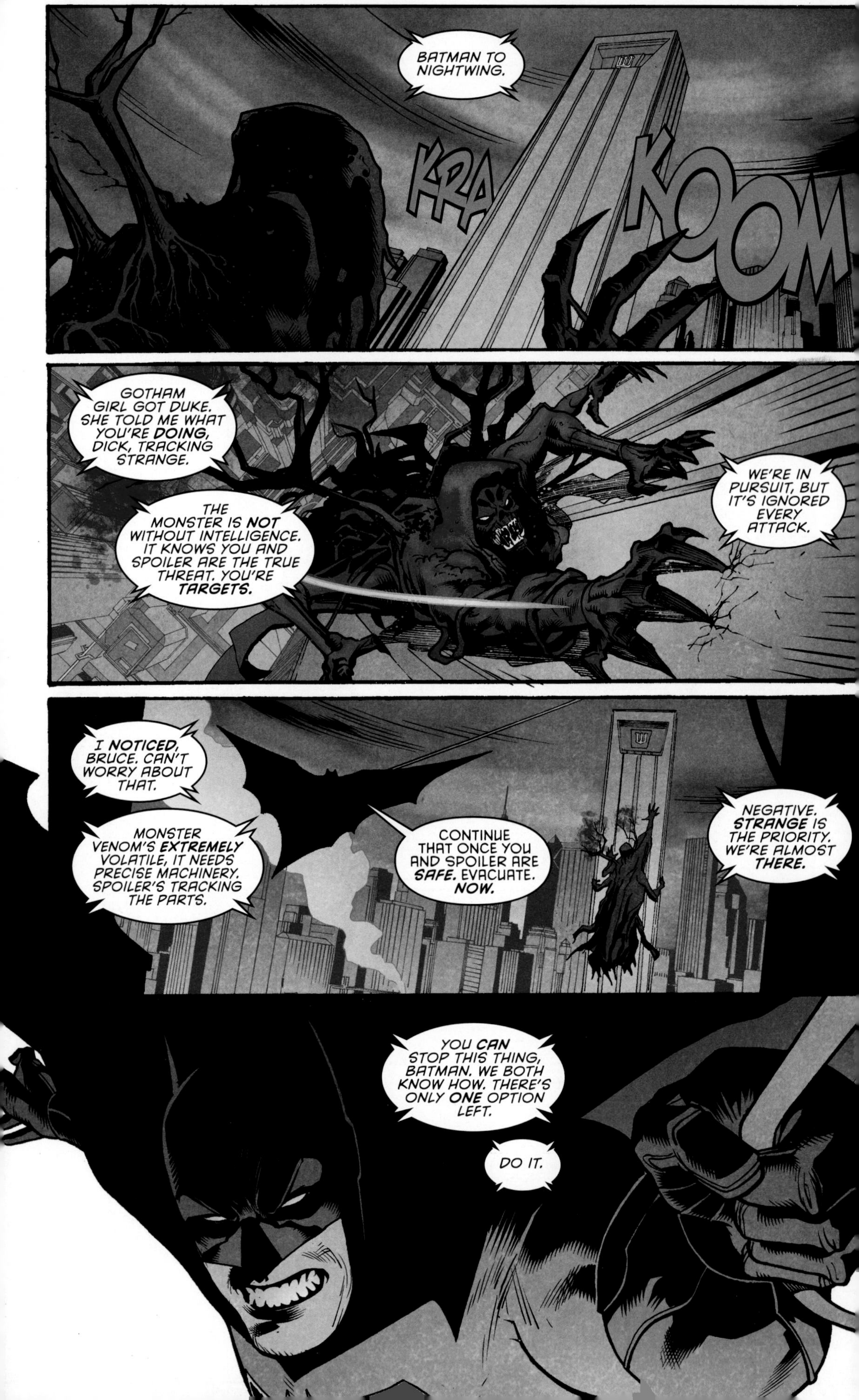
BATMAN TO NIGHTWING.
KRA
KOOM
GOTHAM GIRL GOT DUKE. SHE TOLD ME WHAT YOU'RE DOING, DICK, TRACKING STRANGE.
THE MONSTER IS NOT WITHOUT INTELLIGENCE. IT KNOWS YOU AND SPOILER ARE THE TRUE THREAT. YOU'RE TARGETS.
WE'RE IN PURSUIT, BUT IT'S IGNORED EVERY ATTACK.
I NOTICED, BRUCE. CAN'T WORRY ABOUT THAT.
MONSTER VENOM'S EXTREMELY VOLATILE, IT NEEDS PRECISE MACHINERY. SPOILER'S TRACKING THE PARTS.
CONTINUE THAT ONCE YOU AND SPOILER ARE SAFE. EVACUATE. NOW.
NEGATIVE. STRANGE IS THE PRIORITY. WE'RE ALMOST THERE.
YOU CAN STOP THIS THING, BATMAN. WE BOTH KNOW HOW. THERE'S ONLY ONE OPTION LEFT.
DO IT.

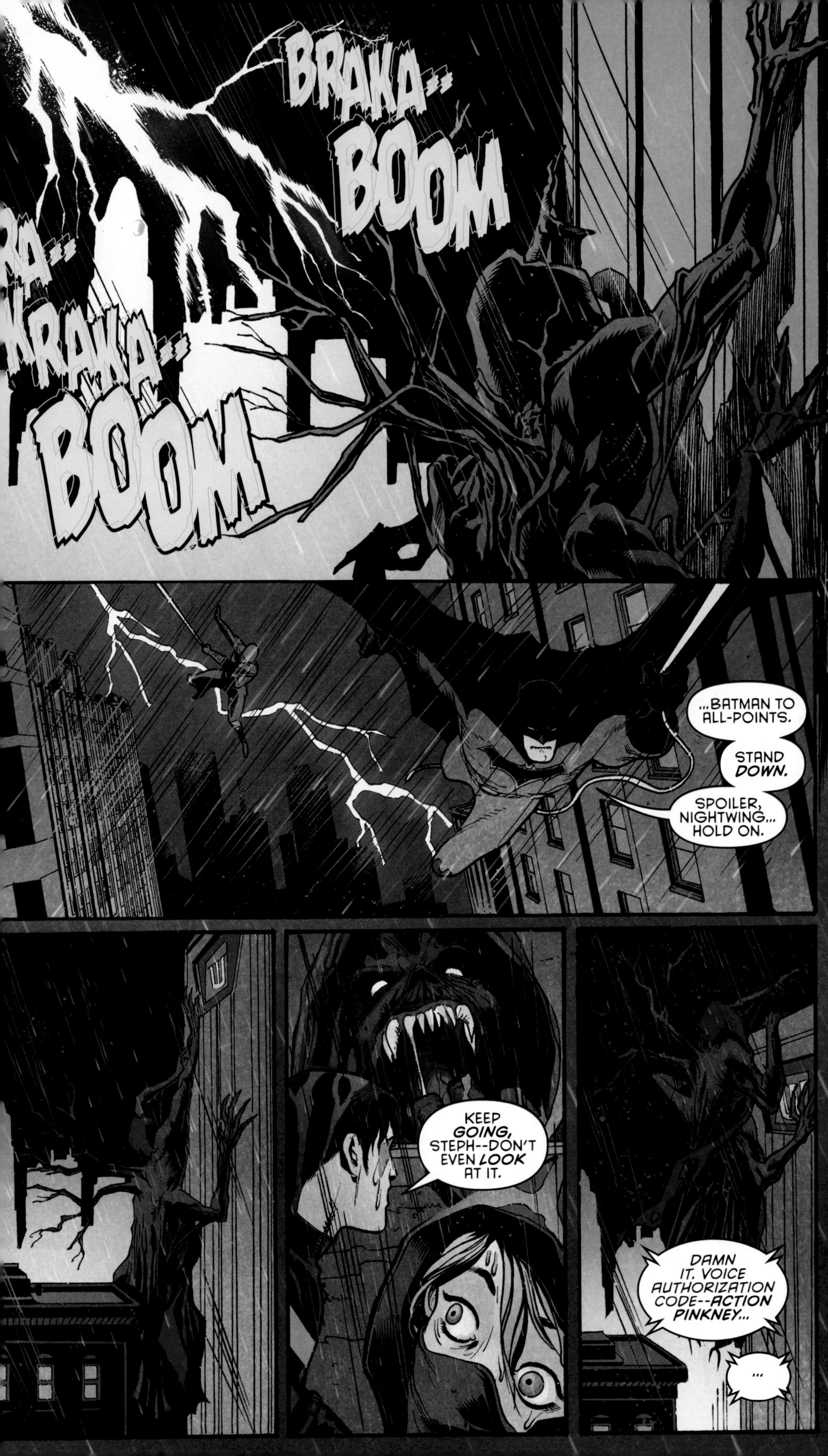
BRAKA... BOOM
RA... KRAKA... BOOM
...BATMAN TO ALL-POINTS.
STAND DOWN.
SPOILER, NIGHTWING... HOLD ON.
KEEP GOING, STEPH--DON'T EVEN LOOK AT IT.
DAMN IT. VOICE AUTHORIZATION CODE--ACTION PINKNEY...
...

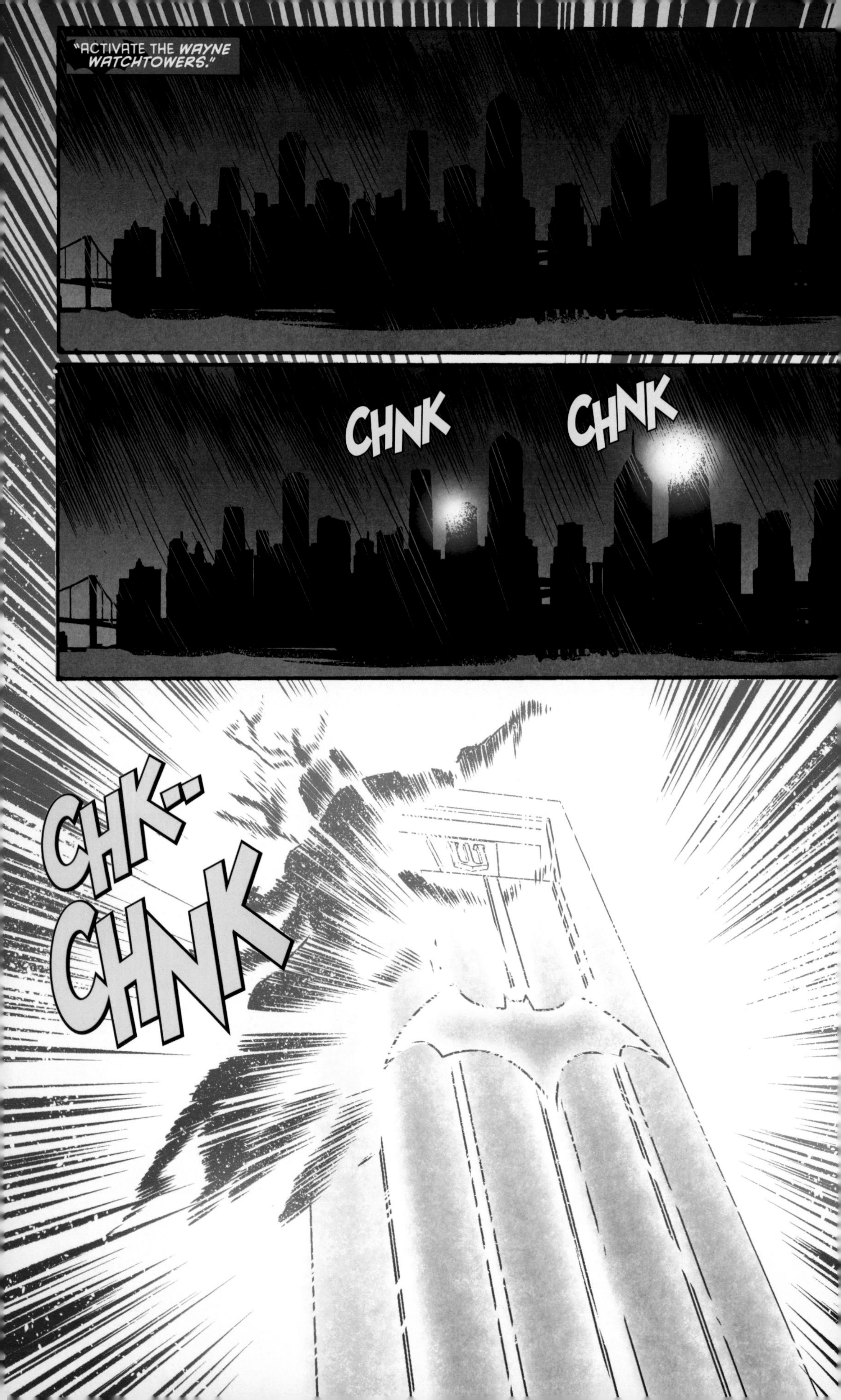
"ACTIVATE THE WAYNE WATCHTOWERS."
CHNK
CHNK
CHK--
CHNK

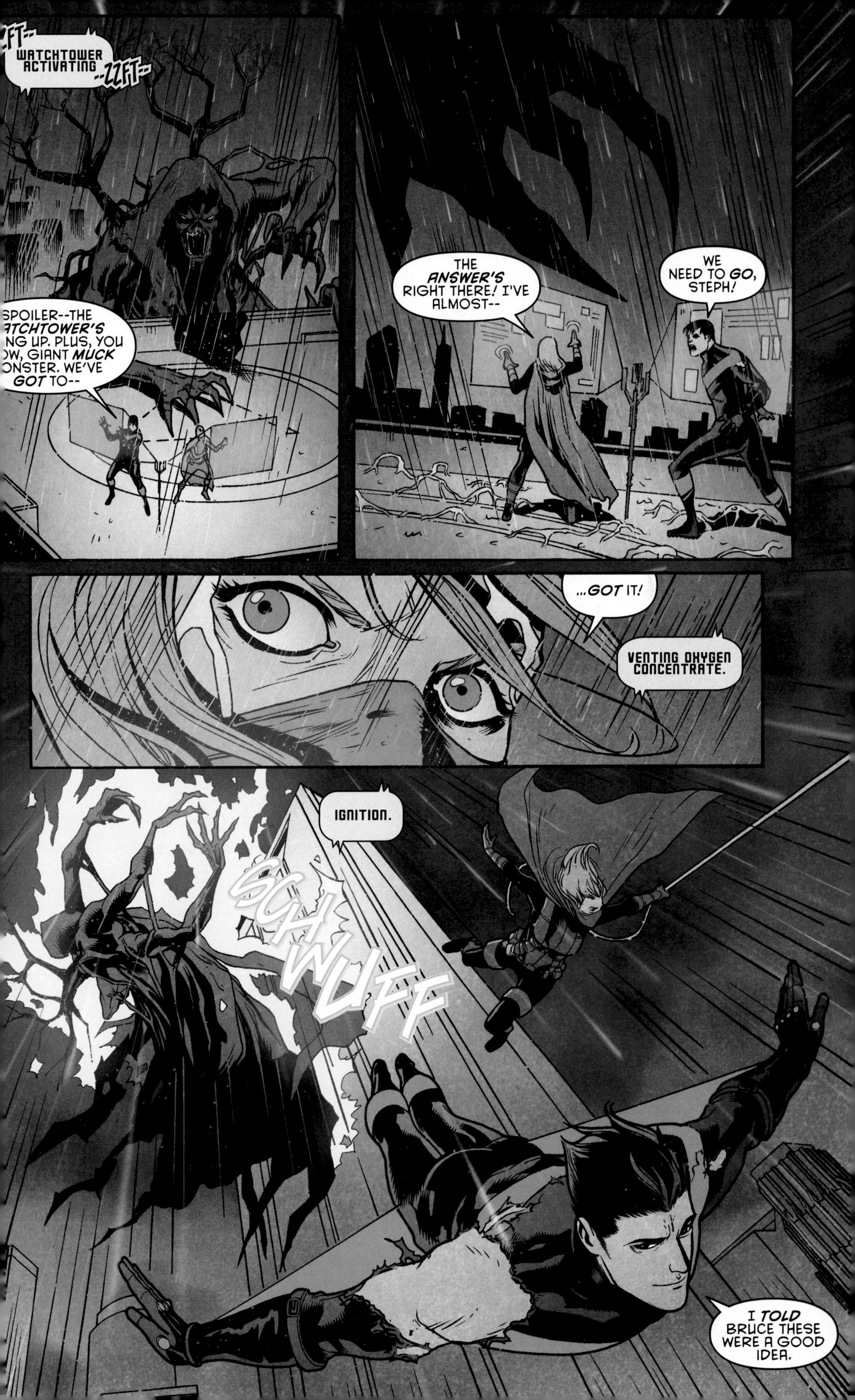

--ZZFT-- WATCHTOWER ACTIVATING --ZZFT--
SPOILER--THE WATCHTOWER'S ...NG UP. PLUS, YOU ...OW, GIANT MUCK ...ONSTER. WE'VE GOT TO--
THE ANSWER'S RIGHT THERE! I'VE ALMOST--
WE NEED TO GO, STEPH!
...GOT IT!
VENTING OXYGEN CONCENTRATE.
IGNITION.
SCHWUFF
I TOLD BRUCE THESE WERE A GOOD IDEA.

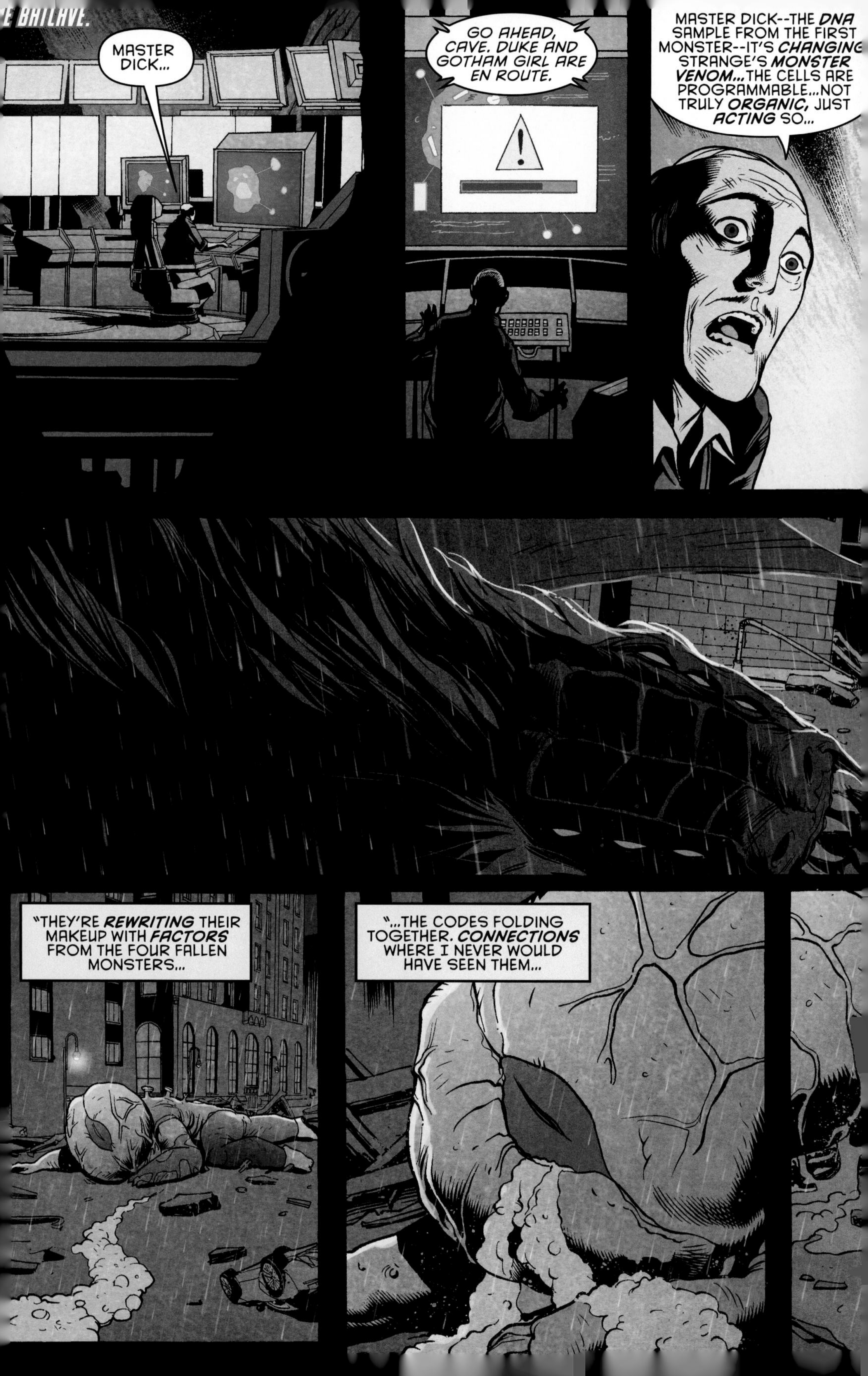

E BATCAVE.
MASTER DICK...
GO AHEAD, CAVE. DUKE AND GOTHAM GIRL ARE EN ROUTE.
MASTER DICK--THE DNA SAMPLE FROM THE FIRST MONSTER--IT'S CHANGING STRANGE'S MONSTER VENOM...THE CELLS ARE PROGRAMMABLE...NOT TRULY ORGANIC, JUST ACTING SO...
"THEY'RE REWRITING THEIR MAKEUP WITH FACTORS FROM THE FOUR FALLEN MONSTERS...
"...THE CODES FOLDING TOGETHER. CONNECTIONS WHERE I NEVER WOULD HAVE SEEN THEM...

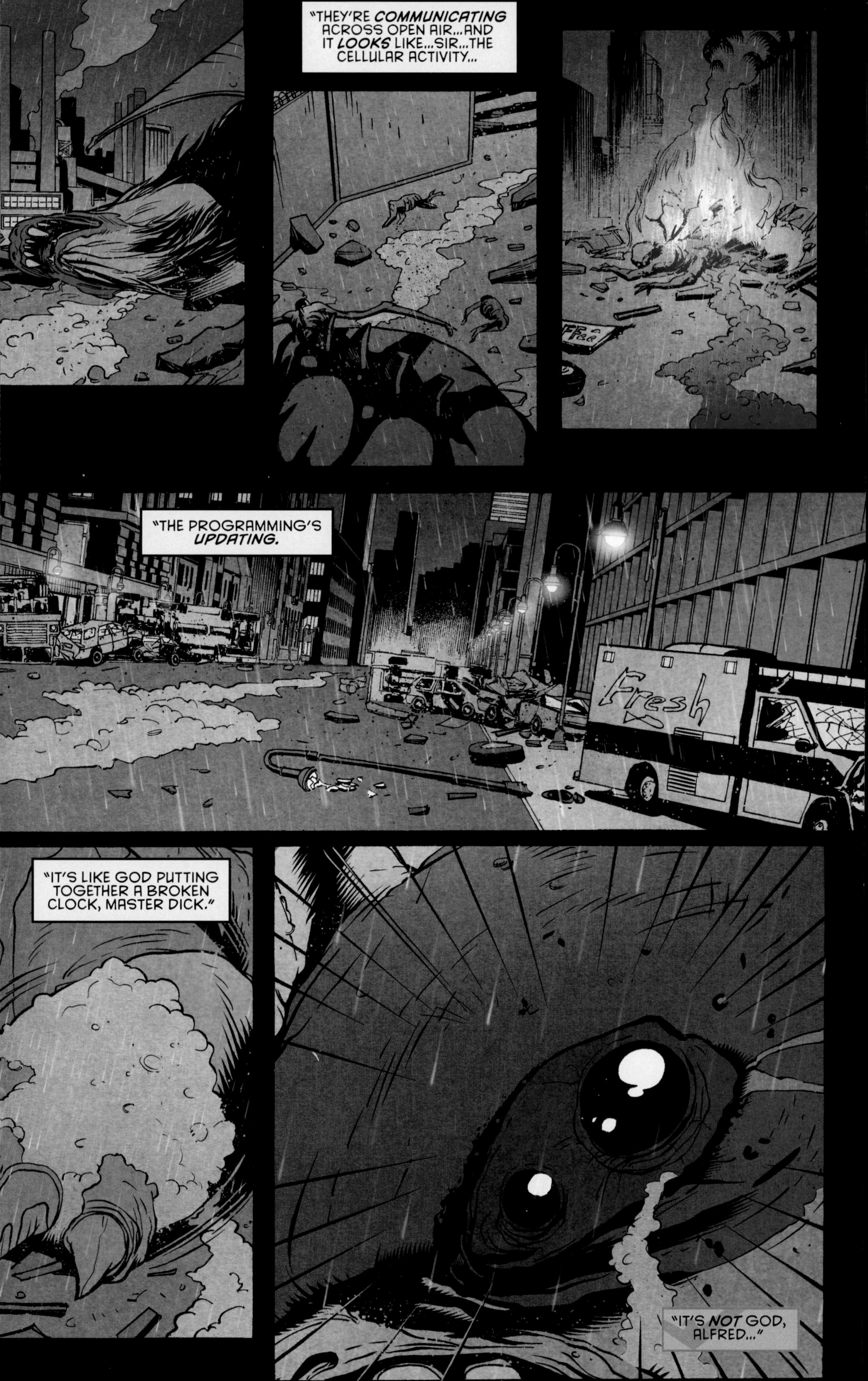
"THEY'RE COMMUNICATING ACROSS OPEN AIR...AND IT LOOKS LIKE...SIR...THE CELLULAR ACTIVITY...
"THE PROGRAMMING'S UPDATING.
Fresh
"IT'S LIKE GOD PUTTING TOGETHER A BROKEN CLOCK, MASTER DICK."
"IT'S NOT GOD, ALFRED..."

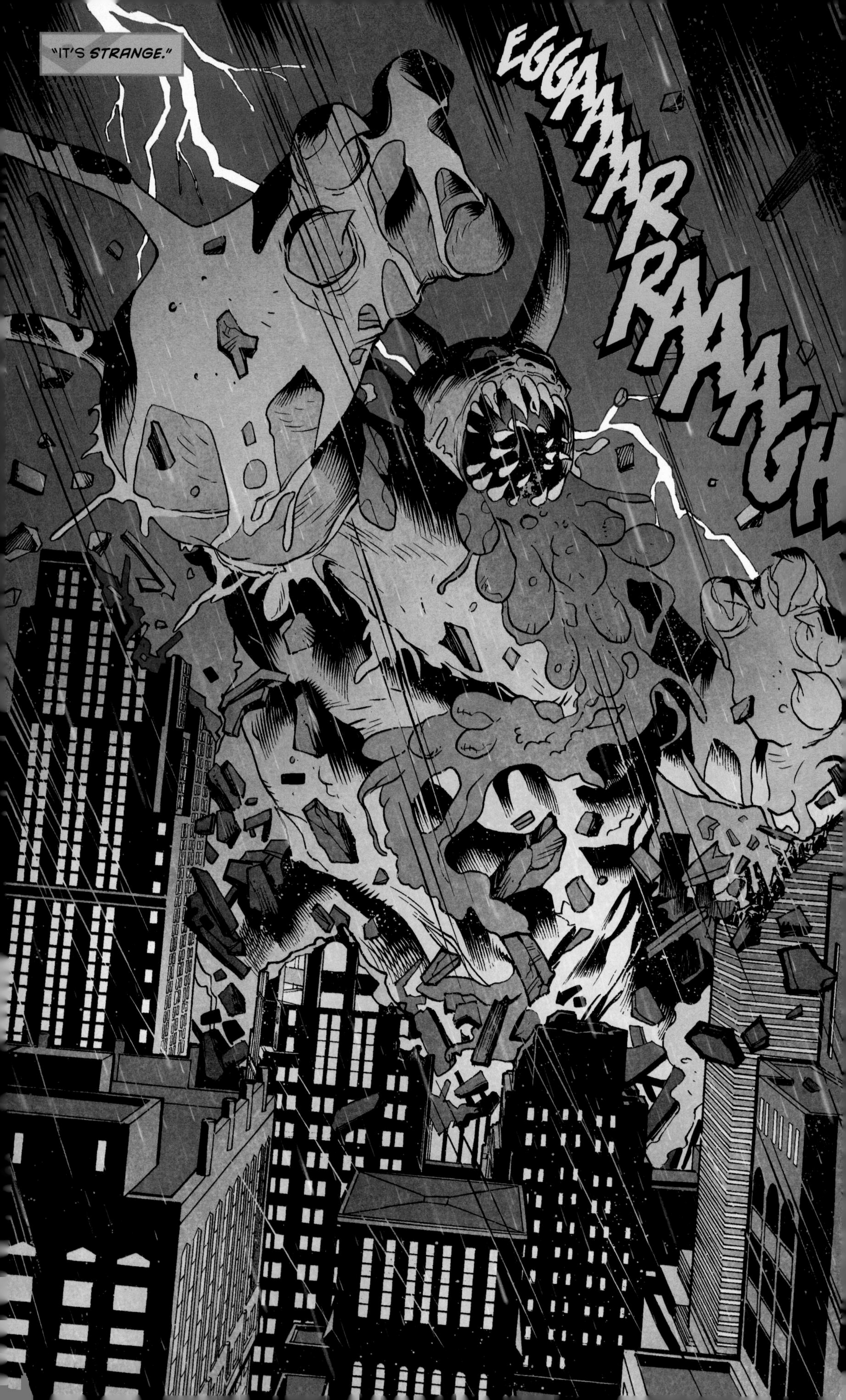
"IT'S STRANGE."
EGGAAAARRRAAAGH

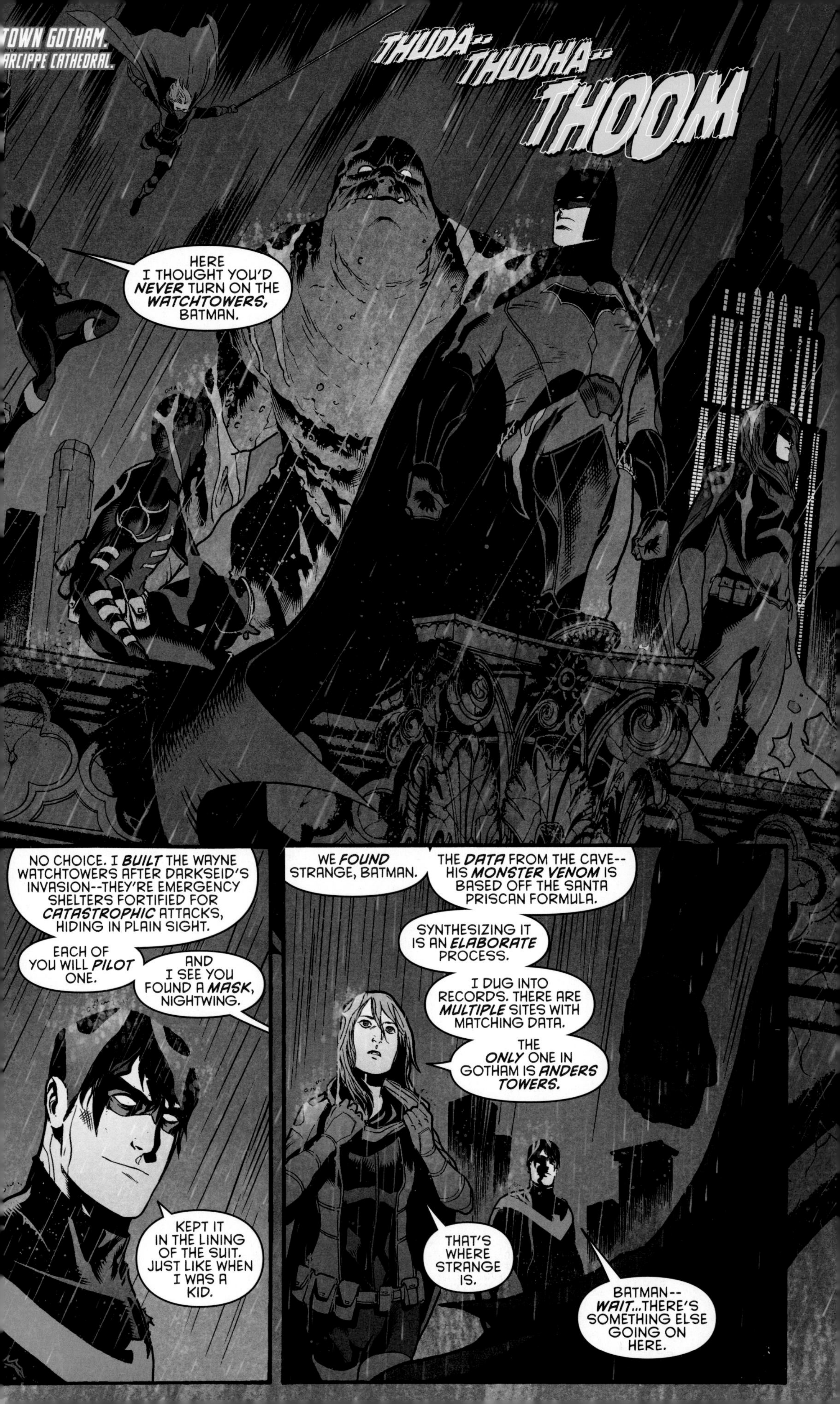
TOWN GOTHAM.
ARCIPPE CATHEDRAL.
THUDA-- THUDHA-- THOOM
HERE I THOUGHT YOU'D NEVER TURN ON THE WATCHTOWERS, BATMAN.
NO CHOICE. I BUILT THE WAYNE WATCHTOWERS AFTER DARKSEID'S INVASION--THEY'RE EMERGENCY SHELTERS FORTIFIED FOR CATASTROPHIC ATTACKS, HIDING IN PLAIN SIGHT.
EACH OF YOU WILL PILOT ONE.
AND I SEE YOU FOUND A MASK, NIGHTWING.
KEPT IT IN THE LINING OF THE SUIT. JUST LIKE WHEN I WAS A KID.
WE FOUND STRANGE, BATMAN.
THE DATA FROM THE CAVE-- HIS MONSTER VENOM IS BASED OFF THE SANTA PRISCAN FORMULA.
SYNTHESIZING IT IS AN ELABORATE PROCESS.
I DUG INTO RECORDS. THERE ARE MULTIPLE SITES WITH MATCHING DATA.
THE ONLY ONE IN GOTHAM IS ANDERS TOWERS.
THAT'S WHERE STRANGE IS.
BATMAN-- WAIT...THERE'S SOMETHING ELSE GOING ON HERE.

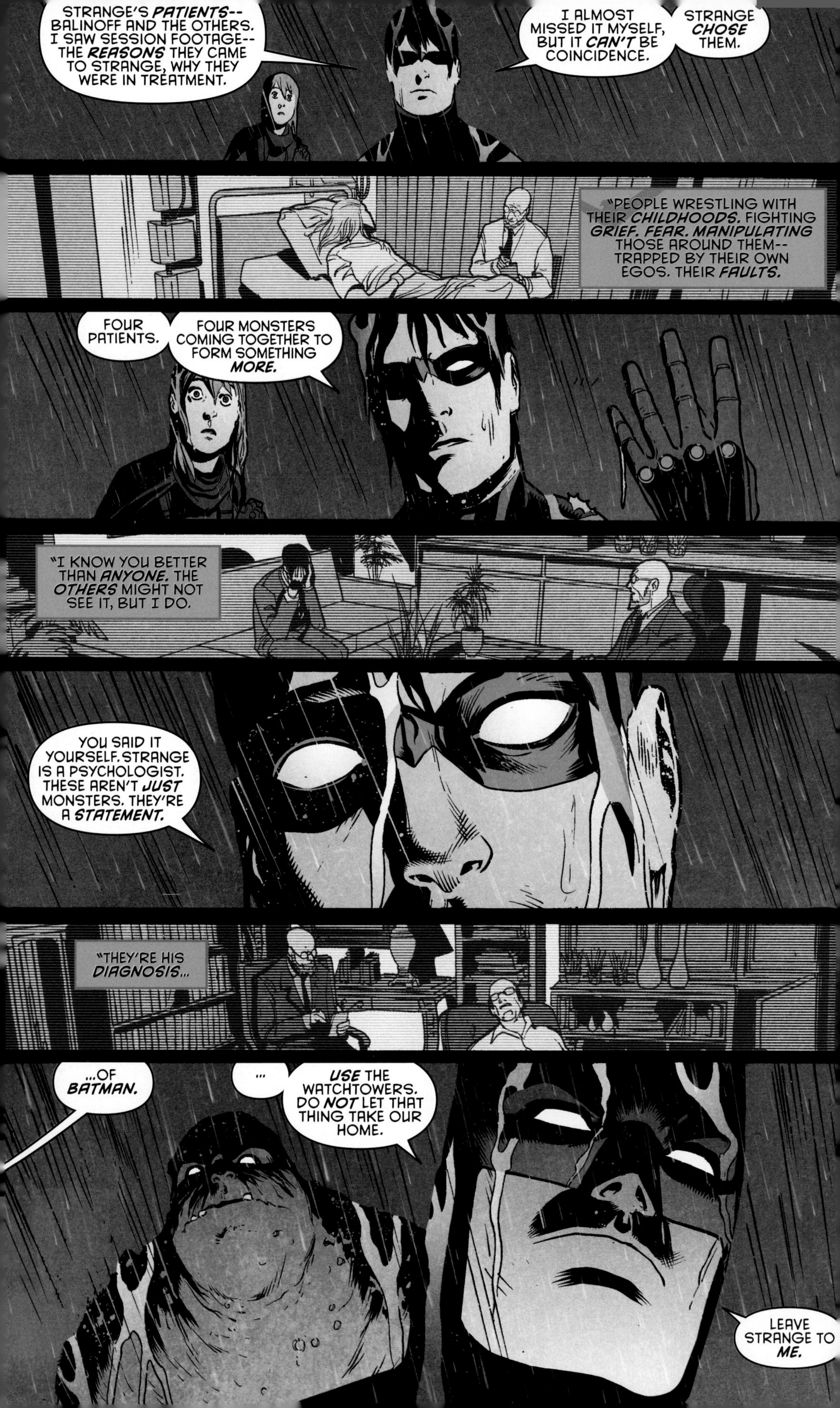

STRANGE'S PATIENTS-- BALINOFF AND THE OTHERS. I SAW SESSION FOOTAGE-- THE REASONS THEY CAME TO STRANGE, WHY THEY WERE IN TREATMENT.
I ALMOST MISSED IT MYSELF, BUT IT CAN'T BE COINCIDENCE.
STRANGE CHOSE THEM.
"PEOPLE WRESTLING WITH THEIR CHILDHOODS. FIGHTING GRIEF. FEAR. MANIPULATING THOSE AROUND THEM-- TRAPPED BY THEIR OWN EGOS. THEIR FAULTS.
FOUR PATIENTS.
FOUR MONSTERS COMING TOGETHER TO FORM SOMETHING MORE.
"I KNOW YOU BETTER THAN ANYONE. THE OTHERS MIGHT NOT SEE IT, BUT I DO.
YOU SAID IT YOURSELF. STRANGE IS A PSYCHOLOGIST. THESE AREN'T JUST MONSTERS. THEY'RE A STATEMENT.
"THEY'RE HIS DIAGNOSIS...
...OF BATMAN.
...
USE THE WATCHTOWERS. DO NOT LET THAT THING TAKE OUR HOME.
LEAVE STRANGE TO ME.

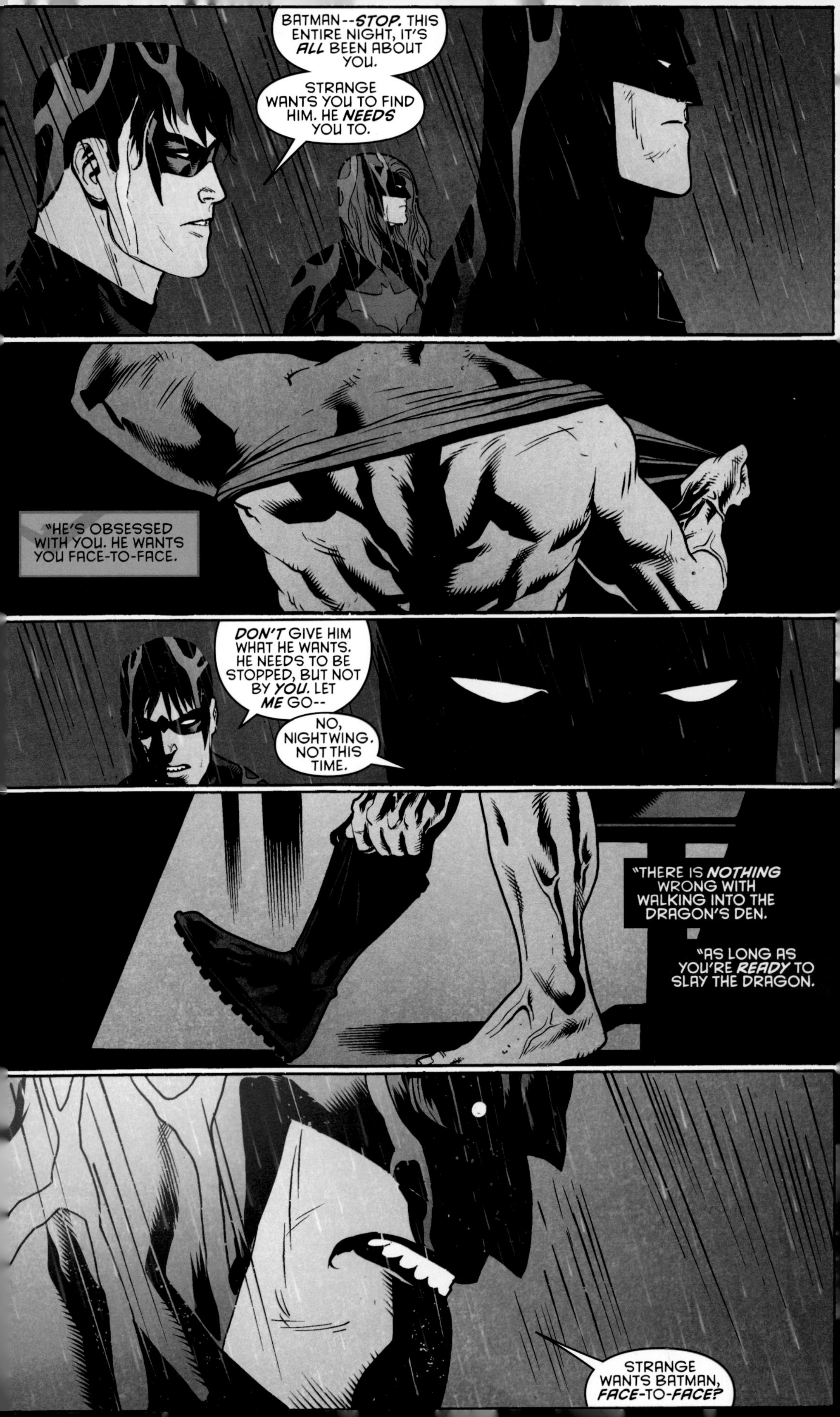
BATMAN--*STOP.* THIS ENTIRE NIGHT, IT'S *ALL* BEEN ABOUT YOU.
STRANGE WANTS YOU TO FIND HIM. HE *NEEDS* YOU TO.
"HE'S OBSESSED WITH YOU. HE WANTS YOU FACE-TO-FACE.
DON'T GIVE HIM WHAT HE WANTS. HE NEEDS TO BE STOPPED, BUT NOT BY *YOU*. LET *ME* GO--
NO, NIGHTWING. NOT THIS TIME.
"THERE IS *NOTHING* WRONG WITH WALKING INTO THE DRAGON'S DEN.
"AS LONG AS YOU'RE *READY* TO SLAY THE DRAGON.
STRANGE WANTS BATMAN, *FACE*-TO-*FACE?*

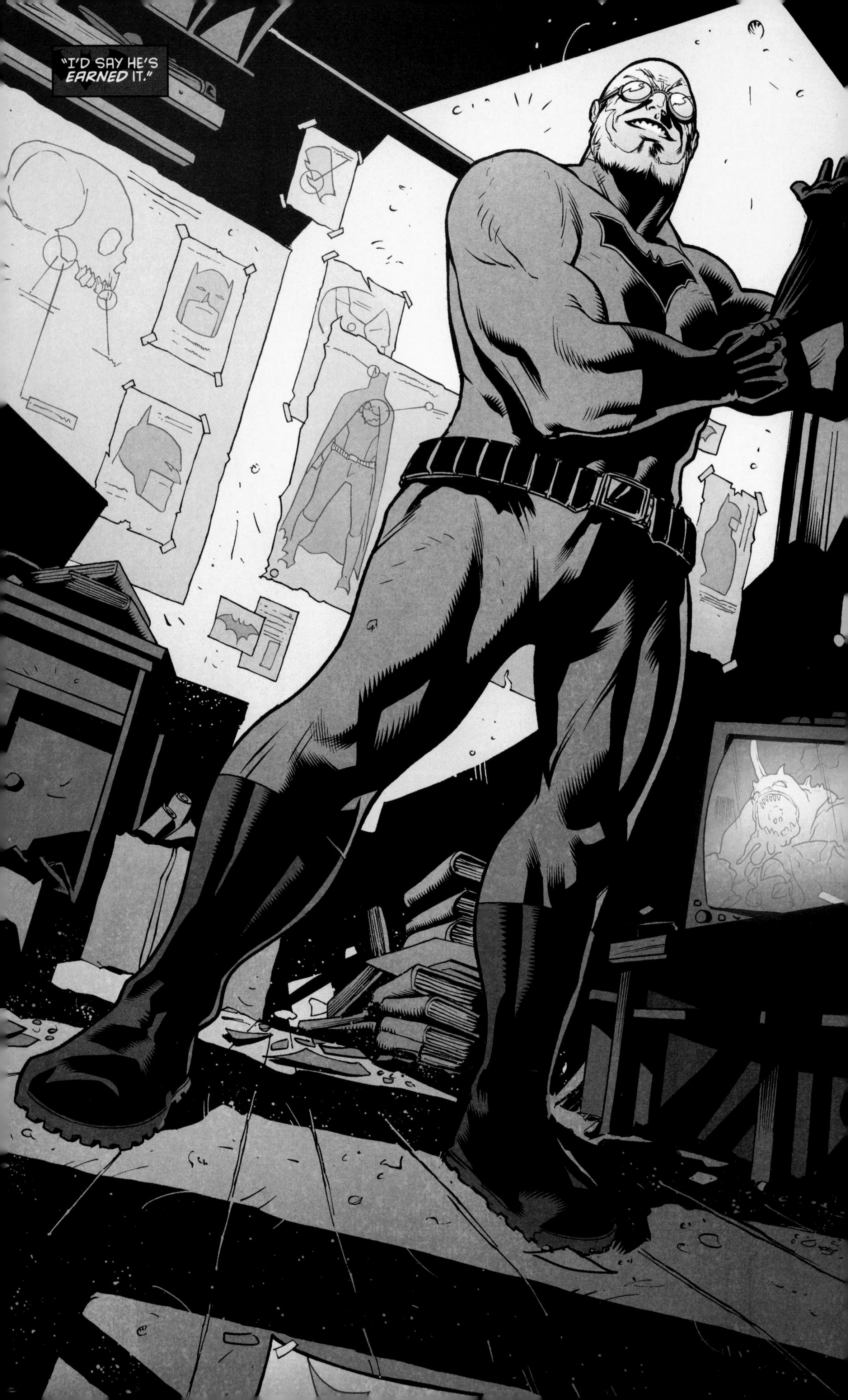
"I'D SAY HE'S EARNED IT."

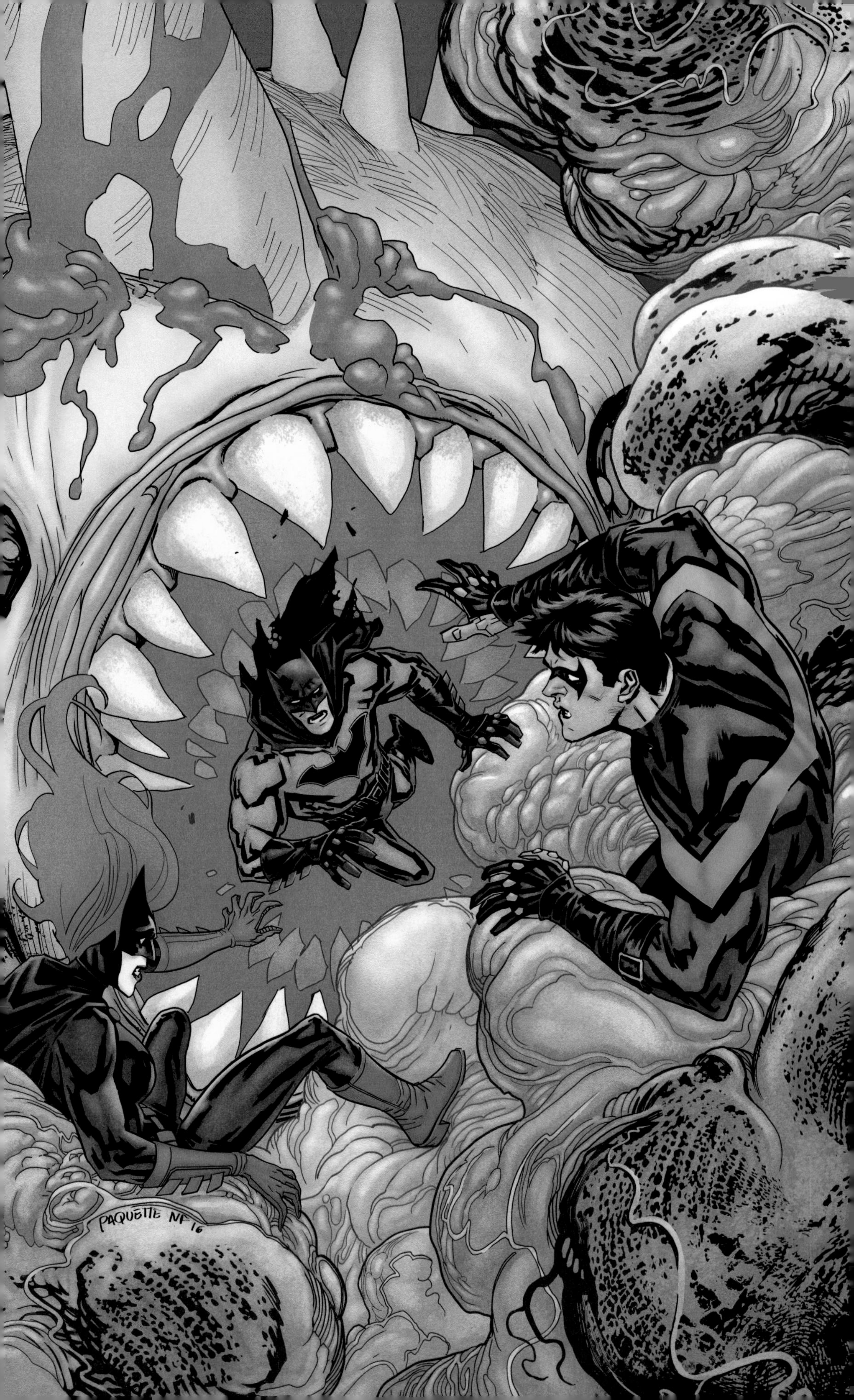
PAQUETTE NF 16

STEVE ORLANDO & JAMES TYNION IV plot * STEVE ORLANDO script * ANDY MacDONALD art * JOHN RAUCH colors
MARILYN PATRIZIO letters * YANICK PAQUETTE & NATHAN FAIRBAIRN cover art

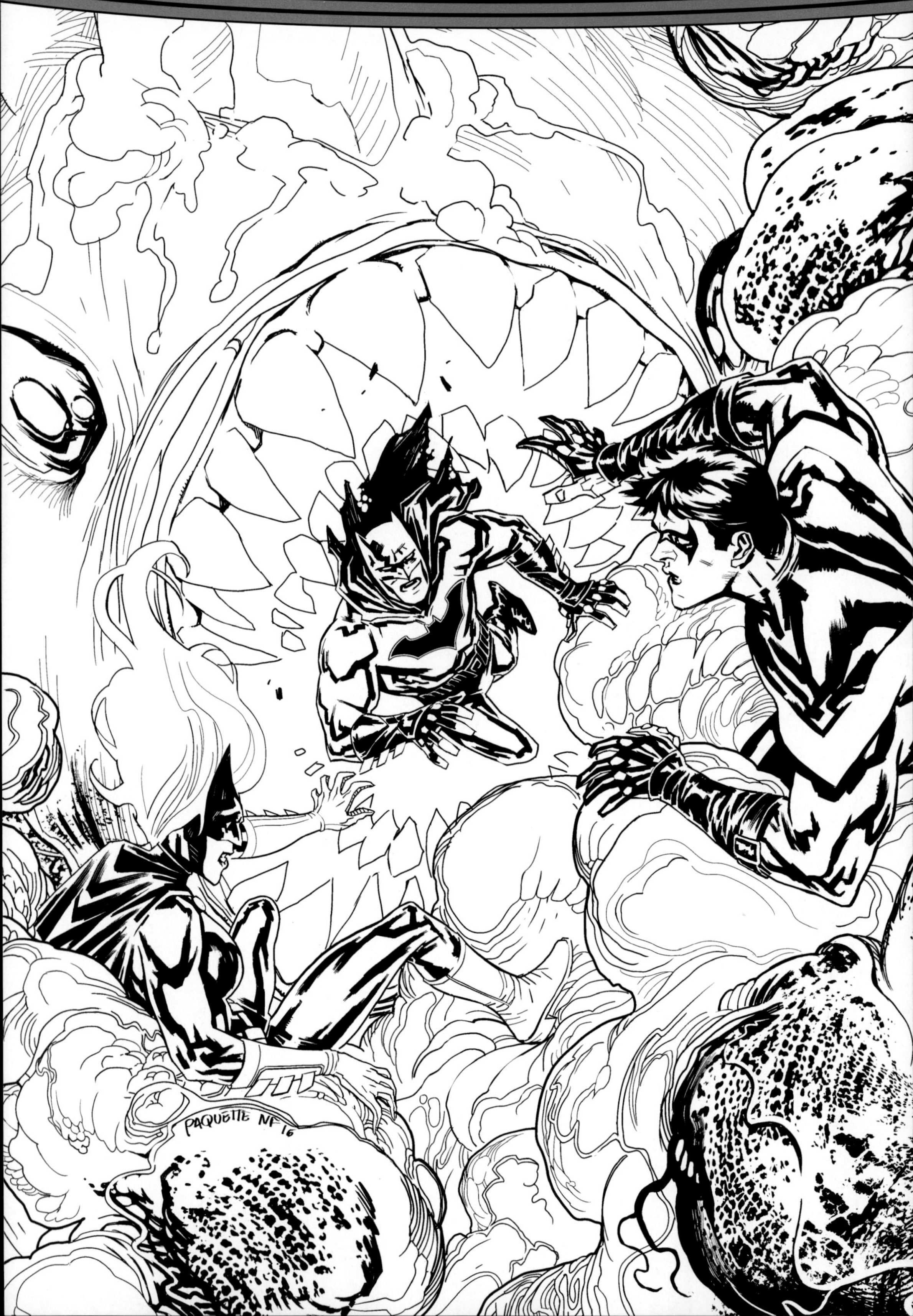
PAQUETTE NF'16

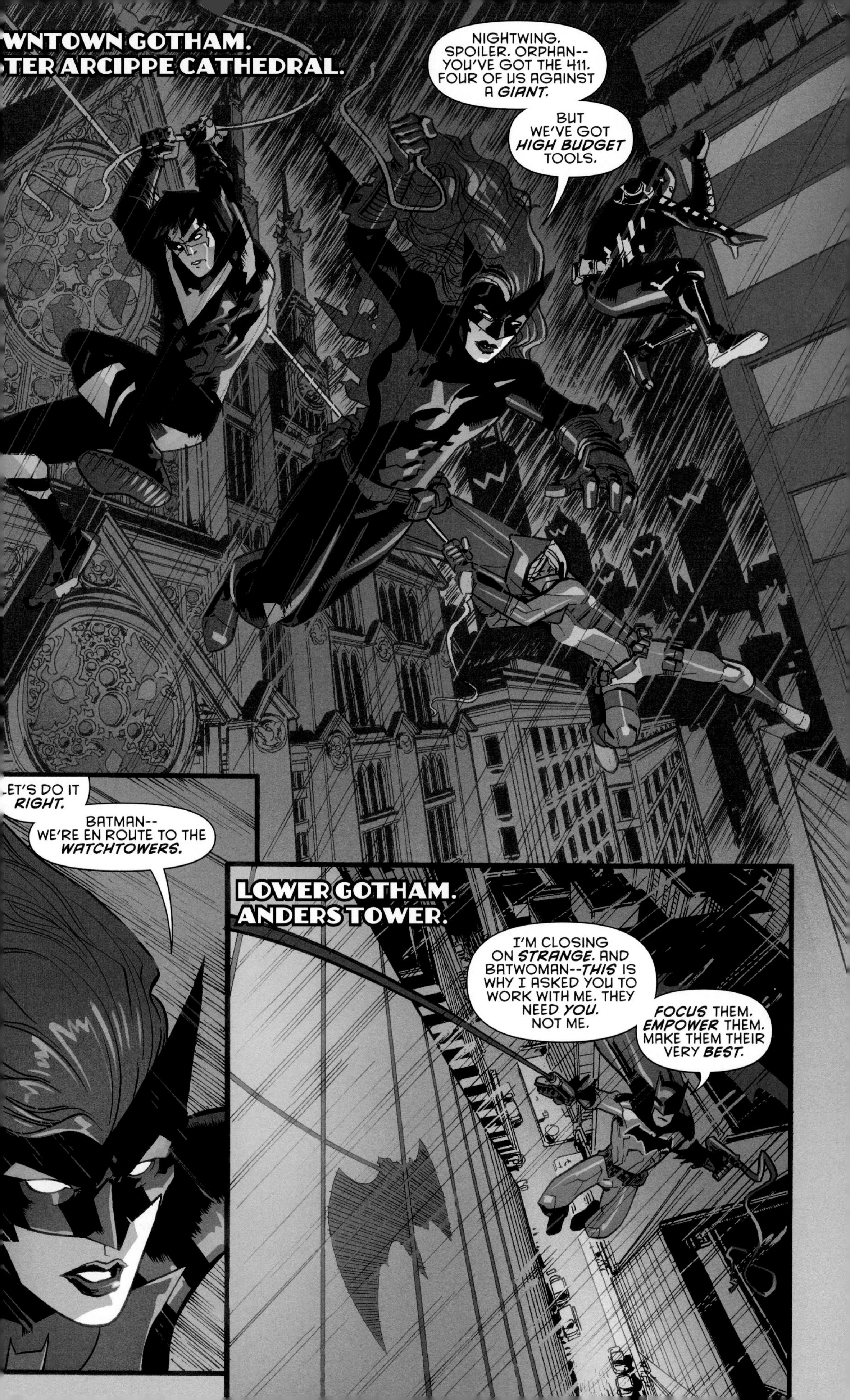
WNTOWN GOTHAM.
TER ARCIPPE CATHEDRAL.
NIGHTWING. SPOILER. ORPHAN-- YOU'VE GOT THE 411. FOUR OF US AGAINST A GIANT.
BUT WE'VE GOT HIGH BUDGET TOOLS.
ET'S DO IT RIGHT.
BATMAN-- WE'RE EN ROUTE TO THE WATCHTOWERS.
LOWER GOTHAM. ANDERS TOWER.
I'M CLOSING ON STRANGE. AND BATWOMAN--THIS IS WHY I ASKED YOU TO WORK WITH ME. THEY NEED YOU. NOT ME.
FOCUS THEM. EMPOWER THEM. MAKE THEM THEIR VERY BEST.

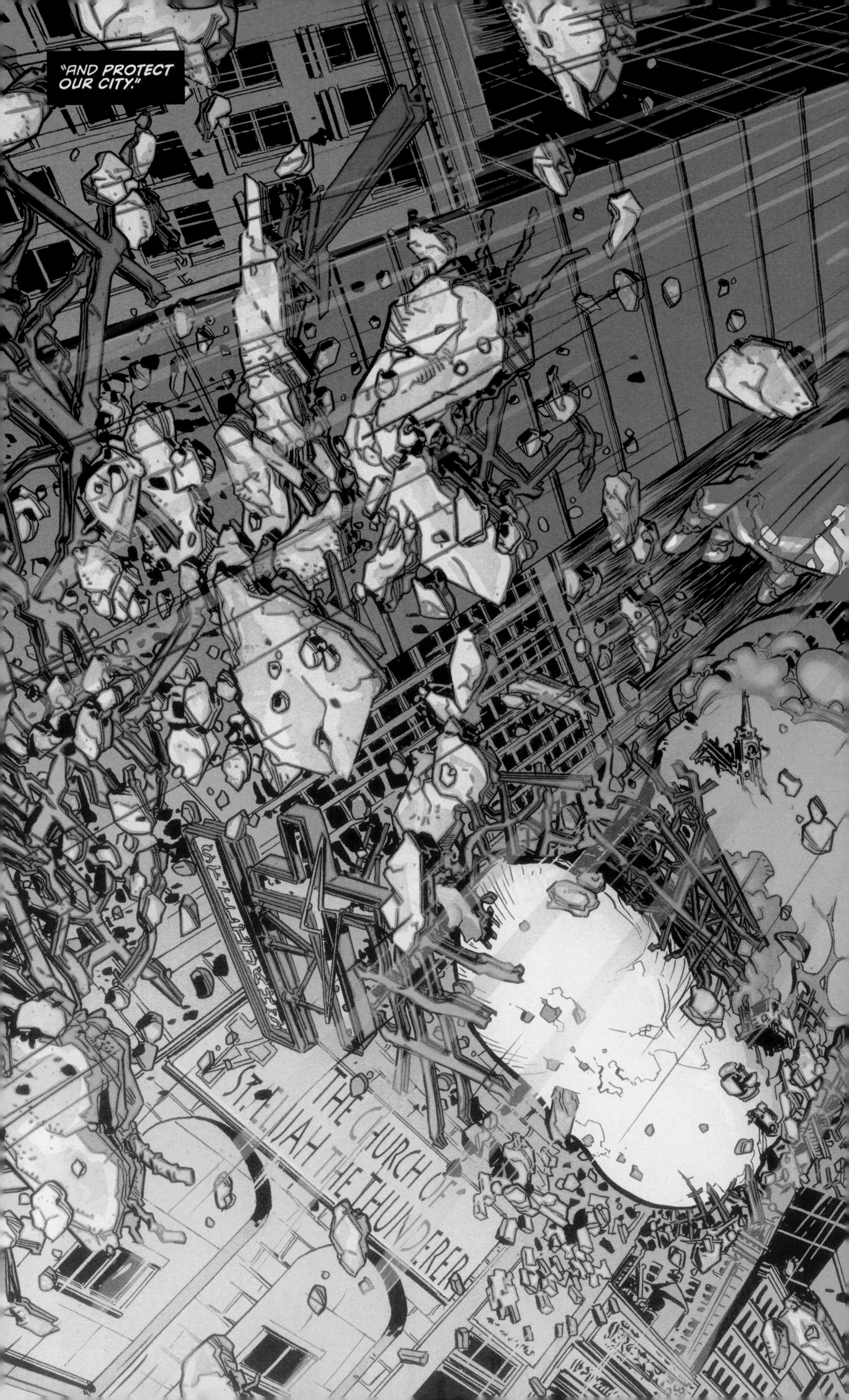
"AND PROTECT OUR CITY."
THE CHURCH OF
ST. ELIJAH THE THUNDERER

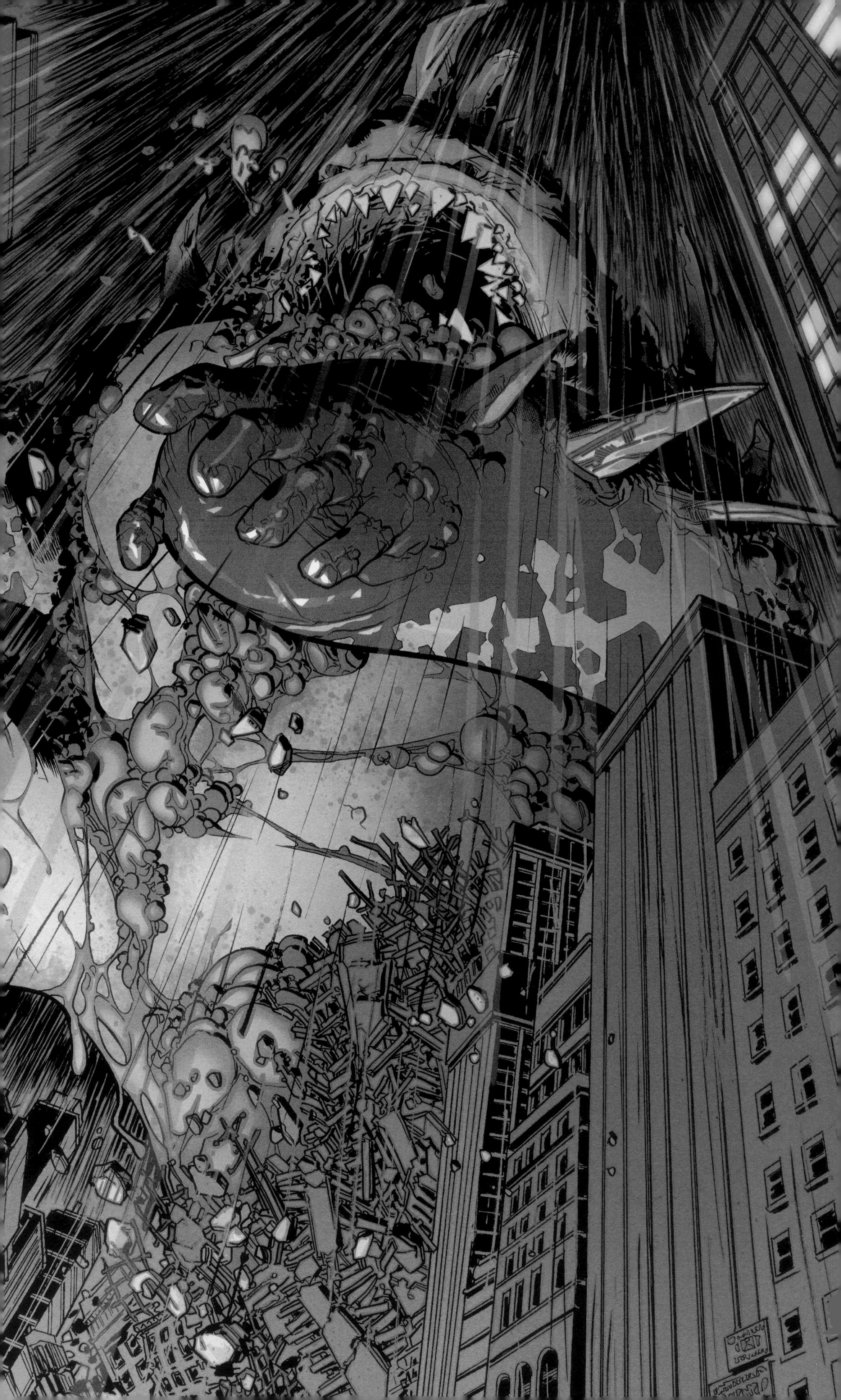

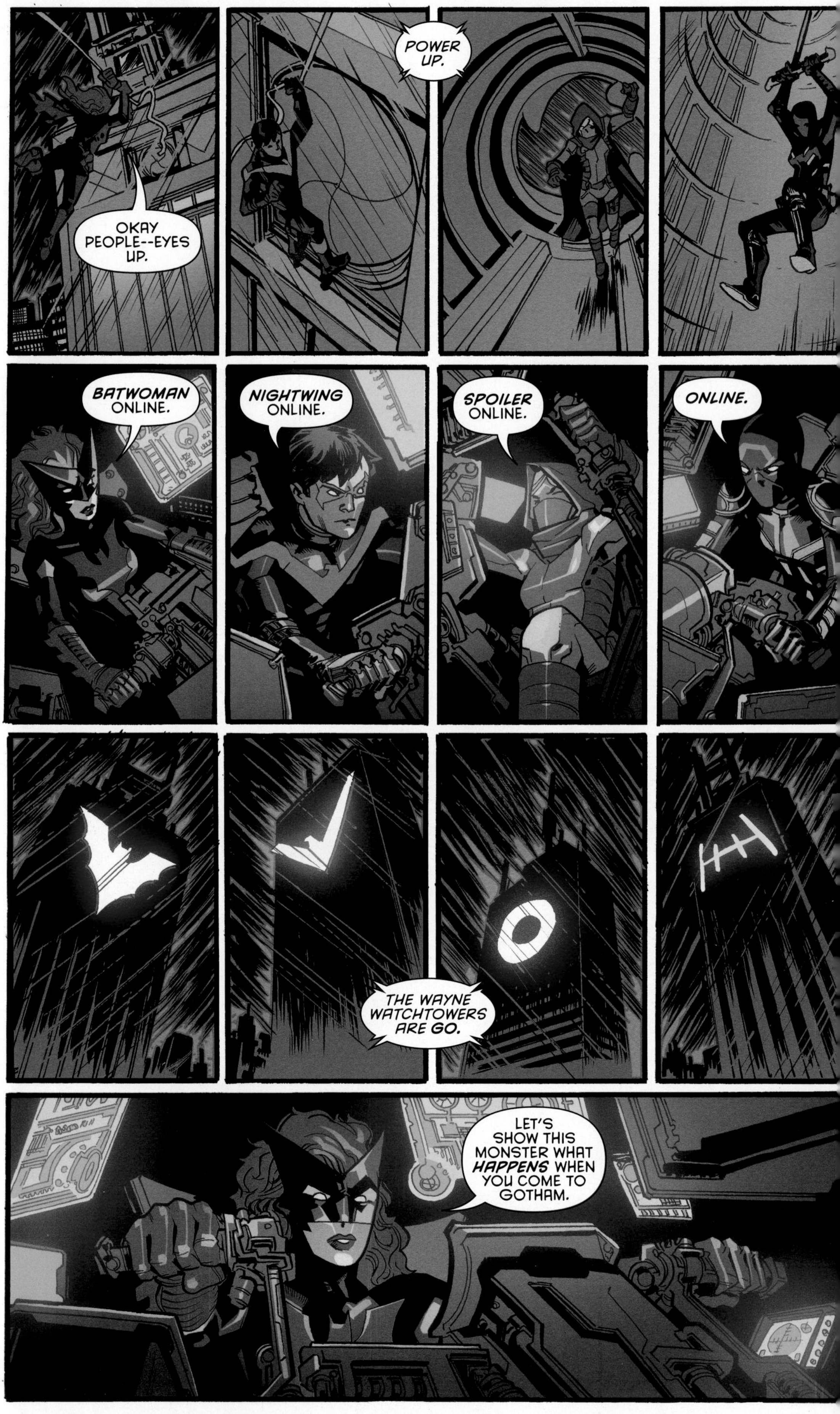
OKAY PEOPLE--EYES UP.
POWER UP.
BATWOMAN ONLINE.
NIGHTWING ONLINE.
SPOILER ONLINE.
ONLINE.
THE WAYNE WATCHTOWERS ARE GO.
LET'S SHOW THIS MONSTER WHAT HAPPENS WHEN YOU COME TO GOTHAM.

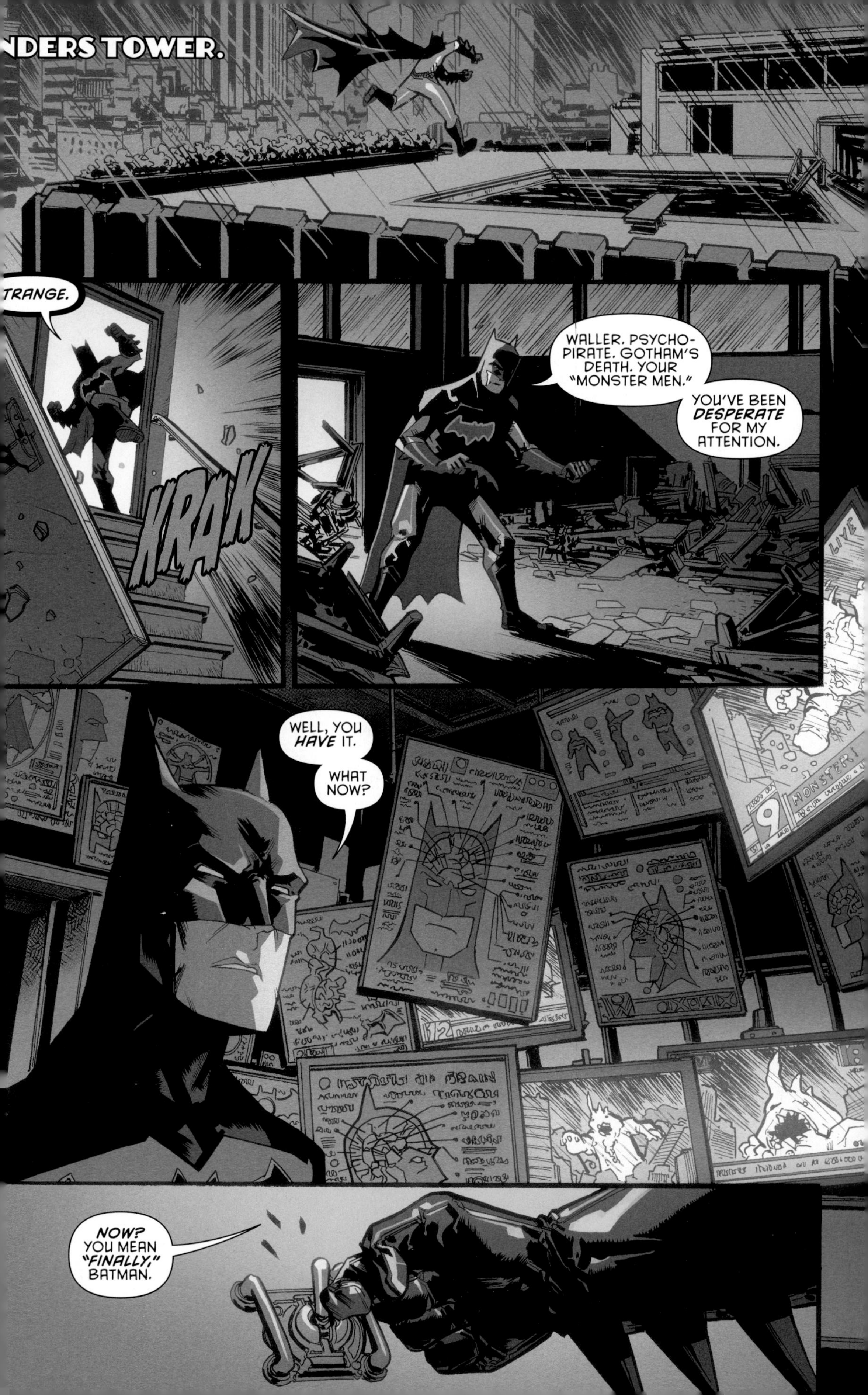

NDERS TOWER.
TRANGE.
KRAK
WALLER. PSYCHO-PIRATE. GOTHAM'S DEATH. YOUR "MONSTER MEN."
YOU'VE BEEN *DESPERATE* FOR MY ATTENTION.
WELL, YOU *HAVE* IT.
WHAT NOW?
NOW? YOU MEAN *"FINALLY,"* BATMAN.

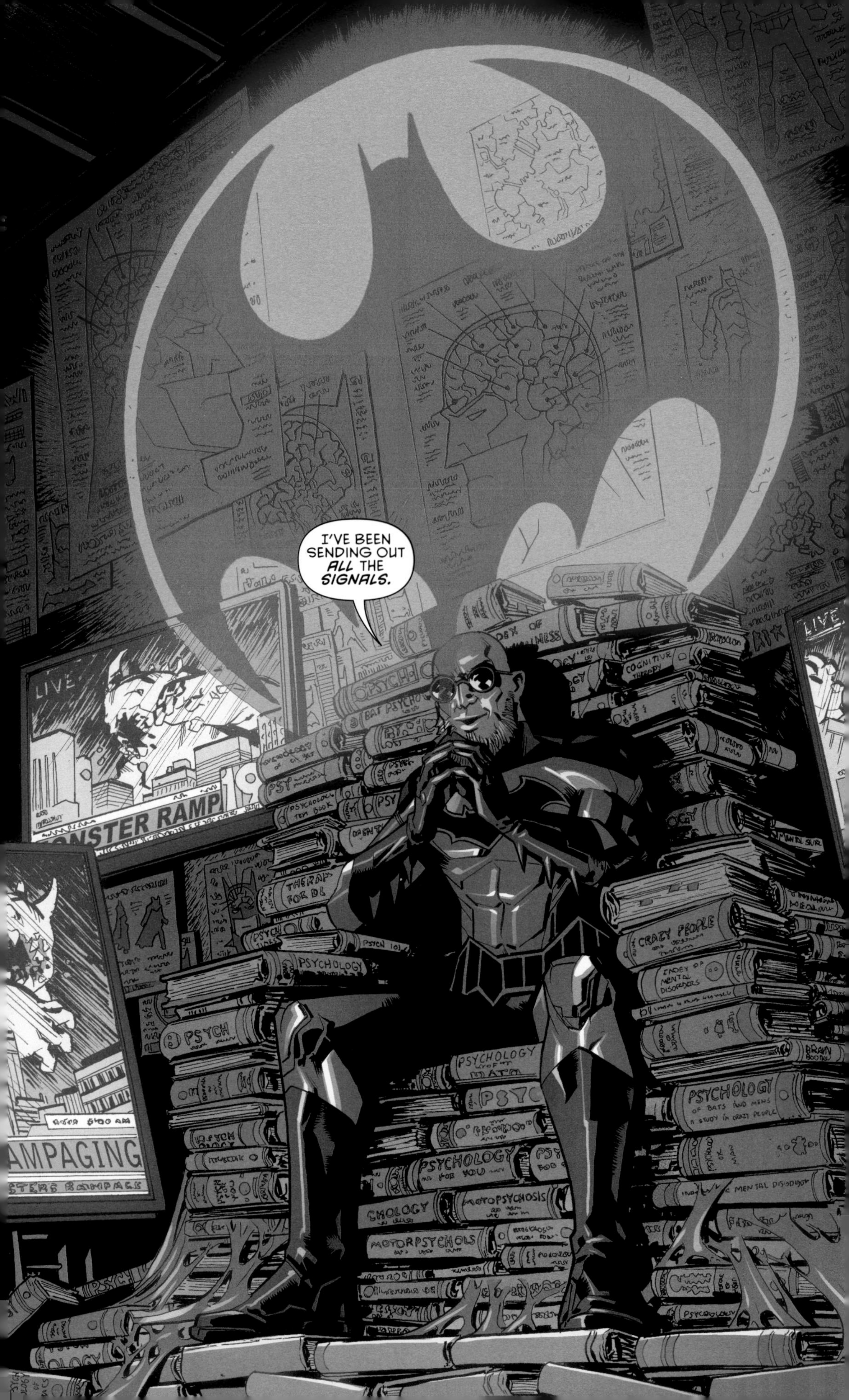
I'VE BEEN SENDING OUT ALL THE SIGNALS.
COGNITIVE THERAPY
CRAZY PEOPLE
INDEX OF MENTAL DISORDERS
PSYCHOLOGY OF BATS AND MENS A STUDY IN CRAZY PEOPLE
PSYCHOLOGY FOR YOU
MOTOPSYCHOSIS
PSYCH 101
PSYCHOLOGY TEXT BOOK
BAT PSYCHO
LIVE
ONSTER RAMP
AMPAGING

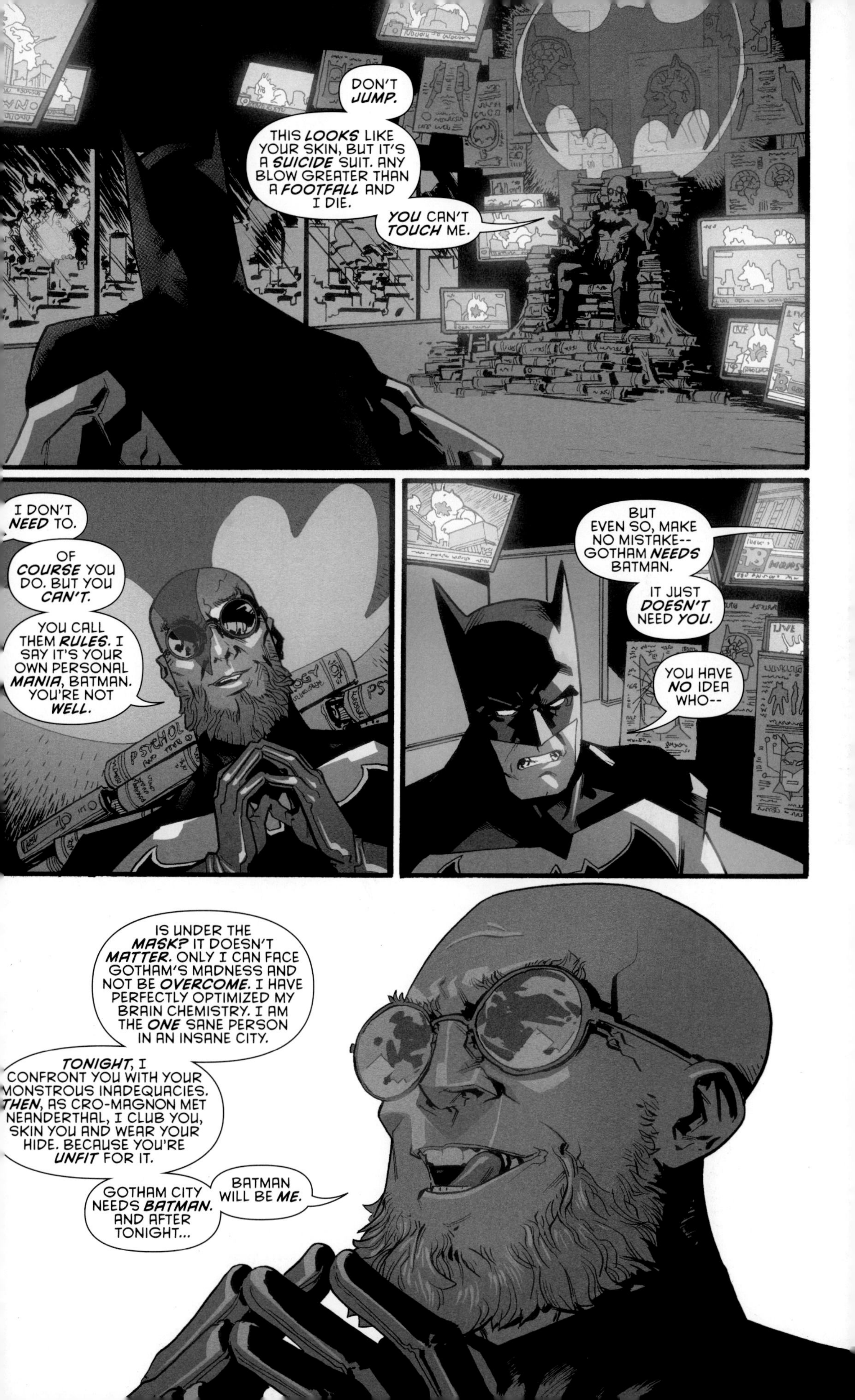
DON'T JUMP.
THIS LOOKS LIKE YOUR SKIN, BUT IT'S A SUICIDE SUIT. ANY BLOW GREATER THAN A FOOTFALL AND I DIE.
YOU CAN'T TOUCH ME.
I DON'T NEED TO.
OF COURSE YOU DO. BUT YOU CAN'T.
YOU CALL THEM RULES. I SAY IT'S YOUR OWN PERSONAL MANIA, BATMAN. YOU'RE NOT WELL.
BUT EVEN SO, MAKE NO MISTAKE-- GOTHAM NEEDS BATMAN.
IT JUST DOESN'T NEED YOU.
YOU HAVE NO IDEA WHO--
IS UNDER THE MASK? IT DOESN'T MATTER. ONLY I CAN FACE GOTHAM'S MADNESS AND NOT BE OVERCOME. I HAVE PERFECTLY OPTIMIZED MY BRAIN CHEMISTRY. I AM THE ONE SANE PERSON IN AN INSANE CITY.
TONIGHT, I CONFRONT YOU WITH YOUR MONSTROUS INADEQUACIES. THEN, AS CRO-MAGNON MET NEANDERTHAL, I CLUB YOU, SKIN YOU AND WEAR YOUR HIDE. BECAUSE YOU'RE UNFIT FOR IT.
GOTHAM CITY NEEDS BATMAN. AND AFTER TONIGHT...
BATMAN WILL BE ME.

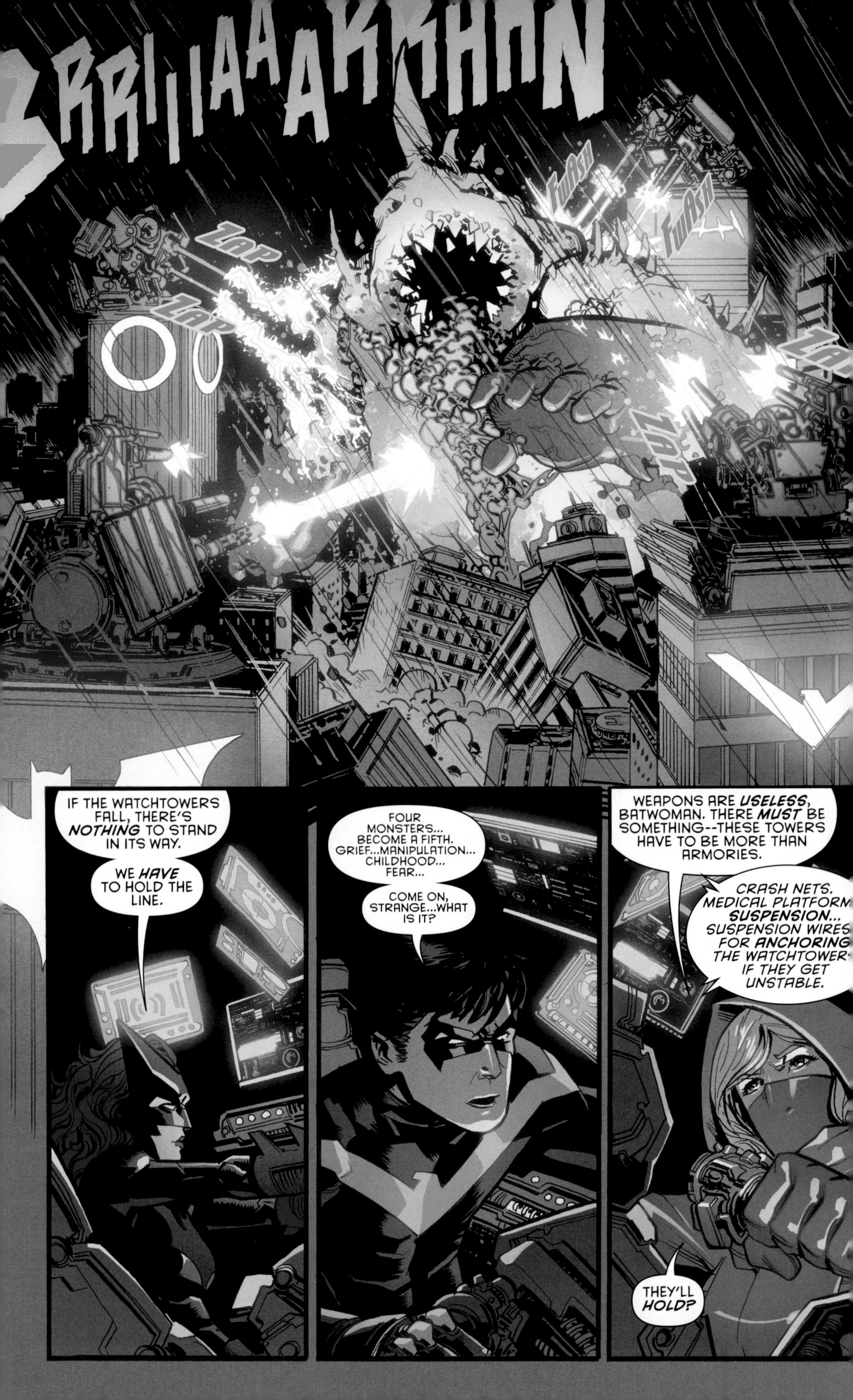
BRRIIIAAAKKHHN
ZAP
ZAP
FWASH
FWASH
ZAP
ZAP
IF THE WATCHTOWERS FALL, THERE'S *NOTHING* TO STAND IN ITS WAY.
WE *HAVE* TO HOLD THE LINE.
FOUR MONSTERS... BECOME A FIFTH. GRIEF...MANIPULATION... CHILDHOOD... FEAR...
COME ON, STRANGE...WHAT IS IT?
WEAPONS ARE *USELESS*, BATWOMAN. THERE *MUST* BE SOMETHING--THESE TOWERS HAVE TO BE MORE THAN ARMORIES.
CRASH NETS. MEDICAL PLATFORM *SUSPENSION*... SUSPENSION WIRES FOR *ANCHORING* THE WATCHTOWER IF THEY GET UNSTABLE.
THEY'LL *HOLD?*

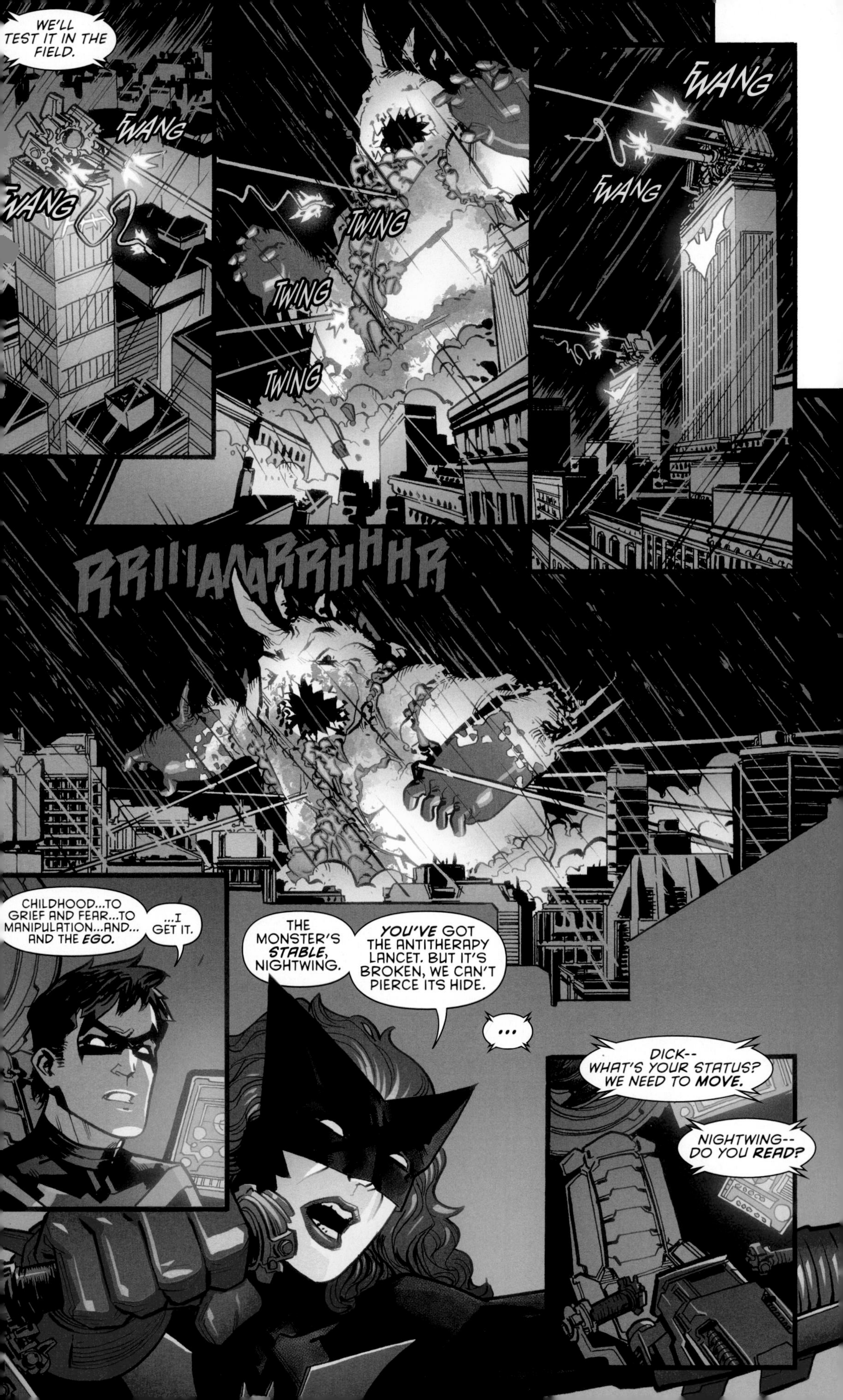

WE'LL TEST IT IN THE FIELD.
FWANG
FWANG
TWING
TWING
TWING
FWANG
FWANG
RRIIIAAARRRHHHHR
CHILDHOOD...TO GRIEF AND FEAR...TO MANIPULATION...AND... AND THE *EGO.*
...I GET IT.
THE MONSTER'S *STABLE,* NIGHTWING.
YOU'VE GOT THE ANTITHERAPY LANCET. BUT IT'S BROKEN, WE CAN'T PIERCE ITS HIDE.
...
DICK-- WHAT'S YOUR STATUS? WE NEED TO *MOVE.*
NIGHTWING-- DO YOU *READ?*

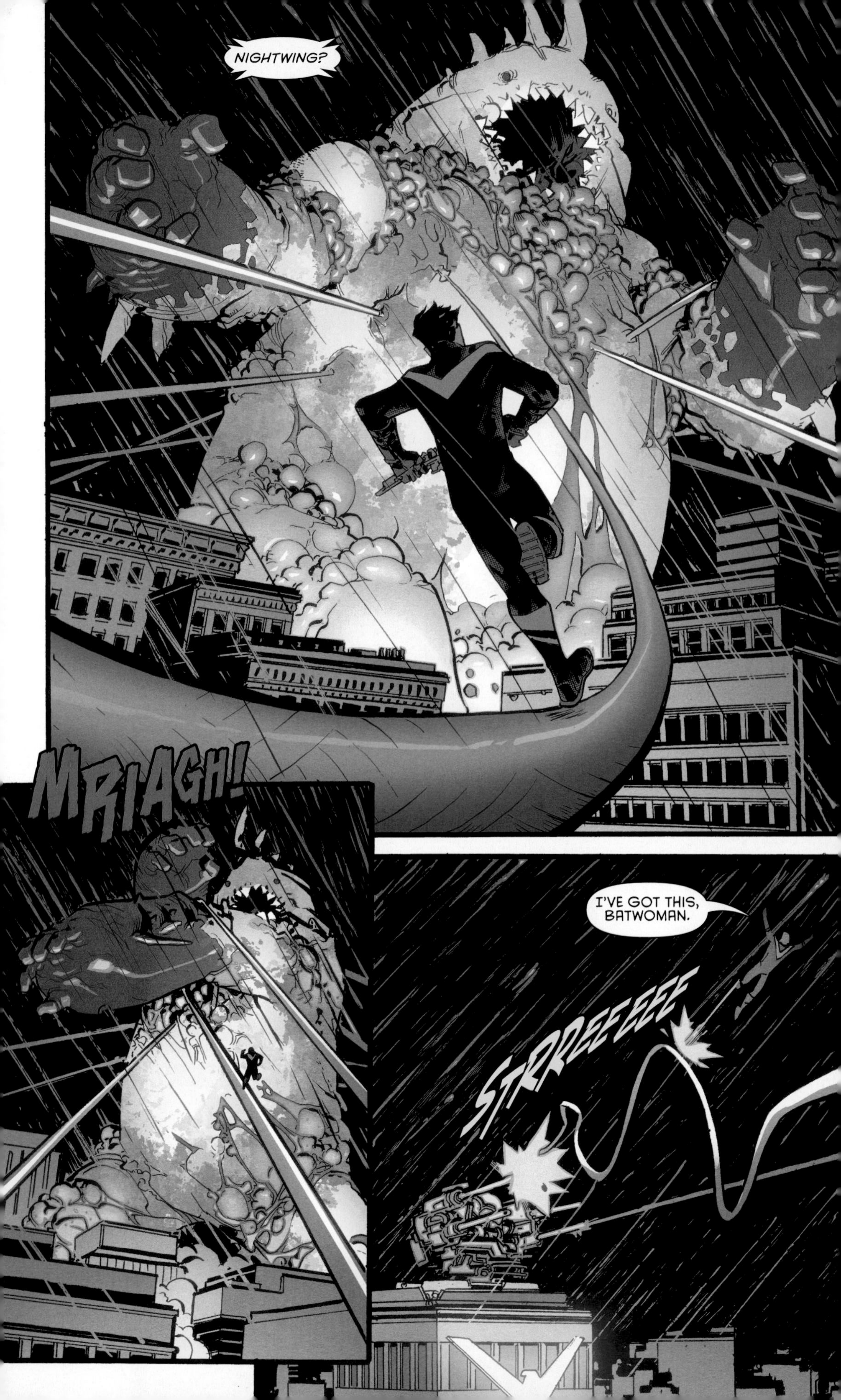
NIGHTWING?
MRIAGH!
I'VE GOT THIS, BATWOMAN.
STRREEEEEEE

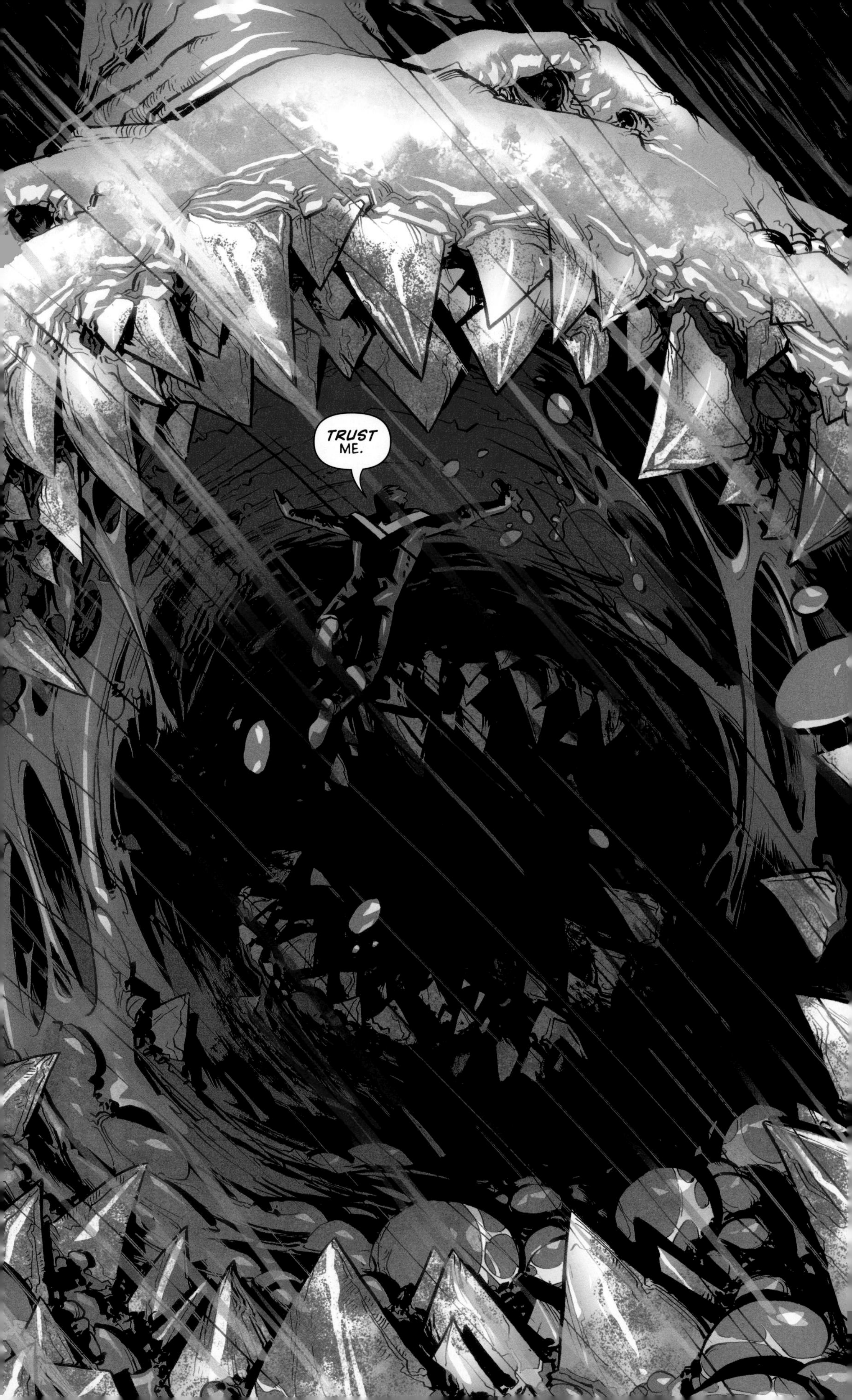
TRUST ME.

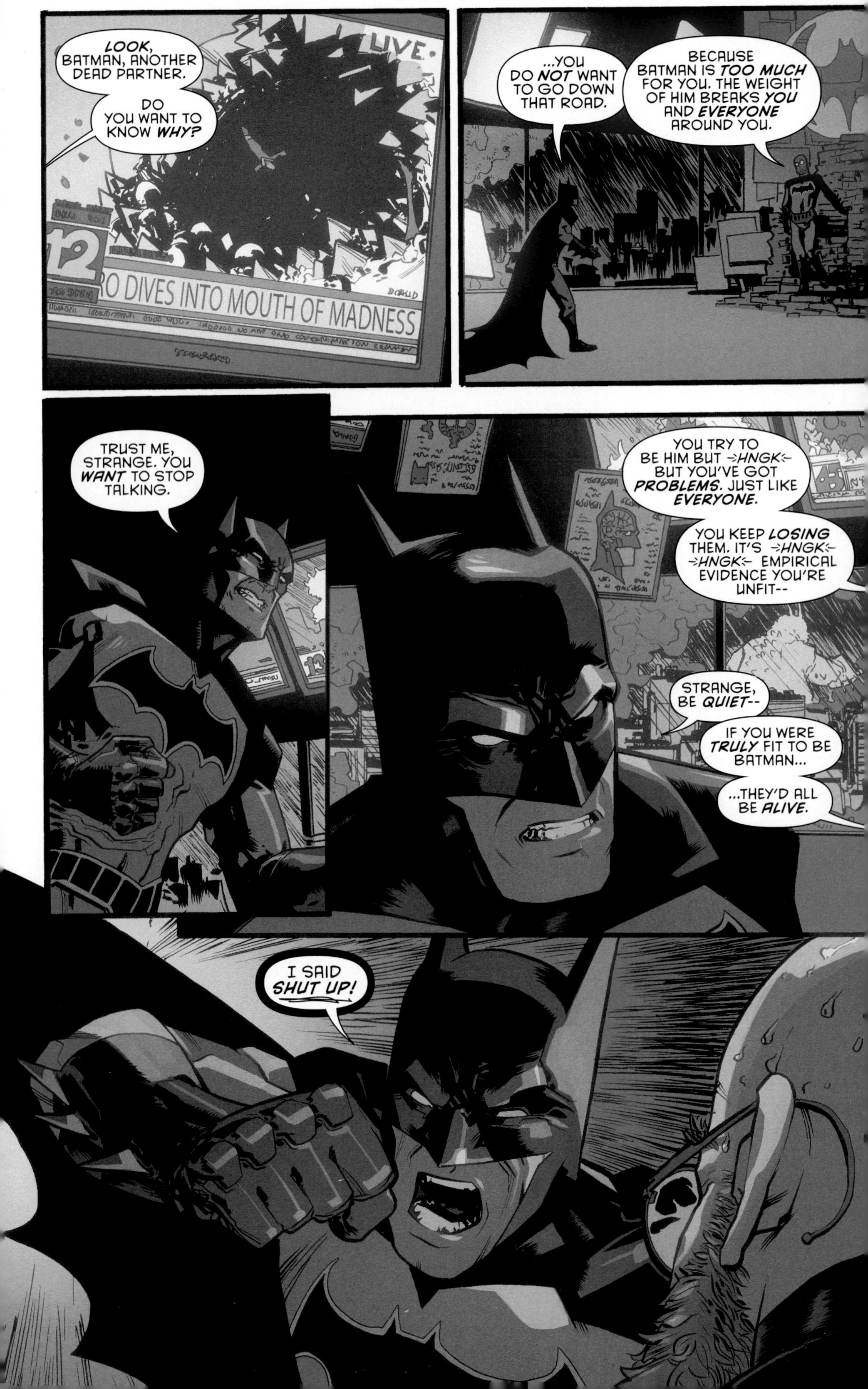
LOOK, BATMAN, ANOTHER DEAD PARTNER.
DO YOU WANT TO KNOW WHY?
LIVE
12
RO DIVES INTO MOUTH OF MADNESS
...YOU DO NOT WANT TO GO DOWN THAT ROAD.
BECAUSE BATMAN IS TOO MUCH FOR YOU. THE WEIGHT OF HIM BREAKS YOU AND EVERYONE AROUND YOU.
TRUST ME, STRANGE. YOU WANT TO STOP TALKING.
YOU TRY TO BE HIM BUT ⇒HNGK⇐ BUT YOU'VE GOT PROBLEMS. JUST LIKE EVERYONE.
YOU KEEP LOSING THEM. IT'S ⇒HNGK⇐ ⇒HNGK⇐ EMPIRICAL EVIDENCE YOU'RE UNFIT--
STRANGE, BE QUIET--
IF YOU WERE TRULY FIT TO BE BATMAN...
...THEY'D ALL BE ALIVE.
I SAID SHUT UP!

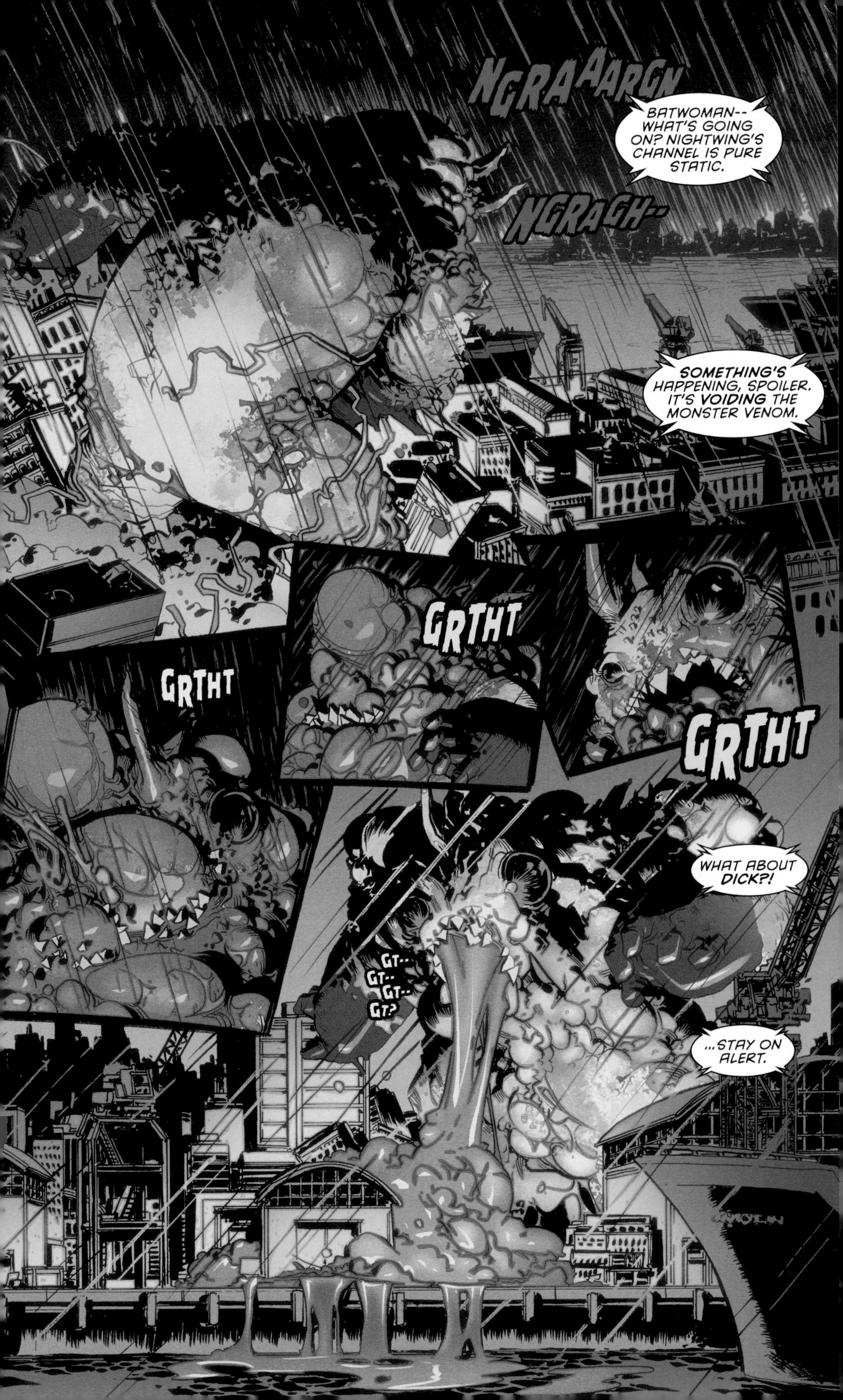

NGRAAARGN
BATWOMAN-- WHAT'S GOING ON? NIGHTWING'S CHANNEL IS PURE STATIC.
NGRAGH--
SOMETHING'S HAPPENING, SPOILER. IT'S VOIDING THE MONSTER VENOM.
GRTHT
GRTHT
GRTHT
WHAT ABOUT DICK?!
GT-- GT-- GT-- GT?
...STAY ON ALERT.

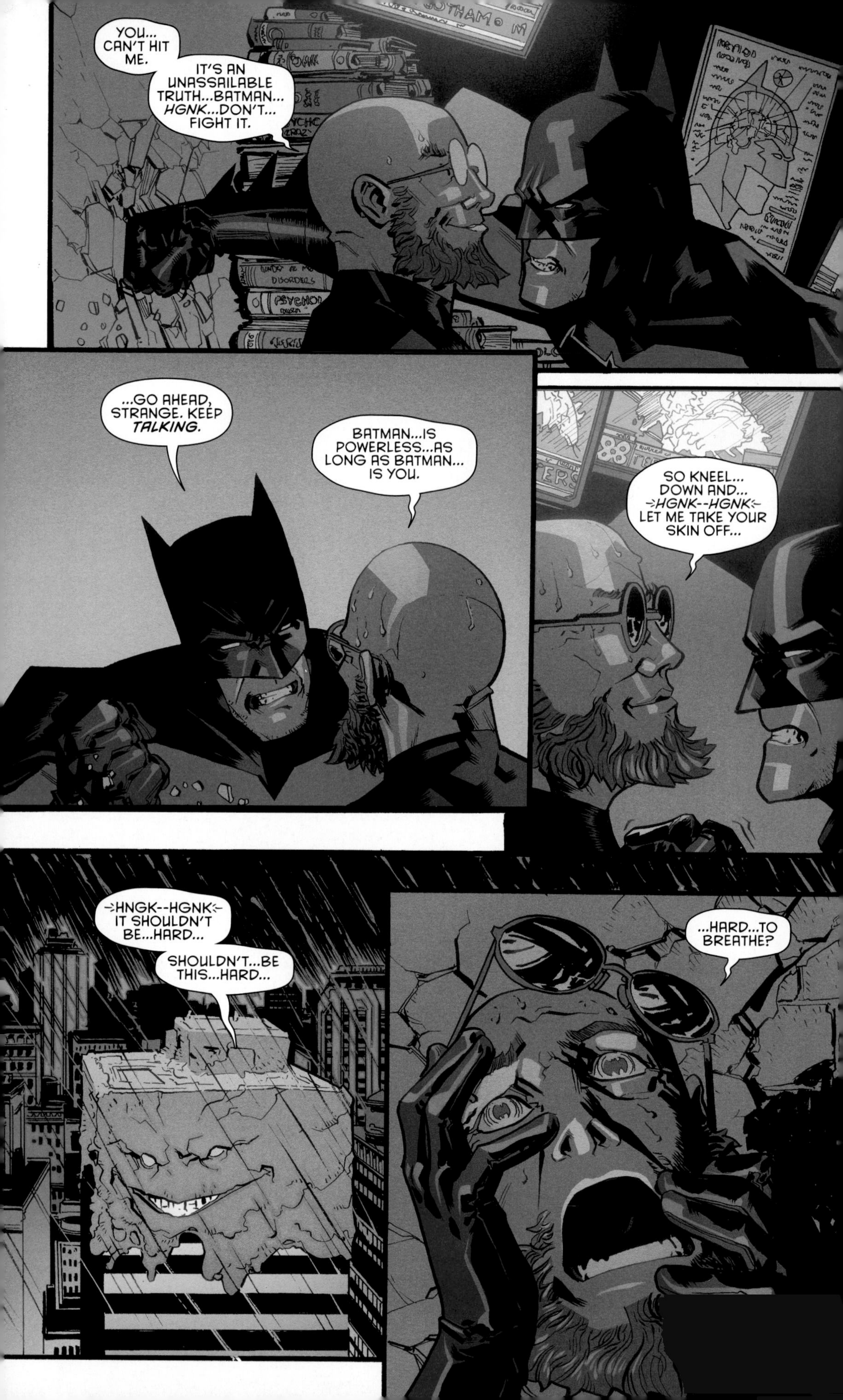
YOU... CAN'T HIT ME.
IT'S AN UNASSAILABLE TRUTH...BATMAN... HGNK...DON'T... FIGHT IT.
...GO AHEAD, STRANGE. KEEP TALKING.
BATMAN...IS POWERLESS...AS LONG AS BATMAN... IS YOU.
SO KNEEL... DOWN AND... HGNK--HGNK LET ME TAKE YOUR SKIN OFF...
HNGK--HGNK IT SHOULDN'T BE...HARD...
SHOULDN'T...BE THIS...HARD...
...HARD...TO BREATHE?

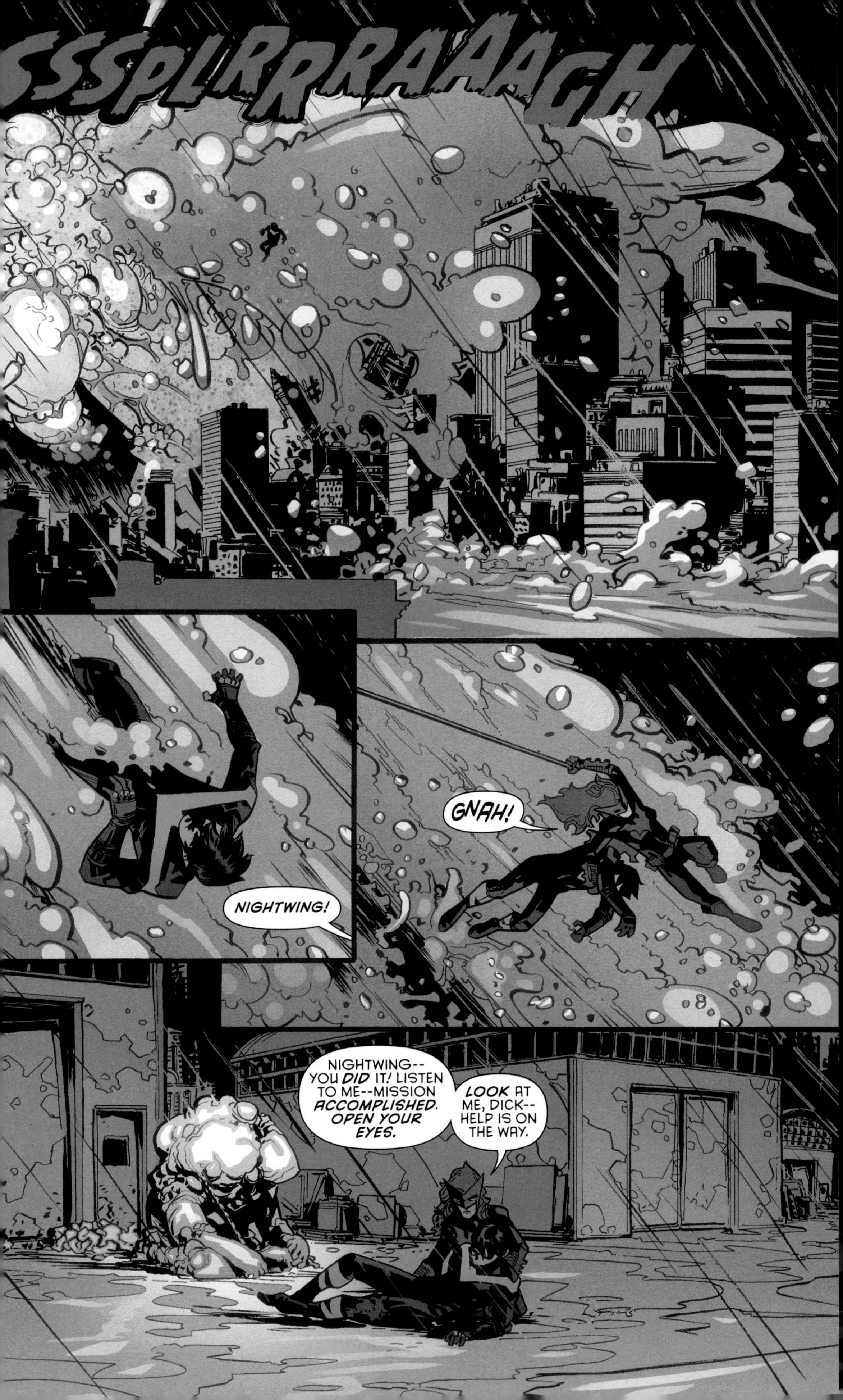
SSSPLIRRRAAAACH
NIGHTWING!
GNAH!
NIGHTWING-- YOU DID IT! LISTEN TO ME--MISSION ACCOMPLISHED. OPEN YOUR EYES.
LOOK AT ME, DICK-- HELP IS ON THE WAY.

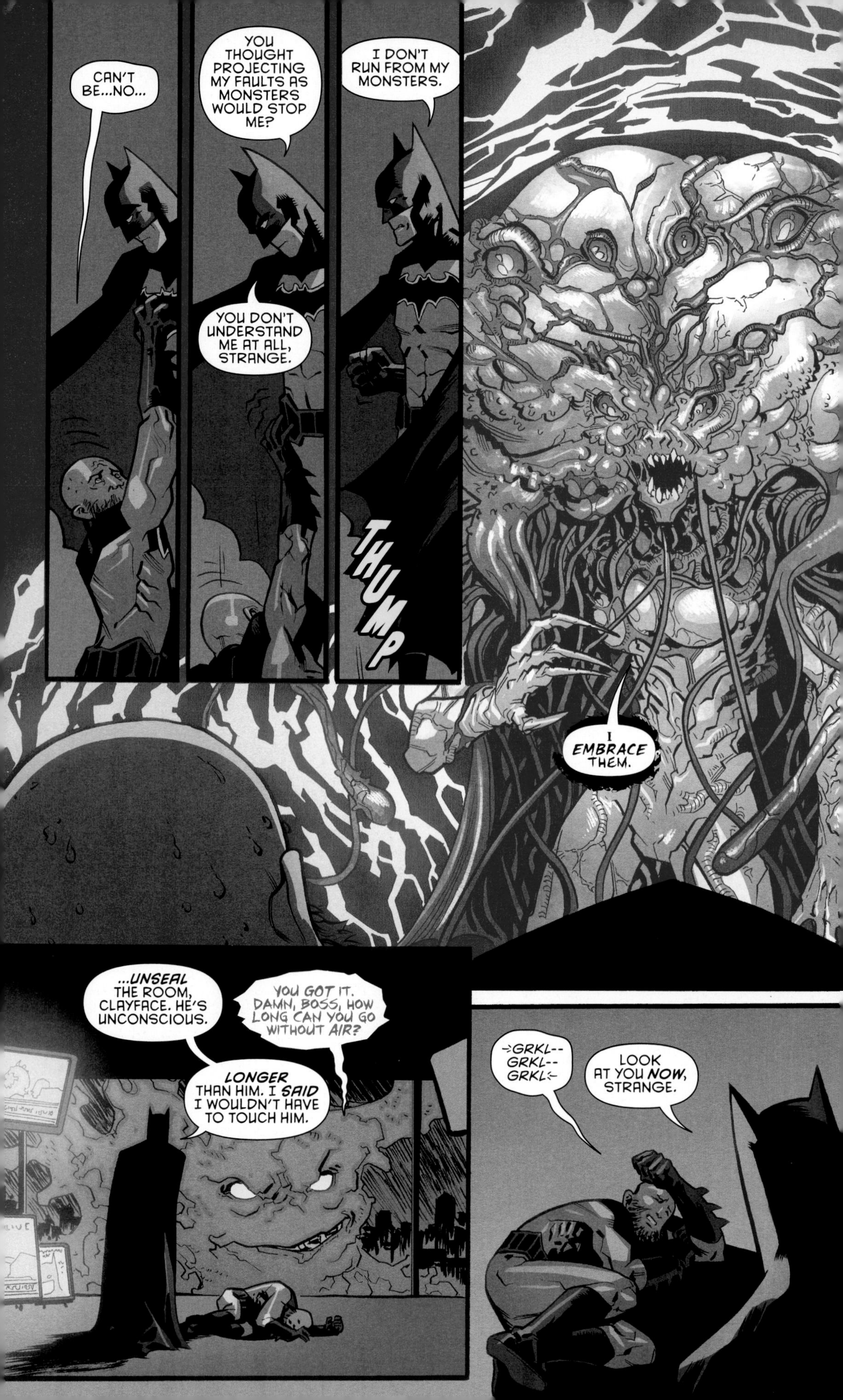
CAN'T BE...NO...
YOU THOUGHT PROJECTING MY FAULTS AS MONSTERS WOULD STOP ME?
YOU DON'T UNDERSTAND ME AT ALL, STRANGE.
I DON'T RUN FROM MY MONSTERS.
THUMP
I EMBRACE THEM.
...UNSEAL THE ROOM, CLAYFACE. HE'S UNCONSCIOUS.
YOU GOT IT. DAMN, BOSS, HOW LONG CAN YOU GO WITHOUT AIR?
LONGER THAN HIM. I SAID I WOULDN'T HAVE TO TOUCH HIM.
-GRKL-- GRKL-- GRKL-
LOOK AT YOU NOW, STRANGE.

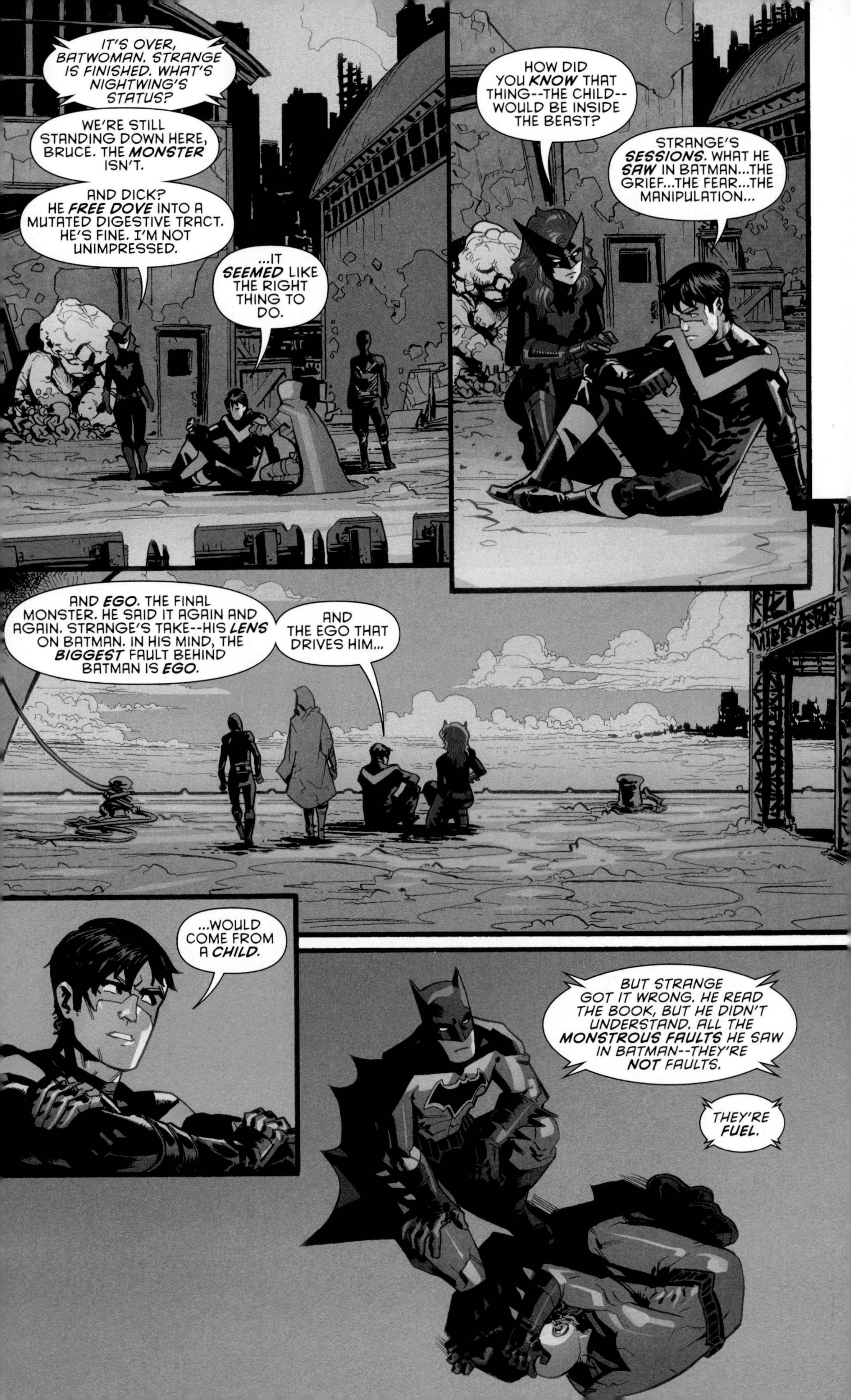
IT'S OVER, BATWOMAN. STRANGE IS FINISHED. WHAT'S NIGHTWING'S STATUS?
WE'RE STILL STANDING DOWN HERE, BRUCE. THE MONSTER ISN'T.
AND DICK? HE FREE DOVE INTO A MUTATED DIGESTIVE TRACT. HE'S FINE. I'M NOT UNIMPRESSED.
...IT SEEMED LIKE THE RIGHT THING TO DO.
HOW DID YOU KNOW THAT THING--THE CHILD--WOULD BE INSIDE THE BEAST?
STRANGE'S SESSIONS. WHAT HE SAW IN BATMAN...THE GRIEF...THE FEAR...THE MANIPULATION...
AND EGO. THE FINAL MONSTER. HE SAID IT AGAIN AND AGAIN. STRANGE'S TAKE--HIS LENS ON BATMAN. IN HIS MIND, THE BIGGEST FAULT BEHIND BATMAN IS EGO.
AND THE EGO THAT DRIVES HIM...
...WOULD COME FROM A CHILD.
BUT STRANGE GOT IT WRONG. HE READ THE BOOK, BUT HE DIDN'T UNDERSTAND. ALL THE MONSTROUS FAULTS HE SAW IN BATMAN--THEY'RE NOT FAULTS.
THEY'RE FUEL.

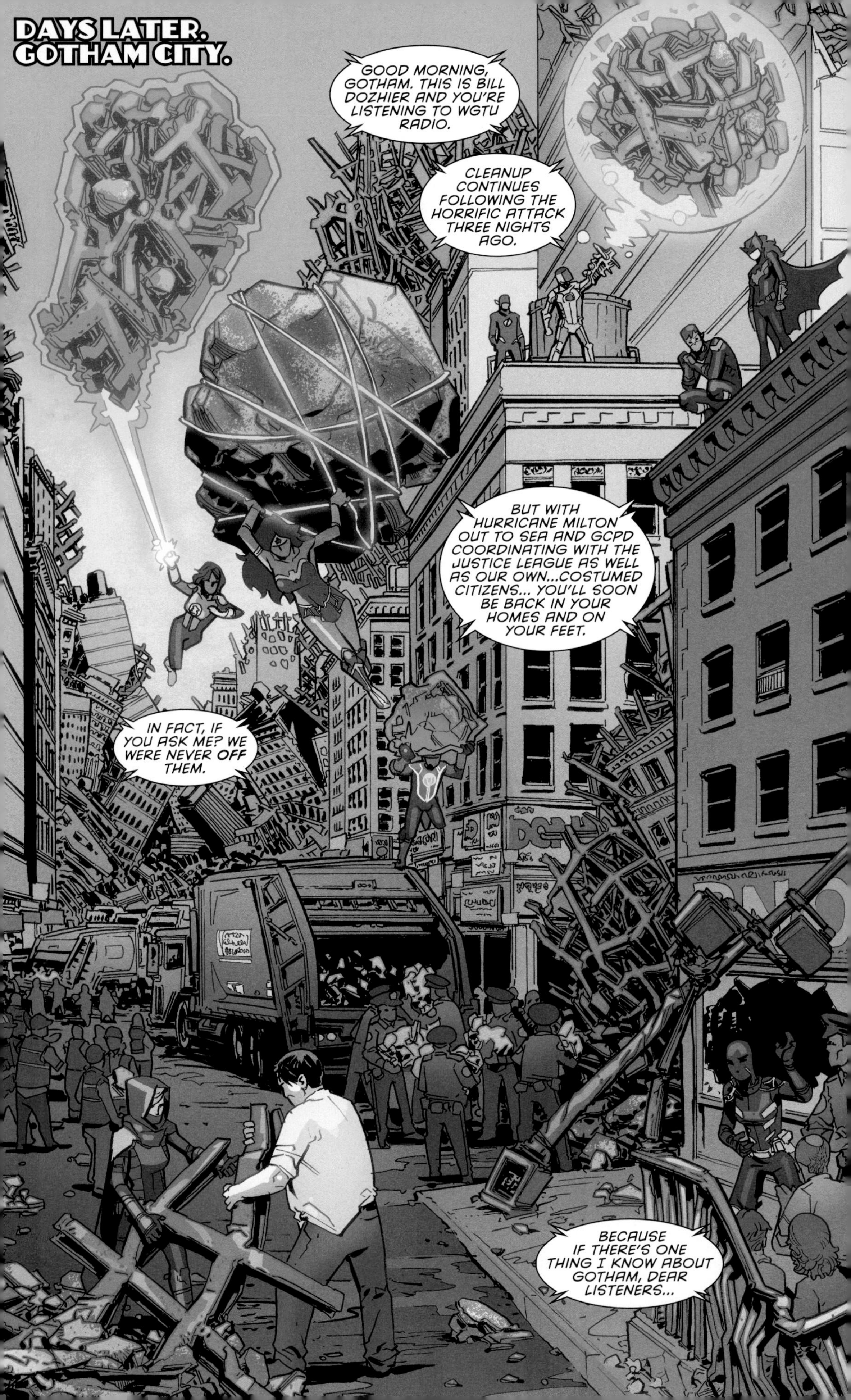
DAYS LATER. GOTHAM CITY.
GOOD MORNING, GOTHAM. THIS IS BILL DOZHIER AND YOU'RE LISTENING TO WGTU RADIO.
CLEANUP CONTINUES FOLLOWING THE HORRIFIC ATTACK THREE NIGHTS AGO.
BUT WITH HURRICANE MILTON OUT TO SEA AND GCPD COORDINATING WITH THE JUSTICE LEAGUE AS WELL AS OUR OWN...COSTUMED CITIZENS... YOU'LL SOON BE BACK IN YOUR HOMES AND ON YOUR FEET.
IN FACT, IF YOU ASK ME? WE WERE NEVER **OFF** THEM.
BECAUSE IF THERE'S ONE THING I KNOW ABOUT GOTHAM, DEAR LISTENERS...

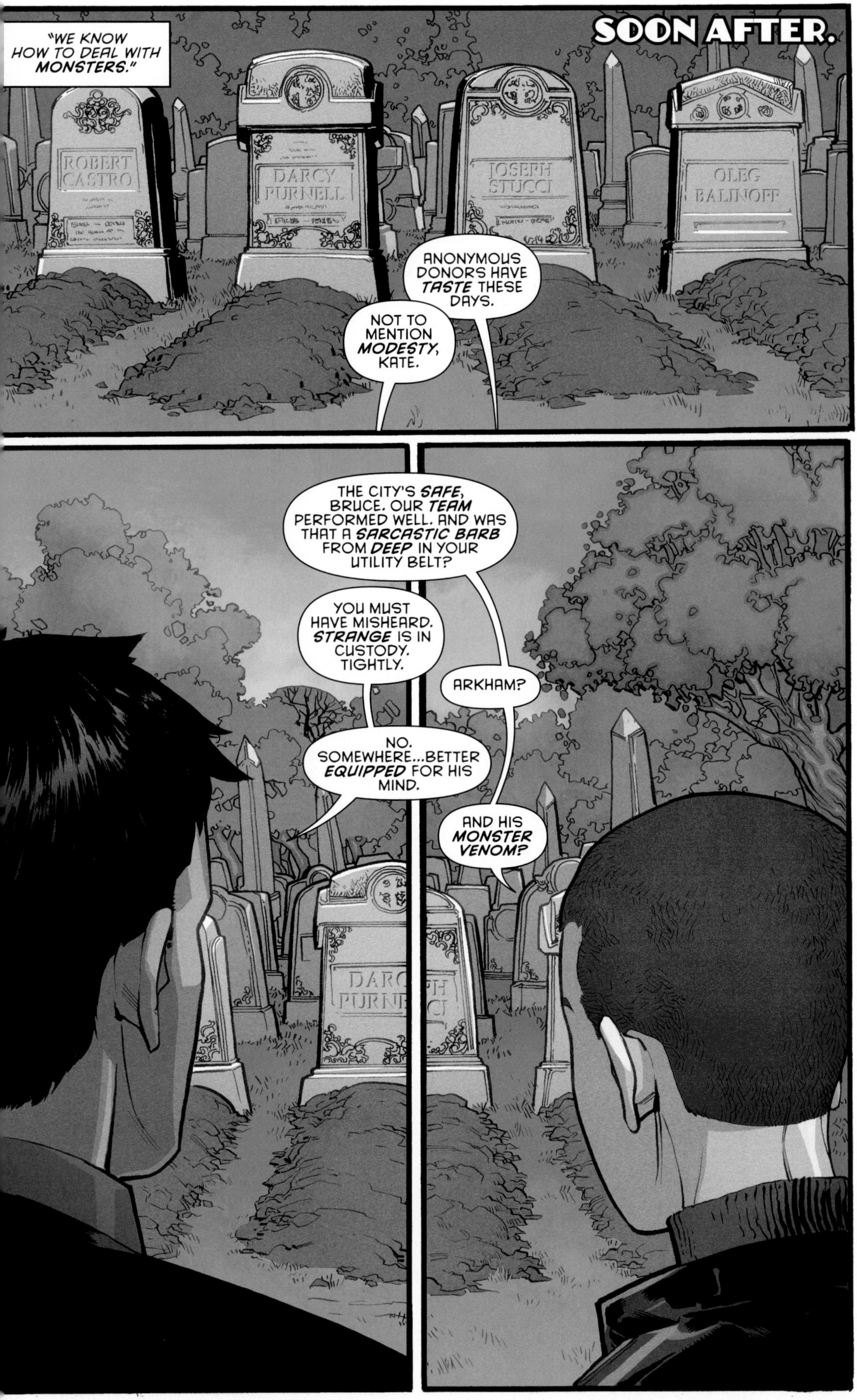
"WE KNOW HOW TO DEAL WITH MONSTERS."
SOON AFTER.
ROBERT CASTRO
DARCY PURNELL
JOSEPH STUCCI
OLEG BALINOFF
ANONYMOUS DONORS HAVE TASTE THESE DAYS.
NOT TO MENTION MODESTY, KATE.
THE CITY'S SAFE, BRUCE. OUR TEAM PERFORMED WELL. AND WAS THAT A SARCASTIC BARB FROM DEEP IN YOUR UTILITY BELT?
YOU MUST HAVE MISHEARD. STRANGE IS IN CUSTODY. TIGHTLY.
ARKHAM?
NO. SOMEWHERE...BETTER EQUIPPED FOR HIS MIND.
AND HIS MONSTER VENOM?

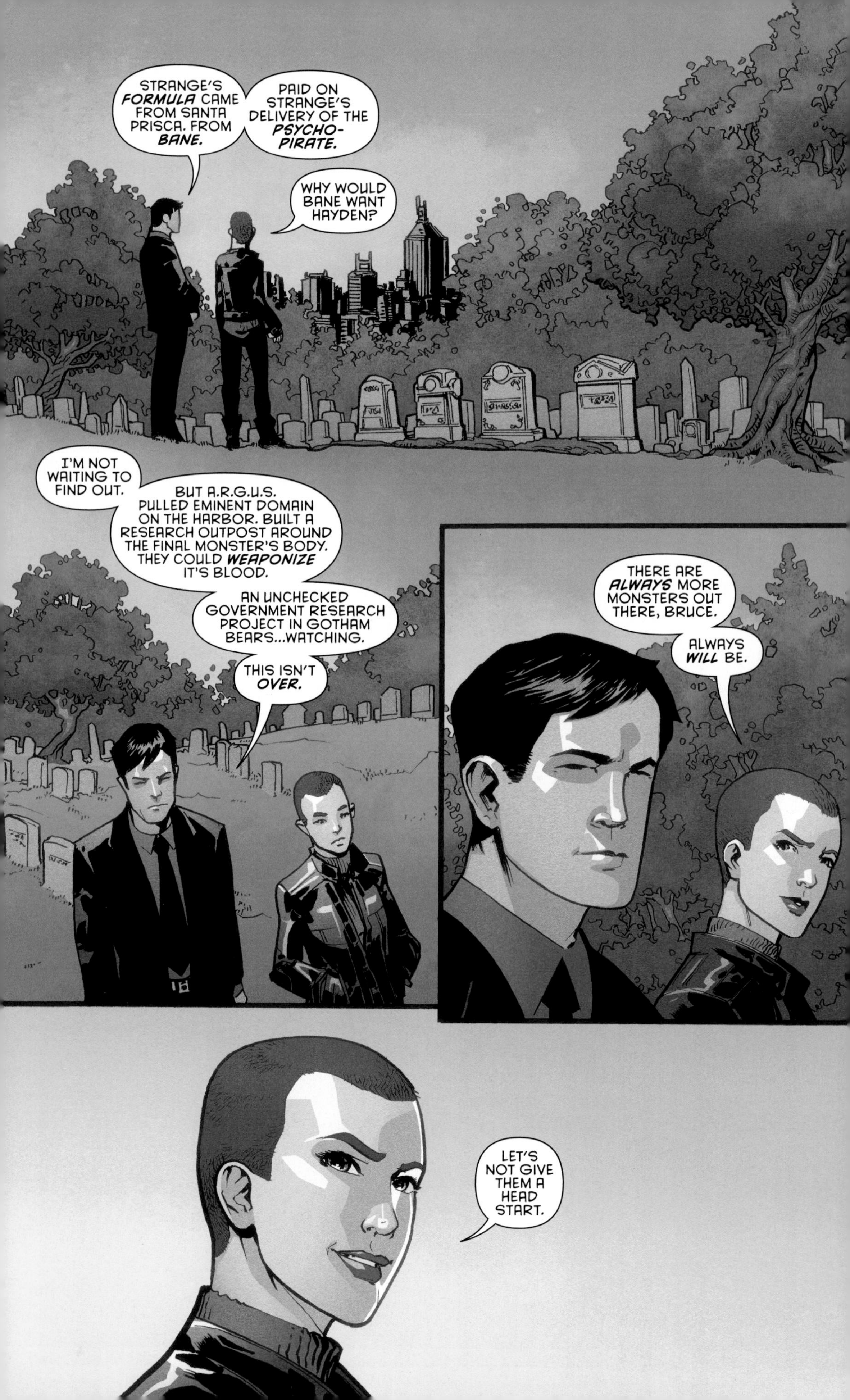
STRANGE'S FORMULA CAME FROM SANTA PRISCA. FROM BANE.
PAID ON STRANGE'S DELIVERY OF THE PSYCHO-PIRATE.
WHY WOULD BANE WANT HAYDEN?
I'M NOT WAITING TO FIND OUT.
BUT A.R.G.U.S. PULLED EMINENT DOMAIN ON THE HARBOR. BUILT A RESEARCH OUTPOST AROUND THE FINAL MONSTER'S BODY. THEY COULD WEAPONIZE IT'S BLOOD.
AN UNCHECKED GOVERNMENT RESEARCH PROJECT IN GOTHAM BEARS...WATCHING.
THIS ISN'T OVER.
THERE ARE ALWAYS MORE MONSTERS OUT THERE, BRUCE.
ALWAYS WILL BE.
LET'S NOT GIVE THEM A HEAD START.

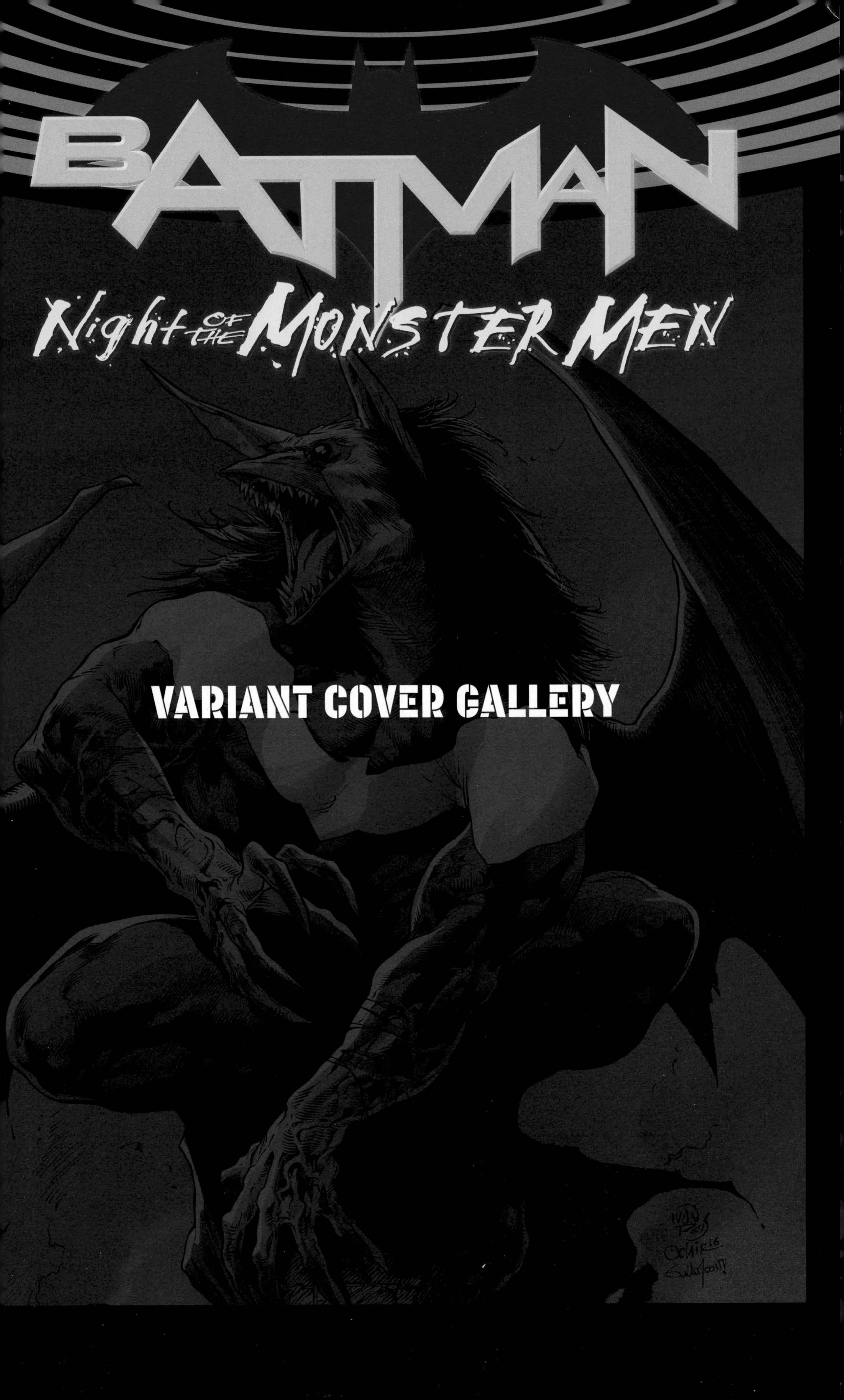
BATMAN
Night OF THE MONSTER MEN

VARIANT COVER GALLERY

BATMAN #7 variant cover by TIM SALE & BRENNAN WAGNER

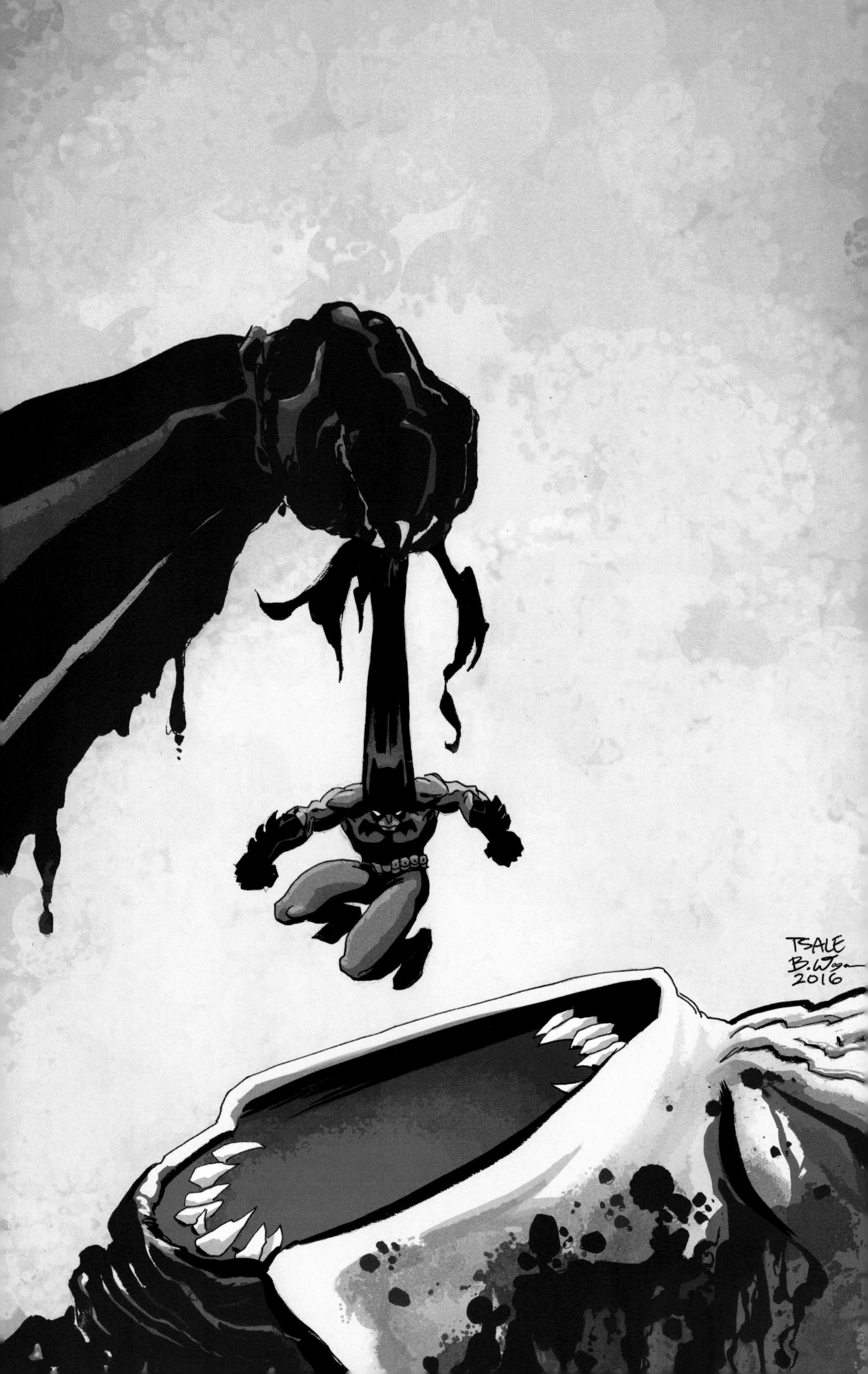
TSALE
B.Wagner
2016

BATMAN #8 variant cover by TIM SALE & BRENNAN WAGNER

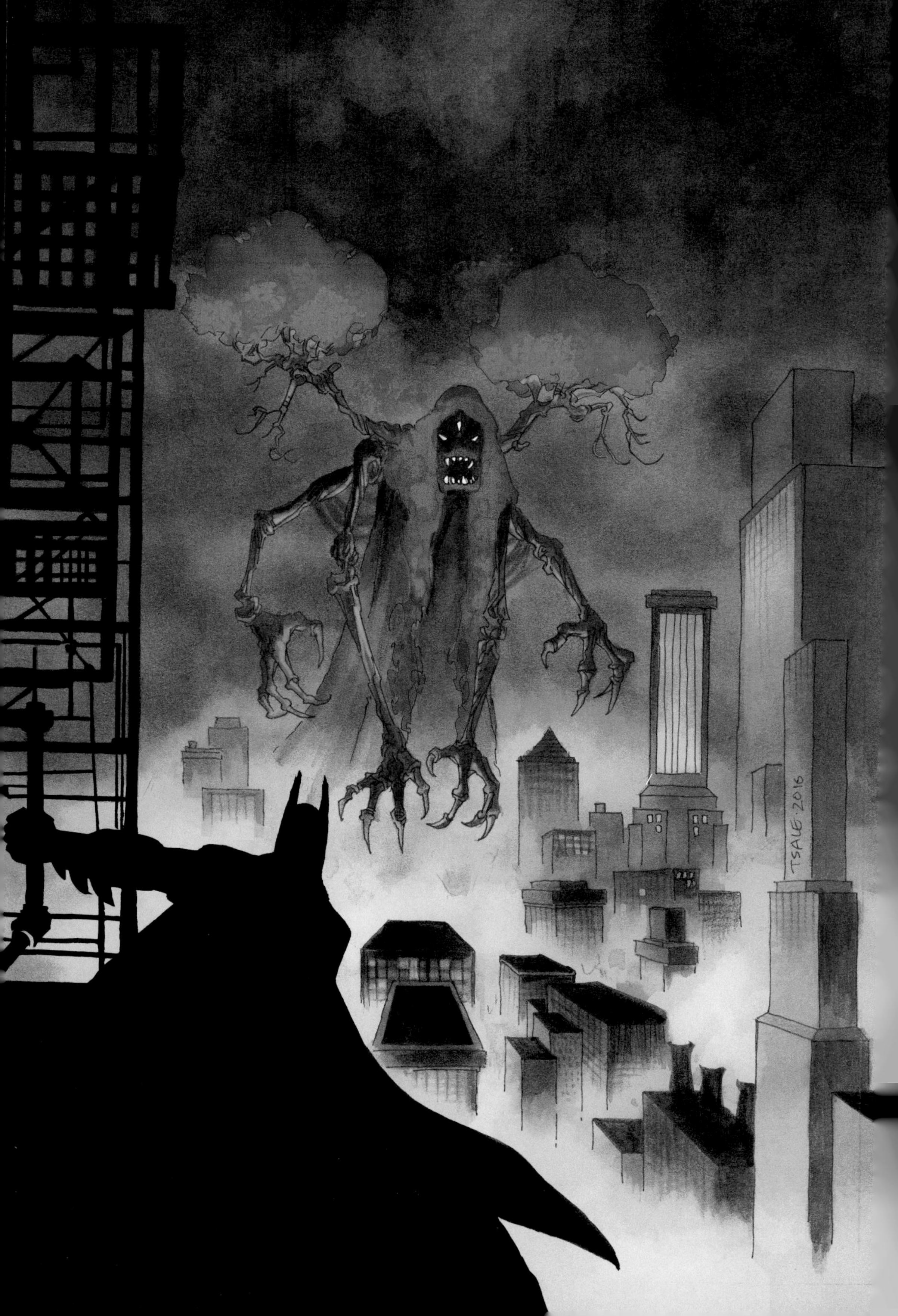
TSALE·2016

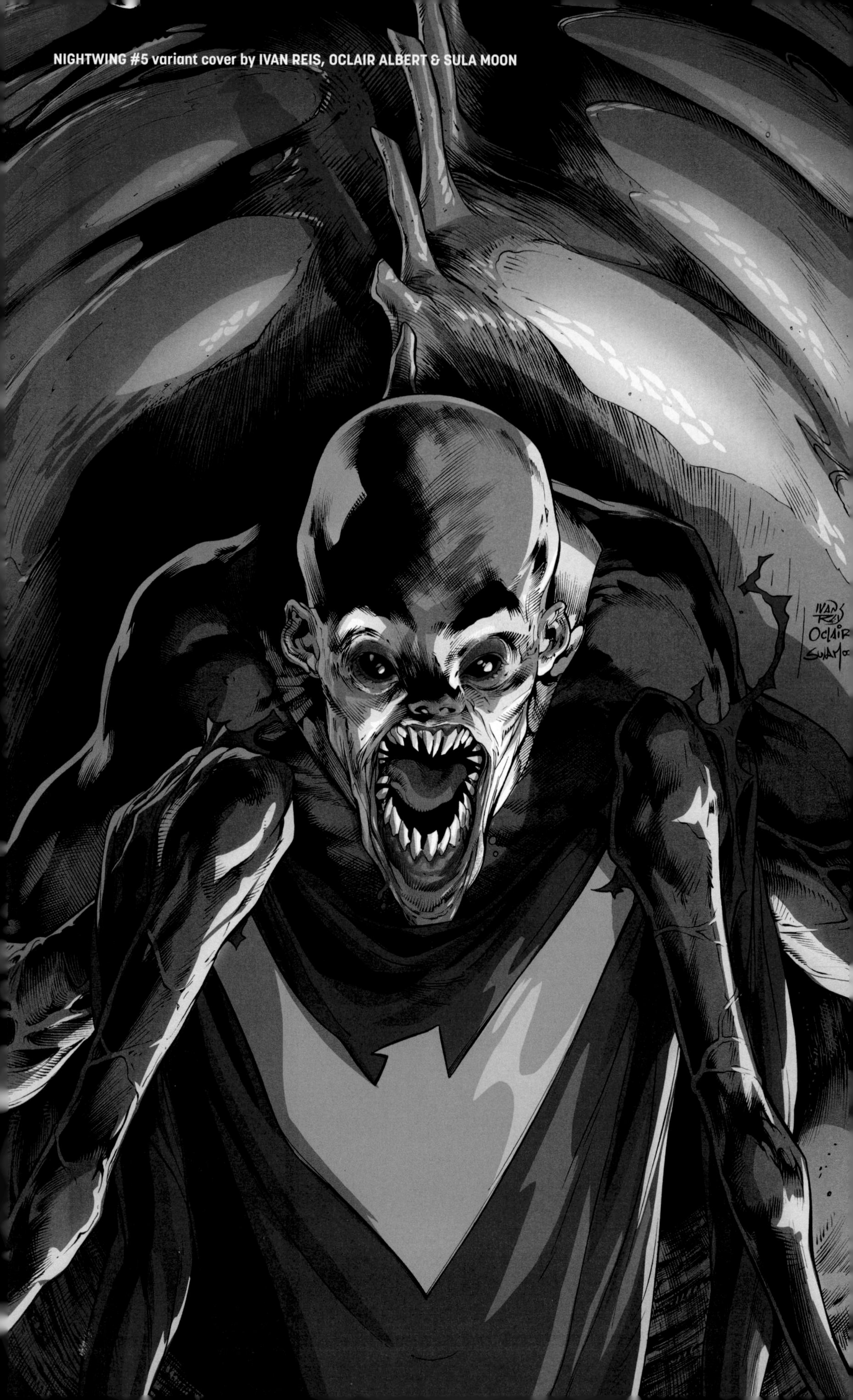

NIGHTWING #5 variant cover by IVAN REIS, OCLAIR ALBERT & SULA MOON

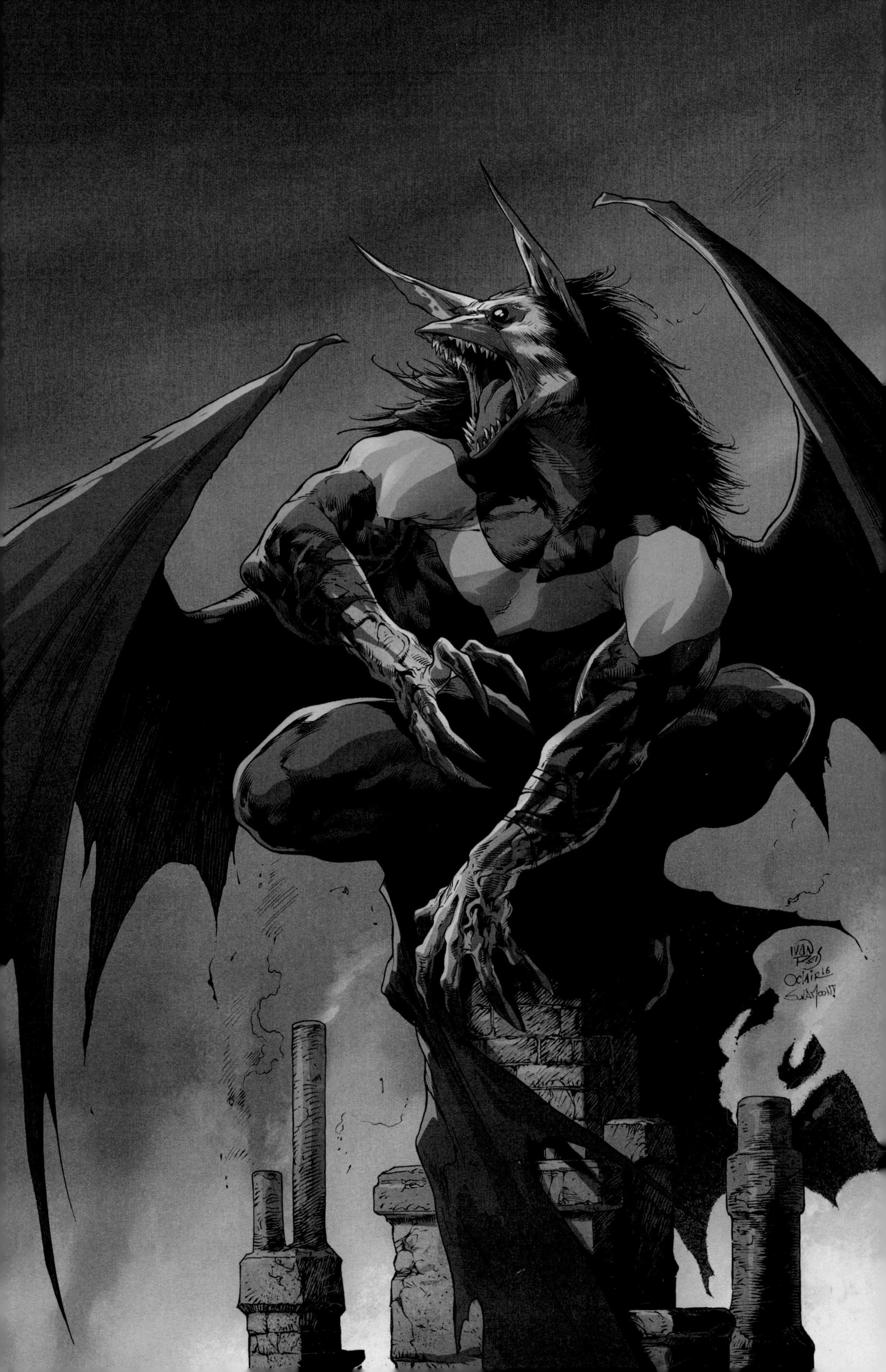

NIGHTWING #6 variant cover by IVAN REIS, OCLAIR ALBERT & SULA MOON

DETECTIVE COMICS #941 variant cover by RAFAEL ALBUQUERQUE

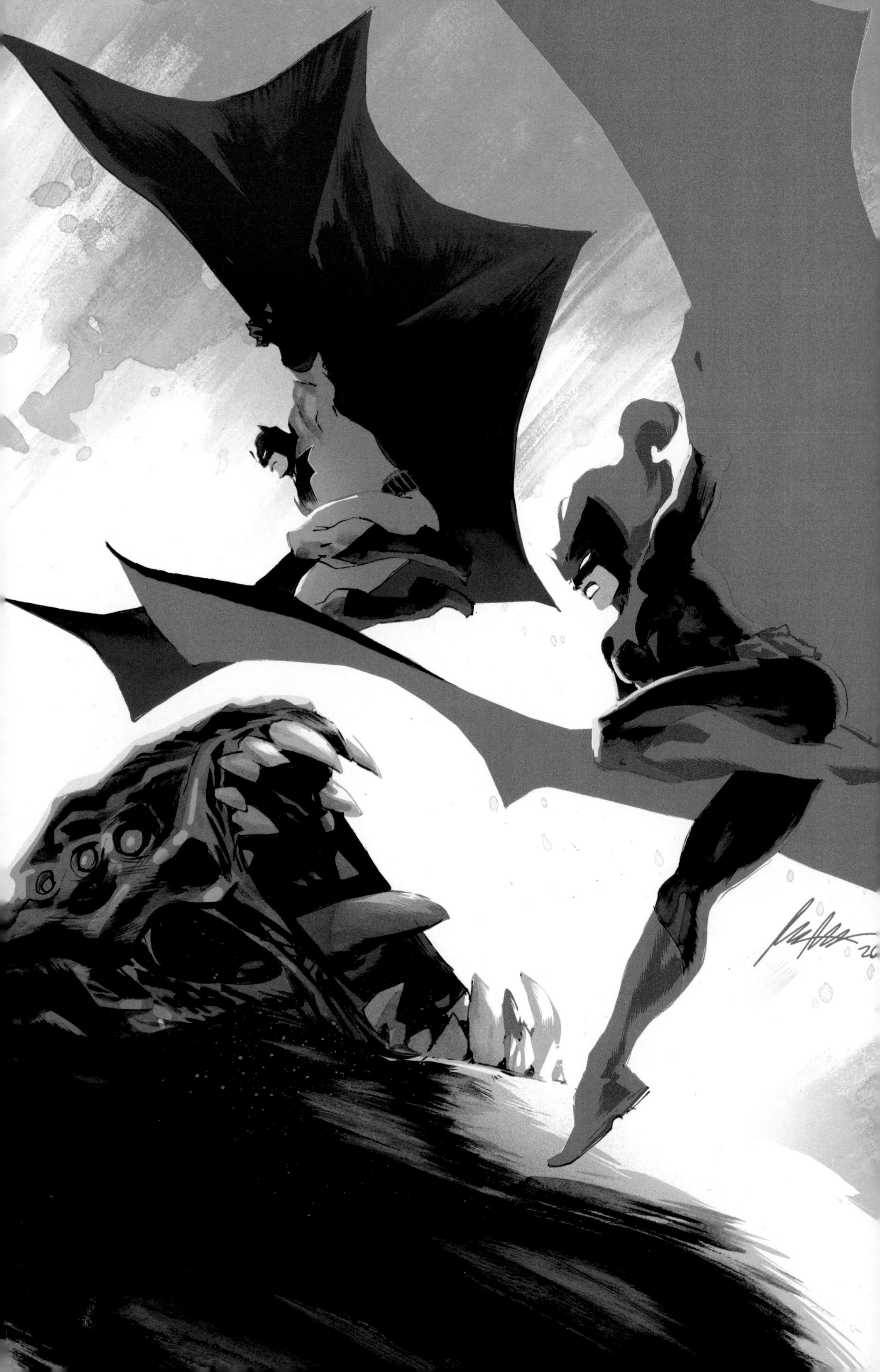

ECTIVE COMICS #942 variant cover by RAFAEL ALBUQUERQUE

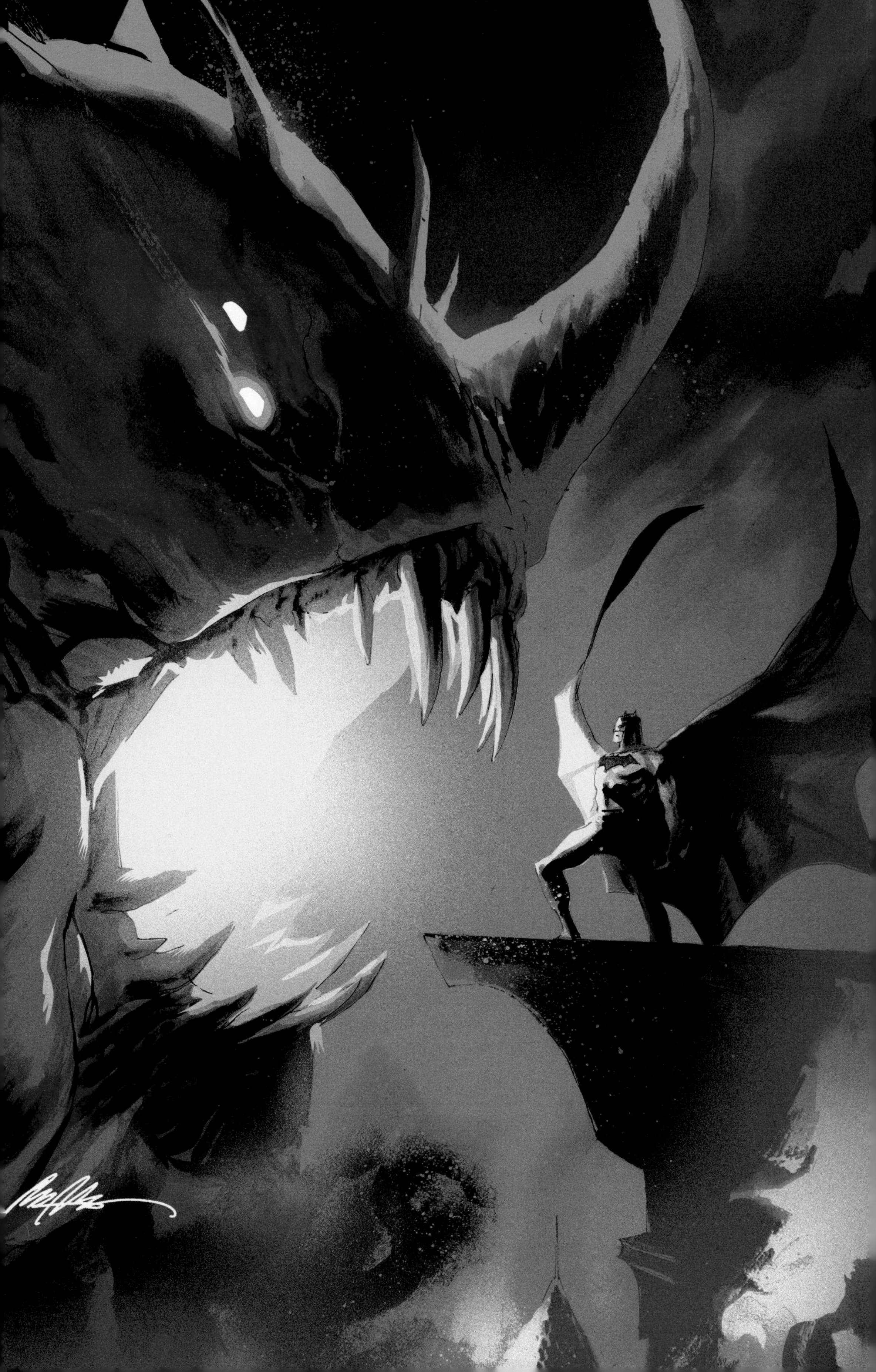

NIGHT OF THE MONSTER MEN promotional art by RILEY ROSSMO

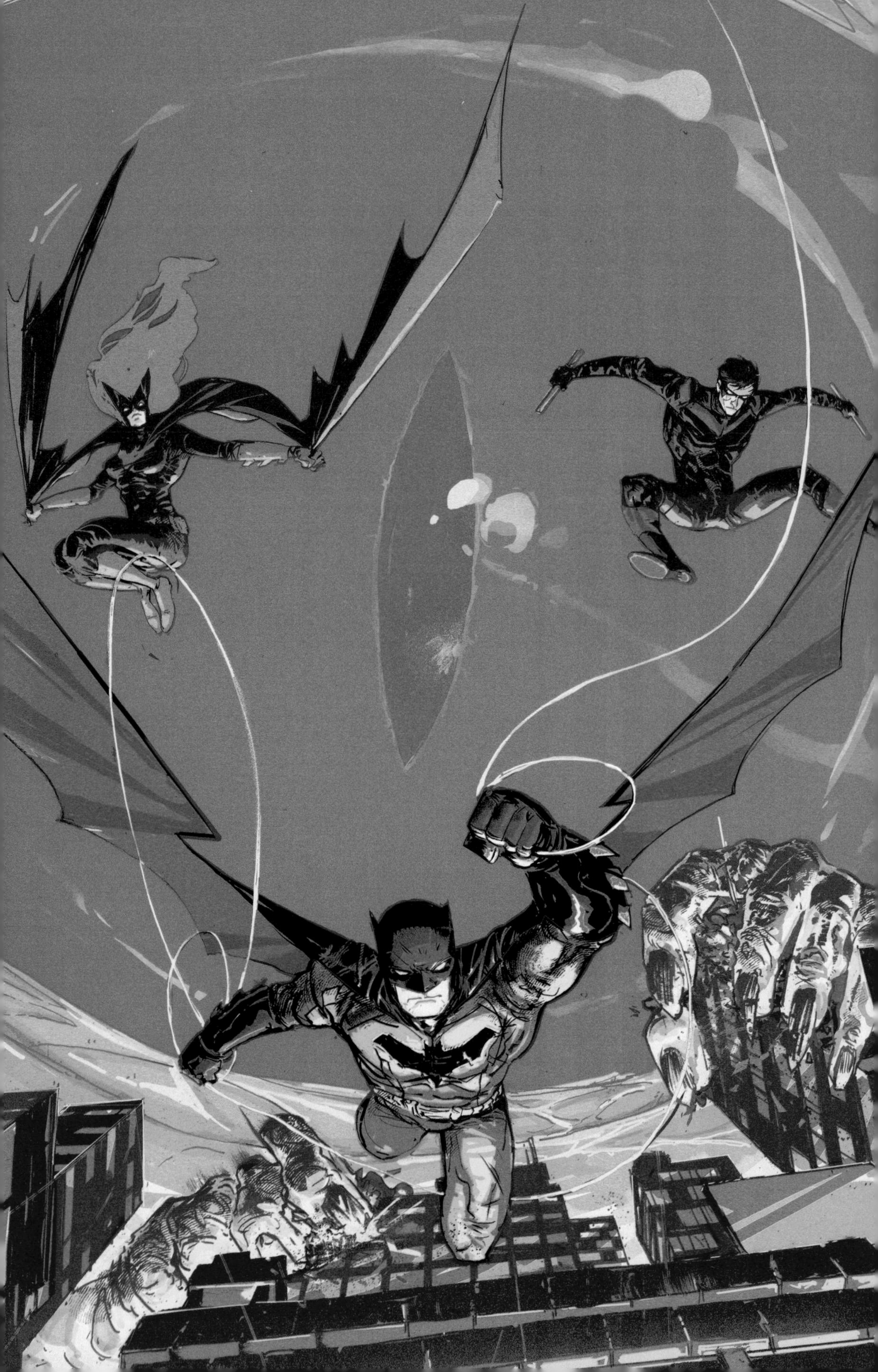

MONSTER MEN DESIGNS
by RILEY ROSSMO

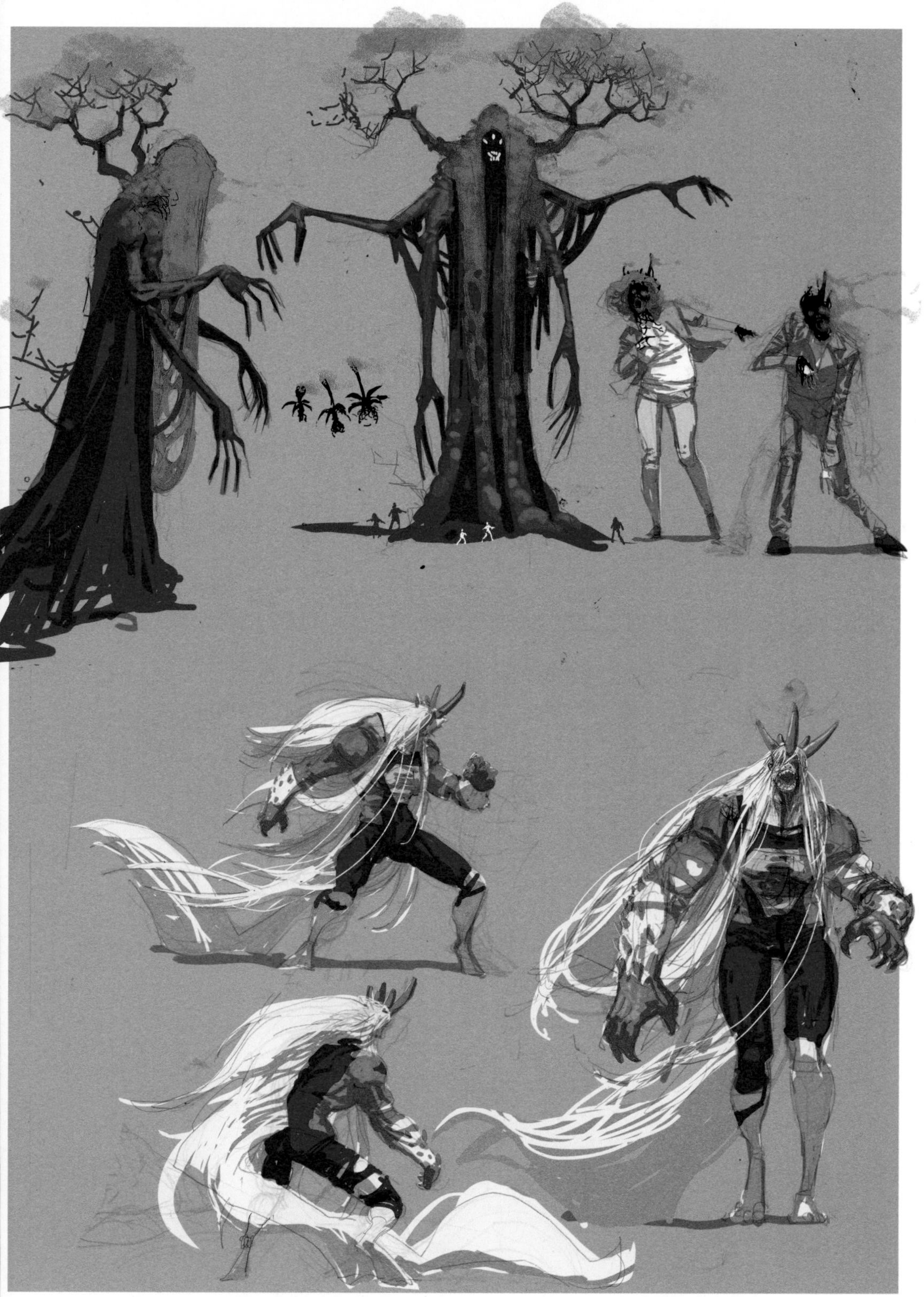

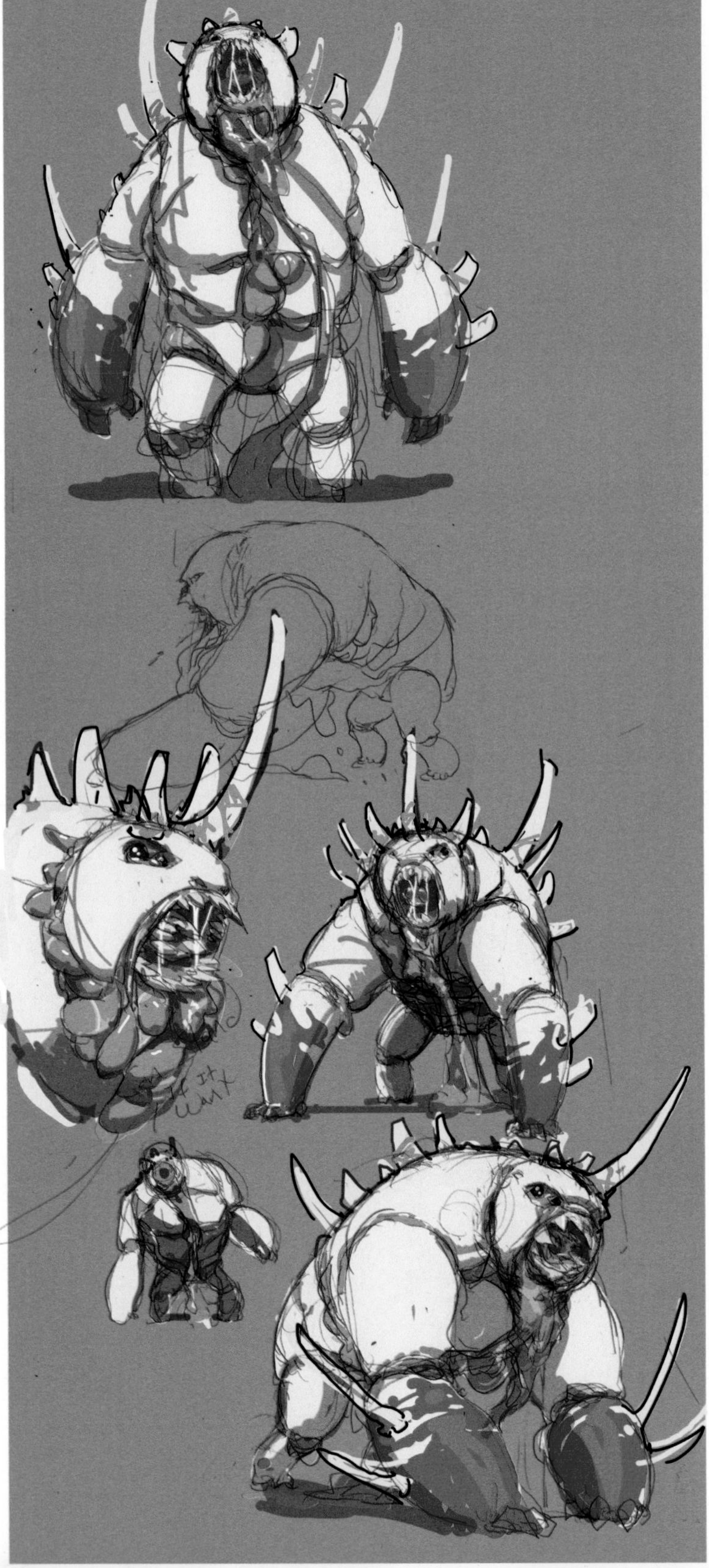

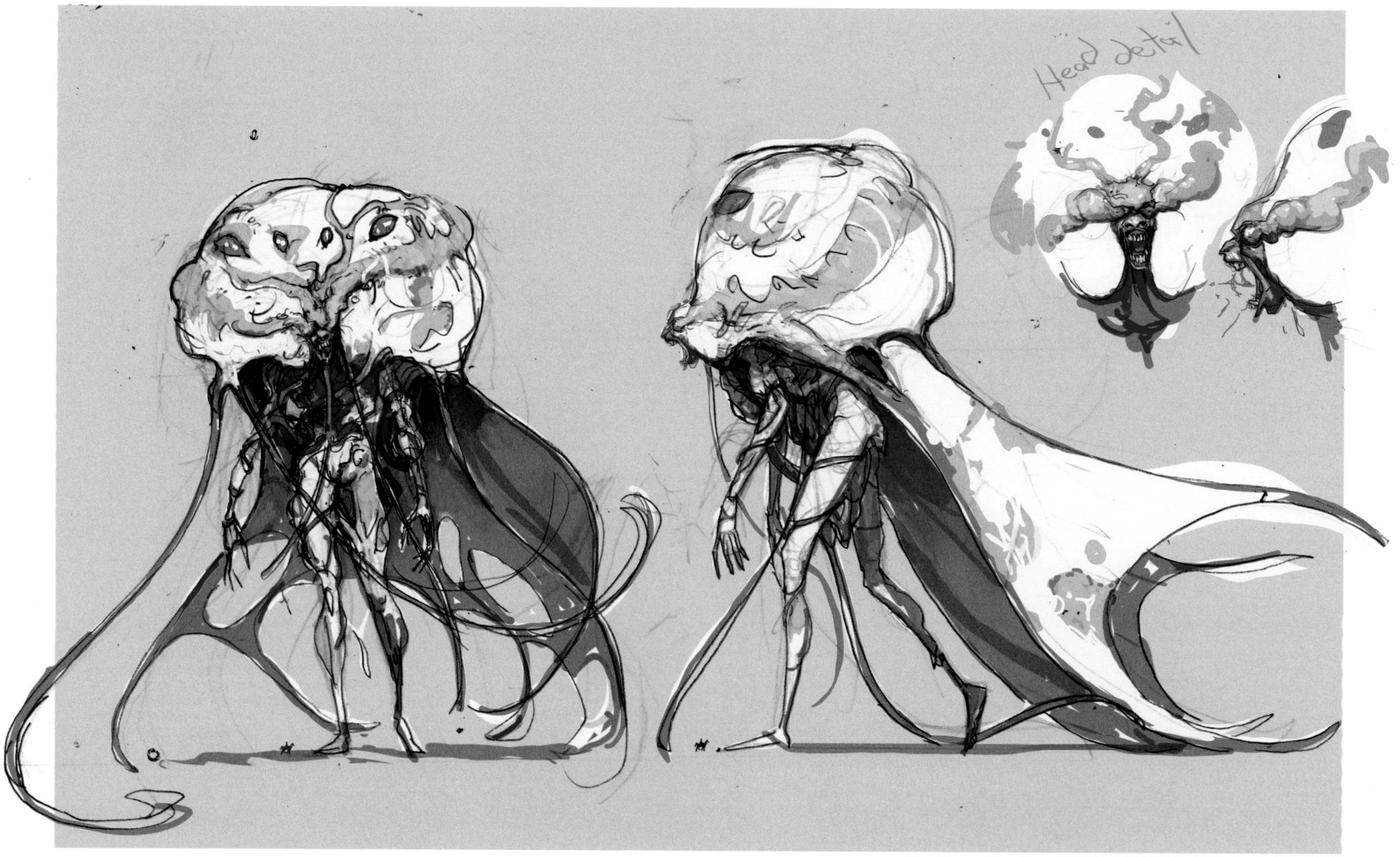
Head detail

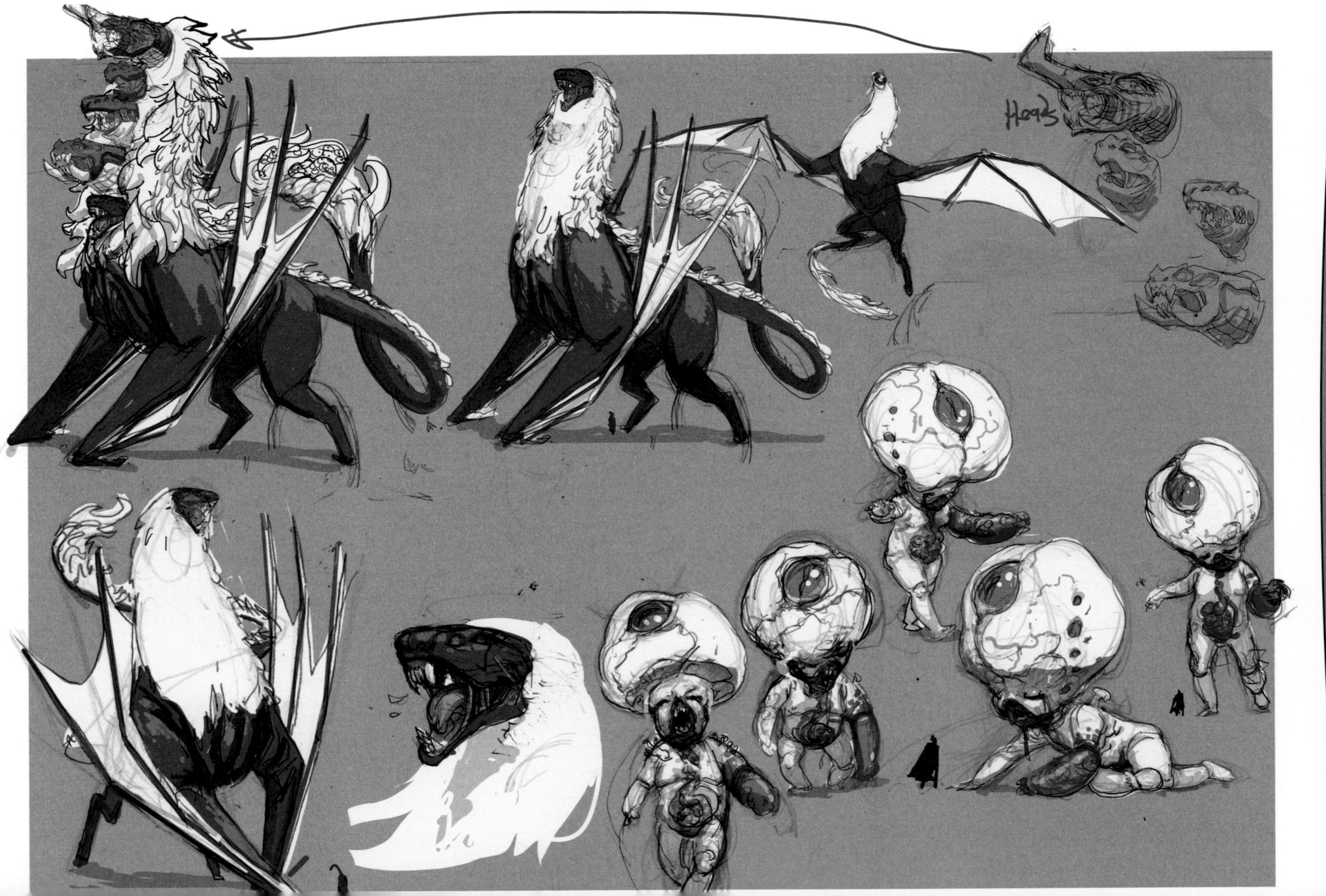
Heads

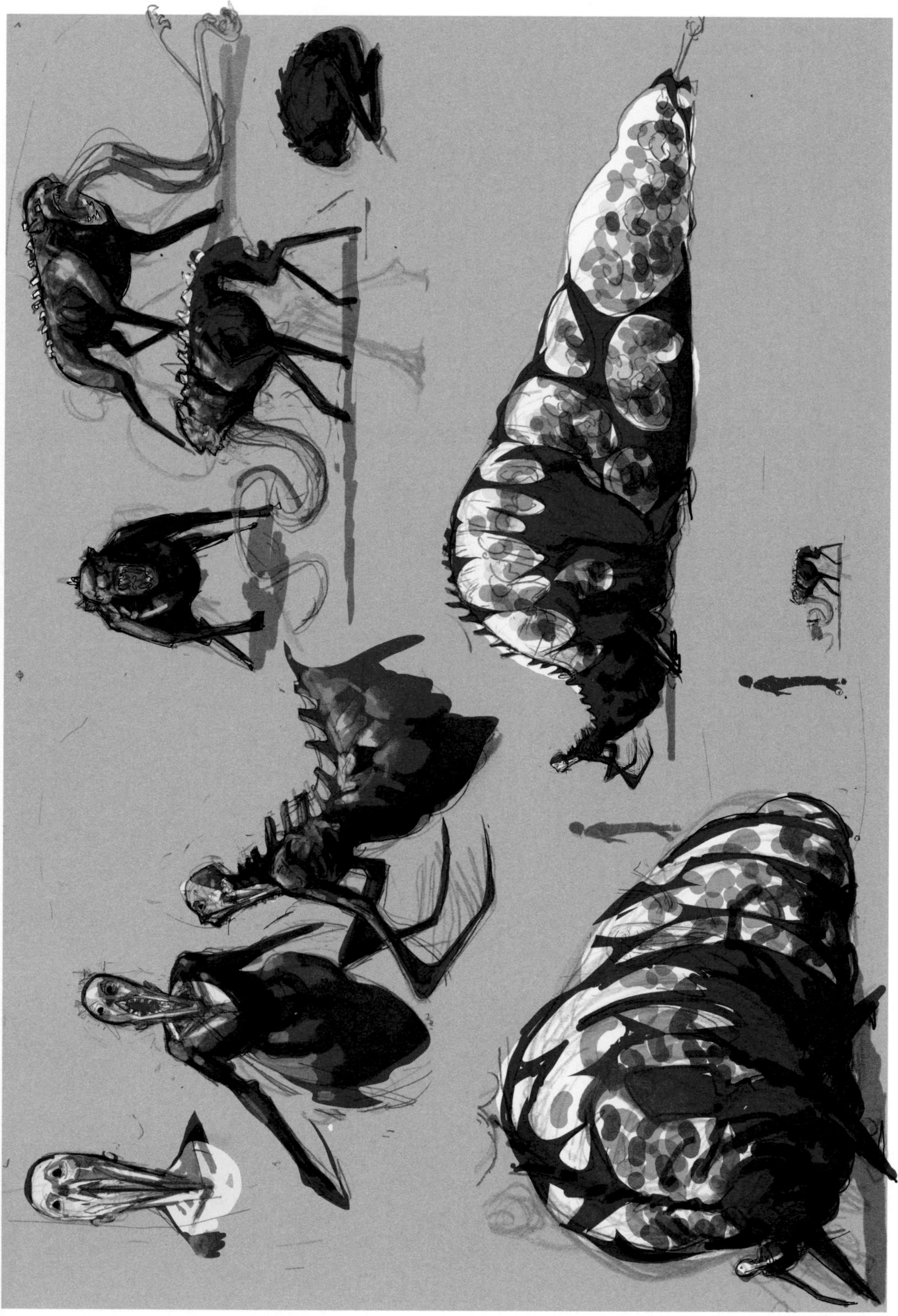

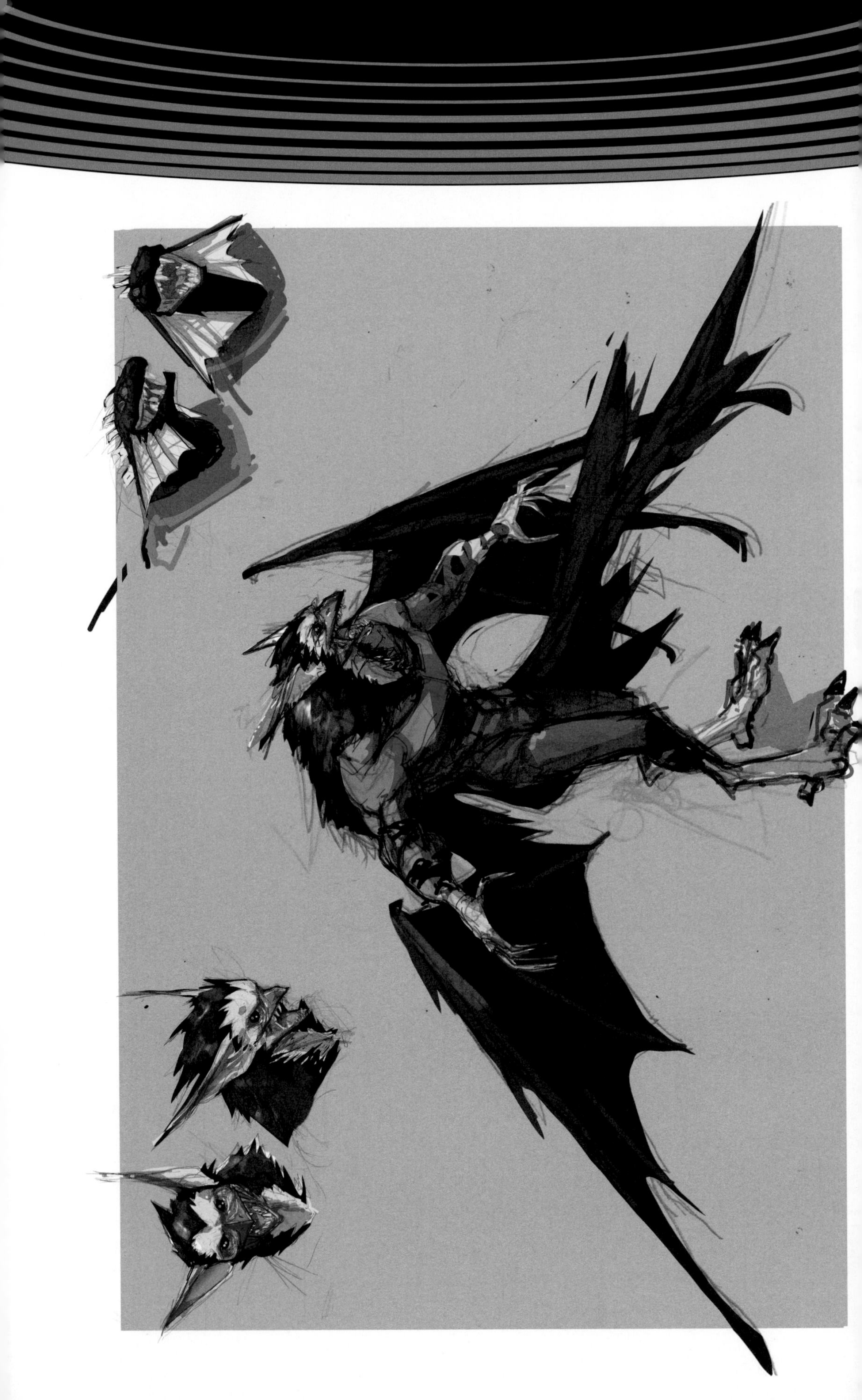

...an is getting a brand-new voice."

...SA TODAY

...eat showcase for the new team as well
...vering a taste of the new flavor they'll be
...ing to Gotham City." — **IGN**

...UNIVERSE REBIRTH

...ATMAN

...1: I AM GOTHAM

...M KING
...th DAVID FINCH

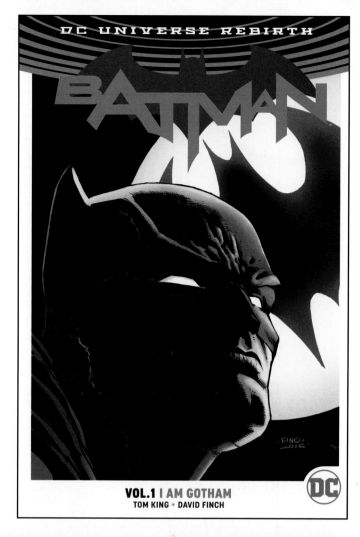

VOL. 1 I AM GOTHAM
TOM KING * DAVID FINCH

ALL-STAR BATMAN VOL. 1:
MY OWN WORST ENEMY

NIGHTWING VOL. 1:
BETTER THAN BATMAN

DETECTIVE COMICS VOL. 1:
RISE OF THE BATMEN

Get more DC graphic novels wherever comics and books are sold!

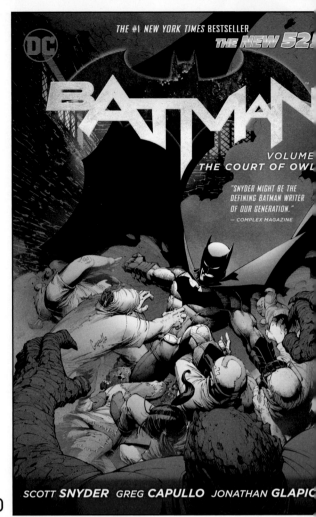

THE #1 *NEW YORK TIMES* BESTSELLER
THE NEW 52!

BATMAN
VOLUME
THE COURT OF OWL

"SNYDER MIGHT BE THE
DEFINING BATMAN WRITER
OF OUR GENERATION."
— COMPLEX MAGAZINE

SCOTT **SNYDER**   GREG **CAPULLO**   Jonathan **GLAPIC**

*"[Writer Scott Snyder] pulls from
the oldest aspects of the Batman
myth, combines it with sinister-
comic elements from the series'
best period, and gives the whole
thing terrific forward-spin."*
– ENTERTAINMENT WEEKLY

START AT THE BEGINNING!
BATMAN
VOL. 1: THE COURT OF OWLS
SCOTT SNYDER with GREG CAPULLO

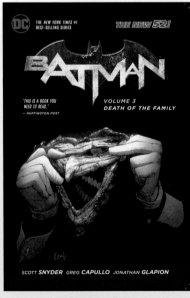

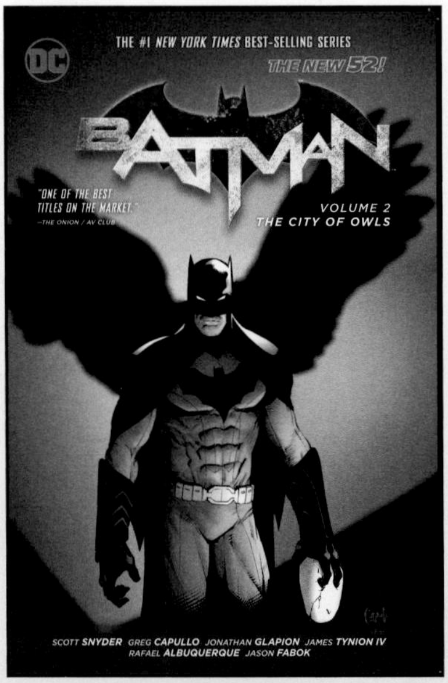

THE #1 *NEW YORK TIMES* BEST-SELLING SERIES
THE NEW 52!

BATMAN
VOLUME 2
THE CITY OF OWLS

"ONE OF THE BEST
TITLES ON THE MARKET."
– THE ONION / AV CLUB

SCOTT **SNYDER**   GREG **CAPULLO**   JONATHAN **GLAPION**   JAMES **TYNION IV**
RAFAEL **ALBUQUERQUE**   JASON **FABOK**

**BATMAN VOL. 2:
THE CITY OF OWLS**

THE *NEW YORK TIMES* #1
BEST-SELLING SERIES
THE NEW 52!

BATMAN
VOLUME 3
DEATH OF THE FAMILY

"THIS IS A BOOK YOU
NEED TO READ."
– HUFFINGTON POST

SCOTT **SNYDER**   GREG **CAPULLO**   JONATHAN **GLAPION**

**BATMAN VOL. 3:
DEATH OF THE FAMILY**

READ THE ENTIRE

BATMAN
ZERO YEAR – SECR

BATMAN
ZERO YEAR – DA

BATMAN
GRAVEYAR

BATMAN
EN

BATMAN
SUPER

BATMAN

BATMAN
EP

Get more DC graphic novels wherever comics and books are sold.